THE ASSUMED AUTHORIAL UNITY OF LUKE AND ACTS

For nearly 1,900 years, few have questioned the single authorship of Luke and Acts. A careful reassessment of the internal and external evidence, however, reveals this assumption to be built on a shakier foundation than was previously thought. Patricia Walters' innovative study offers a newly designed statistical analysis of Luke and Acts, pointing to the existence of highly significant differences in their prose style. In particular, a comprehensive survey and re-examination of the two books' least contested authorial stratum – their seams and summaries – brings to light ancient prose compositional patterns that distinguish Luke and Acts beyond a reasonable doubt. Walters' application of statistical analysis is unique in biblical scholarship and will provide impetus for using similar methods in other areas of the field. This book will therefore be of great interest to academic researchers and students of early Christianity, classical literature and rhetoric, and New Testament studies.

PATRICIA WALTERS is an assistant professor and Coordinator of the Religious Studies program at Rockford College, Illinois.

SOCIETY FOR NEW TESTAMENT STUDIES

MONOGRAPH SERIES

General Editor: John M. Court

145

THE ASSUMED AUTHORIAL UNITY OF LUKE AND ACTS

SOCIETY FOR NEW TESTAMENT STUDIES

MONOGRAPH SERIES

Recent titles in the series

The Assumed Authorial Unity of Luke and Acts

A Reassessment of the Evidence

PATRICIA WALTERS

CAMBRIDGE
UNIVERSITY PRESS

CAMBRIDGE UNIVERSITY PRESS
Cambridge, New York, Melbourne, Madrid, Cape Town, Singapore, São Paulo, Delhi

Cambridge University Press
The Edinburgh Building, Cambridge CB2 8RU, UK

Published in the United States of America by Cambridge University Press, New York

www.cambridge.org
Information on this title: www.cambridge.org/9780521509749

First published 2009

Printed in the United Kingdom at the University Press, Cambridge

A catalogue record for this publication is available from the British Library

Library of Congress Cataloguing in Publication data
Walters, Patricia, 1947–
The assumed authorial unity of Luke and Acts : a reassessment of the evidence / Patricia Walters.
    p.   cm. – (Society for New Testament studies monograph series ; 145)
Includes bibliographical references and index.
ISBN 978-0-521-50974-9 (hardback)
1. Bible. N.T. Luke – Criticism, interpretation, etc. 2. Bible. N.T.
Acts – Criticism, interpretation, etc. I. Title. II. Series.

BS2589.W35   2008
226.4′066 – dc22   2008034149

ISBN 978-0-521-50974-9 hardback

BS2589
, W35
2009
0231580890

CONTENTS

FIGURES

ACKNOWLEDGMENTS

Originating in a dissertation, awarded a PhD at Loyola University Chicago in May 2005, this book has been a total labor of love. The argument that evidence for the authorial unity of Luke and Acts ought to be reassessed and, if necessary, challenged has intrigued me since my early days in graduate school. Without the guidance and inspiration of those at Loyola, however, this book would not have come to fruition. Hence, it is with the most sincere gratitude and admiration that I wish to thank my dissertation director, Thomas H. Tobin, S. J., who steadfastly and patiently guided me through the process. Dr. James Keenan provided a classical studies perspective and inspired me to find precedents for my methodological approach. With inimitable conscientious guidance and support, Dr. Wendy Cotter, C. S. J. showed me how to reach beyond myself to produce not only a cogent argument but also, I hope, a worthy one. These three and Dr. Martin Buntinas of Loyola's Department of Mathematics and Statistics, who generously helped on the statistical sections, as well as many other fine scholars in Loyola's Department of Theology, formed the intellectual soil from which my ideas grew and developed.

This book is dedicated to my mother, Cleora Susan Wadsworth Walters, and *in memoriam* to my father, Robert Earl Walters. My parents taught me to pursue goals with diligence and loyalty, all the while allowing me to follow my own muses. Also, my five sisters have cheered me along the way more than they know. Finally, on the road of self-discovery, the trudge to Happy Destiny, many trusted friends have provided more spiritual, mental, and emotional sustenance than can ever be returned or acknowledged.

My thanks are also due to Dr. Katharina Brett and all the staff at Cambridge University Press who have so kindly helped me organize, revise, and finish this manuscript.

ABBREVIATIONS

The abbreviations for ancient writers and their works have been taken from Simon Hornblower and Antony Spawforth (eds.), *The Oxford Classical Dictionary*, 3rd edition (Oxford: Oxford University Press, 1996), pp. xxix–liv.

AB	Anchor Bible
ABRL	Anchor Bible Reference Library
AJP	*The American Journal of Philology*
BASPSup	Bulletin of the American Society of Papyrologists: Supplement
BENT	Beiträge zur Einleitung in das Neue Testament
BETL	Bibliotheca Ephemeridum Theologicarum Lovaniensium
BZ	*Biblische Zeitschrift*
CBR	*Currents in Biblical Research*
CP	*Classical Philology*
CQ	*Classical Quarterly*
ET	English translation
ETL	*Ephemerides Theologicae Lovanienses*
EusSup	Eus Supplementa
EvQ	*Evangelical Quarterly*
FN	*Filologia Neotestamentaria*
HSCP	*Harvard Studies in Classical Philology*
HTR	*Harvard Theological Review*
HTS	Harvard Theological Studies
ITQ	*Irish Theological Quarterly*
JBL	*Journal of Biblical Literature*
JCACSup	Journal of the Classical Association of Canada Supplementary
JSNT	*Journal for the Study of the New Testament*
JSNTSup	Journal for the Study of the New Testament Supplement Series

JTS	*Journal of Theological Studies*
LCL	Loeb Classical Library
LEC	Library of Early Christianity
LXX	Septuagint
NT	*Novum Testamentum*
NTOA	Novum Testamentum et Orbis Antiquus
NTS	*New Testament Studies*
RB	*Revue Biblique*
SBLDS	Society of Biblical Literature Dissertation Series
SBLMS	Society of Biblical Literature Monograph Series
SBEC	Studies in the Bible and Early Christianity
SBS	Sources for Biblical Study
SNTA	Studiorum Novi Testamenti Auxilia
SNTSMS	Society for New Testament Studies Monograph Series
SPIB	Scripta Pontificii Instituti Biblici
SSD	Seam and summary data
TAPA	*Transactions of the American Philological Association*
TCR	*The Classical Review*
TL	*Theologische Literaturzeitung*
TLG	*Thesaurus Linguae Graecae*
TPAPA	*Transactions and Proceedings of the American Philological Association*
TZ	*Theologische Zeitschrift*
ZTK	*Zeitschrift für Theologie und Kirche*

1

BACKGROUND AND METHODOLOGY

Today, the discussion on the common authorship of [Luke] and Acts, which is to be distinguished from that on the identity of the author, is *closed*. Of course, "resolution of this basic issue does not determine that the same author could not have written in different genres, employed different theological constructs in the two volumes, or used different narrators" (Parsons-Pervo, *Rethinking*, p. 116). But it is a necessary condition to allow for a reflection on the way Luke has composed both writings [emphasis added].[1]

Rarely do scholars make the startling and uncompromising declaration that a topic is *closed* to further investigation. Such a statement defies the search and research objectives of any systematic, critical inquiry. So universally held is the above opinion[2] that few have opted to challenge

[1] J. Verheyden, "The Unity of Luke-Acts" in J. Verheyden (ed.), *The Unity of Luke-Acts*, BETL 142 (Leuven: Leuven University Press, 1999), pp. 6–7 note 13. For the reference cited, see Mikeal C. Parsons and Richard I. Pervo, *Rethinking the Unity of Luke and Acts* (Minneapolis, Minn.: Fortress Press, 1993), p. 116.

[2] See, e.g., David E. Aune, *The New Testament and Its Literary Environment* (Philadelphia, Pa.: Westminster Press, 1987), p. 77; F. F. Bruce, *The Acts of the Apostles* (Grand Rapids, Mich.: Wm. B. Eerdmans, 1990), pp. 1–9; Henry J. Cadbury, *The Making of Luke-Acts*, 2nd edition (Peabody, Mass.: Hendrickson Publishers, 1958; reprint, 1999), p. 8; Hans Conzelmann, *Acts of the Apostles*, trans. James Limburg, A. Thomas Kraabel, and Donald H. Juel, Hermeneia (Philadelphia, Pa.: Fortress Press, 1987), pp. xl–xlv; Frederick W. Danker, *Luke*, Proclamation Commentaries (Philadelphia, Pa., Fortress Press, 1987), p. 2; Martin Dibelius, *From Tradition to Gospel*, trans. Bertram Lee Woolf from the 2nd edition (New York: Charles Scribner's Sons, 1935), p. 3; originally published as *Die Formgeschichte des Evangeliums* (Tübingen: Mohr/Siebeck, 1919); "Style Criticism in the Book of Acts" in Heinrich Greevan (ed.), *Studies in the Acts of the Apostles*, trans. Mary Ling (London: SCM Press, 1956; reprint, Mifflintown, Penn.: Sigler Press, 1999), pp. 174f.; originally published as "Stilkritisches zur Apostelgeschichte" in H. Schmidt (ed.), *Eucharisterion: Studien zur Religion und Literatur des Alten und Neuen Testaments*, Festschrift Hermann Gunkel, vol. II (Göttingen: Vandenhoeck & Ruprecht, 1923), pp. 27–49; Joseph A. Fitzmyer, *The Gospel According to Luke I–IX*, AB 28 (New York: Doubleday, 1970), pp. 35–41; *The Acts of the Apostles: A New Translation with Introduction and Commentary*, AB 31 (New York:

the hypothesis – and it is a hypothesis – that Luke and Acts were written and compiled by a unitary author-editor. Here "author-editor" denotes a writer who not only composed independently but also redacted and compiled inherited sources and traditions, be they written or oral.

Although few, challenges to the single authorship of Luke and Acts follow two trajectories. The first understands Luke and Acts as the *fulfillment of different writers' theological agendas*, a proposition with little currency among scholars. On this trajectory, which is profiled later, are examples of two nineteenth-century exegetes, F. C. Baur and J. H. Scholten, whose complex theological interpretations of the early Christian religious milieux treat the possible extenuating historical circumstances from which conflicting theologies emerged.[3] The second trajectory of challenges to single authorship differentiates compositional styles in Luke and Acts, primarily through word study analysis. On this trajectory, also summarized later, are the lone examples of Albert C. Clark and A. W. Argyle, two twentieth-century scholars, who base their authorship testing on literary-critical analysis without factoring in theological motivations.[4] Tracing challenges to the single authorship hypothesis along the two trajectories shows none has so far persuaded scholars to abandon the common authorship hypothesis.

Why does the hypothesis enjoy such unequivocal agreement, as we shall see, in the face of some significant counter-evidence? One purpose of this book is to re-examine the evidence for single authorship and, by doing so, reveal certain problems in the research. The other purpose is to conduct a new authorial analysis based on ancient literary criticism in order to reconfirm or challenge the prevailing opinion – in short, it is a study of passages in Luke and Acts virtually certain to be authorial, that is, seams and summaries, and how they map the elements of ancient prose composition criticism such as euphony, rhythm, and sentence structure, documented by ancient literary critics. Said another way, this authorial analysis searches patterns of ancient compositional conventions in the

---

Doubleday, 1998), pp. 49–51; Ernst Haenchen, *The Acts of the Apostles: A Commentary*, trans. Basil Blackwell (Philadelphia, Pa.: Westminster Press, 1971), pp. 90–112; John C. Hawkins, *Horae Synopticae: Contributions to the Study of the Synoptic Problem*, 2nd edition (Oxford: Clarendon Press, 1909; reprint, 1968), p. 174; Alfred Plummer, *A Critical and Exegetical Commentary on the Gospel According to S. Luke*, 5th edition (Edinburgh: T. & T. Clark, 1922; reprint 1969), pp. xi–xii; Gerhard Schneider, *Das Evangelium nach Lukas: Kapitel 1–10*, vol. I (Würzburg: Gütersloher Verlagshaus Gerd Mohn, Gütersloh und Echter Verlag, 1977), pp. 32–33; and W. C. van Unnik, "The 'Book of Acts' – The Confirmation of the Gospel" in David E. Orton (ed.), *The Composition of Luke's Gospel: Selected Studies from "Novum Testamentum"* (Leiden: Brill, 1999), pp. 184f.

[3] See pp. 24f. and pp. 25f., respectively.   [4] See pp. 26ff. and pp. 33ff., respectively.

seams and summaries of Luke and Acts. The patterns – when identified, tabulated, and statistically compared – will reveal the prose compositional style in each book, an authorial handprint, as it were. The differences in compositional style when statistically compared will either verify or challenge the received opinion of single authorship.

State of the question

The single authorship hypothesis rests on three "pillars" of evidence, presented as standard fare in many commentaries. First, the *preface* of each book (Lk 1:1–4; Acts 1:1–5)[5] dedicates it to one named Theophilus, and the Acts preface refers to "the first book" (Τὸν . . . πρῶτον λόγον, Acts 1:1), assumed to be the gospel of Luke. As a literary hinge, these connective devices fasten Acts to Luke. Hence, commentators and exegetes cite the prefaces as evidence for single authorship, as shown in the following examples. In *The Beginnings of Christianity*, F. J. Foakes Jackson and Kirsopp Lake write:

> On one point there is practical agreement – the author of the two works [Luke and Acts] is the same. *This seems to be proved by the common address to Theophilus, by the description in Acts i. of a book corresponding to the Third Gospel,* and by the identity of the two books in style and language, even in subtle details and mannerisms [emphasis added].[6]

In *The Making of Luke-Acts*, Henry J. Cadbury suggests:

> In any study of Luke and Acts, their unity is a fundamental and illuminating axiom. Among all the problems of New Testament authorship no answer is so universally agreed upon as is the common authorship of these two volumes. *Each is addressed in its opening words to the same Theophilus, the second volume refers explicitly to the first,* and in innumerable points of style the Greek diction of each shows close identity with the other. Whatever the difference in subject matter and sources, each

---

[5] The length of the Acts preface is a matter of dispute. In fact, all the following have been proposed: Acts 1:1; 1:1–2; 1:1–5; 1:1–8; 1:1–11; 1:1–14; 1:1–26; 1:1–2:41; 1:1–2:47. I have chosen Acts 1:1–5, so Aune, *Literary*, p. 117. See also Steve Walton, "Where Does the Beginning of Acts End?" in Verheyden, *Unity of Luke-Acts*, p. 447.

[6] F. J. Foakes Jackson and Kirsopp Lake, *The Beginnings of Christianity: Part 1: The Acts of the Apostles: Prolegomena II*, vol. II (London: Macmillan and Co., 1922), p. 207.

volume is in its present form the work of the same ultimate editor [emphasis added].[7]

While W. C. van Unnik believes there is no reason to doubt the correctness of Acts 1:1,[8] F. F. Bruce sums up a conservative view of common authorship:

> Suffice it to say that, from the late second century on, the consentient witness of all who write on the subject is that the author of the two volumes *Ad Theophilum* (anonymous as they are in the form in which they have come down to us, and the form in which those writers knew them) was *one and the same person, and that his name was Luke* [emphasis added].[9]

Finally and most explicitly, in *The Acts of the Apostles*, Joseph A. Fitzmyer writes:

> The authorship of Acts is related to that of the Third Gospel, *because* Acts begins, "In my first account, Theophilus, I dealt with all that Jesus did and taught from the beginning (1:1). *It* [Acts] *is dedicated to the "Theophilus," for whom the author wrote an account of Jesus' words and deeds (Luke 1:3). The dedication to the same person implies a common authorship of both the Gospel and Acts* [emphasis added].[10]

So strong is the authority of prefatory evidence that virtually no one suggests the Luke and Acts prefaces come from other than one author-editor. Indeed, investigation of extra-biblical Hellenistic and Greco-Roman prefaces such as Josephus *Contra Apionem* I.1; II.1 and numerous others appear to support this view.[11] Loveday Alexander's extensive study of ancient preface conventions has convinced many that the Luke and Acts prefaces are more closely related to technical treatise or manual preface

---

[7] Cadbury, *Making of Luke-Acts*, p. 8.

[8] Van Unnik, "The 'Book of Acts' – The Confirmation of the Gospel," p. 184.

[9] Bruce, *Acts of the Apostles*, pp. 2f.

[10] Fitzmyer, *Acts of the Apostles*, p. 49. For an excursus on proems, see Conzelmann, *Acts of the Apostles*, p. 4.

[11] E.g., Fitzmyer, *Luke I–IX*, p. 288. For a comprehensive treatment of extra-biblical prefaces, see reference in note 12 as well as Loveday Alexander, "Formal Elements and Genre: Which Greco-Roman Prologues Most Closely Parallel the Lukan Prologues?" in David P. Moessner (ed.), *Jesus and the Heritage of Israel: Luke's Narrative Claim upon Israel's History* (Harrisburg, Pa.: Trinity Press International, 1999).

formulations than to those in historical texts, Hellenistic Jewish literature, or other Greek literary works.[12] Whatever the generic implications,
when analyzed without the presumption of common authorship, the Luke
and Acts prefaces give rise to a nagging question. Why is the range of
stylistic variation between them so enormous? One look at an analysis of
the Josephus *Contra Apionem* prefaces as well as others suggests a stylistic variation much narrower than that in the prefaces to Luke and Acts.
The structural and stylistic differences between sophisticated and basic
Greek in the latter prefaces are so great as to make their attribution to one
author-editor, well, problematic. Due to the entrenched nature of the single authorship hypothesis, however, never considered is the idea the Luke
and Acts prefaces may have originated from different author-editors.

The second "pillar" on which the single authorship hypothesis rests
is early Christian *external evidence*. Second- to fourth-century Christian writers attribute the authorship of "a" gospel and the book of Acts
to one named "Luke," variously identified as the "Luke" of tradition
(Col 4:14; 2 Tim 4:11; Phlm 24), a physician (Col 4:14; *Muratorian
Canon* fragment), a follower of Paul (Irenaeus, *Adversus haereses* III.1.1;
10.1; 14.1), or a combination of these. The two earliest pieces of extant
external evidence date from the latter part of the second century, Irenaeus' *Adv. haer.* (ca. 175–180 CE) and the *Muratorian Canon* fragment.
In the case of Irenaeus, scholars writing about the authorship of Luke and
Acts often cite Irenaeus *Adv. haer.* III.1.1: "Καὶ Λουκᾶ δέ, ὁ ἀκόλουθος
Παύλου, τὸ ὑπ' ἐκείνου κηρυσσόμενον εὐαγγέλιον ἐν βίβλῳ κατέθετο.
[Then, Luke, the follower of Paul, set down in a book the gospel proclaimed by him.]"[13] Additionally, Irenaeus *Adv. haer.* III.13.3; III.14.1, 4
attribute to "Luke" a substantial amount of material corresponding to the
contents of the book of Acts.[14] The significance should not be missed:
Irenaeus appears to *differentiate* the two texts; *although he attributes both
to "Luke," their original unity is open to question.* Irenaeus, it seems, did
not consider Luke and Acts to be two parts of a one-volume work. In the
case of the *Muratorian Canon* fragment, a difficult and error-filled Latin
text, the "third book of the gospel" and "the Acts of all the apostles" are

---

[12] Loveday Alexander, *The Preface to Luke's Gospel: Literary Convention and Social
Context in Luke 1.1–4 and Acts 1.1*, SNTSMS 78 (Cambridge: Cambridge University Press,
1993), p. 167.

[13] Eusebius, *The Ecclesiastical History*, trans. Kirsopp Lake, LCL 153 (Cambridge,
Mass.: Harvard University Press, 1926; reprint 1949, 1953, 1959, 1965), 5.8.3. Unless
otherwise indicated, the English translations are my own.

[14] The original Greek of a possible title for Acts (*Adv. haer.* III.13.3) is not extant; the
Latin translation is *doctrina apostolorum*.

attributed to "Luke" the physician, a companion of Paul (10.2–8, 34–39). While a majority of scholars dates the *Muratorian Canon* ca. 170–210 CE, a minority argues for the fourth century.[15] About Luke and Acts, the *Muratorian Canon* says:

> The third book of the gospel: according to Luke.

> After the ascension of Christ, Luke the physician, whom Paul had taken along with him as a companion [*iuris studiosum*], composed in his own name on the basis of report. He himself, however, did not see the Lord in the flesh and therefore, as far as he could follow, he wrote down [the story]. He began to tell it from the nativity of John (10.2–8).

> . . . The Acts of all the apostles have been written in one volume. Compiled for the most excellent Theophilus, Luke includes in detail the things that were done in his own presence, as he shows plainly by omitting both the death of Peter and also Paul's departure from the city when he was setting out for Spain (10.34–39).[16]

Despite the fact that extant external evidence dates to the latter part of the second century, interpretation of the external evidence seems at best contradictory, at worst problematic. *Adversus haereses*, the *Muratorian Canon* fragment, and indeed all external evidence that identifies "Luke" as the author-editor of the third gospel and Acts notwithstanding, scholars today consider Luke, the other gospels, and Acts to be *anonymous* texts, author unknown. At the very same time, scholars do not question the early evidentiary attribution of Luke and Acts to *one* author-editor. Why do scholars doubt the external evidence for "Luke" as the author-editor of the gospel and Acts but readily accept the evidence for single authorship? Why do scholars declare Luke and Acts to be anonymously written texts but faithfully attribute them to that one author-editor? The answer may be that external evidence does not provide the whole story. Scholars rely on internal evidence in conjunction with external evidence.

---

[15] For the majority opinion, see Bruce M. Metzger, *The Canon of the New Testament: Its Origin, Development, and Significance* (Oxford: Clarendon Press, 1987), pp. 191–201. For the minority opinion, see Geoffrey Mark Hahneman, *The Muratorian Fragment and the Development of the Canon* (Oxford: Clarendon Press, 1992), pp. 215–218. See also A. C. Sundberg, Jr., "Canon Muratori: A Fourth-Century List," *HTR* 66 (1973), 1–41.

[16] The English translation comes from Henry J. Cadbury, "The Tradition," in F. J. Foakes Jackson and Kirsopp Lake (eds.), *The Beginnings of Christianity, Part 1: The Acts of the Apostles, vol. II. Prolegomena II: Criticism* (London: Macmillan and Co., 1922), pp. 210–211. For the Latin text, see Hahneman, *The Muratorian Fragment*, p. 6.

Thus, the third and most impressive "pillar" on which the single author-ship hypothesis rests is *internal evidence*, presented in summarized form below. Single authorship advocates point to the "remarkable similari-ties"[17] between Luke and Acts in vocabulary, style, themes, and the-ology; and admittedly the two books do reveal a striking number of parallels and correspondences in structure, theme, style, and portrayal of key figures. For example, the two books frame large portions of text by means of a journey motif, the so-called travel narrative in Luke (Lk 9:51–19:27) and the travels of Paul and other missionaries in Acts (Acts 13:1–28:31). Similarly, numerous syntactic and lexical correspondences such as the ἐγένετο constructions, the definite article+infinitive, and the use of κύριος to refer to Jesus have been extensively investigated. Most often noted are the apparently parallel portrayals of key figures in the two books, e.g., Jesus' noble, dignified death (Lk 23:33–49) and Stephen's heroic martyrdom (Acts 7:54–60), or Jesus' miracle working (e.g., Lk 5:17–26; 7:11–17; 8:41–42, 49–56) and Peter's and Paul's miraculous accomplishments of healing and resuscitation (e.g., Peter: Acts 3:1–10; 9:36–42; Paul: 14:8–11; 20:7–12).

Although the undisputed acceptance of single authorship still obtains, scholars question the once-understood, inextricably linked theological, generic, and narrative unity of Luke and Acts, as J. Verheyden, editor of *The Unity of Luke-Acts* (1999), notes:

> In their recent monograph Parsons and Pervo joined forces to "rethink" the unity of Lk and Acts. They feel uneasy about the way many scholars tend to speak of unity without sufficiently clarifying their model, their arguments for it, or its implications. They list five levels on which the relationship has to be studied: the author and the canon (*two issues which do not need a lot of discussion*), the genre, the narrative, and the theology of the work [emphasis added].[18]

In *Rethinking the Unity of Luke and Acts* (1993), Mikeal C. Parsons and Richard I. Pervo suggest scholarly opinion on the tight integration of Luke and Acts is often based on insufficient or unclear supporting criteria. They ask us, for example, to re-examine the reasoning for an author-editor with one *Weltanschauung* to compose a "present" theology of salvation informing Luke but a "future" theology informing Acts.[19] Theories about and problems with the literary and theological unity of

---

[17] Verheyden, "The Unity of Luke-Acts," p. 6 note 13.   [18] Ibid., pp. 5–6.
[19] Parsons and Pervo, *Rethinking the Unity of Luke and Acts*, pp. 88f.

Luke and Acts are summarized below, but the overriding point is that scholars who distinguish features of theology, genre, or subject matter *never* suggest different authorship. In other words, the hypothesis that Luke and Acts come from the hand of one author-editor is a *sine qua non* in New Testament studies.[20] Attested to by the prefaces and early church writers who reinforced the claim and by correspondences in language, style, and theology, the single authorship hypothesis enjoys an almost invulnerable position. Thus, the state of the question cannot be fully grasped until the external and internal evidence are evaluated.

External evidence for single authorship

The external evidence consists of authorial references in second- to fourth-century manuscripts. Note the extant fragments of Papias' five-volume work (ca. early second century CE) contain no references to Luke or Acts.[21] As mentioned, Irenaeus *Adv. haer.* (ca. 175–180 CE) contains the earliest extant references to a gospel and to apostolic teaching (Lat. *doctrina apostolorum*) written by "Luke," while in nearly the same period, Clement of Alexandria's *Stromata* 5.12.82.4 contains the earliest extant Greek titular reference to *Acts of the Apostles*, also given to "Luke."[22] As shown too, the *Muratorian Canon* fragment clearly links Luke and Acts to the same author-editor. Although some scholars find words and phrases from Acts in the works of earlier second-century writers such as Polycarp or Clement of Rome, they admit these so-called borrowings may simply reflect the language and spirit of the age.[23]

In addition to Irenaeus and the *Muratorian Canon* fragment, the external evidence for single authorship of Luke and Acts includes:[24] Clement

---

[20] For a comprehensive treatment of recent scholarly contributions to the issue of Luke and Acts unity, see Michael F. Bird, "The Unity of Luke-Acts in Recent Discussion," *JSNT* 29 (2007), pp. 425–448. Scholars focus on questions of whether Luke and Acts comprise a literary whole or whether reception-history studies have relevance. For the former, see Andrew Gregory, "The Reception of Luke and Acts and the Unity of Luke-Acts" *JSNT* 29 (2007), pp. 459–472; for the latter, see Luke Timothy Johnson, "Literary Criticism of Luke-Acts: Is Reception-History Pertinent?" *JSNT* 29 (2007), pp. 159–162.

[21] Eusebius, *Hist. eccl.* II.15.2; III.39.1–7, 14–17 (III CE). The five fragments include: Jerome, *De viris illustribus* 18 (V CE); Philippus Sidetes, *Hist. eccl.* fragments in Codex Barocci 142 (V CE); Codex vaticanus Reg. Lat. 14 (IX CE); Georgius Monachus, *Chronicon*, Codex Coisl. 305 (IX CE); Catena on John, ed. Corderius (1630 CE).

[22] The Latin translation of Irenaeus *Adv. haer.* contains the earliest extant reference to the book of Acts: *doctrina apostolorum* (III.13.3).

[23] Haenchen, *Acts of the Apostles*, p. 9.

[24] For a list, although slightly expanded here, see Cadbury, "The Tradition," pp. 209–264. The Greek texts have been taken from the *Thesaurus Linguae Graecae*, CD ROM

of Alexandria *Stromata* 5.12.82.4;[25] Tertullian *Adversus Marcionem* 4.2.4;[26] Origen *Contra Celsum* 6.11;[27] *Commentarii in evangelium Joannis* 1.23.149,[28] 150;[29] *Commentarium in evangelium Matthaei* 15.15;[30] 17.25;[31] *Selecta in Psalmos* 12.1632;[32] *In epistulam ad Hebraeos homiliae* 14.1309;[33] and Eusebius *Historia ecclesiastica*

vol. E, University of California Irvine, 1999. Where the Greek edition is unavailable or Latin is the original language, I follow the *Corpus Scriptorium Ecclesiasticorum Latinorum* used by Cadbury. The exception is the *Muratorian Canon* fragment, where I use Hahneman, *The Muratorian Fragment*.

[25] λείπεται δὴ θείᾳ χάριτι καὶ μόνῳ τῷ παρ' αὐτοῦ λόγῳ τὸ ἄγνωστον νοεῖν, καθὸ καὶ ὁ Λουκᾶς ἐν ταῖς Πράξεσι τῶν ἀποστόλων ἀπομνημονεύει τὸν Παῦλον λέγοντα· ἄνδρες Ἀθηναῖοι, κατὰ πάντα ὡς δεισιδαιμονεστέρους ὑμᾶς θεωρῶ [It is left then by God's grace and only by the Word from him to consider the unknown, just as also Luke in the Acts of the Apostles recounts Paul saying: "Men of Athens, in all ways I observe that you are very religious"]

[26] Nam ex iis commentatoribus, quos habemus, Lucam videtur Marcion elegisse quem caederet. Porro Lucas non apostolus, sed apostolicus, non magister, sed discipulus, utique magistro minor, certe tanto posterior quanto posterioris apostoli sectator, Pauli sine dubio ... [For from the gospel writers whom we have Marcion is seen to have selected Luke for mutilation. Luke, not an apostle but a follower of the apostles, not a master but a disciple, at any rate inferior to a master and so far later than the others as he was the follower of a later apostle, of course, of Paul ...]; translation from Cadbury, "The Tradition," p. 225.

[27] Καὶ "Ἰούδας" δὲ "ὁ Γαλιλαῖος," ὡς ὁ Λουκᾶς ἐν ταῖς Πράξεσι τῶν ἀποστόλων ἔγραψεν, ἐβουλήθη ἑαυτόν τινα εἰπεῖν μέγαν, καὶ πρὸ ἐκείνου "Θευδᾶς" ["Judas of Galilee," as Luke wrote in the Acts of the Apostles, wanted to call himself someone great, as did Theudas before him]

[28] Δηλοῖ δὲ τὸ εὐαγγέλιον καὶ ἐν ταῖς Πράξεσιν ὁ Λουκᾶς, οὐκ ἄλλον ἢ τὸν Χριστόν εἶναι τὸν λίθον [Luke made the gospel clear also in the Acts; none other than Christ is the stone]

[29] ἐν δὲ ταῖς Πράξεσιν ὁ Λουκᾶς γράφει· "Οὗτός ἐστιν ὁ λίθος ὁ ἐξουδενωθεὶς ὑφ' ὑμῶν τῶν οἰκοδόμων, ὁ γενόμενος εἰς κεφαλὴν γωνίας" [In the Acts, Luke writes: "He is the stone rejected by you, the builders; he has become the cornerstone"]

[30] ἀκουσάτω τῶν ἱστορουμένων ὑπὸ τοῦ Λουκᾶ ἐν ταῖς τῶν ἀποστόλων Πράξεσι περὶ τῶν προτραπέντων ὑπὸ τῆς ἐν τοῖς ἀποστόλοις δυνάμεως πιστεύειν καὶ βιοῦν τελείως κατὰ τὸν Ἰησοῦ λόγον [let one hear the narrations by Luke in the Acts of the Apostles about those encouraged by the power of the apostles to believe and live fully according to the word of Jesus]

[31] καὶ ἱστόρηται ὅτι Ἰούδας μὲν ὁ Γαλιλαῖος, οὗ μέμνηται καὶ Λουκᾶς ἐν ταῖς τῶν ἀποστόλων Πράξεσιν [He recounted that Judas of Galilee, of whom Luke makes mention in the Acts of the Apostles]

[32] ἔχει γὰρ καὶ οὗτος "ἐπιθυμίαν τοῦ ἀναλῦσαι καὶ σὺν Χριστῷ εἶναι, πολλῷ μᾶλλον κρείσσονα· τὸ δὲ ἐπιμένειν τῇ σαρκὶ" ἀναγκαιότερους διὰ τοὺς ὠφελημένους, εἴπερ ὁ Δαυῒδ κατὰ τὸν Λουκᾶν ἐν ταῖς Πράξεσι τῶν Ἀποστόλων, ἢ καὶ κατὰ Παῦλον "ἰδίᾳ γενεᾷ ὑπερετήσων" ἐξαπεστάλη [For he had a "desire to depart and be with Christ, for that is far better; but to remain in the flesh" is more necessary on account of the benefits, since according to Luke in the Acts of the Apostles or also according to Paul, David was sent "to provide for his own generation"]

[33] Ἡ δὲ εἰς ἡμᾶς φθάσασα ἱστορία, ὑπό τινων μὲν λεγόντων, ὅτι Κλήμης ὁ γενόμενος ἐπίσκοπος Ῥωμαίων ἔγραψε Ἐπιστολήν· ὑπό τινων δὲ, ὅτι Λουκᾶς ὁ γράψας τὸ Εὐαγγέλιον, καὶ τὰς Πράξεις [The story reached us, by means of some who said that Clement,

1.5.3;[34] 2.8.2;[35] 2.11.1;[36] 2.22.1,[37] 6;[38] 3.4.1,[39] 4;[40] 3.31.5.[41] The so-called Anti-Marcionite prologue to the gospel of Luke appears to be of a later, though uncertain, date.[42] To repeat, few scholars today question the *anonymity* of Luke and Acts authorship, but even fewer, remarkably, question the authorial unity of these two anonymous works. Thus external evidence will not suffice for "proof" of single authorship, so scholars rely on internal evidence.

Internal evidence for single authorship

The internal evidence consists of an array of lexical, stylistic, thematic, and theological correspondences between Luke and Acts. Often vast in scope and vivid in acuity, centuries' worth of critical analysis hardly fits into neat categories, but a cautious attempt to summarize the scholarship produces two rudimentary groupings: stylistic evidence and

who was made bishop of Rome, wrote the Epistle, by others that Luke, who wrote the gospel and the Acts]; see Eusebius *Hist. eccl.* 6.25.14.

[34] ἧς καὶ παρ᾽ ἡμῖν ὁ Λουκᾶς ἐν ταῖς Πράξεσιν μνήμην ὧδέ πως λέγων πεποίηται . . . [of this our own Luke has also made mention here in the Acts saying . . .]

[35] Τὸν δὲ κατὰ Κλαύδιον λιμὸν ἐπισημηνάμενος ἐν ταῖς Πράξεσιν ὁ Λουκᾶς ἱστορήσας τε [Luke in the Acts reports the famine in the time of Claudius]

[36] Ἐπεὶ δὲ πάλιν ὁ Λουκᾶς ἐν ταῖς Πράξεσιν εἰσάγει τὸν Γαμαλιήλ [Since again Luke in the Acts introduces Gamaliel]

[37] Καὶ Λουκᾶς, ὁ καὶ τὰς Πράξεις τῶν ἀποστόλων γραφῇ παραδούς, ἐν τούτοις κατέλυσε τὴν ἱστορίαν [Luke, who also committed to writing the Acts of the Apostles, stopped his narrative with this]

[38] ὅθεν εἰκότως τὰς τῶν ἀποστόλων Πράξεις ἐπ᾽ ἐκεῖνον ὁ Λουκᾶς περιέγραψε τὸν χρόνον [wherefore in all likelihood Luke wrote the Acts of the Apostles at that time]

[39] Ὅτι μέν οὖν τοῖς ἐξ ἐθνῶν κηρύσσων ὁ Παῦλος τοὺς ἀπὸ Ἰερουσαλὴμ καὶ κύκλῳ μέχρι τοῦ Ἰλλυρικοῦ τῶν ἐκκλησιῶν καταβέβλητο θεμελίους, δῆλον ἐκ τῶν αὐτοῦ γένοιτ᾽ ἂν φωνῶν καὶ ἀφ᾽ ὧν ὁ Λουκᾶς ἐν ταῖς Πράξεσιν ἱστόρησεν [Therefore, it is clear from Paul's own words and from what Luke recounted in Acts that Paul, when preaching to the Gentiles, laid the foundations of the churches from Jerusalem and the area surrounding Illyricum]. The English translation relies on Eusebius *Historia ecclesiastica*, trans. Kirsopp Lake, LCL 153 (Cambridge, Mass.: Harvard University Press, 1926), p. 195.

[40] οὐ μὴν ἀλλὰ καὶ ὁ Λουκᾶς ἐν ταῖς Πράξεσιν τοὺς γνωρίμους αὐτοῦ κατὰ λέγων ἐξ ὀνόματος αὐτῶν μνημονεύει [moreover even Luke in the Acts records a list of those known to him and mentions them by name]

[41] ὁ δὲ Λουκᾶς ἐν ταῖς Πράξεσιν τῶν ἀποστόλων τῶν Φιλίππου θυγατέρων ἐν Καισαρείᾳ τῆς Ἰουδαίας ἅμα τῷ πατρὶ τότε διατριβουσῶν προφητικοῦ τε χαρίσματος ἠξιωμένων μνημονεύει [Luke in the Acts of the Apostles mentions the daughters of Philip living in Caesarea of Judea with their father and vouchsafed with the gift of prophecy]

[42] "And afterwards this same Luke wrote the Acts of the Apostles"; see Haenchen, *Acts of the Apostles*, p. 10 note 1.

theological-thematic evidence.[43] Stylistic evidence covers a range of *linguistic features* – from diction, grammar, and syntax to sentence structure; as will be shown, it makes the stronger case for single authorship. Theological-thematic evidence covers a spectrum of *topics* – from parallels in the miracle-working ministries of Jesus, Peter, and Paul to symmetrical themes such as salvation history, Christology, or the Spirit. The research in this grouping makes a less formally probative case for the single authorship of Luke and Acts, since views of the theological and thematic unity operate at a level more interpretive and inferential, albeit often supported by stylistic features, than that at which stylistic analysis is conducted. As a result, of these two groups, stylistic evidence is given primary attention.

Stylistic evidence

Luke and Acts scholars who study style often focus on one or more of the following aspects: diction, syntax, grammar, linguistic influences, sources, and the arrangement of material – all of which divide into two methodologically distinct sub-groupings.[44] On the one hand, diction implies not only creative word choice by the author-editor but also deliberate or even unintentional use of grammatical or syntactic patterns.

---

[43] See Werner Georg Kümmel, *The New Testament: The History of the Investigation of its Problems*, trans. S. McLean Gilmour and Howard C. Kee (Nashville, Tenn.: Abingdon Press, 1972) who surveys the history of research contributing to the development of New Testament scholarship. See also Haenchen, *Acts of the Apostles*, pp. 14–50, who details a survey of Acts scholarship; W. Ward Gasque, *A History of the Criticism of the Acts of the Apostles* (Grand Rapids, Mich.: William B. Eerdmans, 1975), who traces the historical development of research in Acts from the pre-critical era through the Tübingen school and its scholarly "descendants" through twentieth-century German, British, and North American influences; Colin J. Hemer, *The Book of Acts in the Setting of Hellenistic History* (Winona Lake, Ind.: Eisenbrauns, 1990; reprint 2001), pp. 308–364; and Fitzmyer, *Luke I–IX*, pp. 1–34.

[44] To view style from a more hermeneutical or narrative critical perspective, scholars such as J. Dawsey call upon the work of Robert Tannehill and Robert Alter in which features of fiction-writing are used to study the style of Luke and Acts. Due to the assumptions that must be made with respect to authorial and narrative unity, I have not included discussion of this type of approach. See J. Dawsey, "The Literary Unity of Luke-Acts: Questions of Style – A Task for Literary Critics," *NTS* 35 (1989), 48–66; Robert Tannehill, *The Narrative Unity of Luke-Acts: A Literary Interpretation*, 2 vols. (Philadelphia, Pa.: Fortress Press, 1986), especially vol. I; and Robert Alter, *The Art of Biblical Narrative* (New York: Basic Books, 1981). Further, for an evaluation of the stylistic relationship between Acts and the Pastoral Epistles, see Jean-Daniel Kaestli, "Luke-Acts and the Pastoral Epistles: The Thesis of a Common Authorship," in C. M. Tuckett (ed.), *Luke's Literary Achievement: Collected Essays*, JSNTSup 116 (Sheffield: Sheffield Academic Press, 1995), pp. 117–120.

In this case, a well-known stylistic research method is *word studies*, which identify lexical or other characteristic patterns. On the other hand, stylistic influences reflecting the writer's background, language orientation, and linguistic preferences manifest as common phraseology, for example, LXX-like language, or linguistic remnants of Aramaic or Hebrew. Source and arrangement of material also inform the analysis of an author-editor's redactional activity. By and large, research methods for analyzing these stylistic influences vary by scholar.

Word studies in Luke and Acts. A number of twentieth-century scholars have produced notable word studies. Although word studies cull out vocabulary and phrases characteristic of Luke, Acts, or both, the line between analysis of diction and grammar or syntax is often blurred. For example, the word καλούμενος indicates both the lexical choice of the verb καλέω and the grammatical choice of a participial construction. The word εἴη indicates selection of the verb εἰμί as well as grammatical use of the optative mood. To be sure, a familiar word study belongs to Henry J. Cadbury,[45] who compared "unusual"[46] vocabulary items in Luke and Acts with their occurrence in texts of classical Attic writers and in post-classical, extra-biblical literary works. An undertaking of great magnitude, Cadbury's list spans Greek words beginning with α to ε,[47] and he concluded "Lukan" vocabulary reflects an Attic literary style as well as the commonly acknowledged LXX-like language. In another word study based on the style and vocabulary in the Acts material encompassing the major summaries (Acts 2:41–5:42), Lucien Cerfaux[48] produced a list of characteristic words and expressions in Luke or Acts representative of the earliest Christian community in Jerusalem. Cerfaux found

[45] Henry J. Cadbury, *The Style and Literary Method of Luke* (Cambridge, Mass.: Harvard University Press, 1920; reprint, Eugene, Ore.: Wipf and Stock Publishers, 2001), pp. 4–39.

[46] "Unusual" vocabulary means uncommon words, i.e., those *not* frequently used by most writers; see ibid., pp. 6, 8.

[47] Ibid., pp. 4–39, studies: (a) common Attic words found in certain Attic writers, e.g., ἄγνωστος, βαθύνω, γεύομαι, δεινῶς, ἐγκάθετος; (b) words found only or mainly in one prose writer before Aristotle, e.g., from Plato, ἀνάγνωσις, βαπτίζω, γεννητός, διαμερισμός, ἐπισφαλής; others include Xenophon, Herodotus, Hippocrates, Thucydides, Demosthenes, Isocrates, Hyperides; (c) words found in poetry but not Attic prose, e.g., ἀγέλη, βαρέω, γέν(ν)ημα, δαιμονίζομαι, ἔα; (d) words belonging to post-classical prose, including Aristotle, e.g., ἄβυσσος, βάπτισμα, γάζα, δεισιδαιμονία, ἐγγίζω; and (e) words used first or only by "Luke," e.g., αἰτίωμα, βλητέον, δεξιολάβος, ἐξομολογέω.

[48] Lucien Cerfaux, "La première communauté chrétienne à Jérusalem: Act. II, 41–V, 42," *ETL* 16 (1939), 6–14. See also Lucien Cerfaux, "La composition de la première partie du Livre des Actes" (first published in *ETL* 13 [1936], pp. 667–691) in *Receuil Lucien Cerfaux: études d'exégèse et d'histoire religieuse de Monseigneur Cerfaux*, vol. II (Leuven: 1954).

hapax legomena, other exclusive expressions, non-exclusive expressions, "Lukanisms," and "Semitisms."[49] More recently, Frans Neirynck and F. van Segbroeck[50] have analyzed stylistic characteristics in Luke and Acts in light of the *Index des caractéristiques stylistiques*[51] produced by M.-É. Boismard and A. Lamouille in their schema of the Occidental and Alexandrian text traditions of Acts. Neirynck and van Segbroeck condense the Boismard–Lamouille index to a list of approximately 615 words and expressions typical of the writer "Luke" in the Luke and Acts manuscripts of the Alexandrian text tradition.[52] While the works of Cadbury, Cerfaux, and Neirynck and van Segbroeck fulfill diverse functional requirements and represent some of the most detailed word studies ever compiled for Luke and Acts, perhaps the most pre-eminent word study was compiled by Sir John C. Hawkins, earlier than all the above and worthy of special attention.

[49] See: (a) *hapax legomena* in the Acts summaries, e.g., κτῆμα, ὕπαρξις, ἀφελότης, ἐνδεής, κτήτορες, κλινάριον, πέριξ, ὀχλέομαι; (b) other characteristic expressions from the summaries, e.g., προστίθημι, ψυχαί, ὁμοθυμαδόν, κατ᾽ οἶκον, μετελάμβανον, αἰνοῦντες τὸν θεόν, ἔχοντες χάριν, οἱ σωζόμενοι, καρδία καὶ ψυχὴ μία, ἀπεδίδουν τὸ μαρτύριον, πωλοῦντες, ἐτίθουν παρὰ τοὺς πόδας τῶν ἀποστόλων, προσκαρτεροῦντες, κοινωνία, κλάσις του ἄρτου, φόβος, τέρατα καὶ σημεῖα, ἐπὶ τὸ αὐτό, ἅπαντα (πάντα) κοινά, πιπράσκω, διαδίδωμι, τιμή, μεγαλύνω, σκιά, ἐπισκιάζω; (c) three examples of forty-four found exclusively in Acts 2:41–5:42 but able to be found elsewhere in the NT: αἰτεῖν ἐλεημοσύνην, ἐπέχω, θάμβος, as well as three examples of eighteen not found exclusively in Acts 2:41–5:42: στερεόω, ἄλλομαι, ἀρνέομαι; (4) of principal "Lukanisms" in Acts 2:41–5:42, four examples from the major Acts summaries out of a total of fifty-seven expressions from Acts 2:41–5:42: διαμερίζω, καθ᾽ ἡμέραν, λαός, κολλᾶσθαι; (5) of Semitisms in Acts 2:41–5:42, two examples from the major Acts summaries out of a total of thirteen: φόβος, ἔχοντες χάριν.

[50] Frans Neirynck and F. van Segbroeck, "Caractéristiques stylistiques," *ETL* 61 (1984), 304–339. Neirynck and van Segbroeck use inventories from other works as guides to obtain scholarly agreement, including Plummer, *Luke*, pp. lii–liii, lix–lx; Hawkins, *Horae Synopticae*; T. Vogel, *Zur Charakteristik des Lukas nach Sprache und Stil: eine philologische Laienstudie*, 2nd edition (Leipzig: 1899), pp. 61–68; Adolf von Harnack, *Lukas der Arzt, der Verfasser des dritten Evangeliums und der Apostelgeschichte* (Leipzig: 1906), pp. 29–46, 51–54, 69–72, 138–150; *Sprüche und Reden Jesu. Die zweite Quelle des Matthäus und Lukas* (Leipzig: 1907), pp. 6–87; Cadbury, *Style and Literary Method*; R. Morgenthaler, *Statistik des neutestamentlichen Wortschatzes* (Zurich: Gotthelf-Verlag, 1958), pp. 51, 181, 182–183; J. Jeremias, *Die Sprache des Lukasevangeliums: Redaktion und Tradition im Nicht-Markus-Stoff des dritten Evangeliums* (Göttingen: Vandenhoeck & Ruprecht, 1980).

[51] Cf. M.-É. Boismard and A. Lamouille, *Texte occidental des Actes des Apôtres: reconstitution et réhabilitation*, vol. II (Paris: Éditions Recherche sur les Civilisations, 1984), pp. 197–209.

[52] E.g., ἀγαλλίασις, βάπτισμα, Γαλιλαῖος, δέ+genitive absolute, ἐᾶν, ζηλωτῆς, ἡγούμενος, θάμβος, ἰᾶσθαι (in its proper sense), καθαιρεῖν, λαλεῖν, μάρτυς (εἶναι/γίνεσθαι)+genitive, Ναζωραῖος, ὁ τε+substantive+καὶ ὁ+substantive, παιδεύειν, ῥῆμα, σάββατον, τάσσειν, υἱοὶ Ἰσραήλ, Φαρισαῖος (singular), χαίρων (at the end of a proposition), ψαλμός, ὥρα.

In his vintage but authoritative *Horae Synopticae*, Sir John C. Hawkins (1909) lists 151 words and phrases "characteristic of Luke" and Acts, contrasted primarily with Matthew and Mark, but also with John, the Pauline letters, and the rest of the New Testament.[53] Hawkins defines "characteristic of Luke" as a word or phrase that occurs at least four times in Luke *and* that is (a) not found in Mark or Matthew at all or (b) found in Luke at least twice as often as Matthew and Mark combined.[54] As a sign of its enduring value, Hawkins' list is reproduced almost three-quarters of a century later in Joseph A. Fitzmyer's commentary on Luke.[55] Included also in Hawkins' work are two shorter lists of words characteristic of the *combined* vocabulary of Luke and Acts contrasted with (a) Matthew and Mark together and (b) Luke alone.[56]

[53] Hawkins, *Horae Synopticae*, pp. 15–24. The 151 terms follow; note that parentheses indicate a word may be accounted for by the subject matter: ἀγαθοποιέω, ἀδικία, ἄδικος, ἀθετέω, ἄν+optative, ἀναστας/ἀναστάντες, ἀνήρ, ἄνθρωπε, ἀπὸ τοῦ νῦν, ἀπολαμβάνω, ἀπόστολος, ἄρχοντες (of the Jews), αὐτὸς ὁ, ἀφαιρέω, ἀφίστημι, ἄχρι, βαλλάντιον, βίος, βρέφος, γε, τό γεγονός, γίνομαι w/ἐπί+acc., γονεῖς, δέομαι, (δέκα), δὲ καί, διαλογισμός, διανοίγω, διατάσσω, διέρχομαι, δικαιόω, δοξάζω τὸν θεόν, ἐγένετο+καί, ἐγένετο+finite verb, ἐγένετο+infinitive, εἰ δὲ μήγε, εἴη (optative), εἰμί w/dat., εἶναι after preposition+article, εἶπεν παραβολήν, εἶπεν δέ/εἶπαν δέ, εἰρήνη, εἰσφέρω, ἐλάχιστον (neut. w/o noun), ἔλεγεν δέ/ἔλεγον δέ, ἔλεος, ἐν μιᾷ τῶν, ἐν ταῖς ἡμέραις ταύταις, ἐν τῷ+infinitive, ἐνώπιον, ἐξαποστέλλω, ἐξέρχομαι ἀπό, ἐπαίρω, ἐπιδίδωμι, ἐπιθυμέω, ἐπιλαμβάνομαι, ἐπιστάτης, ἐρωτάω, ἕτερος, ἔτος, εὐαγγελίζομαι, εὐφραίνω, ἐφίστημι, ἔχω+infinitive, θαυμάζω ἐπί, θεραπεύω ἀπό, (θύω), ἰάομαι, ἰδοὺ γάρ, Ἱερουσαλήμ, καθ'ἡμέραν, καί in apodosis, καὶ αὐτός, καὶ οὗτος, καλούμενος w/names or appellations, κατακλίνω, κατανοέω, κεῖμαι, κλαίω, κλίνω, κοιλία (=womb), κριτής, κρούω, ὁ Κύριος (of Jesus in narrative), λαός, λέγω παραβολήν, λίμνη, (λιμός), ὁ λόγος τοῦ θεοῦ, λύχνος, μετὰ ταῦτα, (μήν), μιμνήσκομαι, (μνᾶ), νομικός, νῦν, (οἰκονόμος), οἶκος (=household/family), ὁμοίως, ὄνομα (nom.), ὀνόματι (=by name), ὅς in attraction, ἀλλὰ οὐχί, παρά (=beyond), παρὰ τοὺς πόδας, παραγίνομαι, παραχρῆμα, παρέχω, πᾶς/πας ὁ λαός, πειρασμός, πέμπω, πίμπλημι, πλῆθος, πλήν, πλούσιος, πράσσω, πρός used of speaking to, προσδέχομαι, προσδοκάω, προστίθημι, προσφωνέω, ῥῆμα, στραφείς, συγγενεύς/ συγγενής/συγγενίς, (συλλαμβάνω), σύν, συνέχω, συνκαλέω, σωτηρία, τε, τίς w/optative, τίς ἐξ ὑμῶν, τις w/nouns, τό before τίς or τί, τό/τά before prepositions, τοῦ before infinitives, τοῦτον (=him), ὑπάρχω, ὑποστρέφω, ὕψιστος, ὑψόω, (φάτνη), φίλος, φοβέομαι of fearing God, φυλάσσω, φωνή with γίνομαι, χαίρω (=rejoicing, not greeting), χάρις, χήρα, ὡς (=when), ὡσεί.

[54] Ibid., p. 15.   [55] Fitzmyer, *Luke I–IX*, pp. 109–114.

[56] Hawkins, *Horae Synopticae*, pp. 27ff. The list for (a) includes words and phrases found in Luke and Acts four times more often than in Matthew and Mark together: ἅγιος, ἄγω, ἱκανός, ὁ+noun, with words inserted in between, οὖ. The list for (b) includes words and phrases that occur at least six times in Luke and Acts taken together and not at all in Matthew or Mark or else at least four times more often in Luke and Acts taken together than in Matthew and Mark together: αἰνέω, ἀνάγω, ἀναιρέω, ἀποδέχομαι, ἀπολογέομαι, ἀτενίζω, βουλή, γνωστός, διότι, ἐάω, ἔθος, εἰσάγω, ἐπέρχομαι, ἡμέρα with γίνομαι, κατέρχομαι, λατρεύω, (ἡ) οἰκουμένη, παράκλησις, παύομαι, περιτέμνω, πόλιν or πόλεις after κατά distributive, πυνθάνομαι, σιγάω, σταθείς and σταθέντες, στρατηγός, συνβάλλω, χαρίζομαι, χρόνοι plural.

Intriguingly, Hawkins discovers there exist between Luke and Acts not only similarities[57] but also substantial *differences*.[58] The differences, not often considered by other scholars, include: (1) words and phrases characteristic of Luke but found at least three times as often in Acts: ἀνήρ, (ἀπόστολος),[59] ἄχρι, ἐγένετο+infinitive, ὀνόματι (="by name"), and τε, as well as (ἀνάγω), ἀπολογέομαι, ἀτενίζω, βουλή, κατέρχομαι, μὲν οὖν, πνεῦμα ἅγιον; (2) words and phrases that never occur in Luke but are found at least five times or more in Acts: αἵρεσις, ἀναλαμβάνω, (ἀνθύπατος), γένος, διαλέγομαι, ἐπαύριον, ἐπικαλέομαι (=being named), ἐπικαλέομαι (=being called), ἐπιμένω, ἐπίσταμαι, μεταπέμπομαι, ὁμοθυμαδόν, ὅραμα, παρρησιάζομαι, προσκαρτερέω, προσλαμβάνομαι, τέρας, τηρέω, (χιλίαρχος), χωρίον; (3) words and phrases rarely occurring in Luke but occurring at least three times or more in Acts: βούλομαι, γνωστός, ἡγεμών, κατά (="against"), κελεύω, μόνον, νομίζω, παρίστημι (transitive), συνέρχομαι, τροφή, υἱοὶ Ἰσραήλ, φημί; (4) words and phrases that occur seven or more times in Luke but never in Acts: ἀγαπάω, ἁμαρτωλός, ἐγένετο+finite verb, ὁμοίως, πλούσιος, στραφείς; and (5) words and phrases occurring at least two or more times more often in Luke than Acts: ἑαυτοῦ, ἐγένετο+καί, εἶπεν δέ or εἶπον δέ, ἐν τῷ+infinitive, ἐξέρχομαι ἀπό, καὶ αὐτός, αὐτὸς ὁ, πλήν. The robustness of the differences leads Hawkins to suggest a remarkable explanation, namely, that a significant *time lapse* occurred between the writing of Luke and Acts!

But I do not know that much attention has been paid to the linguistic *differences* between the two [Luke and Acts]. These, however, are important in their way; for, while quite insufficient to throw doubt on the common authorship, they seem to suggest

---

[57] Ibid., pp. 175–176. Methodologically, Hawkins tabulates figures for the following: (a) the fifty-eight words peculiar to Luke and Acts; (b) seventeen words peculiar to Matthew and Acts; (c) fourteen words peculiar to Mark and Acts; and (d) thirteen words peculiar to John and Acts. The number of words peculiar to Luke and Acts (58) exceeds the other three gospels and Acts combined (17 + 14 + 13 = 44). See also ibid., p. 176, where Hawkins shows that of the 151 words and phrases characteristic of Luke, 115 (76 percent) are found in Acts. Finally, Hawkins, ibid., pp. 183–185, addresses the ninety-seven verses of the "We"-Sections of Acts and shows that, when comparing the frequency of words and phrases characteristic of each gospel with their frequency of occurrence in the "We"-Sections of Acts, those characteristic of Luke are more than twice as likely to be found in the "We"-Sections than those characteristic of Matthew or Mark.

[58] Ibid., pp. 177–182.

[59] Parentheses around a word indicate the subject matter may well be a significant factor in its use.

that *a considerable time must have elapsed between the writing of the two books* [emphasis added].[60]

Said another way, Hawkins concludes:

the two books, though the works of the same writer, could *not* have proceeded from him at the same, or very nearly the same, time [emphasis added].[61]

If the expressions likely dependent on the passages' subject matter are not counted,[62] there exist some fifty-five curious disparities between Luke and Acts. The time-lapse theory, a remarkable but essentially forgotten explanation for these differences, implies that over time the author-editor's compositional circumstances changed, resulting in a degree of non-uniformity in diction and phraseology significant enough to warrant the claim of chronological distance. For Hawkins, however, the differences never suggest different author-editors.

To date, word studies alone do not make the strongest case for or against single authorship; problematic is the tendency to favor one book over the other in regard to depth of coverage or analysis of sources and authorial redaction. The lists of Hawkins and Cadbury, for example, show a preference toward Luke, whereas the lists of Cerfaux and Neirynck and van Segbroeck appear to have a bias toward Acts. As a result, stylistic evidence other than word choice must inform the single authorship hypothesis most unambiguously.

Stylistic evidence other than word choice. Word studies aside, the preponderance of evidence demonstrating stylistic correspondences between Luke and Acts focuses on the writer "Luke's" redactional activity. Built on the works of Sir John C. Hawkins and Alfred Plummer, arguably the most comprehensive redactional study of "Lukan" style belongs to Henry J. Cadbury in *The Style and Literary Method of Luke*.[63]

---

[60] Ibid., p. 177.

[61] Ibid., p. 180. Henry G. Russell, "Which was Written First, Luke or Acts?" *HTR* 48 (1955), 167–174, explores the possibility of Acts' priority.

[62] See footnote 58.

[63] See Cadbury, *Style and Literary Method*, pp. 73–205; for the reference to Hawkins' work, see footnote 2; Plummer, *A Critical and Exegetical Commentary on the Gospel According to S. Luke*, p. 45. Plummer was one of the first to classify the three well-known types of the ἐγένετο structure in Luke and Acts (i.e., ἐγένετο+finite verb, ἐγένετο+καί+finite verb, and ἐγένετο+infinitive). He defended as "practically certain" (p. xi) that the author-editor of the third gospel is the author-editor of Acts by citing the dedication of both books to Theophilus as well as their similar language, style, and

In this landmark work, which presupposes the Two-Document Hypothesis,[64] Cadbury examines the way Luke's author-editor alters and supplements his sources, Mark and "Q." Ably demonstrated is how Luke's author-editor apparently takes editorial liberties with some Markan passages but remains faithful to the original in others. For example, in the "openings" of pericopes, one finds freely altered patterns such as the introduction of καὶ ἐγένετο (e.g., Lk 6:6; 8:40; 9:28, 37; 18:35) and ἐγένετο ἐν μιᾷ (e.g., Lk 5:12, 17; 8:22; 20:1). In the summaries, one also often finds a loose re-wording and re-ordering of the source, for example, the summary in Lk 4:40–41 depends on the sequence Mk 1:14, 28, 21, 39, or Lk 4:4 on Mk 1:39, or Lk 19:28 on Mk 10:32.[65] Cadbury identifies elements of syntax and sentence structure, for example, use of particles such as καί, δέ, and τε, in selected portions of Luke and Acts, as well as lexical preferences in Luke such as the use of θάλασσα or λαός and the avoidance of ὀψία or the diminutive –ιον.[66] Due to the emphasis on "Luke's" redaction of Mark and "Q," references to "Luke's" style in Acts occur less frequently, occasionally found in the footnotes.[67] Indeed, Cadbury's analysis of style in Luke tends to eclipse that in Acts.

Balanced analysis of style in Luke and Acts is represented by two consummate examples, the works of Joseph A. Fitzmyer and Nigel Turner. The first volume of Fitzmyer's Anchor Bible commentary on Luke, *The Gospel According to Luke, I–IX*, thoroughly particularizes the subject of "Lukan" style,[68] building on the works of Hawkins, Cadbury, Eduard Norden,[69] and Nigel Turner.[70] In his careful fashion, Fitzmyer

---

arrangement. Plummer identified the author-editor of Luke and Acts as "Luke the beloved physician," a companion of Paul, basing this opinion on the "voice of the first eight centuries" (p. xiii).

[64] The Two-Document (or Two-Source) Hypothesis posits that Luke is dependent on the Markan gospel and the Sayings Source "Q." Text peculiar to Luke, the so-called "Special L" material, is presumed to represent single or multiple sources of pre-Lukan tradition or be composed by the author-editor himself.

[65] Cadbury, *Style and Literary Method*, pp. 106–110.

[66] Ibid., pp. 142–147, 186–191.

[67] Ibid., e.g., pp. 111, 113f. (and 113 note 2), 129 note 1, 142, 146, 155 (and 155 note 1), 173ff., 178, 188 note 3, 189, 200.

[68] Fitzmyer, *Luke I–IX*, pp. 107–127; cf. *Acts of the Apostles*, pp. 114–118.

[69] Eduard Norden, *Agnostos Theos: Untersuchungen zur Formengeschichte religiöser Rede* (Darmstadt: Wissenschaftliche Buchgesellschaft, 1956); *Die antike Kunstprosa von vi. Jahrhundert v. Chr. bis in die Zeit der Renaissance*, vol. II (Stuttgart: B. G. Teubner, 1958), pp. 480–492.

[70] Nigel Turner, "The Quality of the Greek of Luke-Acts" in J. K. Elliot (ed.), *Studies in New Testament Language and Text: Essays in Honour of George D. Kilpatrick on the Occasion of his Sixty-Fifth Birthday*, Supplements to *Novum Testamentum* 44 (Leiden: Brill, 1976).

studies "Lukan" style from a variety of perspectives. The first analyzes stylistic redaction of Mark, for example, replacement of Mark's historical present with a past tense;[71] elimination of parataxis – Markan or otherwise – replacing it with a genitive absolute;[72] substitution of δέ or τε for καί;[73] introduction of the literary μέν . . . δέ pairings;[74] elimination of superfluous personal pronouns;[75] introduction of relative pronoun attraction to its antecedent;[76] the optative mood;[77] and use of the definite article in indirect questions and with the infinitive to convey result or purpose.[78] Noteworthy is that for many of these Fitzmyer provides corresponding patterns in Acts. Second, Fitzmyer includes Hawkins' vintage list of 151 words and phrases characteristic of Luke and Acts, accenting the durability of Hawkins' work.[79] Lastly, Fitzmyer analyzes twenty-three "Lukan" Septuagintisms, for example, δοξάζειν τὸν θέον (e.g., Lk 2:20; 5:25f.; 7:16; 13:13), or πρὸ προσώπου+genitive (e.g., Lk 7:27; 9:52; 10:1), or πρός+accusative after a verb of speaking (e.g., Lk 1:13; 4:36; 5:22; 7:24, 40; 15:3, 22; 22:15, 70; 23:4; 24:18, 44), as well as so-called Aramaisms, Hebraisms, or Semitisms.[80] Hebraisms, curious since according to Fitzmyer "[t]here is no evidence that Luke knew any Hebrew,"[81] include the three ἐγένετο constructions, the articular infinitive, the unstressed καὶ αὐτός, the introductory καὶ ἰδού, and periphrasis. Fitzmyer identifies similar patterns in Acts, that is, the ἐγένετο+καί+finite verb and ἐγένετο+infinitive constructions,

---

[71] Fitzmyer, *Luke I–IX*, p. 107; e.g., Lk 19:27, 29; 20:20; 22:8, 45. See Hawkins, *Horae Synopticae*, pp. 144ff., for 151 occurrences of the historic present in Mark with their parallels in Matthew and Luke; see also Cadbury, *Style and Literary Method*, pp. 142–145.

[72] E.g., Lk 2:2, 42; 3:21; 4:2, 40, 42; 8:49; 9:37.

[73] Fitzmyer, *Luke I–IX*, p. 108. See also Cadbury, *Style and Literary Method*, pp. 158–159.

[74] Fitzmyer, *Luke I–IX*, p. 107; e.g., Lk 3:16, 18f.; 10:2; 11:48. See also Cadbury, *Style and Literary Method*, pp. 145–146; Turner, "The Quality of the Greek of Luke-Acts," pp. 388f.

[75] Fitzmyer, *Luke I–IX*, p. 107. See also Cadbury, *Style and Literary Method*, pp. 191–192; and Nigel Turner, *Style*, vol. IV of James Hope Moulton (ed.), *A Grammar of New Testament Greek* (Edinburgh: T. & T. Clark, 1976), p. 58.

[76] Fitzmyer, *Luke I–IX*, p. 107; e.g., Lk 1:20, 72f.; 5:9; Acts 1:22; 10:36; 13:2, 38. See also Turner, "The Style of Luke-Acts," p. 59.

[77] Fitzmyer, *Luke I–IX*, p. 107; e.g., Lk 1:28; Acts 8:20 (in wishes); Lk 22:23; Acts 17:11, 27 (in indirect discourse); Lk 1:29; Acts 5:24 (in indirect questions); Acts 24:19 (in conditions); Lk 1:62; Acts 8:31 (in potential expressions, with ἄν). See also Cadbury, *Style and Literary Method*, pp. 191–192; and Turner, "The Style of Luke-Acts," p. 58.

[78] Fitzmyer, *Luke I–IX*, p. 107; e.g., Lk 1:62; 9:46; Acts 4:21; 22:30 (accusative neuter definite article to introduce an indirect question); Lk 1:9; 10:19; Acts 7:19; 26:18 (genitive definite article+infinitive).

[79] See footnote 52 for Hawkins' complete list.

[80] Fitzmyer, *Luke I–IX*, pp. 114–125.   [81] Ibid., p. 118.

the ἐν+dative of the articular infinitive, and the introductory καὶ ἰδού. Fitzmyer's subsequent Anchor Bible commentary on Acts condenses the discussion of style by referring readers to his commentary on Luke.[82] That is to say, Fitzmyer considers the style of Acts so tightly interwoven with Luke's that, except for a few Acts-only elements, he has placed the whole discussion of Acts style in the Luke commentary.[83] A closely integrated style is thus confirmed.

Nigel Turner, author of "The Style of Luke-Acts" in *A Grammar of the Greek New Testament* and "The Quality of the Greek of Luke-Acts" in *Studies in New Testament Language and Text*, analyzes the style of Luke and Acts in meticulously balanced fashion.[84] He samples data from seven types of passage in Luke and Acts, each roughly 250–270 lines in the Nestle-Aland *Novum Testamentum Graece*; see Figure 1.1.

Turner's analysis of sentence structure, syntax, and diction in these passages integrates two additional comparisons: first, the influence of pre-first-century Aramaic,[85] Hebrew,[86] and Semitic[87] sources; and second, the presence of literary elements in comparable passages of roughly contemporaneous Greek writers such as Josephus, Polybius, Plutarch, Epictetus, Lucian, and Philostratus, as well as the authors of LXX prophetic literature, the book of Revelation, and the Didache. Although more justice is due Turner's analysis than can be given here, a few relevant conclusions are as follows. Many so-called literary elements, such as use of μέν . . . δέ . . . , genitives absolute, and relative pronoun attraction, are also found

---

[82] Fitzmyer, *Acts of the Apostles*, p. 114, writes:
> The following remarks will simply supplement what is already found in *Luke*, 113–25, for the most part adding references to Acts that supply further examples of what is already given there.

Two additional Septuagintisms are presented in the Acts commentary, namely, εἰ introducing a direct question and ἐπαίρειν τὴν φωνήν meaning to raise one's voice, as well as allusions to the frequent use of genitives absolute and Latin words.

[83] Moreover, in support of single authorship, Fitzmyer relies on internal as well as patristic evidence; see e.g., Fitzmyer, *Luke I–IX*, pp. 35–53; Although mentioning the challenges to single authorship, he fully accepts single authorship, arguing that to "dismiss the substance of the tradition – that Luke wrote the Third Gospel and Acts – seems gratuitous" (p. 41). That opinion remains unchanged in his subsequent AB commentary on Acts in 1998 (*Acts of the Apostles*, pp. 49–51). See also Fitzmyer's "The Authorship of Luke-Acts Reconsidered" in *Luke the Theologian: Aspects of His Teaching* (New York: Paulist Press, 1989), pp. 1–26.

[84] For the full reference to the first article, see footnote 74; for the second, see footnote 70.

[85] Turner, "Style of Luke-Acts," pp. 45f.   [86] Ibid., pp. 46ff.

[87] Ibid., pp. 50ff. Examples include πρός after verbs of speaking or the definite article+noun without any qualifying phrase in between.

	Type	Text	Approximate length
1	Infancy narrative	Lk 1:5–2:52	269 lines
2	Lukan "Q"	Lk 6:20–7:10; 7:18–35; 9:57–62; 10:2–15, 21–24; 11:2–4, 9–26, 29–36	277 lines
3	Text redacted from Mark	Lk 8:4–9:50	276 lines
4	"Special L" material	Lk 15:1–16:15; 16:19–31; 17:7–21; 18:1–14; 19:1–27	268 lines
5	First part of Acts, i.e., Acts 1–15	Acts 3:1–5:42	268 lines
6	Second part of Acts, i.e., Acts 16–28	17:1–19:40	275 lines
7	"We"-Sections	16:10–18; 20:5–15; 21:1–18; 27:1–28:16	253 lines

Figure 1.1 Luke and Acts texts analyzed by Nigel Turner

in biblical Greek, often in the intertestamental material.[88] Quite surprising is that Lk 15:11–32, the parable of the prodigal son in the "Special L" material, frequently considered one of the least Semitic passages in Luke, in fact contains a greater percentage of Semitisms than any other sample passage. To wit, Turner shows, it contains Aramaisms (e.g., ἤρξατο in 15:14; πορευθείς in 15:15), Hebraisms (e.g., εἰς ἑαυτὸν ἐλθὼν in 15:17; general priority of verb over subject in regard to word order), and Septuagintisms (e.g., ἥμαρτον εἰς . . . in 15:18, 21). Turner concludes the style of Luke and Acts contains a Semitic flavor throughout, a fact he attributes at least in part to features inherent in the primitive Christian language. The most comprehensive and balanced of any scholar's work herein discussed, Turner's analysis successfully sidesteps many obstacles by not only including a comparative analysis of a wide range of non-biblical material but also not favoring one book, Luke or Acts, over the other vis-à-vis depth of coverage.

---

[88] Ibid., pp. 57ff. For an investigation of Hellenistic and Attic verb style in Luke and Acts compared with that in the works of Dionysius of Halicarnassus, see David L. Mealand, "Luke-Acts and the Verbs of Dionysius of Halicarnassus," *JSNT* 63 (1996), pp. 63–86.

Problems with the stylistic evidence. Similar patterns of word choice, syntax, grammar, and linguistic influences seem to link Luke and Acts not only inextricably but also unshakably. The single authorship hypothesis, reinforced by the two books' stylistic correspondences, acquires almost shatterproof certainty. Problems with this effectively unassailable position, however, are two-fold. First, with the exception of Turner's work, stylistic analyses of Luke and Acts tend to treat one book more comprehensively than the other. Why? What makes asymmetrical treatment the rule rather than the exception? The answer is unclear. Richard Pervo suggests that, although Luke and Acts ought to be read "against one another," commentaries largely ignoring the other volume continue to be written.[89] This lack of balance discloses a second problem. The investigation of style reveals a notable absence of detailed inquiry into the *differences* between Luke and Acts. Except for Hawkins' work, differences are downplayed or totally ignored. Why? The reason is that single authorship is simply taken for granted; there is no need to hunt for differences when authorial unity is assumed. Therefore, differences must and will be taken into consideration.

Theological-thematic evidence

Although stylistic similarities shape much of the internal evidence on which the single authorship hypothesis is based, scholars also study theological and thematic internal evidence shared by Luke and Acts. An often-noted unifying paradigm, for example, is how the author-editor of Luke and Acts endeavors to anchor events in *concrete* time and place. The concretizing of Jesus' historical context is, according to most scholars, especially visible in Luke, in sharp contrast to Matthew, Mark, and John. In Luke, the author-editor uses such constructs in the preface (Lk 1:1–4) to reveal a chronological distance of two or three generations from the Christ-event. Then the historical and political location of the beginnings of John and Jesus are contextualized in the infancy narrative (1:6; 2:1–2) and at the beginning of John's ministry (3:1–3). In the Passion narrative, Luke's author-editor mentions Jesus' audience with Herod Antipas (23:6–16). Similarly, in Acts, the author-editor uses historical references to concretize the time of the Jewish high-priestly class of Annas, Caiaphas, and others (Acts 4:6) and the administration of Roman government officials such as Gallio (18:12–17), M. Antonius

---

[89] Richard Pervo, "Israel's Heritage and Claims upon the Genre(s) of Luke and Acts: The Problems of a History" in Moessner, *Jesus and the Heritage of Israel*, p. 128.

Felix (24:1–23), and Porcius Festus (24:27–25:27). To acknowledge the wide-ranging contributions to research on the theological and thematic similarities between Luke and Acts and to respond to problems associated with them would require another book-length treatment. Therefore, a cautious and brief summary of the breadth and depth of such research follows two main orientations, one based on structure and the other based on ideation.

Structural orientation. A structural orientation is one where the two books' commonalities follow a *high-level organizing principle.* In this orientation, Luke and Acts are bound together to model a particular unified framework or structural arrangement. One well-rehearsed example is the temporal periodization of salvation history suggested by Hans Conzelmann.[90] Although extensively revised in later years, Hans Conzelmann's three-fold periodization – stretching first from creation of the world to John the Baptist's imprisonment, then from Jesus' baptism to his ascension, and finally from Jesus' ascension to his parousia – has remained a notable contribution to the perspective on theological continuity from Luke to and through Acts. According to Conzelmann and others who revisit his schema, Luke and Acts together form an integrated framework representing the first-century theological *Weltanschauung* of their common author-editor. Inasmuch as the theological structure of Conzelmann's unified periodization presumes the hypothesis of common authorship,[91] he claims theological internal evidence trumps the stylistic: "*If these* [Luke and Acts] *form a self-contained scheme, then for our purpose literary critical analysis is only of secondary importance.* Nevertheless, in this secondary sense it is important, and is therefore not to be despised [emphasis added]."[92]

Quite distinct from Conzelmann's theory, another well-known demonstration of structural orientation is that of Charles H. Talbert, who finds numerous sets of balanced framing and thematic correspondences *within* Luke and Acts and *between* Luke and Acts.[93] In examining them meticulously, he determines in what ways they reveal the author-editor's

---

[90] See Hans Conzelmann, *The Theology of St. Luke*, trans. Geoffrey Buswell (New York: Harper & Row, 1961), pp. 16–17; originally published as *Die Mitte der Zeit* (Tübingen: J. C. B. Mohr, 1953).

[91] Two comprehensive critical examinations of Conzelmann's work may be found in Fitzmyer, *Luke I–IX*, pp. 181–187, and Charles H. Talbert, *Literary Patterns, Theological Themes, and the Genre of Luke-Acts* (Missoula, Mont.: Scholars Press, 1975), pp. 103–107.

[92] Conzelmann, *Theology of St. Luke*, p. 9.

[93] Talbert, *Literary Patterns*, pp. 16–18, 23f., 26f., 35f., 40, 44, 45, 51f., 57f., 58f., 61.

theological perspective,[94] especially the "Lukan" *Heilsgeschichte* and Christology.[95] As theological-thematic internal evidence, Talbert's parallel arrangements show a literary architecture of theme and style, within and between the two books. As two key representatives of structurally oriented research, the Talbert and Conzelmann examples are deeply rooted in the authorial unity of Luke and Acts.

Ideational orientation. An ideational orientation is one that reveals how *a specific theological concept or theme is used or developed in a parallel way in both books.* As defined, the primary difference between a structural and ideational orientation is one of ratio: the structural maps the two books to one structure (2:1), whereas the ideational maps one concept or theme to the two books (1:2). Analyzed synthetically, ideational evidence typically supports an over-arching theological-thematic construct, e.g., Christology, soteriology, or eschatology, and appears in parallel strands in Luke and Acts. Skillfully represented examples are found in J. A. Fitzmyer's commentary on Luke.[96] In a balanced theological-thematic treatment of both Luke and Acts, Fitzmyer's sketch is derived from the Lukan kerygma, redaction of traditional material, geographical and historical emphases, and soteriology, all of which allow him to produce a broad outline of "Lukan" theology.

Scholarship especially in genre and narrative criticism has seen a veritable sea change in theological perspective, from understanding Luke and Acts as a sequence of two books to treating "Luke-Acts" as a narrative unity.[97] The one-book-in-two-parts view has had the effect of cementing even more strongly the single authorship hypothesis. Even a study devoted completely to Acts does not acknowledge there could be questions of disunity between Luke and Acts; Colin J. Hemer suggests the case for the authorial unity requires minimal attention, as it is a mere "datum of the problem."[98] As noted above, Mikeal Parsons and Richard Pervo, in contrast, argue that the unity of the two books may not be as tightly

---

[94] Ibid., pp. 89–124.

[95] For an opinion on the divergent Christological portraits in Luke and Acts, see Erwin R. Goodenough, "The Perspective of Acts," in Leander E. Keck and J. Louis Martyn (eds.), *Studies in Luke-Acts: Essays Presented in Honor of Paul Schubert, Buckingham Professor of New Testament Criticism and Interpretation at Yale University* (Nashville, Tenn.: Abingdon Press, 1966; London: SPCK, 1968, 1976, 1978; Philadelphia, Pa.: Fortress Press, 1980; reprint, Mifflintown, Penn.: Sigler Press, 1999), pp. 51–59.

[96] Fitzmyer, *Luke I–IX*, pp. 143–270.

[97] For a full treatment of this perspective, see Tannehill, *The Narrative Unity of Luke-Acts*.

[98] Hemer, *The Book of Acts in the Setting of Hellenistic History*, p. 30.

woven as thought: "There are theological themes and threads that extend through Luke and Acts, but to speak of a monolithic theological unity would be an exaggeration."[99] Parsons and Pervo convincingly suggest that a fully integrated Christology, eschatology, theological anthropology, soteriology, or ecclesiology has yet to be demonstrated. Although they presume single authorship, Parsons and Pervo rightly conclude that this premise does not alone guarantee a coherent unity:

> *Acceptance of the authorial unity of Luke and Acts should not imply acceptance of unity on other levels.* All types of unity are hypotheses rather than assured results. The canonical disunity deserves a bit more than curt dismissal. Luke and Acts may belong to one genre, but the explorations of separate genres have thus far yielded interesting data and should not be excluded. As narratives they are independent yet interrelated works. Theological unity ought not be a brush with which to efface particularity [emphasis added].[100]

The import of this citation resonates in many New Testament exegetical circles, yet its underlying integrity rests on the first nine words: "Acceptance of the authorial unity of Luke and Acts . . ." Should we not rethink *all* aspects, *including* authorial unity?

Challenges to the single authorship hypothesis

Although miniscule in number, challenges to authorial unity have been summarily rebutted, rejected, neglected, or ignored. As mentioned above, the challenges follow two major trajectories, the first of which understands Luke and Acts as the fulfillment of differing theological agendas. On this trajectory, for example, is the work of F. C. Baur, an early representative of the Tübingen school, who argued that a follower of Paul wrote Acts but not the gospel of Luke.[101] According to Baur, Acts mitigates Paul's earlier hard-line stance on the Mosaic law and Judaic traditions and serves as an apology for a type of Paulinism that stood in opposition to a powerful Jewish-Christian party.[102] Hence, Acts *harmonizes* the

---

[99] Parsons and Pervo, *Rethinking the Unity of Luke and Acts*, p. 114.

[100] Ibid., p. 126.

[101] Ferdinand Christian Baur, *Paul, the Apostle of Jesus Christ: His Life and Work, His Epistles and His Doctrine*, vol. I, trans. Eduard Zeller (London: Williams and Norgate, 1873), pp. 12–13.

[102] Ibid., p. 12. It should be noted that Baur uses Matthias Schneckenburger, *Über den Zweck der Apostelgeschichte* (Berne: Chr. Fischer, 1841), pp. 92–95 but carries further

conflicted relations between two competing Christianities, a controversy that lasted well into the second century. Granting the "We"-Sections and other Acts narratives could have been composed by the author-editor of Luke, Baur claims the on-going conflict between the two Christianities not only implies a later date for the composition of Acts but also substantiates its uniqueness, as well as the anonymity of its author-editor:

> If we carefully consider these relations and the order in which they must have arisen, and remember that not for some time could they acquire such importance, we shall be carried on by them to a point when *we can no longer maintain the authorship of Luke for the Acts of the Apostles, at least in the form in which we possess the work* [emphasis added].[103]

Baur's different authorship hypothesis rests on a complex theological interpretation of the early Christian religious milieu. Although for his time he added depth and strength to a critical perspective on the distinction of early Gentile and Jewish Christianity, later scholars argue Baur's hypothesis of different authorship may be drawn from an oversimplification of the historical situation.[104]

In 1873, J. H. Scholten published another challenge to single authorship.[105] Largely based on his interpretation of two strands of Pauline Jewish-Christianity not altogether unlike Baur's, Scholten argues against the homogeneity of Luke and Acts. On the one hand, the third gospel, not yet in the canon, occupies itself far more than Acts with the points of faith, good works, Christology, soteriology, and eschatology. On the other hand, Acts is seen essentially as a Paulinist apology to convince the Jewish-Christian "party" of the legitimacy of Gentile Christianity. A more original Paulinist gospel of Luke came from the hand of a *verzoenenden* (reconciling) Paulinist, and the Marcion version from the hand of an ultra-Paulinist. The former became canonical, the latter heretical. Scholten's argument against the tradition of single authorship, radical for

---

the idea that the Luke of Church tradition as author of both the third gospel and Acts is contradictory to his (Baur's) analysis. See H. Windisch, "The Case Against the Tradition" in F. J. Foakes Jackson and Kirsopp Lake (eds.), *The Beginnings of Christianity, Part 1: The Acts of the Apostles, vol. II.: Prolegomena: Criticism* (London: Macmillan and Co., 1922), p. 298 note 2. See also Kümmel, *The New Testament: The History of the Investigation of Its Problems*, pp. 133ff.

[103] Baur, *Paul, the Apostle of Jesus Christ*, p. 12.

[104] So Haenchen, *Acts of the Apostles*, p. 17. For his survey of critical research on Acts, see pp. 14–50.

[105] J. H. Scholten, *Is de derde evangelist de schrijver van het boek der Handelingen? Critisch onderzoek* (Leiden: Academische Boekhandel van P. Engels, 1873), pp. 95–99.

its time, shifts the question of authorship to the second century CE and bases it in a more political milieu.[106]

In the twentieth century, two scholars critically challenged the single authorship hypothesis. To be sure, they may be called χωρίζοντες, a term in antiquity for those who supposed the Iliad and Odyssey had different authors![107] Whereas commentaries on Luke or Acts occasionally mention the two challenges and their rebuttals, voices in opposition to the *opinio communis* remain faint indeed.[108]

Challenge by Albert C. Clark (1933)

Published in 1933 by the Clarendon Press at Oxford, Albert C. Clark's critical edition of Acts advanced the study of ancient Acts manuscripts, especially those connected to *D* (*codex Bezae*).[109] The appendix entitled "Authorship of Luke and Acts"[110] challenges single authorship by means of three observations: (1) similarities between Luke and Acts are overstated; (2) similarities between Acts and the Pauline Epistles are

---

[106] For a discussion of the "radical Holland" view, see H. Windisch, "The Case Against the Tradition," pp. 307f. For a vintage perspective, see J. MacRory, "The Authorship of the Third Gospel and the Acts," *ITQ* 2 (1907), 190–202.

[107] Hemer, *The Book of Acts in the Setting of Hellenistic History*, p. 30.

[108] Also mentioned occasionally is J. Wendham, "The Identification of Luke," *EvQ* 63 (1991), 3–44, who argues a conservative point of view that Luke and the other synoptic gospels had been written by 55 CE and *that Luke was present during Jesus' lifetime and death*. Wendham appears to attribute to possible corrupted transmission or to faulty interpretation such statements as the one in the Lukan preface (Lk 1:1–4) stating or implying that Luke was not an eye-witness.

[109] Albert C. Clark, *The Acts of the Apostles: A Critical Edition with Introduction and Notes on Selected Passages* (Oxford: Clarendon Press, 1933; reprint 1970), offers evidence that *D* as most representative of the longer "Western text" has been mislabeled and misjudged, since it can be shown that similar texts existed in the East; e.g., Egypt in IV CE (pp. xv–xix). In a clever attempt to promote objective treatment of *D* and similar manuscripts (e.g., the Fleury palimpsest 𝔏^h and Old Latin manuscripts, translated from Greek versions older than any extant ones), Clark substitutes a neutral symbol Z for them and Γ (=*Graeci*) for the earliest Greek uncials (ℵ A B C). At the risk of over-simplification, Clark's argument may be summarized as follows: the direction of dependence is Z → Γ rather than Γ → Z (pp. xv–lxiv). That is, instead of viewing the longer Z readings as interpolations into Γ, Clark argues that numerous instances of the shorter Γ passages represent omission of a *D* στίχος due to *homoeoteleuton*, many of which then have been "botched" or amended in Γ "to make a construction after an omission" to generate good Greek (pp. xxiv–xxxii). Examples of simple omission include Acts 4:32 and 11:1–2. Examples of omission and "botching" include Acts 2:30, 37; 3:3; 14:19; 15:12; and 21:25. For a review of Clark's work, see Kirsopp Lake and Silva Lake, "The Acts of the Apostles," *JBL* 53 (1934), 34–45. For a review of others who give priority to the "Western" tradition, see J. Delobel, "The Text of Luke-Acts: A Confrontation of Recent Theories" in Verheyden, *Unity of Luke-Acts*, pp. 83–108.

[110] Clark, *Acts of the Apostles*, pp. 393–408.

understated; and (3) differences between Luke and Acts signal the work of different writers.[111] Although problematic to Clark's second observation is the presupposition of thirteen authentic Pauline epistles, this difficulty does not fatally flaw his challenge if one focuses on the first observation, that is, his figures for Luke and Acts. À propos the first and third observations, Clark tabulates differences in four general categories:[112] (1) particle and preposition use and the case of ἀνήρ and ἄνθρωπος; (2) lexical differences between Acts and all four gospels; (3) the ἐγένετο argument; and (4) singular features of Acts. Details will be laid out shortly after an introduction of the major rebuttal to Clark.

Rebuttal by Wilfred L. Knox (1942)

The chief refutation of Clark's different authorship proposal came from Wilfred L. Knox[113] in a lecture series on Acts delivered at Oxford in 1942. Knox's critique, which rightly criticizes many of Clark's statistics primarily for a neglect of source issues, will be included below when appropriate to explaining the details of Clark's four-pronged challenge. An assessment of their analytical methodologies follows that.

Category 1: Particle and preposition use: τε; μέν; σύν/μετά+genitive; and the case of ἀνήρ and ἄνθρωπος

Clark detects a striking divergence in the use of particles and prepositions between Luke and Acts, suggesting to him styles singular enough to challenge common authorship. It is, he claims, the patterns of small parts of speech, i.e., particles and prepositions, which contain the most

---

[111] Ibid., p. 394.

[112] Clark obtains his figures from the concordance by Carl Hermann Bruder, *Concordantiae omnium vocum Novi Testamenti graeci: primum ab Erasmo Schmidio editae, nunc secundum critices et hermeneutices nostrae aetatis rationes emendata auctae meliori ordine dispositae* (Lipsiae: Sumptibus Ernesti Bredtii, 1867). Bruder's counts differ slightly from the counts in the W. F. Moulton and A. S. Geden (hereafter "Moulton-Geden") concordance, also used by Clark. See W. F. Moulton and A. S. Geden, *A Concordance to the Greek New Testament*, 3rd edition (Edinburgh: T. & T. Clark, 1926). Further, I noticed a slight difference is also obtained if Clark's numbers are checked against a concordance of the Nestle-Aland *Novum Testamentum Graece* 27th edition. For all intents and purposes, however, the degree of disparity does not affect the force of Clark's arguments.

[113] The lectures were published two years later; see Wilfred L. Knox, *Some Hellenistic Elements in Primitive Christianity*, The Schweich Lectures on Biblical Archaeology, 1942 (London: Oxford University Press, 1944; Munich, Kraus Reprint, 1980), pp. 1–15. For more details on his position, see Knox, *The Acts of the Apostles* (Cambridge: Cambridge University Press, 1948).

valuable authorship evidence,[114] yet they rarely appear on the research "radar screen." For example, Clark finds 8 occurrences of τε in Luke but a stunning 158 in Acts.[115] Of those in Luke, all are in the τε καί construction. Of those in Acts, 59 are in the τε καί construction and 99 in others. The case of μέν is also striking, as there are 11 occurrences in Luke and 51 in Acts,[116] including the special case, μὲν οὖν, of which Luke contains 1 and Acts 27, and the special class, μὲν *solitarium*,[117] of which Luke contains 1 and Acts 15. In the case of σύν+genitive or μετά+genitive, Luke favors μετά, 52 occurrences to 26 of σύν, whereas Acts favors σύν, 51 occurrences to 37 of μετά.[118] As for ἀνήρ and ἄνθρωπος, Luke has 27 occurrences of ἀνήρ and 100 of ἄνθρωπος, whereas Acts has 101 occurrences of ἀνήρ and 46 of ἄνθρωπος. Finally, Clark reports that διά+genitive occurs in Acts over three times as often as in Luke (Lk=15; Acts=51). While impressive, Clark's figures hide inherent problems that disallow their use "as is."

To rebut Clark's challenge, Knox, although admitting the τε patterns make a *prima facie* case for different authorship,[119] remarks that in Luke, because τε occurs 4 times in the "Special L" material, 2 in the redaction of Mark, and 2 in the redaction of "Q," the author-editor would have liked to use τε more freely (!), a rather speculative critique. About Clark's other figures, however, Knox's criticism is decidedly persuasive. Concerning the three μέν constructions, μέν (Lk=11; Acts=51), μὲν οὖν (Lk=1; Acts=27), and μὲν *solitarium* (Lk=1; Acts=15), Knox shows the author-editor of Luke introduced the first type 6 times in redaction or independent composition and kept 4 occurrences already in his sources,[120] which implies of course that μέν is part of the author-editor's stylistic

---

[114] Clark, *Acts of the Apostles*, p. 395.

[115] Ibid., p. 396. The eight occurrences in Luke are Lk 2:16; 12:45; 15:2; 21:11 (*bis*); 22:66; 23:2; 24:20, found in the Bruder concordance. Clark points out that Moulton-Geden shows another τε in Lk 14:26, which to Clark is "an obvious error for δέ." The Nestle-Aland *Novum Testamentum Graece* 27th edition also reads τε in Lk 14:26 (B L Δ 33. 892 *pc*) and δέ in the critical apparatus (𝔓45 ℵ A D W Θ Ψ f1,13 𝔐 lat syh samss bo) or an omission of the particle altogether (𝔓75 sams). The reading from the earliest witnesses, i.e., δέ in 𝔓45 and omitted in 𝔓75 respectively, appear to be more difficult than τε and so deserve re-consideration. Clark points out that in Acts the Moulton-Geden concordance shows 134 occurrences of τε, whereas the Bruder shows the 158 total that Clark used.

[116] Clark, *Acts of the Apostles*, pp. 397f.

[117] That is, μέν occurs without an accompanying δέ.

[118] The preposition σύν is somewhat rare in the other gospels (Mt 4, Mk 5, and Jn 3, according to Bruder), and it does not appear in Hebrews or the Pastoral Epistles at all.

[119] Knox, *Acts of the Apostles*, p. 11.

[120] Ibid., p. 10. This is an instance of a divergence in the Bruder vs. Moulton-Geden concordances, i.e., eleven occurrences to ten.

repertoire. In Acts, the first type occurs once in the preface, 16 times in the first half (Acts 1:5–12:25), and 31 times in the second.[121] Moreover, the second type, μὲν οὖν, occurring only once in Luke, occurs 9 times in the first half of Acts and 18 times in the second. Knox concludes either there exists no reason to propose different authorship of Luke and the *first* part of Acts or else the first part of Acts had a different author-editor from the *second* part,[122] a witty but also speculative assertion. Differences in the use of ἀνήρ (Lk=27; Acts=101) and ἄνθρωπος (Lk=100; Acts=46) may not be so striking either, opines Knox, because in Acts ἀνήρ occurs 29 times in the vocative, while in Luke ἄνθρωπος appears 24 times in the "Son of Man/Humanity" title. Concluding that particle and preposition differences, as well as differences in the use of ἀνήρ / ἄνθρωπος, should be considered no more than moderate, Knox considers Clark's figures markedly inflated owing to Clark's neglect of the sources used in Luke.

Category 2: Lexical differences between Acts and the four gospels

Independent of subject matter, ordinary words found in Luke and the other three gospels are used in Acts, if at all, in a different way.[123] Albert Clark records 4 common words found in the four gospels but not in Acts;[124] 6 found in the four gospels but *rarely* in Acts;[125] 8 found in Acts but not in the four gospels;[126] and 7 found in Acts but *rarely* in the four gospels.[127] In general, these differences support Clark's challenge, although in the

---

[121] Knox's use of the Moulton-Geden concordance means his figures differ slightly from those in the Bruder concordance used by Clark. For the full references to these concordances, see footnote 114.

[122] Knox, *Acts of the Apostles*, p. 10.   [123] Clark, *Acts of the Apostles*, pp. 399–400.

[124] πόθεν (Lk=4), μακρόθεν (Lk=4), ποτέ (Lk=4), and ὑπάγω (Lk=6).

[125] ἀκολουθεῖν (Lk=17, Acts=4), ἀφιέναι (Lk=34, Acts=3), βάλλειν (Lk=19, Acts=5), μνημεῖον (Lk=10, Acts=1), παιδίον (Lk=14, Acts=0), and ὧδε (Lk=16, Acts=2).

[126] ἐλπίς (Acts=8), ἐπικαλεῖσθαι (+acc) (Acts=11), ἡμέτερος (Acts=3), καταντᾶν (Acts=9), μάλιστα (Acts=3), ξενίζειν (Acts=7), παρρησιάζεσθαι (Acts=11), and χρῆσθαι (Acts=2).

[127] ἀναλαμβάνειν (Lk=0; Acts=8), ἄχρι (Lk=4; Acts=16), βούλεσθαι (Lk=2; Acts=14), διό (Lk=2; Acts=10), ἐπιμένειν (Lk=0; Acts=8), συνέρχεσθαι (Lk=2; Acts=17), and τέρος (Lk=0; Acts=9). With respect to βούλεσθαι, Clark contrasted it with figures for its Hellenistic Greek replacement θέλειν (Lk=28, Acts=16). In Luke, the difference in the counts for βούλεσθαι (2) and θέλειν (28) is striking. In Luke, βούλεσθαι occurs in Lk 10:22, a "Q" passage, and in Lk 22:42, a redaction of the beginning of Jesus' prayer in Gethsemene. In Acts, βούλεσθαι is found in Acts 5:28, 5:33; 12:4; 15:37; 17:20; 18:15, 27; 19:30; 22:30; 23:28; 25:20, 22; 27:43; 28:18, all but three of which occur in the second half.

Type		Lk	Acts	Mt	Mk	Jn
1	ἐγένετο+finite verb	22	0		2	
2	ἐγένετο+καί+finite verb	11	1 (?)	1		
3	ἐγένετο+infinitive	5	16		1	

Figure 1.2 Clark's tabulations for the three types of ἐγένετο construction

third list of 8 words found in Acts but not in the four gospels, certain words in Acts appear only infrequently at best: χρῆσθαι appears only twice, and ἡμέτερος and μάλιστα 3 times.[128] On these differences Knox remains silent.

Category 3: The ἐγένετο argument

Long known to be characteristic of Luke and Acts,[129] three types of [καί] ἐγένετο or ἐγένετο [δέ], shown in Figure 1.2, occur with varying frequency in Luke and Acts, according to Clark.[130]

In Luke, Clark finds a total of 33 (33=22+11) occurrences of the first two constructions and 5 of the third.[131] By contrast, in Acts, he finds a total of 0 occurrences of the first construction and perhaps 1 of the second, but 16 of the third. While these are rather striking differences, counters Knox, what argues *against* Clark's numbers is this: in showing the first type is peculiar to Luke but not to Acts, Clark omits Matthew's five hieratic uses of ἐγένετο ὅτε that terminate the five major discourses

[128] In the same list of eight above, Clark points out the conspicuous absence of ἐλπίς in all four gospels. It is worth noting, however, that of the eight occurrences of ἐλπίς in Acts, all but two occur in the last five chapters (Acts 23:6; 24:15; 26:6, 7; 27:20; 28:20) and one in a quote from Joel (2:26).

[129] Clark, *Acts of the Apostles*, p. 401. Other scholars' descriptions of the three classifications include, e.g., Plummer, *A Critical and Exegetical Commentary on the Gospel According to S. Luke*, p. 45, considered the first to so categorize; Cadbury, *Style and Literary Method*, p. 132; Turner, "The Style of Luke-Acts," pp. 46–47; and Fitzmyer, *Acts of the Apostles*, p. 115.

[130] Clark states that he draws upon the work of Plummer, *A Critical and Exegetical Commentary on the Gospel According to S. Luke*, p. 45.

[131] Clark, *Acts of the Apostles*, p. 401. In fact, Knox, *Acts of the Apostles*, p. 6, describes Types 1 and 2 as ungrammatical Greek constructions or barely so and Type 3 as acceptably grammatical.

(Mt 7:28; 9:1; 13:53; 19:1; 26:1).[132] According to Knox, this paradigm might have influenced the author-editor of Luke enough to infuse the gospel with a hieratic sense, since the gospel of Luke was likely read in early Christian worship services.[133] Planting Hebraisms in ungrammatical or barely acceptable Greek would "produce a biblical ring"[134] that did not require a working knowledge of the LXX. To Knox these ἐγένετο discrepancies prove nothing, since their presence can be explained, albeit somewhat weakly, without any appeal to different authorship.

Category 4: Singular features of Acts

To support his challenge, Clark introduces characteristics peculiar to Acts: (1) the rarity of ἐάν, ὅς ἄν, and ὅταν in Acts compared with Luke;[135] (2) contrasting use of ὅπως and ἵνα;[136] (3) rare types of the optative in Acts;[137] (4) unusual constructions in Acts;[138] (5) contrasting types of negation;[139] and (6) contrasting sets of synonym choices.[140] Except for the last set involving synonym choice, the first five contrast syntax and grammar, for example, the use of negation, conjunctions, or verbal mood. Again, Knox remains silent, no rebuttal or critique of any of the sets.

In sum, to Clark the evidence when viewed together overwhelmingly confirms his suggestion that the *understatement* of differences between Luke and Acts is subordinated to an *overstatement* of similarities:

---

[132] Knox, *Acts of the Apostles*, p. 7. According to Knox, the following two circumstances may argue *for* the validity of Clark's claim of different authorship: (1) in Luke, Type 1 occurs eight (of twenty-two) times in the characteristically Semitic infancy narrative and six (of twenty-two) times in intentional redactions of Markan material that have no corresponding construct; and (2) in Luke, Type 2 occurs six (of eleven) times in intentional redactions of Markan material that have no corresponding construct.

[133] Ibid.   [134] Ibid.

[135] Clark, *Acts of the Apostles*, pp. 401ff.: ἐάν (Lk=30; Acts=6), ὅς ἄν (Lk=20; Acts=4), and ὅταν (Lk=29; Acts=2).

[136] Ibid.: ὅπως (Lk=38; Acts=12), and ἵνα (Lk=7; Acts=15).

[137] Ibid.: Acts 8:20, 31; 17:18, 27; 20:16; 24:19; 25:16; 26:29; 27:12; see Clark, *Acts of the Apostles*, 402.

[138] Ellipse of ἔφη and εἶπεν (Acts=9); καὶ νῦν (Acts=9); future infinitive (Acts=5); future participle to express purpose (Acts=1).

[139] Clark, *Acts of the Apostles*, pp. 401ff.: μή (Lk=94; Acts=52); μηδείς (Lk=9; Acts=23); οὐ μή (Lk=18; Acts=3); οὐχί (Lk=15; Acts=2).

[140] Words for: field/countryside: ἀγρός (Lk=10; Acts=1), χωρίον (Lk=0; Acts=6); killing: ἀναιπεῖν (Lk=2; Acts=19), ἀπολλύναι (Lk=28; Acts=2), ἀποκτείνειν (Lk=13; Acts=6); speaking: εἰπεῖν (Lk=308; Acts=136), λαλεῖν (Lk=30; Acts=63), λέγειν (Lk=227; Acts=105), φάναι (Lk=6; Acts=27); and knowing: γινώσκειν (Lk=28; Acts=12), εἰδέναι (Lk=24; Acts=20), ἐπιστασθαι (Lk=0; Acts=10).

> It appears from this discussion that *unity of authorship cannot
> be proved, as generally stated, by linguistic evidence*, which,
> on the contrary, reveals very great differences between the two
> works. On the other hand, the prologues to Lk. and Acts most
> distinctly imply that both were the work of one author. We are
> therefore in face of a grave problem [emphasis added].[141]

Moreover, the contradiction between the two prefaces' content and the
linguistic quality causes Clark to doubt the originality of the Acts preface, as he concludes it was added later when the two books' stylistic
similarities were recognized. For his part, Knox rightly criticizes Clark's
statistics on the grounds he failed to discriminate sources, but Knox
falls victim to the occasional speculative enterprise of interpreting what
Luke's author-editor might have wanted to write.

Assessment of Clark's challenge and Knox's rebuttal

Upon close inspection, problems with Clark's challenge soon emerge.
In certain cases, Clark's analysis seems too grammatically fixed; for
example, he compares καλούμενος but not other forms of καλέω, εἶπεν
δέ but not εἶπον δέ, and ὀνόματι but not ὄνομα in other cases or in
the plural.[142] Furthermore, although not pertinent to the present authorship study, problematic for today's scholars is that Clark used a single
combined tabulation for the authentic and disputed Pauline letters.[143]

In spite of Knox's criticism, Clark's challenge is cited in commentaries because his method is meticulous, as well as grounded in
linguistics. In fact, in one case Clark's evidence may be stronger than he
or Knox noticed. In the analysis of linguistic agreements between Acts
and the Pauline material and how they differ from Luke, Clark fails to
point out the noticeable lexical and syntactical *disagreements* between
Luke and Acts, for example, ὁ+word before noun (Lk=7; Acts=20); ὅς
attracted (Lk=11; Acts=23); τις+substantive (Lk=33; Acts=70); and

---

[141] Clark, *Acts of the Apostles*, p. 406.
[142] Ibid., pp. 400f. In table (c) on p. 400, in the list of words not found in the gospels, it
appears that Clark also miscalculated the instances of ξενίζειν, which occurs in "Paul" not
four times but zero, and once in Hebrews.
[143] Scholars generally acknowledge Paul's authentic letters to include Romans, 1
Corinthians, 2 Corinthians, Galatians, Philippians, 1 Thessalonians, and Philemon. Disputed Pauline letters generally include 2 Thessalonians, Colossians, Ephesians, 1 Timothy,
2 Timothy, and Titus. New Testament scholars almost unanimously agree that the Letter to
the Hebrews is non-Pauline.

ὑπάρχειν (Lk=7; Acts=26). Aided by these figures, Clark's work cautiously but convincingly supports the notion that the differences between Luke and Acts have been understated.

Challenge by A. W. Argyle (1974)

In a *New Testament Studies* article, "The Greek of Luke and Acts,"[144] A. W. Argyle offers another twentieth-century critical challenge to single authorship through the presentation of synonym evidence. Finding over sixty Greek synonym pairs, Argyle claims that where the author-editor of Luke used one, the author-editor of Acts used the other. Furthermore, in many cases one or the other author-editor declined to use a particular synonym at all. Three examples suffice to show the direction of Argyle's argument: (1) Luke attests ὠφελέω (Lk 9:25, not in Acts), whereas Acts βοηθέω (Acts 16:9; 21:28, not in Luke);[145] (2) Luke attests δαπάνη (Lk 14:28; not in Acts), whereas Acts τιμή (Acts 4:34; 5:2, 3; 7:16; 19:19; 28:10; not in Luke);[146] and (3) Luke attests διαλογίζομαι (Lk 1:29; 3:15; 5:21, 22; 12:17; 20:14; not in Acts), but Acts φρονέω (Acts 28:22; not in Luke) and ἐπίσταμαι (Acts 10:28; 15:7; 18:25; 19:15, 25; 20:18; 22:19; 24:10; 26:26; not in Luke).[147] Carefully detailing over sixty synonym pairs, Argyle establishes a challenge to the one-author hypothesis: different synonym choices point to different author-editors. Moreover, like Clark, he alleges different authorship casts doubt on the authority of the prefaces as evidence of common authorship:

> Acts i.1–2 no more prove that the author of Acts was the author of the third Gospel than II Peter i.1, iii.1 prove that the author of II Peter was the same person as the author of I Peter.[148]

Rebuttal by B. E. Beck (1977)

The major rebuttal to Argyle's work was proffered by B. E. Beck in an *NTS* article, "The Common Authorship of Luke and Acts," where he not only admits Argyle's list appears to serve as evidence of different authorship but also adds over ten synonym pairs to Argyle's list.[149] While admiring the precision of Argyle's analysis, Beck counters with the argument that synonym identification is unreliable: one scholar's synonym is

---

[144] A. W. Argyle, "The Greek of Luke and Acts," *NTS* 20 (1974), 441–445.
[145] Ibid., 442.   [146] Ibid.   [147] Ibid.   [148] Ibid., 444–445.
[149] B. E. Beck, "The Common Authorship of Luke and Acts," *NTS* 23 (1977), 346.

not another's. Argyle's challenge, argues Beck, is built on three dubious premises: (a) the word pairs are actual synonyms; (b) the problem of sources may be neglected; and (c) synonym pairs of comparable use do not exist *within* each book.[150] To answer the first question of whether Argyle's word pairs are actual synonyms, Beck applies this test: may the words be substituted for one another and still keep the same meaning? In over ten cases, Beck says no. Three examples, parallel to those above, show Beck's objection: (1) βοηθεῖν (Acts 16:9; 21:28) does not fit in Lk 9:25, where the idea of "benefit" rather than "assist" is required;[151] (2) δαπάνη meaning "cost" or "expense" (Lk 14:28) is not a suitable synonym for τιμή implying the "price" paid for property (Acts 7:16) or value realized from its sale (Acts 4:34; 5:2, 3; 19:19) or value added by honor (Acts 28:10), not to mention the fact that both Luke and Acts use the verb δαπανᾶν (Lk 15:14; Acts 21:24);[152] and (3) διαλογίζεσθαι (Lk 1:29; 3:15; 5:21f.; 12:17) meaning "to consider, debate, or question," often followed by an indirect question, is not interchangeable with either the more general ἐπίστασθαι (Acts 10:28; 15:7; 18:25; 19:15, 25; 20:18; 22:19; 24:10; 26:26) meaning "to know or understand" or φρονεῖν (Acts 28:22) meaning "to think."[153] To Beck, these and other cases present insurmountable difficulties in Argyle's approach to synonym identification.

Second, Beck contends, the problem of sources may not be ignored, given Argyle's position on the unrestrained nature of redaction by Luke's author-editor,[154] namely, Luke's author-editor so freely changed the vocabulary and syntax of his sources that a cautious character to his redaction is implausible. Mistakenly perhaps, Beck takes this to mean Argyle would disagree Luke's author-editor also freely *kept* his sources' vocabulary and syntax. For example, claims Beck, although Luke's author-editor replaced Mark's ἀπῆλθον with ὑπεχώρησεν in Lk 9:10 and replaced Mark's ἀπῆλθεν with ἐν τῷ ὑπάγειν in Lk 8:42, he kept Mark's verb ἀπελθεῖν in Lk 8:37, 39.[155] These and other examples cause Beck to conclude Argyle's synonym differences may be due to the *retention* of source vocabulary.

Third, Beck demonstrates Argyle's synonym pairs also occur *within* a book, thus diluting Argyle's challenge. In Luke, the author-editor used the synonym combinations: (a) ἀγανακτεῖν (Lk 8:14) and ὀργίζεσθαι (Lk

[150] Ibid., 347.   [151] Ibid., 348.   [152] Ibid., 347.   [153] Ibid.
[154] Argyle, "The Greek of Luke and Acts," 441. Cf. Knox, *Acts of the Apostles*, pp. 10–11.
[155] Beck, "The Common Authorship of Luke and Acts," 348–349.

14:2; 15:28); and (b) the three synonyms: ἅπτεσθαι (middle voice; Lk 5:13; 6:19; 7:14, 39; 8:44, 45, 46, 47; 18:15; 22:51), ψηλαφᾶν (Lk 24:39; cf. Acts 17:27) and προσψαύειν (Lk 11:46). In Acts, the author-editor used the synonym combinations: (a) πωλεῖν (Acts 4:37; 5:1; cf. Lk 12:6, 33; 17:28; 18:22; 19:45; 22:36) and πιπράσκειν (Acts 2:45; 5:4), once both in one verse (Acts 4:34); and (b) the four synonyms: ἀναστατοῦν (Acts 17:6; 21:38), ἐκταράσσειν (Acts 16:20), συνκινεῖν (Acts 6:12), and ἐπίστασιν ποιεῖν (Acts 24:12; cf. ἀνασείειν in Lk 23:5). To suggest many of Argyle's synonym combinations are not exclusive to the inter-book relationship but are reflected even within Luke or Acts weakens Argyle's challenge significantly.

Assessment of Argyle's challenge and Beck's rebuttal

With little or no attention to sources, studies such as Argyle's (and Clark's before this) function with difficulty as challenges to the single author hypothesis, even when meticulously planned and executed. Accounting for sources would provide the required robustness to word studies of Luke and Acts. Moreover, a close examination of Beck's rebuttal reveals how detailed the work must be. That is to say, Beck[156] objects to Argyle's[157] pairing λιμός in Lk 15:14 with ἀσιτία in Acts 27:21 and ἄσιτος in Acts 27:33 but not [Argyle's] mentioning that λιμός is also used in Lk 4:25; 15:17; 21:11 and Acts 7:11; 11:28. Here both Argyle's evidence and Beck's objection include a lexicographical error, to wit, since λιμός can mean either a famine (Lk 4:25; 15:14; 21:11; Acts 7:11; 11:28) or an individual's experience of hunger (Lk 15:17), Argyle should have contrasted the word λιμός in Lk 15:17, *not* 15:14; and Beck should have discovered that error.

Why re-examine the single authorship hypothesis?

To many, revisiting single authorship not only flies in the face of long-held tradition and scholarship but also squanders time and effort better spent elsewhere.[158] Although Clark's challenge to single authorship focuses on the use of Greek particles and other common linguistic elements and

---

[156] Ibid.   [157] Argyle, "The Greek of Luke and Acts," 442.

[158] Although this is anecdotal evidence only, I was told by a conservative scholar at the 2005 Society of Biblical Literature annual meeting that "it makes no difference *at all* whether Luke and Acts were written by the same man, the result is the same."

Argyle's challenge claims distinctive synonym use, both prove inconclusive because they do not adequately address the question of sources.

Methodology and precedents

> [W]e must distinguish between the stylistic peculiarities of the *sources* on the one hand and the stylistic peculiarities, if any, which we can ascribe to the *compiler* on the other [emphasis added].[159]

What does "single authorship" mean? To accept the composite nature of Luke and in all likelihood Acts begs the following source-related question: *To what extent is a given passage an independent composition by the author-editor, a redaction of inherited material, or an exact copy of inherited material?* Idiosyncrasies in *authorial* style must be differentiated from stylistic features of the inherited *sources*.[160] To investigate authorship, what passages in Luke and Acts best serve as authorial data, and how are they identified? Further, what prose compositional elements offer the most valid evidence of an author-editor's characteristic style, and how are they identified and analyzed? Investigation of these key questions has led to the development of the following three-stage methodology.

Stage One: Select data appropriate for analysis of authorial style

Data for an authorial analysis must consist of evidence that irrefutably reveals an author-editor's stylistic repertoire. Although no Luke or Acts passage may be given "authorial" status without any reservation whatsoever, one set of passages lies closest to or at the authorial stratum, namely, the two books' *seams and summaries*.[161] As framework passages linking pericopes or complexes of pericopes in Luke and Acts, seams and summaries should reveal unity and coherence in the author-editor's prose compositional style for three major reasons. First, seams and summaries point to the literary junctures or transitions where two pieces of material are joined to form a larger narrative. As a result, seams and summaries exemplify text composed *later* than the material they connect. Therefore, they are by definition *closer to or at the authorial*

---

[159] Knox, *Acts of the Apostles*, p. 9.   [160] Ibid.

[161] For a full discussion of the history of seam and summary research, refer to Chapter Two.

stratum of text.[162] Second, because seams and summaries represent neutral text that conforms neither to the traditional forms of Luke nor to the traditional forms of Acts, they effectively lie outside the interpretive boundaries of traditional forms. Hence, this attribute guarantees a commonality of style other forms in the two texts may not enjoy. Third, the seams and summaries from Luke and Acts have been identified by expert scholars who not only (a) designate a particular text as a seam or summary from the hand of the author-editor but also (b) include in their work either an explicit list of all seams and summaries in Luke or Acts or a list deducible by specific references to such passages. In other words, it is Luke and Acts scholars who supply the most informed opinion on exactly what passages should be designated seams and summaries (sometimes called "transitional texts" or "connective formulae" or the like). To maintain methodological integrity and control, *only when a majority of a select but representative group of expert scholars identify a particular seam or summary should it be included.* That is to say, the best data are the seams and summaries identified *in common* by a majority of experts. In mathematics, this is called the intersection of data sets rather than their union, and the net result is a set of methodologically valid seams and summaries from Luke and Acts, where the authorial "handprint" is most likely to be discovered. Chapter Two details the history of seam and summary research in Luke and Acts, culling from that the principles and criteria by which to recognize seams and summaries as authorial data.

Stage Two: Recover prose compositional conventions from antiquity

After the selection of valid authorial data, the second stage focuses on a search of ancient prose composition criticism to recover the conventions attended to by those in antiquity who learned to read and write Greek. After Aristotle, prose composition criticism was separated into two major components: word choice or diction (ἐκλογή ὀνομάτων) and word arrangement (σύνθεσις), the latter of which informs the present authorship analysis. In the literary "workshops"[163] of early prose composition critics there are extant examples of linguistic sensitivities adhered to by writers of Hellenistic Greek – for example, paradigms of euphony,

---

[162] For definitions along with criteria for identification, refer to Chapter Two.

[163] D. A. Russell, *Criticism in Antiquity* (Berkeley, Calif.: University of California Press, 1981), p. 5, writes of how we may in retrospect "glimpse the inside of the workshop."

dissonance, and rhythm evident in good Greek prose. Detailed in Chapter Three, four early critics stand out for their contributions: Aristotle in *The Art of Rhetoric* (*Rhetorica*) Book III, Pseudo-Demetrius in *On Style* (*De elocutione*), Dionysius of Halicarnassus in his *On Composition* (*De compositione verborum*) and other critical essays, and Pseudo-Longinus in *On the Sublime* (*De sublimitate*). Collecting actual examples from antiquity results in an array of elements optimally suited for authorial analysis. When analyzed synoptically, they describe the unique markers of an author-editor's stylistic "handprint."

> Stage Three: Analyze stylometrically the seams and
> summaries in light of the prose compositional
> conventions of antiquity

Upon completion of the first two stages, the authorial analysis includes, on the one hand, a set of valid authorial data, and on the other, a set of ancient prose compositional conventions with actual examples. The third stage, the subject of Chapter Four, simply merges the first two in order to (1) tabulate in what quantities and patterns the compositional conventions are present in the seams and summaries and (2) determine, by stylometric analysis, whether the patterns confirm single authorship as they should.

Stylometry defined

Before proceeding, it may be helpful to point out that stylometry in general is understood as the science of measuring literary style.[164] With regard to the New Testament, Anthony Kenny offers the following appreciation of stylometric study:

> Stylometry is the study of quantifiable features of style of a written or spoken text. Such a study may be undertaken for several different reasons. One may wish to study the statistics of word usage or word order with a view to understanding a text better, to catch nuances of meaning and perhaps to render them into a different language . . . Or one may hope to use the

---

[164] Erica Klarreich, "Bookish Math: Statistical Tests are Unraveling Knotty Literary Mysteries," *Science News* 164 (2003), 392. A new type of computer architecture called a "neural network," modeled after the human brain, can now "learn" to identify literary style.

quantifiable features of a text as an indication of authorship of a text when this is in question.[165]

As an analytical tool, stylometry is hardly new to biblical studies. In 1851 Augustus de Morgan carried out a stylometric study of *word length* to determine the authenticity of Pauline letters, although today scholars often measure sentence length, not word length, as a criterion of Pauline authenticity.[166] Presently, the most commonly measured stylometric feature is *word frequency*. Even though unusual words, *hapax legomena*, often capture the spotlight as authorship evidence, ironically the frequency of small, everyday words provides more information about the characteristics of an author-editor's compositional style and hence authorship.[167] As criteria the present authorship analysis uses neither *hapax legomena* nor the small, everyday words but rather, as mentioned above, the prose compositional elements culled from the works of ancient critics. To that end, the investigation seeks to answer but one question: *Based on a prose compositional analysis of seams and summaries, does the gospel of Luke appear to be written by the same person as the Acts of the Apostles?*

Precedents for the authorship analysis methodology

Even with attempts to identify a text's author, precedents for the suggested methodology exist in both the ancient and modern eras. In the first century BCE, Dionysius of Halicarnassus wrote a critical essay analyzing the speeches of Dinarchus (d. 240 BCE), a poet and librarian in Alexandria:[168] "Therefore I have decided that he [Dinarchus] should not be passed over, but that for serious students of rhetoric ... it is imperative ... to examine his life and style and *to distinguish between his genuine and spurious speeches* [emphasis added].[169] By not studying Dinarchus thoroughly, suggests Dionysius, the great Pergamum

---

[165] Anthony Kenny, *A Stylometric Study of the New Testament* (Oxford: Clarendon Press, 1986), p. 1.

[166] Ibid.   [167] Albert C. Clark's work is a premier example; see footnote 110.

[168] See Usher's comment in Dionysius of Halicarnassus, "On Literary Composition" in *Dionysius of Halicarnassus: Critical Essays*, vol. II, trans. Stephen Usher, LCL 466 (Cambridge, Mass.: Harvard University Press, 1985), pp. 250f. note 2. As a librarian in Alexandria, Dinarchus was also involved in the problem of authorship ascription and identification.

[169] Dion. Hal. *Dinarchus* 1. The English translation belongs to Stephen Usher; see footnote 168.

grammarians frequently attributed speeches either *to* him falsely or *by* him to someone else. According to Dionysius, the most valuable criterion of authenticity is applying a generalized category, viz., *authorial uniformity*, to the specifics of Dinarchus' style.[170] That is to say, since Dinarchus evidently had no clearly detectible style, as did a Lysias or a Demosthenes, speeches by Dinarchus could be recognized by their *lack* of uniformity! Lysias' works, Dionysius opines, show self-consistency in diction, lucidity, and smoothness.[171] So when Lysianic authorship is questioned, simply look for a consistency in excellence, charm, diction, and animation; if consistency exists, confidently attribute the speech to Lysias; if little or no consistency exists with regard to these qualities, attribute the speech to Dinarchus. Likewise, the consistency of Demosthenes' impressive diction, vivid portrayal of emotion, keenness of mind, vitality, and vehemence, advises Dionysius, serves as a criterion of authorship attribution; if the highest degree of each of these qualities is lacking, attribute the speech to Dinarchus.[172] With a developed literary taste far removed from modern sensibilities, Dionysius' standards clearly concentrate on the qualitative rather than the quantitative, but they apparently served his and his students' needs well. Today such a methodology appears less than unbiased and impartial; indeed, it seems quite subjective and idiosyncratic.

In the modern era in a variety of literary fields, stylometric and other quantitative analysis precedents exist that have brought the power of statistics to bear on authorship. The best known is undoubtedly Shakespeare. A brief search of the library shelf or Internet will surprise the casual observer. Statistical analyses of Shakespearean texts measure the gamut of characteristics: punctuation, hyphenation patterns, word length, diction, spelling, syntax, line length, and rhythm. Of note is an authorship study belonging to Donald W. Foster in *Elegy by W. S.: A Study in Attribution*,[173] the analysis of a funeral elegy whose author's initials, W. S., appear both on the title page and following the dedication. Foster analyzes the funeral elegy's prosody (e.g., pentameter lines; open lines), rhyme (e.g., identical rhymes; analogous rhymes), diction (e.g., unique words; hyphenation; proper nouns), spelling, accidence (e.g., "more severer" or "more braver"), syntax (e.g., use of "who" and "whom"; incongruent antecedent), and word length. Based on a meticulous examination of the

---

[170] Dion. Hal. *Dinarchus* 6.   [171] Ibid., 7.   [172] Ibid.

[173] Donald W. Foster, *Elegy by W. S.: A Study in Attribution* (Newark, Del.: University of Delaware Press, 1989).

data, Foster argues W. S. stands for William Shakespeare, not William Strachey, a contemporaneous author.[174]

Almost as well studied as Shakespeare's style is another authorship dilemma involving twelve *Federalist Papers*, composed and published anonymously under the pseudonym "Publius" in 1788–89 at the founding of the United States. Often used as an example in statistical texts, the *Federalist Papers* quandary provides a "real-life" authorship problem, that is, deciding whether "Publius" was Alexander Hamilton or James Madison. In their article, "Deciding Authorship," Frederick Mosteller of Harvard University and David L. Wallace of the University of Chicago detail a systematic analysis[175] in which they tabulate marker words (e.g., "while" and "whilst") and measure the frequency of differentiating words (e.g., "commonly," "innovation," and "war"), as well as ordinary words (e.g., "by," "from," and "to"). Based on statistical comparisons of the disputed and undisputed papers, Mosteller and Wallace conclude James Madison authored the twelve *Federalist Papers* in question.

To recapitulate, the present authorship analysis does *not* seek to identify the author-editor of Luke and Acts but rather tries in a methodologically robust, valid, rigorous, and controlled way to answer the simple yes–no question: *Based on a prose compositional analysis of seams and summaries, what is the probability the author-editor of Luke is the same person as the author-editor of Acts?*

Concluding considerations

So deeply entrenched is the *opinio communis* on single authorship that changing it may be impossible. A stylometric study of ancient prose composition criticism applied to the seams and summaries in Luke and Acts by all accounts ought to reveal stylistic patterns similar enough to

---

[174] Foster documents his fateful journey into authorship analysis in *Author Unknown: On the Trail of Anonymous* (New York: Henry Holt, 2000).

[175] Frederick Mosteller and David L. Wallace, "Deciding Authorship," in J. M. Tanur *et al.* (eds.), *Statistics: A Guide to the Unknown* (San Francisco, Calif.: Holden-Day, 1972), pp. 207–219. A sophisticated statistical analysis of the *Federalist Papers* authorial dilemma is found in Glenn Fung, *The Disputed Federalist Papers: SVM Feature Selection via Concave Minimization* (New York: ACM Press, 2003); at the time of writing, a nine-page "pdf" file at www.cs.wisc.edu/~gfung/federalist.pdf. Fung also concludes that Madison is the author of the disputed texts. A comprehensive pre-computer-age text on the problems, methods, and measurements of numerical and mathematical authorial analysis may be found in C. B. Williams, *Style and Vocabulary: Numerical Studies* (London: Charles Griffin, 1970).

warrant continued support for single authorship. If the patterns differentiate the two books in a statistically significant way, the sharp divergence requires further investigation. Indeed, if the above-described methodology succeeds, critical analysis should be conducted of other allegedly single-authored material in Luke and Acts, e.g., the Acts speeches or the so-called "We"-Sections. Even the most meager willingness to reconsider single authorship opens the door to long-sought answers such as resolution of Luke and Acts conundra (e.g., the divergent ascension stories), the author-editor's unparalleled capability for stylistic variation, and the length of the Acts preface.

2

AUTHORIAL DATA: SEAMS AND SUMMARIES

> Of late we have seen an endeavour to apportion the Acts of the
> Apostles by source-criticism in such a way that very little
> remains for Luke, who yet was certainly no mere compiler...
> Yet the fact remains that often enough the documentary infor-
> mation used by Luke floats like *croûtons* in the soup... joints
> and seams are discernible at many points.[1]

Julius Wellhausen's *croûtons*-in-the-soup simile aptly describes the evidence and data paradigm needed to re-examine the single authorship
of Luke and Acts. While "joints and seams" form the literary intersec-
tions that unite segments of written material, they simultaneously define
the boundaries where those segments have been linked. That is to say,
functionally they both unite and divide.[2]

As noted in the previous chapter, these literary junctures, called "seams
and summaries," represent by definition not only a stratum of text composed *later* than the material they connect but also *neutral* text, unaligned
with the traditional forms of Luke and Acts.[3] Whether re-worked or independently composed, seams and summaries represent the most fecund
textual layer in which to "excavate" an author-editor's style. With an eye
toward gathering authorial data from Luke and Acts, this chapter seeks to
identify seams and summaries in both books using a four-fold approach:
(1) sketch the historical development of "seam" and "summary" research;
(2) weigh its relevance to Luke and Acts with an eye toward identifying
any resultant problems; (3) compile a list of seams and summaries in

---

[1] From Julius Wellhausen, *Nachrichten von der königlichen Gesellschaft der Wissenschaften zu Göttingen, Philosophie-Historie Klasse* (1907), pp. 1–21, cited by Haenchen,
Acts of the Apostles, p. 32.

[2] Henry J. Cadbury, "The Summaries in Acts" in F. J. Foakes Jackson and Kirsopp Lake
(eds.), *The Beginnings of Christianity, Part I: The Acts of the Apostles, vol. V: Additional
Notes to the Commentary* (London: Macmillan and Co., 1933), pp. 401–402.

[3] See Chapter One for the full rationale.

Luke identified by a majority of select but representative experts; and
(4) do the same for Acts.

Historical roots of "seam" and "summary" in Markan studies

Seam and summary categories originated in Markan studies based on the
Two-Document Hypothesis. From this perspective, except for the LXX
there exist no verifiable extant sources with which to compare and trace
Markan editorial changes and thus isolate the first evangelist's preferences in style, grammar, syntax, and theology. Many *Über*-scholars have
contributed to the development of such research in Mark. In the early
twentieth century, Karl Ludwig Schmidt in *Der Rahmen der Geschichte
Jesu* demonstrated how Markan seams and summaries constituted a literary framework for complexes of traditional material, joined together
to create a continuous whole. Schmidt used the familiar term *Sammelbericht* ("summary report") to label the framework passages, and in so
doing, differentiated inherited material from the way it was contextualized. Schmidt, in fact, claimed the evangelist created the framework
as the very means to present the tradition. Throughout *Der Rahmen*,
Schmidt's definition of *Sammelberichte* evolved and built, as he observed
that summary reports framed pericopes or complexes of pericopes in the
gospel, represented a later stage of development, and implied compositional activity on the part of the evangelist. Of Mk 3:7–12, for example,
Schmidt wrote:

> Das ist eine ganz allgemeine Schilderung, ein Sammel-
> bericht . . . Als allgemeines Urteil dürfte feststehen, daß solch
> ein Sammelbericht jünger ist als die Einzelanekdote . . . ist der
> Sammelbericht das Erzeugnis eines bestimmten Autors, also
> ein künstliches Produkt, dessen Existenz durch schriftliche Fix-
> ierung gesichert ist. [So a general proposition must be estab-
> lished, that this sort of a summary report is *later than the indi-
> vidual anecdotes* . . . the summary report is the *creation of
> a definite author*, an artistic product whose existence is fixed
> through textual addition] [emphasis added].[4]

---

[4] Karl Ludwig Schmidt, *Der Rahmen der Geschichte Jesu: Literarkritische Untersuchungen zur ältesten Jesusüberlieferung* (Berlin: Nachdruck aus Ausgabe, 1919; reprint,
Darmstadt: Wissenschaftliche Buchgesellschaft, 1965), p. 105.

Later on, Schmidt differentiated summary reports and introductory notes, whereby the latter established chronology or topology and the former extended Jesus' fame and influence to wider regions and greater numbers of people.[5] Using the term *Naht* ("seam") as well as *Zwischennotiz* ("connective note") and *Zwischenbemerkung* ("connective remark"),[6] Schmidt defined the boundary between two sets of material. It was a matter of taste, he argued, whether one viewed the transition as attached to the preceding pericope or the following one. He deduced, for example, that Mk 6:6b (καὶ περιῆγεν τὰς κώμας κύκλῳ διδάσκων "He went around among the villages teaching") was attached to the pericope following it, namely, the Sending Forth (6:7–13), not the one preceding it, Jesus' Rejection at Nazareth (6:1–6a).[7] Taste notwithstanding, the direction of attachment was determined on a case-by-case basis. All things considered, Schmidt's treatment of *Sammelbericht* and *Naht* contributed in an absolutely prototypical way to later work on Markan seams and summaries.[8]

After Schmidt, and with the advent of *Formgeschichte* (form history), others ably demonstrated how Markan seams and summaries revealed the evangelist's own theological perspective. Ernst Lohmeyer in *Galiläa und Jerusalem*,[9] for instance, explored the significance of Galilee as the locale for the Markan Jesus' expected post-resurrection appearance, a setting that epitomized both the ministerial beginning and eschatological endpoint of God's plan in Jesus.[10] As Lohmeyer did, British scholar Robert Henry Lightfoot in *Locality and Doctrine in the Gospels* also claimed Galilee, not Jerusalem, served as the endpoint of Markan theology.[11] In light of *Formgeschichte*, these arguments largely derive from the theology-laden seams and summaries. Then, a few years later in the mid-twentieth century, noted scholar Willi Marxsen brought the Markan literary structure into much sharper focus in *Der Evangelist Markus*,[12]

---

[5] Ibid., p. 13.   [6] Ibid., pp. 8, 160.   [7] Ibid., p. 159.

[8] For a more current view of Schmidt's work, see Charles W. Hedrick, "The Role of 'Summary Statements' in the Composition of the Gospel of Mark: A Dialog with Karl Schmidt and Norman Perrin," *NT* 4 (1984), 289–311.

[9] Ernst Lohmeyer, *Galiläa und Jerusalem* (Göttingen: Vandenhoeck & Ruprecht, 1936).

[10] Ibid., pp. 26ff.

[11] Robert Henry Lightfoot, *Locality and Doctrine in the Gospels* (London: Hodder and Stoughton, 1938), p. 125.

[12] Willi Marxsen, *Mark the Evangelist: Studies on the Redaction History of the Gospel*, trans. James Boyce, Donald Juel, William Poehlmann with Roy A. Harrisville (Nashville, Tenn.: Abingdon Press, 1969); originally published as *Der Evangelist Markus – Studien zur Redaktionsgeschichte des Evangeliums* (Göttingen: Vandenhoeck & Ruprecht, 1956, 1959).

where he distinguished the Markan hand from inherited material, in other words, the redaction history of Mark from its form history. By a process of "[s]upplementation and redaction," Marxsen argued, the evangelist Mark transformed the inherited into the contemporaneous.[13] On account of their "framework" functionality, Marxsen showed Markan seams and summaries, whose theological *teleos* was shown to be Galilee, represented a textual stratum composed later than the traditional material they connect.

During the mid-twentieth century, Ernest Best in *The Temptation and the Passion: The Markan Soteriology* brilliantly extended the work of previous scholars when he isolated and examined Markan "seams," defining them as "words, phrases, sentences which join together the various incidents of the Gospel."[14] As Best described it, pieces of pre-Markan tradition were inherited by the evangelist Mark (or his community), who stitched them together either by redacting the tradition or by creating new, supplementary text to connect the traditional material.[15] The latter technique, for instance, moves Jesus from one locale to another (e.g., Mk 6:6b; 9:2, 9, 14, 30; 11:1, 11). Markan "seams," both introductory and summarizing, Best explained, not only shape the literary arrangement but also reveal the evangelist's focus on Jesus' teaching mission.

Later, Wilhelm Egger in *Frohbotshaft und Lehre* painstakingly identified thirteen Markan summaries (Mk 1:14f., 21f., 32–34, 39, 45; 2:1f., 13; 3:7–12; 4:1f.; 6:6b; 30–34, 53–56; 10:1), further categorized as those about healing and the crowds (1:32–34; 6:53–56); those about proclamation (1:14f., 39); those that describe Jesus' teaching activities (1:21f.; 2:1f., 13; 4:1f.; 6:6b, 30–34; 10:1); and general statements about Jesus' fame (1:45; 3:7–12).[16] Taken together, the summaries reveal not so much a geographical trajectory through the second gospel but a christological development of Jesus as proclaimer and teacher, in which the author-editor of Mark assembles pieces of textual "mosaic" to fashion an underlying transition from concealment to revelation. In introducing his concept of *Sammelbericht*, Egger noted the difficulty in discovering a

---

[13] Marxsen, *Mark the Evangelist*, p. 65.

[14] Ernest Best, *The Temptation and the Passion: The Markan Soteriology* (Cambridge: Cambridge University Press, 1965), p. 63.

[15] Ibid.

[16] Wilhelm Egger, *Frohbotschaft und Lehre: Die Sammelberichte des Wirkens Jesu im Markusevangelium* (Frankfurt am Main: Josef Knecht, 1976). For a broad-brush perspective on Markan summaries in dialogue with Egger, see Geert Van Oyen, *De summaria in Marcus en de compositie van Mc 1,14–8,26*, SNTA 12 (Leuven: Leuven University Press/Peeters, 1987). For a recent overview of the structure of Mark, see Kevin W. Larson, "The Structure of Mark's Gospel: Current Proposals," *CBR* 3 (2004), 140–160.

unifying principle ("Da der Begriff «Sammelbericht» sehr weit ist . . . läßt sich nur schwer ein einheitliches Prinzip für die Anordnung des Stoffes ableiten").[17]

Most recently, scholar Robert Stein has extended the work of Best and other predecessors by differentiating the "seam" and "summary" categories far more definitively, most particularly vis-à-vis function. Stein explains the evangelist Mark composed "seams" to unite either individual pericopes or pre-Markan "complexes" of pericopes by using literary threads such as frequent mention of Galilee (*pace* Lohmeyer, Lightfoot, Marxsen) or repeated reference to Jesus' teaching mission (*pace* Best). Stein carefully constructs a definition of "seam":

> Although these [the isolated pre-Markan-gospel pericopes or "complexes" of pericopes] must have had introductions of some sort, *they did not possess seams uniting them to one another.* In order to join these pericopes together Mark had either to create the seams we find in the Gospel or rework the original introductions that introduced the isolated pericopes. *There may have been occasions when the introductions to the isolated pericopes would have served as seams, but frequently this would not have been so . . .* The cement he [Mark] used to bind these materials together reveals something of his own particular theological emphasis [emphasis added].[18]

In Stein's view, Markan seams hold the vocabulary, style, and themes that pinpoint authorial intervention; seamic examples include: Mk 1:21–22; 2:2; 3:14; 5:34; 6:2, 12, 30; 7:14, 17, 24, 36–37; 8:26, 30, 31, 34; 9:9, 30, 31; 12:1, 35, 38a; 13:1.[19] In the case of summaries, Stein suggests the evangelist appended material to the end of an individual pericope or pre-Markan "complex" of pericopes and offers this carefully constructed definition of "summary":

> In the Gospel of Mark there frequently appear statements that summarize Jesus' activity, message, or fame . . . It is almost certain that the *summaries* found in Mark did not circulate independently during the oral period . . . In other words, in these

---

[17] Egger, *Frohbotschaft und Lehre*, p. 3.

[18] Robert Stein, *Gospels and Tradition: Studies on Redaction Criticism of the Synoptic Gospels* (Grand Rapids, Mich.: Baker Book House, 1991), pp. 51f.

[19] Ibid., p. 76 notes 23, 24. He contrasts these examples of seams with Markan insertions in 1:44; 3:23a; 6:34; 11:17a, 18.

> summaries Mark did not simply write down a traditional
> pericope. He personally composed these summaries and selected
> the particular material he wanted to insert into them . . . They
> did not exist before him . . . *His selection of material here is*
> *far more important than his selection of the individual peri-*
> *copes that he wished to include in his Gospel, because the latter*
> *did not require the amount of creative activity comparable to*
> *the creation of the various summaries out of diverse traditional*
> *material* [emphasis added].[20]

In agreement with his predecessors, Stein understands summaries, like
seams, to come directly from the hand of the evangelist; short summaries
include Mk 1:28, 39; 2:13; 6:6b, longer ones 1:14–15; 3:7–12; 6:53–56;
9:30–32; 10:32–34.

According to Stein, seams establish the context for an individual pericope or "complex" of pericopes; summaries recapitulate them. Seams
stand "in front of," summaries "after." To complete his exploration of
authorial intervention, Stein even identifies a textual unit he names the
Markan "insertion," that is, text added *in the middle of* a pericope (e.g.,
Mk 14:28; 16:7); by definition, however, the insertion does not function
as a seam or summary. To recapitulate, although without a doubt Stein
contributes solidly to the functional differentiation of Markan seams,
summaries, and insertions, he also avoids the debate over using solely
theological-thematic threads to distinguish seams and summaries from
other types of text. By doing so, he strengthens the methodological
objectivity of his work.

Relevance to Luke and Acts research and resultant problems

It is hardly an overstatement to say seam and summary research in Luke
and Acts has been unbalanced. Regarding the third gospel, the degree of
in-depth attention given to seams and summaries in Mark has not been
afforded to those in Luke. Perhaps because the Two-Document Hypothesis understands Lukan dependency on Mark and "Q," the remaining
traditional forms, often called "Special L," are usually given to the third
evangelist's community. Thus, from the hand of Luke's author-editor
comes the evangelist's own "gospel," revealed in the differences among

---

[20] Ibid., p. 53.

the various source materials.[21] That said, distinguishing seams from summaries in Luke remains a murky affair.

Contrariwise, summaries in Acts have not suffered the same fate, for close scrutiny of the major summaries (Acts 2:42–47; 4:32–35; 5:12–16) has had a long history. Yet functionally seams and summaries in Acts pose the same, or a similar, problem as that in Mark: except for the LXX, no extant source survives that either author-editor might have used. The lack of verifiable sources for Acts complicates efforts to determine the book's composition, observes Jacques Dupont: "Despite the most careful and detailed research, it has not been possible to define any of the sources used by the author of Acts in a way which will meet with widespread agreement among the critics."[22] Nonetheless, Henry Cadbury rightly suggests the use of written sources by the author-editor of Acts must not be discounted, even though until now none has been uncovered: "The means of demonstration [that written sources existed] are less available, but the probability is still very great."[23]

The complexity of the Acts compositional framework is nowhere more evident than in a glimpse at the history of Acts source theories, summarized fully in Dupont's *Sources of Acts*. From the eighteenth century on, source theories about pre-Acts traditions were argued, rejected, re-argued, adapted, and expanded with varying degrees of success. Traced by Ernst Haenchen in *The Acts of the Apostles*,[24] early research on Acts source criticism provided the foundation for later, more sophisticated theories resonant with complex nuances that account for the difficulty in source detection and provenance. Nineteenth-century scholar Adolf von Harnack proposed the existence of "doublets," suggesting two pre-Acts sources in Acts 1–5.[25] Harnack's discovery of "doublet" subject matter led scholars to suggest the provenance for one pre-Acts source was Jerusalem (e.g., Acts 3:1–5:16; 8:5–40; 9:32–11:18; 12:1–23) and the other Antioch (e.g., 6:1–8:4; 11:19–30; 12:25–15:35).[26] At that time,

---

[21] In the case of "Q" material, the reconstruction has, in large measure, depended on the way the third evangelist redacts Markan material.

[22] Jacques Dupont, *The Sources of Acts*, trans. Kathleen Pond (New York: Herder and Herder, 1964), p. 166.

[23] Cadbury, *Style and Literary Method*, p. 66.

[24] Haenchen, *Acts of the Apostles*, pp. 24–50, 81–90.

[25] Adolf von Harnack, *The Acts of the Apostles*, 2nd edition, trans. J. R. Wilkinson (London: Williams & Norgate; New York: G. P. Putnam's Sons, 1909), pp. 132ff., 182; originally published as *Die Apostelgeschichte*, BENT 3 (Leipzig: J. C. Hinrichs, 1908). According to Harnack, the second half of Acts was written by an eye-witness to Paul.

[26] The first is often referred to as Jerusalem-Caesarea, the second as Antioch-Jerusalem. The *Beginnings of Christianity* editors propose a similar source theory; see F. J. Foakes

while source-critical research relied more on theological-thematic ratio-
nales than purely stylistic features, composition of the so-called three
major Acts summaries (2:42–47; 4:32–35; 5:12–16) was given to the
hand of the author-editor.

Early in the twentieth century, as Schmidt was examining the
Markan framework, Acts scholars constructed source theories by identifying transition points where one literary tradition appears to change
to another. In at least one case, these transition points are called seams.
F. J. Foakes Jackson and Kirsopp Lake in *The Beginnings of Christianity*
write about Acts seams:

> The only method of discovering internal evidence in a book
> which, as its treatment of Mark shows, cannot be expected easily
> to reveal its composition by its style, is to consider the 'seams,'
> not of language but of narrative, which suggest that the editor
> has passed from one tradition to another. Of course such 'seams'
> do not in themselves prove the use of documentary sources: they
> only indicate that it is possible.[27]

Defining "seam" as a transition point to a new section of material,
Foakes Jackson and Lake build their Acts source-critical theory on ear-
lier work such as Harnack's "doublets" in Acts 1–5 and Charles Cutler
Torrey's idea of Aramaic pre-Acts sources in 1:11–15:35.[28] Of special
note are two types of enigmatic source material: (1) the so-called "We"-
Sections (Acts 16:10–17; 20:5–15; 21:1–28; 27:1–28:16; and 11:28

Jackson and Kirsopp Lake, "The Internal Evidence of Acts" in *Beginnings of Christianity,
vol. II*, pp. 121–204, a somewhat dated but extensive treatment of the source question in
Acts.

[27] Foakes Jackson and Lake, "The Internal Evidence of Acts," *Beginnings of Christianity*, vol. II, p. 137.

[28] See Harnack, *Acts of the Apostles*, pp. 132ff., 182, and Charles Cutler Torrey, *The
Composition and Date of Acts*, HTS 1 (Cambridge, Mass.: Harvard University Press, 1919;
reprint, New York: Kraus reprint, 1969), pp. 10–22. For a discussion of the perceived
non-persuasiveness of Torrey's arguments in particular, see Haenchen, *Acts of the Apostles*,
pp. 73–75, who points out Torrey's lack of attention to LXX wording as responsible for the
"Aramaicisms" he found and his failure to notice the similarity of the presumed Semitisms
in the first part of Acts to those in the second. Fitzmyer, *Acts of the Apostles*, pp. 82,
116 further points out that Torrey's work appeared before the discovery of the Dead Sea
Scrolls, the Aramaic texts of which show themselves to be of an earlier and distinctive
dialect than the later Aramaic that Torrey used for his theory (ca. fourth to sixth centuries
CE). Like Haenchen and others, Fitzmyer brings to light the fact that many of Torrey's
Aramaicisms are actually Septuagintisms. For another scholar's perspective, see Matthew
Black, *An Aramaic Approach to the Gospels and Acts*, 3rd edition (Oxford: Clarendon Press,
1967).

in D),[29] a source conundrum involving a shift from third person singular and plural to first person plural; and (2) three versions of Paul's call (9:3–18; 22:6–16; 26:12–18). Like the pentimento effect in a vintage painting, pre-Acts sources, although they remain strangely elusive, are sometimes detectable through "cracks" in the narrative.

While less likely to identify seams and summaries by partitioning Acts into fragments, segments, or complexes, the so-called genre-based theories and in particular that of Richard Pervo in *Profit with Delight* show that Acts scholars must take seriously the different kinds of ancient novels, "free-wheeling" narratives, which were popular in Greco-Roman society.[30] Demonstrating how Acts may be understood as a set of genre traditions joined in a unified framework, Pervo points to a number of narratives that do not display the smaller and neater shape of apophthegms, miracle stories, and parables such as those found in the gospel; thus, the location of summaries and transition points in Acts is often not obvious.

Most recently, Joseph A. Fitzmyer in his Anchor Bible commentary on Acts makes a distinction between seams (often called "sutures" by Fitzmyer) and summaries. In doing so, he both expands the research of French scholar Pierre Benoit and others[31] and reminds us that there is precious little tradition on which to draw in regard to pre-Acts sources; any Acts source theory is really a speculative question; and as a result, Acts is by and large understood to consist of free composition.[32] *So by what standards may seams and summaries in Luke and Acts be selected as data for an authorship analysis?*

Criterion of majority consensus

Luke and Acts scholars at times identify seams and summaries based on the collective research of their predecessors, and as a result, inconsistencies arise. Whereas on certain passages there is total agreement, for example, the major Acts summaries, on other passages there is less scholarly accord. Where one scholar finds a summary statement, another does not; where one scholar identifies a seam or transition point, another

---

[29] Fitzmyer, *Acts of the Apostles*, p. 81. "D" is the siglum for Codex Bezae Cantabrigiensis, also known simply as Codex Bezae. See also Ernst Haenchen, "Das 'Wir' in der Apostelgeschichte und das Itinerar," *ZTK* 58 (1961), 329–366.

[30] Richard Pervo, *Profit with Delight: The Literary Genre of the Acts of the Apostles* (Philadelphia, Pa.: Fortress Press, 1987).

[31] Fitzmyer, *Acts of the Apostles*, pp. 85ff. See also Pierre Benoit, "La deuxième visite de saint Paul à Jérusalem," *Biblica* 40 (1959), 778–792.

[32] Pervo, *Profit with Delight*, pp. 80, 85.

does not. To undertake an authorial analysis based on seams and summaries requires a set of passages *consistently identified as such by major scholars. It is methodically unsound to analyze data passages whose status as a seam or summary is open to question.* Therefore, the selection of seams and summaries for this authorial analysis is based on scholarly consensus. That is to say, before inclusion in the Luke and Acts seam and summary data set, a majority of select but representative scholars needs to agree a particular passage is actually a seam or summary (sometimes called "transitional text" or "connective formula") *from the hand of the author-editor.* By requiring a majority of experts to agree that a particular passage is a seam or summary, passages selected for authorial analysis are *only* those whose compositional status is assured, or perhaps better, least contested. By contrast, to include a passage on the basis of only one expert who identified it as a seam or summary results in an unbalanced set of authorial data: some passages are included by only one "vote," some by more than one, others by a majority, and still others by unanimous "vote." The criterion of majority consensus allows a set of well-adjudicated and valid authorial data to be compiled.

To that end, two select but representative groups of expert scholars have been chosen, one for Luke and one for Acts. Regarded as major contributors to Luke and Acts studies, each has compiled a *complete list* of seams and summaries, or such a list may be inferred from *explicit references.* For Luke, the group of experts comprises Henry J. Cadbury, Rudolf Bultmann, Joseph A. Fitzmyer, François Bovon, Anicia Co, and Gregory Sterling. Included in a minor way is Martin Dibelius, who in a footnote to his article "Style Criticism in Acts"[33] presents a short list of Lukan "bridge" passages. *The criterion of majority agreement means a passage identified by four or more members of this group will be included in the Luke seam and summary data.* Also cited in the Luke group is Johannis de Zwaan,[34] who identifies a complete set of literary "stops" that "mark stages in the progress of the narrative"[35] in Luke (and Acts). As will be shown, however, de Zwaan relies on content-thematic selection criteria, namely, "incidents" in the life of Jesus in Luke (or in the early church in Acts) and the "feelings" of the multitudes, which do not provide sufficient controls.

---

[33] Dibelius, "Style Criticism," p. 10 note 19. The list of "bridge" passages comprises: Lk 3:15, 19, 20; 8:1–3; 9:9; 21:37, 38.

[34] J. de Zwaan, "Was the Book of Acts a Posthumous Edition?" *HTR* 17 (1924), 95–153.

[35] Ibid., 102.

For Acts, the group comprises Martin Dibelius, Henry J. Cadbury, Pierre Benoit, Hans Conzelmann, and Joseph A. Fitzmyer. The criterion of majority agreement means *a passage identified by three or more of this group will be included in the Acts seam and summary data.* Also cited is a Hastings' *Dictionary of the Bible* article by C. H. Turner. Again cited but not included in the final tally is Johannis de Zwaan for the same reason given above.

The works of these select but representative groups, one for Luke and one for Acts, produce two consistent and balanced lists of seams and summaries. The collected sets of seams and summaries are identified with a high degree of confidence because a preponderance of expert opinion understands them as such. When the lists are made final at the end of this chapter, *judgments of other expert scholars will be cited in the footnotes, thus augmenting the evidence.*

Definition of seam and summary functionality

A cursory glance at Luke and Acts seam and summary research reveals that many definitions and classifications exist – some explicit, many implicit. Before inquiring into individual scholars' work, a cautious attempt will be made to extrapolate a general working definition of seam and summary derived from the functionality described by Robert Stein for Markan seams and summaries.[36] The Stein approach works well because the definitions represent recent and in-depth research and they apply to both a gospel format and a text that lacks, except for the LXX, recognized extant sources. In light of existing terminological inconsistencies, the following definitions for Luke and Acts seams and summaries are offered:

Seam

A seam may be defined as the words, phrases, or sentences that create a transition to a new unit of text and at the same time unite it with antecedent material. Not unlike the boundary created when two pieces of cloth are stitched together, a "seam" functions as the visible line where the edges of two segments of text are joined. At the macro-framework level, seams reveal the author-editor's overall literary structure; at the sub-framework level, seams indicate a new section of text. Although seams sometimes,

---

[36] See pages 47–48.

but not always, signal new topographical, chronological, or historical settings, they may be "lifted off" the pericope or complex of pericopes without diminishing or destroying the content.

Summary

A summary consists of one or more sentences of editorial commentary that round off a pericope or complex of pericopes often by recapitulating or amplifying ideas found in the antecedent material. Following the same textile analogy above, a "summary" forms the boundary where a pericope or complex of pericopes has been finished off, not unlike the way in which a tailor's hem, turned under and sewn down, forms the border of a piece of cloth. Like seams, summaries may be "lifted off," leaving the original form and content intact.

Because of their independence from any required subject matter, these two definitions help to clarify nomenclature occasionally found in individual scholars' seam and summary remarks, especially in relation to "seam," where terminological diversity is the rule rather than the exception. It is hoped the above definitions offer assistance in sorting out how to catalog phrases such as "connective device" or "transitional formula." We begin with Luke.

Collected set of seams and summaries in Luke

Henry J. Cadbury contributed two well-known volumes to the study of Luke (and Acts), both of which inquire into seams and summaries, but not always explicitly. First, in *The Style and Literary Method of Luke*,[37] Cadbury analyzes the stylistic patterns of the evangelist "Luke" with an emphasis on redacted Markan material. Cadbury defines "summary" by *in se* phrases such as "in the brief summaries of Jesus' work and influence" and "in these summaries of Jesus' work or fame,"[38] presuming reader familiarity with the summary concept. Although Cadbury does not specifically use the term "seam," he identifies transition points that function as such in the narrative. With that in mind, Cadbury detects authorial intervention in three locations: (1) at the opening of new sections of material, that is, seams; (2) at the closing of sections; and (3) in summaries.

---

[37] Cadbury, *Style and Literary Method*, pp. 105–115.   [38] Ibid., p. 108.

The opening of sections; prefaces

As partial verses only,[39] section "openings" or seams entail three key patterns: two types of ἐγένετο construction and a formulaic beginning for parables.[40] The evangelist "Luke," notes Cadbury, added to or edited the beginning of pericopes or "complexes" of pericopes inherited from Mark, "Q," or the so-called "Special L" material. Suggesting the Lukan hand at the point of transition to new sections of material, openings contain similar vocabulary and syntax:

1. the [καὶ] ἐγένετο δέ construction in Lk 6:6a; 7:11a; 8:1a, 40; 9:28a, 37a, 51; 10:38; 11:1a; 14:1; 17:11; 18:35a
2. the [καὶ] ἐγένετο ἐν μιᾷ construction in Lk 5:12a, 17a; 8:22; 20:1
3. the parable formula ἔλεγεν or εἶπεν παραβολήν in Lk 5:36a; 6:39a; 12:16a; 13:6a; 14:7a; 15:3; 18:1–2a, 9; 19:11; 20:9a; 21:29a.

Besides showing how the author-editor of Luke has composed the openings in his own style, Cadbury argues something more than style preferences is happening; in fact, many of the openings signal a brand new arrangement of source material, which in turn determines the need for a literary "seam" to connect previously unconnected sections and thus produce a continuous narrative flow. The above three sets of passages, although not labeled as such by Cadbury, should be categorized as Lukan "seams," re-worked or independently composed, which unite pericopes or complexes of pericopes.

Closing of sections; conclusions

Three add-on patterns appear in the closing sections[41] of material inherited from Mark: (1) a nominative circumstantial participial clause with the active δοξάζων or passive δοξαζόμενος (e.g., 4:15; 5:25; 18:43);[42] (2) the aorist passive indicative of πίμπλημι (e.g., 4:28; 5:26; 6:11);

---

[39] Ibid., pp. 106f.
[40] Noted above, the [καὶ] ἐγένετο constructions in Luke and Acts are considered first categorized by Plummer, *A Critical and Exegetical Commentary on the Gospel According to S. Luke*, p. 45.
[41] Cadbury, *Style and Literary Method*, p. 107.
[42] In all cases except 4:15 (where δοξάζων ὑπὸ πάντων appears), the phrase used is δοξάζων τον θεόν. Cadbury, *Style and Literary Method*, p. 107 notes that other syntactical forms of δοξάζω τον θεόν are found in Lk 2:20; 7:16; 13:13; 17:15; 23:47; Acts 4:21; 11:18; 21:20, as well as in Lk 5:26, copied from Mark.

and (3) a variety of other expressions that depict awe or praise of God (e.g., 8:37; 9:34, 43a, 43b; 18:43; 19:37).[43] As clauses or phrases securely woven into the end of pericopes, the closings reveal similar lexical patterns, but they do not function as seams or summaries according to the above definitions.

Summaries of Jesus' ministry and influence

In the Lukan summaries redacted from Mark (e.g., Lk 4:14–15, 31–32, 37, 40–41, 44; 5:15–16; 6:17–19; 7:17, 21; 8:1–4; 13:22; 14:25; 17:11; 19:28, 47, 48; 21:37–38),[44] Cadbury observes that Luke's author-editor took stylistic liberties, not by adding to or intensifying the inherited Markan summaries, but by repeating them at other points in the narrative. In contrast to the stylistic adaptation in openings and closings, the author-editor of Luke not only imported Markan summaries with more fidelity but also repeated them. Notably absent are seams and summaries from both the infancy narrative (Lk 1–2), a situation amended in Cadbury's next major work on Luke and Acts, and the passion and resurrection narratives (Lk 22–24).

In Cadbury's next well-known volume, *The Making of Luke-Acts*,[45] written for an audience who does not necessarily (need to) know Greek, a case is built for the composition of Luke and Acts. As pre-gospel oral forms were circulated, collected, and written down, literary connective devices provided a sense of continuous flow to the narrative arrangement. Cadbury mentions two types of device: first, "new connections" or introductory formulae, that is to say, seams; and second, summaries.[46] Delineating introductory formulae based in part on Schmidt's study of Markan seams and summaries, Cadbury writes:

> These phrases [introductory formulae] serve a double purpose; *they both connect and separate the units . . .* Luke's phrases in

---

[43] Further, Luke's author-editor adds intensification to the disciples' inability to understand the import of Jesus' second and third passion predictions (e.g., 9:45; 18:34) and also deletes occasional Markan expressions depicting the crowd's or the disciples' amazed response (e.g., 8:39; 9:37; 18:24, 25, 31). See Cadbury, *Style and Literary Method*, p. 107.

[44] Ibid., pp. 108–111.

[45] Henry J. Cadbury, *The Making of Luke-Acts*, 2nd edition (New York: Macmillan Company, 1st edition, 1927; London: S.P.C.K., 2nd edition, 1958; Peabody, Mass.: Hendrickson Publishers, 1958. Reprint, 1999).

[46] Ibid., p. 57. The author-editor of Mark had already woven together various forms to compose a gospel narrative of his own before "Luke" inherited it, "Q," and perhaps other traditional forms.

Cadbury: Lukan seams (i.e., new connections or introductory formulae)
5:12a, 17a, 36a; 6:6a, 39a; 7:11a; 8:1a, 22, 40; 9:28a, 51; 10:38; 11:1a; 12:16a; 13:6a; 14:1, 7a; 15:3; 18:1–2a, 9, 35a; 19:11; 20:1, 9a; 21:29a.
Cadbury: Lukan summaries
1:80; 2:40, 52; 3:18; 4:14–15, 31–32, 37, 40–41, 44; 5:15–16; 6:17–19; 7:17, 21; 8:1–4; 13:22; 14:25; 17:11; 19:28, 47, 48; 21:37–38.

Figure 2.1 Cadbury's list of seams and summaries in Luke

part emphasize the indefiniteness of the setting. On the other hand, the circumstances of the setting seem to be more fully elaborated by Luke, so that the units with him are more intelligible as wholes [emphasis added].[47]

Cadbury also defines summaries:

> The summaries may be regarded as merely an enlargement of the same process. They serve a double purpose – to divide and to connect. *They give continuity and historical perspective, but they are also of a later vintage than the single episodes.* They belong to the stage of collection, representing an editorial need and even an historical interest which cannot be satisfied only with episodes. They are associated with the adjacent incidents which they generalize. They are often merely the conclusion of a single incident expanded. They indicate that the material is typical, that the action was continued, that the effect was general. They fill in the lacunae [emphasis added].[48]

In *The Making of Luke-Acts*, Cadbury identifies two more summaries, one in the infancy narrative (2:52)[49] and one in the John the Baptist material (3:18).[50] Shortly thereafter, included in an article on Acts summaries, he also identifies Lk 1:80 and 2:40.[51] Figure 2.1 recapitulates Cadbury's comprehensive list of Lukan seams and summaries. Without a doubt, Cadbury's contribution should never be underestimated, as he built a solid foundation for later scholarship.

Contemporaneous with Cadbury and deserving of brief mention, Martin Dibelius lists a set of "bridge" passages in Luke (Lk 3:15, 19, 20;

---

[47] Ibid., pp. 57f.   [48] Ibid., p. 58.   [49] Ibid., pp. 329f.   [50] Ibid., p. 58f.
[51] Cadbury, "The Summaries in Acts," p. 395.

8:1–3; 9:9; 21:37, 38) in a footnote to his article "Style Criticism of the Book of Acts."[52] These examples from the author-editor's hand link complexes of traditional material and make Dibelius' point. As in Luke, so in Acts, "in the way in which they [Acts summaries] form bridges between material which is separated in the text, *they are identical with what we have seen in corresponding parts of Luke's Gospel* [emphasis added]."[53] Even though Dibelius emphasizes the style, composition, and arrangement of traditional forms in Acts, he wants to show bridge passages function identically in Acts and Luke, to link material that is (widely) "separated in the text."[54]

How does Dibelius' list correspond to Cadbury's? The two lists have only Lk 8:1–3 and 21:37–38 in common. The first, 8:1–3, recapitulates the itinerancy of Jesus, the Twelve, and his female traveling companions; the second, 21:37–38, sums up Jesus' daily routine, locating him during the day in the Temple, where "all the people" came to hear him, and at night on the Mount of Olives. Because Dibelius' list serves a different function and does not pretend to be comprehensive, it will be used only in a minor way to support the majority opinion on passages identified as seams and summaries in Luke.

A contemporary of Cadbury and Dibelius, Rudolf Bultmann in *The History of the Synoptic Tradition*[55] also considers how sayings and "narrative species" were joined together to form gospel complexes. Specifically, the author-editor of Luke composed "introductions" to speech material as

---

[52] Dibelius, "Style Criticism," p. 10 note 19.   [53] Ibid., p. 10.

[54] Examples of bridge passages in Acts include the introduction of Saul (7:58; 8:1; 8:3) and the persecution in and dispersion from Jerusalem thus setting up the mission in Judea and Samaria (8:1, 4, 25; 11:19); see Dibelius, "Style Criticism," p. 10. On closer examination, Dibelius' examples for Luke do not seem overly strong. If, as Dibelius says, his examples from Acts are paradigmatically similar to those in Luke, the list of Lukan examples should also link (widely) separated material. It is unclear how Lk 3:15, 19–20; 8:1–3; 9:9; 21:37, 38 model this bridging function of the Acts examples. For instance, in Lk 3:15 does the people's question as to whether John is the Messiah link to the pericope on the messengers from John the Baptist (Lk 7:18–23) or Jesus' testimony to John (Lk 7:24–35) or Herod's concern that John had been raised from the dead (Lk 9:7–9) or Peter's confession of Jesus as Messiah (Lk 9:18–20) or the questioning of Jesus' authority (Lk 20:1–8) or all of these? (Other less clearly related pericopes that mention John the Baptist include those on fasting (Lk 5:33–35), the mention of John before the Lord's prayer (Lk 11:1), and the saying about the Law (Lk 16:16).) Furthermore, if Lk 3:15 points forward as Dibelius' Acts examples do, how is the preaching of John the Baptist in Lk 3:1–14 to be accounted for? Similar questions may be asked of other examples in Dibelius' list. The point is that the bridging function appears to connect distantly separated material in Acts, a function not seen as clearly in Luke. The Lukan passages tend to link adjacent material.

[55] Rudolf Bultmann, *The History of the Synoptic Tradition*, trans. John Marsh from 3rd German edition (New York: Harper & Row, 1963); originally published as *Die Geschichte der synoptischen Tradition*, 3rd edition (Göttingen: Vandenhoeck & Ruprecht, 1957).

well as "primitive connective formulae," "transition formulations," and "editorial formulations."[56] Building on the work of Julius Wellhausen, K. L. Schmidt, and others, Bultmann carefully examines the assemblage of pre-gospel traditions joined by independent composition or redaction to form the written gospel. Composing junctures based on similar content, catchwords, or seeming mere happenstance,[57] the author-editor of Luke built a coherent presentation from speech material (e.g., apophthegms or dominical sayings) and narrative material (e.g., miracle stories).[58]

As Bultmann attempts to differentiate introductory and transitional formulae, he opines: "It is only with difficulty that we can distinguish introductions from transition formulations."[59] His list of "introductions" comprise: (1) Lk 10:1, a setup for the mission speech to the seventy-two; (2) Lk 10:17, an orientation to the sayings in vv. 18–20; (3) Lk 11:1, which in connecting Jesus' prayer activity with the disciples' request becomes an introduction to the Lord's prayer; (4) Lk 11:37, a lead-in to the "Pharisaic" discourses from "Q"; and (5) others (Lk 13:22; 14:1–4, 25; 15:1–3; 17:5, 20; 18:1, 9; 19:11; 20:45; 22:24).[60] Transition formulae differ from introductions since, as "artificial" constructions,[61] they imply the linkage of pericopes happens synthetically; thus, they are less intrinsic to the story. Examples of transition formulae include: (1) Lk 10:23a (καὶ στραφεὶς πρὸς τοὺς μαθητὰς κατ᾽ ἰδίαν εἶπεν·) which joins the "Q" passage in vv. 21–22 to the "Q" passage in vv. 23b–24; (2) Lk 11:29a (τῶν δὲ ὄχλων ἐπαθροιζομένων ἤρξατο λέγειν·); and (3) others (Lk 12:1a–c, 15, 41; 14:12a; 16:14; 17:37).[62] Since Bultmann attributes these passages to Luke's author-editor, apart from the reproduction of Markan material, they largely come from the so-called Lukan travel narrative (9:51–19:27). Besides these, Bultmann identifies passages that anchor adjacent material in "secular history,"[63] namely, 1:5a; 2:1–2; 3:1–2a; 3:19–20; the first three introduce; the last recapitulates Herod's πονηρά and his imprisonment of John the Baptist. Unfortunately, the distinction between introductions and transitions is blurred entirely when Bultmann classifies them by motif, as shown in Figure 2.2.

Bultmann also points out "conclusions"[64] (Lk 3:18; 7:1a; 11:53–54; 20:26) as well as "concluding formulae"[65] from the author-editor's hand, some taken over from Mark (5:26; 6:11; 19:47–48; 20:19, 26, 39–40), others composed independently (9:43a; 13:17; 18:43). Are these summaries?

[56] Bultmann, *History of the Synoptic Tradition*, pp. 323, 360. [57] Ibid., p. 322.
[58] Ibid., pp. 337f. [59] Ibid., p. 335. [60] Ibid., pp. 334f. [61] Ibid., p. 335.
[62] Ibid., pp. 335f. [63] Ibid., pp. 361f. [64] Ibid., p. 337. [65] Ibid., p. 361.

Motif	Lukan references
Jesus at prayer	6:12; 9:18; 11:1
Context of a feast	7:36; 11:37; 14:1
Jesus in the synagogue, excluding references to parallel Markan material	4:15; 13:10
Jesus' travel through cities and villages	5:12; 7:11; 8:1; 10:1
Jesus' journey to Jerusalem	9:51, 57; 10:38; 13:22; 14:25; 17:11; 18:35; 19:1, 11
Question and answer context	10:17; 11:1; 12:41; 17:5, 37
Others' words as stimulus to speak	3:10; 11:45; 13:23; 14:15; 15:2; 17:20
Multitudes around Jesus	5:1; 7:11; 8:4; 11:27, 29; 12:1; 14:25; 19:48; 20:1; 21:38
Others' thoughts or behavior as stimulus to speak	11:38; 14:7; 16:14; 18:9; 19:11; 22:24

Figure 2.2 Bultmann's list of introductory and transitional passages

It is unclear; Bultmann's discussion occupies only two paragraphs, indicating a less than extensive amount of attention given to ending formulae over introductions and transitions. Of Bultmann's terms, "introduction" and "transition formulation," the latter may better describe "seam" than the former; but because Bultmann himself expressed difficulty in distinguishing these editorial formulations, it is appropriate to include both in a comprehensive listing, recapitulated in Figure 2.3.

How closely do the lists of Cadbury (and Dibelius) and Bultmann correspond? Not very much, given that Bultmann's list differs from Cadbury's in two significant ways. First, Bultmann tends to highlight passages not redacted from Mark, that is, independent composition, whereas Cadbury focuses on redacted Markan material. Neither viewpoint is more valid than the other; the emphases are simply different. Second, while summaries receive scant attention in Bultmann's analysis, the opposite is true in Cadbury's. It is possible Bultmann's noticeable inattention to summaries may be due to an earlier supposition that Lukan summaries were by and large composed by the evangelist Mark and redacted by the author-editor of Luke, a supposition supported by Cadbury's matching each Lukan summary to a Markan parallel.

Bultmann: Lukan introductions and transition formulations
1:5a; 2:1–2; 3:1–2a, 10, 19–20; 4:15; 5:1, 12; 6:12; 7:11, 36; 8:1, 4; 9:18, 51, 57; 10:1, 17, 23a, 38; 11:1, 27, 29a, 37, 38, 45; 12:1a–c, 15, 41; 13:10, 22, 23; 14:1–4 and vv.1, 7, 12a, 15, 25; 15:1–3 and v. 2; 16:14; 17:5, 11, 20, 37; 18:1, 9, 35; 19:1, 11, 48; 20:1, 45; 21:38; 22:24.
Bultmann: Lukan concluding formulations
3:18; 5:26; 6:11; 7:1a; 9:43a; 11:53–54; 13:17; 18:43; 19:47–48; 20:19, 26, 39–40.

Figure 2.3 Bultmann's list of introduction, transition, and concluding formulations in Luke

In spite of these obvious differences and the fact the terminology does not always coincide precisely, overlap does occur among the seam and summary lists of Cadbury, Bultmann, and to some extent Dibelius, who as expected contributes more fully to the discussion of Acts seams and summaries. Passages identified in common include:

- Lk 4:(14–)15, a transition from the Temptation pericope (4:1–13), sets the stage for Jesus' ministry in Galilee (4:16–9:50). Both Cadbury and Bultmann read 4:14–15 as the redaction and expansion of Mark, perhaps Mk 1:14, 28, 21, 39, in that order. Bultmann dubs these verses an "introduction," Cadbury a "summary."

- Lk 5:12a situates Jesus "in one of the cities" (καὶ ἐγένετο ἐν τῷ εἶναι αὐτὸν ἐν μιᾷ τῶν πόλεων) where he then heals a leper (5:12b–14). Cadbury refers to 5:12a as an "opening," Bultmann as a "transition formula" unconnected to previous material.

- Texts identified as introductory by Cadbury and Bultmann include: Lk 7:11a; 8:1a; 9:51; 10:38; 11:1a; 14:1; 17:11; 18:35; 20:1. Bultmann calls 19:48 introductory, but both he and Cadbury identify 19:47, 48 as summaries (Bultmann: "concluding formulae"). Texts deemed "summaries" by Cadbury but "introductions" or "transition formulae" by Bultmann include: 8:4a; 13:22; 14:25; 17:11; 19:47–48; 21:37–38. Note Cadbury reads 17:11 as an opening as well as a summary. Dibelius draws attention to 8:1 and 21:37–38.

- Lk 3:18 is regarded by Cadbury as a "closing" in *The Style and Literary Method of Luke*, a "summary" in *The Making of Luke-Acts*.[66] Bultmann calls it a "concluding formula."

---

[66] Cadbury, *Making of Luke-Acts*, p. 58.

Because controls on what was identified as a seam or summary appear more fluid than standardized at this time in biblical scholarship history, the practical distinction between them remains murky. It was only later in the twentieth century, as will be seen, that a technical differentiation of seams and summaries came to be accepted more widely.

Another early twentieth-century scholar, Johannis de Zwaan, often cited for his contribution, must be mentioned, although his work is not well-suited to the present authorship analysis. In "Was the Book of Acts a Posthumous Edition?",[67] de Zwaan identifies all passages in Luke (and Acts) that "mark stages in the progress of the narrative."[68] Calling them "stops" rather than summaries, de Zwaan resists the term "summary" on the grounds that "neither in Acts nor in the Gospel do they really summarize the preceding narrative, and it is evident that the cases in Acts belong in the same class as those in the Gospel."[69]

De Zwaan's terminology, it seems, however, complicates rather than clarifies the distinction. He was persuaded literary "stops" in Luke come in two varieties: (1) those mentioning *incidents* in the life of Jesus (or John the Baptist): Lk 1:80; 2:40, 52; 4:44; 7:1; 8:1; 9:51; 11:53–54; 19:48; 24:52–53; and (2) those mentioning the *feelings* of the multitude: Lk 1:65; 2:18; 4:22, 32, 36–37; 7:17; 9:43; 13:17; 23:48.[70] While de Zwaan's approach seeks precision, a *prima facie* inspection of the "stops" reveals problems. First, many Lukan passages other than those he mentions refer to "incidents" in the life of Jesus (or John the Baptist) or the "emotional reaction" of crowds. He includes, for example, (a) Lk 4:44 but not 6:6a, 20:1a; (b) Lk 5:15–16 but not 4:40–41 or 6:17–19; (c) 9:51 but not 13:22, 17:11, 18:35a, 19:1, or 19:28; and (d) 11:53–54 but not 4:28–30, 6:11, or 20:19. Second, if the *function* of "stops" as signpost sentences marks successive stages in the narrative and if the *content* depicts incidents in Jesus' (or John's) life or feelings of the multitudes, which is the *more defining* characteristic? Motif over function appears to control inclusion, since passages that almost certainly function as "stops" (e.g., 5:1a; 7:11a; 9:37a; 11:1a; 12:1a; 14:25; 20:26) are excluded. Third, de Zwaan suggests certain passages function as "stops" in the progress of the narrative, but they lie in the *middle* of a pericope (e.g., Lk 1:65; 2:18; 4:22, 32; 23:48).

---

[67] De Zwaan, "Was the Book of Acts a Posthumous Edition?" 95–153. De Zwaan proposes that Acts is based on the unfinished writings of the author of Luke's gospel and edited by a post-Pauline Christian; thus, the *final* author-editor of Acts is not the author-editor of Luke. This argument does not enjoy wide acceptance today.

[68] Ibid., 102.   [69] Ibid.

[70] Ibid., 102f. De Zwaan also identifies a few cases where the two types seem combined: Lk 4:14, 15; 5:15–16; 21:37–38; 24:36.

All these passages, it seems, are again chosen for content over function, thus by and large diluting the functional precision of "stop" as a marker of narrative progress. In short, de Zwaan fashions new categories to prove a final author-editor touched up many verses in Luke (and Acts), but his categories do not rely on generally well-accepted literary cues. For the purposes of identifying seams and summaries in Luke and Acts, then, de Zwaan's list uses different controls from those required for the present analysis and therefore should not be included.

A half-century later, Joseph A. Fitzmyer expanded the work of Cadbury, Dibelius, and Bultmann in addressing the Lukan seam and summary question in his two-volume *Anchor Bible* commentary on Luke.[71] Like earlier scholars, Fitzmyer identifies Lukan summaries explicitly but uses other terminology for "seams." He notes that summaries in Luke and Acts are analogous. In the commentary on Lk 4:14–15, Fitzmyer defines "summary":

> These verses [4:14–15] are to be regarded as an editorial statement, composed by Luke, who differs with his Marcan source, by which he is otherwise inspired. From the form-critical point of view, they are a "summary" of the sort that Luke uses in Acts (see *JBC*, art. 45 §4). Whereas the summaries in Acts describe (idyllically) the life of early Christians or the growth of the church in its springtime, this one gives an overview of the Galilean ministry of Jesus. Cf. 4:31–32, 40–41; 6:17–19; 8:1–3; 19:47–48; 21:37–38.[72]

As Fitzmyer notes, the *Jerome Biblical Commentary*[73] article (*JBC*, art. 45 §4) defines Lukan summaries in terms of those in Acts, thus neatly packaging the two books' summaries in a tight analogical relationship. When the *New Jerome Biblical Commentary* article on summaries appeared in print, so did a new and separate description of the Lukan summary, indicating not only greater attention to the gospel but a view based on the inherited Markan context as well:

> To fill the gaps between his freestanding episodes, Luke used the generalizing summary, which he had been able to observe in Mark's composition of the episodic Jesus traditions

<hr />

[71] Fitzmyer, *Luke I–IX*; *The Gospel According to Luke X–XXIV*, AB 28A (New York: Doubleday, 1985).

[72] Fitzmyer, *Luke I–IX*, pp. 521f.

[73] Raymond E. Brown, Joseph A. Fitzmyer, and Roland E. Murphy (eds.), *The Jerome Biblical Commentary* (Englewood Cliffs, N.J.: Prentice Hall, 1968), II.45.4.

(Mark 1:32–34, 39; 3:10–12). The summary generalizes single incidents and circumstances of the narrated episodes, making them into the usual and typical traits of a period.[74]

Besides the summaries listed in the first Fitzmyer quotation (i.e., Lk 4:31–32, 40–41; 6:17–19; 8:1–3; 19:47–48; 21:37–38), he identifies other summaries in the commentary (4:14–15; 7:16–17, 21), which, when combined, produce the list: Lk 4:14–15, 31–32, 40–41; 6:17–19; 7:16–17, 21; 8:1–3; 13:22; 19:47–48; 21:37–38.[75] All correspond to Cadbury's list, although with respect to the question of redaction Fitzmyer offers a slightly different perspective. He suggests the author-editor's composition of 4:14–15 is *inspired* by Mk 1:14–15[76] and the composition of 4:40–41 is *more than a redactional modification* of Mk 1:32–34.[77] Except for Lk 6:17–19, understood as a condensed and transposed redaction of Mk 3:7–12, Fitzmyer ascribes the summaries to definite (or probable) composition by the author-editor. Attention to evidence of redactional activity also leads Fitzmyer to identify three other types of editorial intervention: refrains, independent composition in introductory or concluding material, and redacted introductions.

"Refrain" in the infancy narrative: Lk 1:80; 2:40, 52:[78] These verses close the stories of John's birth, Jesus' birth, and the boy Jesus in the Jerusalem Temple, respectively. The recurrence of this aptly named "refrain" within the infancy narrative structure suggests "the infancy narrative was in large part freely composed by Luke" based on earlier models, as well as Hebrew Bible motifs, and thus represents the author-editor's free composition.[79] Because the refrains terminate the pericope and may be lifted off leaving the pericope intact, they function as short summaries and hence should be classified as such.

---

[74] Raymond E. Brown, Joseph A. Fitzmyer, and Roland E. Murphy (eds.), *The New Jerome Biblical Commentary* (Englewood Cliffs, N.J.: Prentice Hall, 1990), II.44.9.

[75] Fitzmyer, *Luke I–IX*, pp. 521f., 542, 552f., 622, 656, 663 (also 667), 695f.; *Luke X–XXIV*, pp. 1021, 1269, 1357. Fitzmyer lists 4:31–32 as a summary in one location in the commentary (*Luke I–IX*, pp. 521f.), but, characterizing it as "resembling the summary of 4:14–15," he suggests it is "best taken with the rest as a simple introduction to the specifically Capernaum ministry" at another location (*Luke I–IX*, p. 542). Thus, this summary anticipates the following material. For a list of Lukan summaries that Fitzmyer compiles retrospectively, see Fitzmyer, *Acts of the Apostles*, p. 97.

[76] Fitzmyer, *Luke I–IX*, pp. 521f.   [77] Ibid., pp. 552f., 663.

[78] Ibid., pp. 388, 432, 446. For Fitzmyer's use of "refrain" in the structure of the infancy narrative, see ibid., p. 314.

[79] Ibid., p. 309.

Independent composition in introductory or
concluding material

Besides the infancy narrative, Fitzmyer identifies authorial composition[80]
in transitional passages not called summaries but located at the beginning
or end of pericopes, including: Lk 1:66c–67; 3:1–3a, 7a, 15–16a, 18;
4:31–32; 7:11; 8:4a; 9:51, 56; 10:1, 17; 11:37–38, 45, 53–54; 12:22a,
41–42a, 54a; 13:23; 14:25; 15:1–3; 17:1a, 11, 19; 18:9; 18:35a; 19:11,
28.[81] Not included are Lukan "insertions" in the middle of a pericope,
for example, 2:19; 19:37. Except for 1:66c, 3:18, 11:53–54, and 17:19,
the uniting thread is they create a transition to a new pericope; that is
to say, they function as "seams." The conclusions, 1:66c, 11:53–54, and
17:19, do not function as independent summaries, since intrinsically they
are tightly woven into the pericope content. "Lukan composition"[82] in
3:18, a "comment of the evangelist," may be understood in effect as a
summary report of John's preaching.

Parable and redacted introductions: *Pace* Cadbury, the introductory
parable formulae are closely tied to following material (5:36a; 6:39;
12:16, 41; 13:6a; 14:7; 15:3; 18:1, 9; 20:9a, 19; 21:29).[83] Meanwhile,
the second category, (non-parable) redacted introductions, consists of
independently composed transitions inserted in the Markan introductions,
e.g., Lk 5:12a, 17; 9:28a, 43b; 20:1.[84] Figure 2.4 shows the entire list of
Lukan seams and summaries taken from Fitzmyer's commentary.

Subsequent to Fitzmyer's work on Luke, François Bovon sets out a
view of the Lukan compositional process in *L'évangile selon saint Luc
1, 1–9, 50*.[85] In the English translation and first volume of the *Hermeneia*

---

[80] He uses various phrases to describe Lukan composition, including from "Luke's pen"
or from "the evangelist's pen," an "introductory" sentence, a "transitional introduction"
composed by Luke, or simply "added by Luke."

[81] Fitzmyer, *Luke I–IX*, pp. 376, 452, 464($\times$3), 542, 656, 700, 826($\times$2); *Luke X–XXIV*,
pp. 842, 859, 943($\times$2), 944, 976, 985, 999, 1021, 1060, 1072, 1136, 1149($\times$2), 1183, 1214,
1231, 1242f. Note Lk 10:20 (*Luke X–XXIV*, p. 859) is categorized as an "introductory foil"
to the use of inherited, isolated sayings in 10:18, 19.

[82] Fitzmyer, *Luke I–IX*, p. 464.

[83] Ibid., pp. 599, 641; *Luke X–XXIV*, pp. 973, 985, 1008, 1044, 1072, 1176, 1183,
1278($\times$2), 1352. (All except 12:41; 20:19 were identified by Cadbury as such.)

[84] Fitzmyer, *Luke I–IX*, pp. 571, 578, 792, 806; *Luke X–XXIV*, p. 1271. All were also
identified by Cadbury and Bultmann as transitional phrases.

[85] François Bovon, *Luke 1: A Commentary on the Gospel of Luke 1:1–9:50*, Helmut
Koester (ed.), trans. Christine M. Thomas, Hermeneia (Minneapolis, Minn.: Fortress Press,
2002); originally published as *L'évangile selon saint Luc 1, 1–9, 50* (Geneva: Labor et
Fides, 1991). The other two volumes so far published are: *L'évangile selon saint Luc 9,
51–14, 35* (Geneva: Labor et Fides, 1996); and *L'évangile selon saint Luc 15, 1–19, 27*
(Geneva: Labor et Fides, 2001).

Fitzmyer: Lukan introductory authorial composition (both independent and redacted)
1:67; 3:1–3a, 7a, 15–16a; 5:12a, 17, 36a; 6:39; 7:11; 8:4a; 9: 28a, 43b, 51, 56; 10:1, 17; 11:37–38, 45; 12:16, 22a, 41–42a, 54a; 13:6a, 23; 14:7, 25; 15:1–3; 17:1a, 11; 18:1, 9; 18:35a; 19:11, 28; 20:1, 9a, 19; 21:29.
Fitzmyer: Lukan concluding authorial composition
1:66c; 3:18; 11:53–54; 17:19.
Fitzmyer: Lukan summaries and refrains
1:80; 2:40, 52; 4:14–15, 31–32, 40–41; 6:17–19; 7:16–17, 21; 8:1–3; 13:22; 19:47–48; 21:37–38.

Figure 2.4 Fitzmyer's list of introductory and concluding authorial composition, summaries, and refrains in Luke

series on Luke, *Luke 1 (1:1–9:50)*, Bovon describes how Luke's author-editor joined and framed the gospel narratives:

> Within the units and passages, Luke employs a simple narrative technique: he strings together smaller self-contained stories, which are intended to instruct and to elicit a response. This so-called episodic style was, of course, prescribed by the sources. But Luke does refine it; *when possible, he inserts short summaries between the episodes; these summaries create transitions, allow the readers to pause, and, above all, effect a generalization of the events* . . . As a rule, the pericopes are longer than the summaries [emphasis added].[86]

This classic approach to Lukan composition describes the editorial nature of summaries and their connective properties, generalized content, and length. Bovon identifies four of them in the infancy narrative (1:66c, 80; 2:40, 52),[87] two in the so-called travel narrative (13:22; 14:25a),[88] and ten in material derived from Mark (Lk 3:18; 4:15, 31–32, 40–41, 44; 5:15–16,

---

[86] Bovon, *Luke 1*, p. 3.

[87] Ibid., pp. 77(×2), 106, 108, 119. For the first summary (1:66c), Bovon seemed to have depended on different punctuation, since he referred to it as 1:66b; clearly he meant the last clause in the verse.

[88] Bovon, *L'évangile selon saint Luc 9, 51–14, 35*, p. 379 ("le sommaire du v. 22 sert de transition et ouvre une nouvelle section" "the summary in v. 22 serves as a transition and opens a new section"); p. 470 ("Le bref sommaire qui l'introduit attire l'attention davantage sur les interlocuteurs de Jésus que sur Jésus lui-même" "The brief summary that introduces it [the scene] draws attention more to the 'interlocutors' of Jesus than to Jesus himself ").

17; 6:17–20a; 8:2–3, 40).[89] In the commentary, Bovon suggests two other types of passage: (1) editorial "transitions" that begin new sections (Lk 3:1–3, 10, 21; 4:14–15; 8:1),[90] and (2) passages alluding to Jesus' journey to Jerusalem (Lk 9:51; 10:38a; 13:22, 33; 14:25; 17:11; 18:35; 19:28).[91] All in the first list and 9:51; 10:38a; 13:22; 14:25; 18:35 in the second are given to free composition by Luke's author-editor. Content and function distinctions occasionally overlap; Bovon calls 4:14–15 a "transition" and 4:15 a "summary,"[92] neither an unfounded designation. While Lk 3:1–3 and 8:1, editorial transitions apparently distinguished from summaries, begin new sections, so do Lk 13:22; 14:25a, allusions to Jesus' progress toward Jerusalem. Bovon designates the latter two as "summaries" that introduce, since *pace* Dibelius summaries may anticipate material.[93] To be sure, for Bovon, both summaries and editorial transitions to new sections anticipate upcoming content, a broadly defined functionality; in a sense, the meaning of seam and summary is presumed known. Finally, in a separate category, Bovon delineates a small set of "frame" passages at the beginning and end of longer passages that "provide a particular direction and interpretation to the narrative";[94] they include 8:4a; 9:1–2, 6, 28a.[95] In the case of 9:1–2, 6, he appears to identify an *inclusio* around the pericope; but in the case of 8:4a; 9:28, he treats both as editorial transitions that set up a new section of material. Figure 2.5 charts a delineation of seams (i.e., editorial transitions) and summaries drawn from Bovon.

Quite evident so far is that Lukan seam and summary definitions and functionality have not manifested extensive scholarly agreement. Summaries, most agree, consist of one or more sentences of authorial commentary that round off a pericope or complex of pericopes and often recapitulate, generalize, or amplify ideas found in antecedent material, although their function is sometimes anticipatory. Seams, more often labeled "transitions" or "connective devices," are the authorial words, phrases, or sentences that not only create a transition to a new section of

---

[89] Bovon, *Luke 1*, pp. 127, 152, 158, 164, 165, 177f., 178, 214, 299, 335 ("The summary passage (v. 40) serves form-critically both as a transition and as an introduction").

[90] Ibid., pp. 120f., 123, 128, 149, 300.

[91] Ibid., p. 7 note 8. Except for 19:28, for which the commentary is forthcoming, see further commentary on each respectively in Bovon, *L'évangile selon saint Luc (9, 51–14, 35)*, pp. 30f. ("redactionnel"), 101, 381, 395, 470; *L'évangile selon saint Luc (15, 1–19, 27)*, p. 131 ("sommaire et localization"), p. 223 ("il écrit ainsi Ἐγένετο δὲ ἐν τῷ . . . typique de sa manière d'écrire") [commentary not yet available for 19:28].

[92] Ibid., pp. 149, 152.

[93] The next section on Acts seams and summaries provides examples of how Dibelius held this position too.

[94] Bovon, *Luke 1*, p. 3.   [95] Ibid., pp. 307, 343(×2), 373.

Bovon: Lukan editorial transitions and allusions to Jesus' journey to Jerusalem
3:1–3, 10, 21; 4:14–15; 8:1; 9:51; 10:38a; 13:22, 33; 14:25; 17:11; 18:35; 19:28.

Bovon: Lukan summaries
1:66c, 80; 2:40, 52; 3:18; 4:15, 31–32, 40–41, 44; 13:22 (see row above); 14:25a (see row above); 5:15–16, 17; 6:17–20a; 8:2–3, 40.

Bovon: Lukan frame passages
8:4a; 9:1–2, 6, 28a.

Figure 2.5   Bovon's list of editorial transitions, allusions to Jesus' journey to Jerusalem, summaries, and frame passages in Luke

text but also unite it with antecedent material. While a standard differentiation of seams (or seam-like text) and summaries (or summary-like text) may not even today be used without caution, the passages identified in common by Cadbury, Fitzmyer, and Bovon include: Lk 1:80; 2:40, 52; 3:18; 4:14–15, 31–32, 40–41; 6:17–19 (20a); 8:1–3(4); 9:51; 13:22; 14:25a; 17:11; 19:28. Other authorial composition identified mostly in common includes: 3:1–3a (except Cadbury); 7:11 (except Bovon); 10:38a (except Fitzmyer); 18:35a (except Bovon); 19:47–48 (except Bovon); 21:37–38 (except Bovon).[96] Bultmann agrees with 3:1–2a, 18; 4:15; 7:11; 8:1, 4; 9:51; 10:38; 13:22; 14:25; 17:11; 18:35; 19:47–48; 21:38.

To conclude this study of scholars who identify seams and summaries in Luke, two recent articles contain comprehensive lists of Lukan summaries, although the focus of each lies elsewhere. First, Maria Anicia Co[97] describes the characteristics of summaries as literary technique. Her position is built on Dibelius' definition of summaries as "generalized descriptions of typical circumstances" and Cadbury's observation that summaries may be "expansions of a conclusion of a single incident or simple deductions from single details or collections."[98] The bulk of Co's article focuses on how summaries help shape narrative progression.

---

[96] The last three will undoubtedly be addressed by Bovon upon publication of the next volume of his commentary on Luke.

[97] Maria Anicia Co, "The Major Summaries in Acts: Acts 2,42–47; 4,32–35; 5,12–16: Linguistic and Literary Relationship," *ETL* 68 (1992), 49–85.

[98] The full quotation from ibid., pp. 55f. is:

> Dibelius maintained that summaries are *generalized descriptions of typical circumstances, formulated by the author*, who, having in mind the composition of a single continuous narrative, set them between the individual stories to

Advancing beyond redaction-critical descriptions of summaries (in Acts) is Co's view that:

> A summary may be described in terms of compression and expansion. It narrates events in a compressed way so that there is a speeding up of the narrative tempo, allowing events which take longer to happen in real-world time to be presented in a relatively short narrative or reading time. In contrast to a scene or scenic representation, it may provide an enlargement of participants, a broadening of time frame, the space of the action or of the action itself. *A summary may be defined as a relatively independent and concise narrative statement that describes a prolonged situation or portrays an event as happening repeatedly within an indefinite period of time. Also an important feature is the* impression *of an extended and open-ended duration. It has an expansive outlook which distinguishes it from a simple résumé of events* [emphasis added].[99]

According to Co, in Luke the literary properties of summaries "serve as a background for understanding Luke's use of summary as a literary technique" in Acts.[100] In a brief but cogent discussion of Lukan summaries, Co describes the third evangelist's redactional methods on Markan summaries, noting that "Luke" borrowed the summary "technique" from Mark to join traditional material into a cohesive flow. Rather than a uniform, literal importation of Markan summaries, "Luke" often reformulates motifs and expressions to compose his own summaries. Most relevant, in a lengthy footnote[101] Co provides three lists of Lukan summaries, shown here and in Figure 2.6:

1. Those with parallels in or dependence on Markan material: Lk 4:15 (par. Mk 1:14b; cf. 1:21, 39); Lk 4:31b–32 (par. Mk 1:21–22); Lk 4:37 (par. Mk 1:28; cf. 1:45; 5:27; 7:25); Lk 4:40b–41 (par. Mk 1:32–34; cf. 3:10–12; 6:5b, 56)[102]; Lk 4:44 (par. Mk

---

provide links and elaborations and to give the impression that these individual stories are but particular examples of what was generally described. Affirming that the summaries are *later than the individual episodes upon which they are based*, Cadbury observed that summaries are *generalizations or expansions of a conclusion of a single incident or simple deductions from single details or collections*. This view largely corresponds to our common idea of a summary as a condensed account, a recapitulation or a presentation of essential points drawn from a previous account or from several reports.

[99] Ibid., pp. 56f. [100] Ibid., p. 57. [101] Ibid., note 36.
[102] Cf. Schmidt, *Der Rahmen*, p. 161, who noticed the connection earlier.

Co: Lukan summaries
1:80; 2:40, 52; 3:18; 4:14b, 15, 31b–32, 37, 40b–41, 44; 5:15, 16, 17b; 6:18b–19; 7:17; 8:1 and vv. 1–3; 9:2, 6, 11; 13:22; 19:47 and vv. 47–48; 21:37–38; 24:53.

Figure 2.6   Co's list of summaries in Luke

    1:39); Lk 5:15 (par. Mk 1:45; cf. 5:27; 7:25); Lk 5:16 (par. Mk 1:45b; cf. 1:35); Lk 6:18b–19 (par. Mk 3:9–12); Lk 9:6 (par. Mk 6:12–13); 19:47 (par. Mk 11:18; cf. 11:17).

2.   Those having linguistic or content affinity with Lukan summaries based on Mark: (1) Lk 3:18; 8:1–3; 13:22 with Lk 9:6; (2) Lk 4:14b; 7:17 with Lk 4:37; 5:15; (3) Lk 8:1–3; 24:53 with Mk 15:40–41; and (4) Lk 19:47–48; 21:37–38 with Lk 5:15–16.

3.   Summaries of parallel composition *within* Luke, many of which are listed above: (1) Lk 5:15, 17b par. Lk 6:18–19; (2) Lk 8:1 par. Lk 9:2, 11; (3) Lk 9:6 par. Lk 8:1; 9:11; 13:22; (4) Lk 1:80; 2:40, 52.

In the second article, Gregory E. Sterling[103] examines the literary relationship between the summaries in Luke redacted from Mark and the summaries in Acts. He writes: "Henry Cadbury argued that *the summaries in Acts could be understood vis-à-vis the summaries in Luke where the evangelist demonstrates dependence on the summaries in Mark* [emphasis added]."[104] Certain Lukan summaries, for example, 1:80; 2:40, 52, function like Markan summaries as "clear structural markers," which "serve to mark the termini of major narrative strands."[105] Using the terms "major" and "minor" for Lukan summaries, Sterling provides two lists. The first list consists of major summaries in Luke, all of which are given to a redacted variation or inspired version of a Markan text: Lk 1:80; 2:40, 52; 4:14–15, 31–32, 40–41; 6:17–19; 8:1–3; 9:6, 10–11.[106] The second list includes three minor summaries derived from or inspired by Mark: 4:37; 5:15–16; 19:47. In a footnote, Sterling also lists sixteen "[o]ther texts in the Gospel of Luke that some consider to be summaries": 1:65; 2:18; 3:18; 4:22, 44; 7:1, 17; 9:43, 51; 11:53–54; 13:17, 22; 19:48; 21:37–38; 23:48;

---

[103] Gregory E. Sterling, "'Athletes of Virtue': An Analysis of the Summaries in Acts (2:41–47; 4:32–35; 5:12–16)" *JBL* 113 (1994), 679–696.
[104] Ibid., 684.   [105] Ibid., 686.   [106] Ibid., 684.

Sterling: Lukan summaries

1:65, 80; 2:18, 40, 52; 3:18; 4:14–15, 22, 31–32, 37, 40–41, 44; 5:15–16; 6:17–19; 7:1, 17; 8:1–3; 9:6, 10–11, 43, 51; 11:53–54; 13:17, 22; 19:47, 48; 21:37–38; 23:48; 24:52.

Figure 2.7 Sterling's list of summaries in Luke

24:52.[107] Of the sixteen, five are identified by de Zwaan alone (1:65; 2:18; 4:22; 23:48; 24:52). The remaining eleven have been identified as summaries or editorial transitions by other scholars, namely: 3:18 (Cadbury, Bultmann, Fitzmyer, Bovon, Co); 4:44 (Cadbury, Bovon, Co); 7:1 (Bultmann); 7:17 (Cadbury, Fitzmyer); 9:43 (Bultmann, Fitzmyer); 9:51 (Cadbury, Bultmann, Fitzmyer, Bovon); 11:53–54 (Bultmann); 13:17 (Bultmann); 13:22 (Cadbury, Bultmann, Fitzmyer, Bovon, Co); 19:48 (Cadbury, Bultmann, Fitzmyer, Bovon, Co); 21:37–38 (Cadbury, Bultmann, Fitzmyer, Bovon, Co). Figure 2.7 shows Sterling's entire list of summaries.

Based on the work of Cadbury, Bultmann, Fitzmyer, Bovon, Co, and Sterling, it is possible to identify a set of Lukan seams and summaries to be used as valid authorial data, agreed on by a majority and hence least open to question. Although the initial plan was to analyze seams and summaries as separate data categories, their delineation by scholars is less than unambiguous. In contrast to the definitions for seam and summary proposed earlier, it has been shown that individual scholars may understand a "summary" to recapitulate *or* anticipate and a "seam" to introduce *or* connect or conclude. Therefore, *for the purposes of this authorship analysis, whether a passage is labeled a seam or summary matters less than whether it is authorial; the key to data selection is authorial composition*, since attempting to untangle the terminology, content, and function will only discourage methodological objectivity. Agreement by a majority of the select but representative group of scholars results in valid authorial data and eliminates the idiosyncratic marks of a lone scholar. Lastly, the list of seams and summaries will include Lk 1:1–4, since the preface is not only independent authorial composition agreed on by all but also sets the stage for the entire gospel. Thus, the final data set consists of the following seams and summaries plus preface, *whose references are provided again in the footnotes and augmented by references*

---

[107] Ibid., note 15.

to works of other noted scholars, as available: Lk 1:1–4;[108] 1:80;[109] 2:40,[110] 52;[111] 3:1–3;[112] 3:18;[113] 4:14–15,[114] 31–32,[115] 40–41,[116]

---

[108] See Foakes Jackson and Lake, *Beginnings of Christianity*, vol. II, p. 136; Cadbury, "Commentary on the Preface of Luke," *Beginnings of Christianity*, vol. II, pp. 489–510; Fitzmyer, *Luke I–IX*, pp. 287–302; Bovon, *Luke 1*, pp. 16–25; Alexander, *Preface to Luke's Gospel*, pp. 91ff., 102–146; David P. Moessner, "The Lukan Prologues in the Light of Ancient Narrative Hermeneutics. Παρηκολουθηκότι and the Credentialed Author" in J. Verheyden (ed.), *The Unity of Luke-Acts*, BETL 142 (Leuven: Leuven University Press, 1999), pp. 399–418.

[109] Cadbury, "The Summaries in Acts," p. 395; Fitzmyer, *Luke I–IX*, pp. 388f. refers to this verse as a "Lucan refrain"; Bovon, *Luke 1*, p. 77; Co, "Major Summaries in Acts," p. 57 note 36; Sterling, "Athletes of Virtue," p. 684. See also Schneider, *Lukas*, vol. I, pp. 62f; Robert C. Tannehill, *Luke*, Abingdon New Testament Commentaries (Nashville, Tenn.: Abingdon Press, 1996), pp. 62f.

[110] Cadbury, "The Summaries in Acts," p. 395; Fitzmyer, *Luke I–IX*, pp. 419, 423, 432 refers to this verse as a "refrain"; Bovon, *Luke 1*, p. 106; Co, "Major Summaries in Acts," p. 57 note 36; Sterling, "Athletes of Virtue," p. 684. See also Schneider, *Lukas*, vol. I, p. 73; Fearghus Ó Fearghail, *The Introduction to Luke-Acts: A Study of the Role of Lk 1,1–4,44 in the Composition of Luke's Two-Volume Work*, Analecta Biblica: Investigationes Scientificae in Res Biblicas 126 (Rome: Editrice Pontificio Institutio Biblico, 1991), p. 14; Tannehill, *Luke*, p. 73.

[111] Cadbury, *Making of Luke-Acts*, p. 329; Fitzmyer, *Luke I–IX*, pp. 435, 446 refers to this verse as a "refrain"; Bovon, *Luke 1*, p. 115; Co, "Major Summaries in Acts," p. 57 note 36; Sterling, "Athletes of Virtue," p. 684. See also Tannehill, *Luke*, p. 77.

[112] Bultmann, *History of the Synoptic Tradition*, p. 361, mentions this as an "editorial formulation" that makes a "connection with secular history" (cf. 2:1ff.); Fitzmyer, *Luke I–IX*, p. 452 sees vv. 1–3a as "clearly of Lucan composition"; Bovon, *Luke 1*, p. 120 writes that this passage "introduces a new section." See also Hawkins, *Horae Synopticae*, p. 197.

[113] Cadbury, *Making of Luke-Acts*, pp. 58f.; Bultmann, *History of the Synoptic Tradition*, p. 337; Fitzmyer, *Luke I–IX*, p. 475 gives it to the author-editor, a "comment of the evangelist"; Bovon, *Luke 1*, p. 127 classifies it as a summary; Co, "Major Summaries in Acts," p. 57 note 36; Sterling, "Athletes of Virtue," p. 684 note 15. See also Ó Fearghail, *Introduction to Luke-Acts*, p. 21.

[114] Cadbury, *Style and Literary Method*, p. 108; Bultmann, *History of the Synoptic Tradition*, pp. 336, 361; Fitzmyer, *Luke I–IX*, pp. 521–522; Bovon, *Luke 1*, p. 152 casts v. 15 as a summary but comments on vv. 14–15; Co, "Major Summaries in Acts," p. 57 note 36 may see vv. 14b and 15 as two summaries; Sterling, "Athletes of Virtue," p. 684. See also Plummer, *Luke*, p. 116; Schneider, *Lukas*, vol. II, p. 104; Ó Fearghail, *Introduction to Luke-Acts*, pp. 24–25; Tannehill, *Luke*, p. 90; J. Delobel, "La rédaction de Lc. IV,14–16a et le 'Bericht vom Anfang' " in Frans Neirynck (ed.), *L'Évangile de Luc: problèmes littéraires et théologiques: mémorial Lucien Cerfaux*, BETL 32 (Gembloux: Duculot, 1978), pp. 203–223. Cf. Mk 6:1–2a; Mt 13:54.

[115] Cadbury, *Style and Literary Method*, p. 108; Fitzmyer, *Luke I–IX*, p. 542, who here refers to this as a "simple introduction" resembling a summary, but elsewhere (e.g., p. 622) includes it in a list of summaries; Bovon, *Luke 1*, p. 158 designates it a summary; Co, "Major Summaries in Acts," p. 57 note 36 designates vv. 31b–32 as the summary; Sterling, "Athletes of Virtue," p. 684.

[116] Cadbury, *Style and Literary Method*, p. 108; Fitzmyer, *Luke I–IX*, p. 552; Bovon, *Luke 1*, p. 164; Co, "Major Summaries in Acts," p. 57 note 36, who designates vv. 40b–41 as the summary; Sterling, "Athletes of Virtue," p. 684. See also Schneider, *Lukas*, vol. II, p. 116.

44;[117] 5:15–16,[118] 17;[119] 6:17–19;[120] 7:11;[121] 8:1–3;[122] 8:4a;[123] 9:51;[124] 10:38a;[125] 13:22;[126] 14:25a;[127] 17:11;[128] 18:35a;[129] 19:28;[130] 19:47–48;[131] 21:37–38.[132]

[117] Cadbury, *Style and Literary Method*, p. 108; Fitzmyer, *Luke I–IX*, p. 556 ("Luke introduces the idea of a wider ministry of Jesus . . . also in Judea (v. 44)"); Bovon, *Luke 1*, p. 165; Co, "Major Summaries in Acts," p. 57 note 36; Sterling, "Athletes of Virtue," p. 684 note 15.

[118] Cadbury, *Style and Literary Method*, p. 109; Bovon, *Luke 1*, pp. 177f.; Co, "Major Summaries in Acts," p. 57 note 36; Sterling, "Athletes of Virtue," p. 684 note 15.

[119] Cadbury, *Style and Literary Method*, p. 106; Fitzmyer, *Luke I–IX*, p. 578; Bovon, *Luke 1*, p. 178; Co, "Major Summaries in Acts," p. 57 note 36; Sterling, "Athletes of Virtue," p. 684 note 15.

[120] Cadbury, *Style and Literary Method*, p. 109; Fitzmyer, *Luke I–IX*, p. 622; Bovon, *Luke 1*, pp. 214, 217 (vv. 17–20a); Co, "Major Summaries in Acts," p. 57 note 36 designates vv. 18b–19 as the summary; Sterling, "Athletes of Virtue," p. 684. See also Schneider, *Lukas*, vol. I, p. 148.

[121] Cadbury, *Style and Literary Method*, p. 106; Bultmann, *History of the Synoptic Tradition*, pp. 336, 360; Fitzmyer, *Luke I–IX*, p. 656 writes that "Luke" is "responsible for the introductory verse (7:11)"; Bovon, *Luke 1*, p. 267. See also Schneider, *Lukas*, vol. I, p. 168. *Contra* Schneider and Fitzmyer, Bovon gives v. 11 to re-working of a source.

[122] Cadbury, *Style and Literary Method*, p. 109; Bultmann, *History of the Synoptic Tradition*, p. 336; Fitzmyer, *Luke I–IX*, pp. 522, 696; Bovon, *Luke 1*, pp. 299, 302; Co, "Major Summaries in Acts," p. 57 note 36; Sterling, "Athletes of Virtue," p. 684. See also Schmidt, *Der Rahmen*, p. 128; Dibelius, "Style Criticism," p. 10 note 19; Ó Fearghail, *Introduction to Luke-Acts*, p. 46; Tannehill, *Luke*, p. 138. All identify 8:1–3 as a summary except Tannehill (and de Zwaan), for whom v. 1 is the summary.

[123] Cadbury, *Style and Literary Method*, p. 109 sees the influence of Mk 4:1 and possibly 6:33; Bultmann, *History of the Synoptic Tradition*, p. 336 observes that this is an "expansion of Mark's original"; Fitzmyer, *Luke I–IX*, p. 700 sees this as an "independent Lucan composition," while 8:4b is seen as "Lukan redaction"; Bovon, *Luke 1*, p. 307 designates v. 4a a "frame" that sets the stage. See also Ó Fearghail, *Introduction to Luke-Acts*, p. 77.

[124] Cadbury, *Style and Literary Method*, p. 106; Bultmann, *History of the Synoptic Tradition*, pp. 360, 361 writes that "Luke clearly marks the transition from the Galilean ministry to the journey to Jerusalem"; Fitzmyer, *Luke I–XI*, p. 826 ascribes this to "almost certainly Lucan composition"; Bovon, *Luke 1*, p. 7 note 8; *L'évangile selon saint Luc (9, 51–14, 35)*, pp. 30f. sees the redactional nature of v. 51: "il est rédactionnel comme l'attestent la syntaxe, le vocabulaire et la théologie"; Sterling, "Athletes of Virtue," p. 684 note 15.

[125] Cadbury, *Style and Literary Method*, p. 106; Bultmann, *History of the Synoptic Tradition*, p. 336; Bovon, *Luke 1*, p. 7 note 8; *L'évangile selon saint Luc (9, 51–14, 35)*, pp. 99, 101, where he notes the first words of v. 38 "rappellent la marche de Jésus vers sa passion."

[126] Cadbury, *Style and Literary Method*, p. 110; Bultmann, *History of the Synoptic Tradition*, p. 334; Fitzmyer, *Luke X–XXIV*, p. 1021 ascribes v. 22 to "almost certainly of Lucan composition"; Bovon, *L'évangile selon saint Luc (9, 51–14, 35)*, p. 379 classifies v. 22 as a "sommaire"; Co, "Major Summaries in Acts," p. 57 note 36; Sterling, "Athletes of Virtue," p. 684 note 15.

[127] Cadbury, *Style and Literary Method*, p. 110 classifies it as a summary; Bultmann, *History of the Synoptic Tradition*, p. 334 sees it as an independent composition; Fitzmyer, *Luke X–XXIV*, p. 1060 argues that this verse "by its vagueness reveals that it comes from the evangelist's pen"; Bovon, *Luke 1*, p. 7 note 8; *L'évangile selon saint Luc (9, 51–14, 35)*, p. 470 also classifies it as a "bref sommaire." See also Schneider, *Lukas*, vol. II, pp. 320f., who calls it a "redaktionelle Situationsangabe."

Collected set of seams and summaries in Acts

Encapsulating a view of the early church in Jerusalem, the three so-called "major Acts summaries" (Acts 2:42–47; 4:32–35; 5:12–16) undoubtedly receive the most attention. Although scholars disagree on whether each is a composite or a completely independent composition, there exists among the three an apparent literary relationship,[133] a "synoptic problem in miniature," as it were. In the entirety of Acts, less richly textured passages also reveal transition points where the author-editor appears to have summarized or joined traditional material by authorial intervention.

Martin Dibelius has contributed two well-known works on seams and summaries in Acts. In the first, his seminal article on "Style Criticism of the Book of Acts," based on a study of compositional style and forms,[134]

---

[128] Cadbury, *Style and Literary Method*, p. 106; Bultmann, *History of the Synoptic Tradition*, pp. 336, 360; Fitzmyer, *X–XXIV*, p. 1149 gives this verse to the author-editor's free composition, i.e., it is "clearly of Lucan composition"; Bovon, *Luke 1*, p. 7 note 8.

[129] Cadbury, *Style and Literary Method*, p. 106; Bultmann, *History of the Synoptic Tradition*, pp. 336, 360; Fitzmyer, *Luke X–XXIV*, p. 1214 sees Luke "fashioning the introduction to this scene"; Bovon, *Luke 1*, p. 7 note 8.

[130] Cadbury, *Style and Literary Method*, p. 110 sees it as a summary; Fitzmyer, *Luke X–XXIV*, p. 1242, sees v. 28 "composed by Luke as a transitional introduction; it connects this episode with the preceding parable"; Bovon, *Luke 1*, p. 7 note 8. This seam is usually given to the free composition of the author-editor but reflects the spelling of "Jerusalem" found in Mk 11:1 (Ἱεροσόλυμα); see Fitzmyer, *Luke X–XXIV*, p. 1247.

[131] Cadbury, *Style and Literary Method*, p. 110; Bultmann, *History of the Synoptic Tradition*, p. 361; Fitzmyer, *Luke X–XXIV*, p. 1269 writes that "Luke sums it up in characteristic fashion (19:47–48), just as he gave a summary of his Galilean ministry at its outset (4:14–15)"; Co, "Major Summaries in Acts," p. 57 note 36; Sterling, "Athletes of Virtue," p. 684 note 15. Both Co and Sterling see this summary as a redaction of Mk 11:18. See also Ó Fearghail, *Introduction to Luke-Acts*, p. 50.

[132] Cadbury, *Style and Literary Method*, p. 111; Bultmann, *History of the Synoptic Tradition*, p. 361; Fitzmyer, *Luke X–XXIV*, p. 1357 also writes that "These verses could be derived from 'L' . . . but they are even more probably to be ascribed to Lucan composition"; Sterling, "Athletes of Virtue," p. 684 note 15. See also Schmidt, *Der Rahman*, p. 287; Schneider, *Lukas*, vol. II, p. 434; Dibelius, "Style Criticism," p. 10 note 19.

[133] E.g., ibid., pp. 9–10; Heinrich Zimmermann, "Die Sammelberichte der Apostelgeschichte," *BZ* 5 (1961), 71–82; Cadbury, "The Summaries in Acts," pp. 397f.; Pierre Benoit, "Some Notes on the 'Summaries' in Acts 2, 4, and 5" in *Jesus and the Gospel*, vol. II, trans. Benet Weatherhead (New York: Seabury Press, 1974), p. 95 note 4; originally published as a paper contributed to the symposium *Aux sources de la tradition chrétienne, mélanges offerts à M. Maurice Goguel* (Neuchâtel-Paris, 1950), pp. 1–10; Fitzmyer, *Acts of the Apostles*, p. 97. For a historical survey of scholarship on the three major summaries in Acts, see Co, "Major Summaries in Acts," pp. 49–55; Andreas Lindemann, "The Beginnings of Christian Life in Jerusalem According to the Summaries in the Acts of the Apostles (Acts 2:42–47; 4:32–37; 5:12–16)" in Julian V. Hills *et al.* (eds.), *Common Life in the Early church: Essays Honoring Graydon F. Snyder* (Harrisburg, Pa.: Trinity Press International, 1998), pp. 202–218.

[134] See summary in Haenchen, *Acts of the Apostles*, pp. 34f.

Dibelius suggests a key difference between Luke and Acts is that Acts displays greater complexity and less homogeneity in its arrangement than the third gospel.[135] In fact, Dibelius all but declares there is no uniform principle of arrangement in Acts. Focusing on the question of what traditional forms were available to the Acts author-editor, Dibelius identifies summaries as transitional texts, pieces of authorial composition whose generalized content is connected to or drawn from individual or specific instances of that content:

> His [the Acts author-editor's] pragmatic endeavours are seen only in *the different general summaries which, interposed between the various scenes and narratives, provide links and elaborations*. In this way individual events reported in those stories are made to appear as particular instances in those parts of the text which give *generalized descriptions of typical circumstances* [emphasis added].[136]

Indeed, according to Dibelius, who did not insist on distinguishing seams and summaries, summaries may recapitulate or anticipate; for example, although both are summaries, Acts 1:13–14 anticipates the selection of Judas' successor (1:15–28), whereas 6:7 recapitulates the scene in which the seven assistants are selected (6:1–6). Because Dibelius examines four sections in Acts, each is treated separately below: (1) 1:1–5:42; (2) 6:1–12:25; (3) 13:1–14:28; 15:35–21:16; and (4) 21:17–28:31.

In the first section (Acts 1:1–5:42), the fractious arrangement of narratives, speeches, and trial scenes shows evidence of linkage through summaries and other transitional texts.[137] Dibelius identifies Acts 1:13–14; 2:42, 43–47; 4:4, 32–35; 5:12–16, 42 as summaries from the hand of the author-editor after the model of Markan summaries. Acts 1:13–14, as mentioned, anticipates the selection of Judas' successor (1:15–28) and 2:43–47 signals the specific miracle that follows, the curing of a crippled beggar (3:1–10). In a similar way, 4:32–35 anticipates the specific stories of property sales by Barnabas (4:36–37) and Annias and Sapphira (5:1–11). Finally, 5:12–16 looks forward to the following trial and imprisonment of the apostles (5:17–42). Dibelius' view on the anticipatory function of summaries applies to the three major summaries and perhaps 2:42, but not 4:4; 5:42.[138] That is, Acts 4:4 is better suited to recapitulate the result of Peter's speech in 3:12b–26 than foreshadow the

---

[135] Dibelius, "Style Criticism," p. 4.   [136] Ibid., p. 9.
[137] Ibid., pp. 8ff.   [138] Ibid., pp. 9f.

Sanhedrin trial of Paul and John in 4:5ff.; similarly, 5:42 more appropriately summarizes the result of the Sanhedrin's release of Paul and John than anticipates the selection of the seven assistants in 6:1–6.

In the second section (Acts 6:1–12:25), comprising "long, connected narratives,"[139] summaries are evident in the "short, independent sentences" at the end of narratives (6:7; 9:31; 12:24).[140] Thus, Acts 6:7 rounds off the selection of the seven assistants (6:1–6); 9:31 anticipates the end of persecution or perhaps recapitulates the result of Saul's conversion (9:1–30) or the mission in Samaria and other parts of Judea (8:5–24, 26–40); and 12:24, following particulars on Herod's persecution of the Christians and his death (12:1–23), depicts the increased spread of God's word.

Further, "bridge" or linking passages, a slightly different case, insert Saul into Stephen's martyrdom (7:58; 8:1a, 3) and connect Stephen's martyrdom with the mission to Samaria and Antioch (8:1b–c, 4, 25; 11:19).[141] On the one hand, 7:58; 8:1, 3 constitute long-distance links to Saul's conversion story (9:1–30) and the entire second part of Acts (13:1–28:31). On the other hand, 8:1b–c, 25 recapitulate the result of the immediately adjacent martyrdom of Stephen (6:8–7:58a; 7:59–60) and the Samaritan mission (8:5–24) respectively, whereas 8:4; 11:19 foreshadow the immediately following new sections of material, specifically, the Samaritan mission (8:5–24) and the Antiochene mission (11:20ff.) respectively. Dibelius mentions no explicit summaries or transition points in the third (13:1–14:28; 15:35–21:16)[142] and fourth (21:17–28:31)[143] sections of Acts.

Years later, in the article "The First Christian Historian,"[144] Dibelius augments his definition of summary.[145] He describes the author-editor of Acts, that is, "Luke," as a writer of early Christian history without the aid of the same amount of traditional material as he had for the gospel. In fact, Dibelius argues, if "Luke" had had more traditions to collect and link together, as he did in the gospel, he could not rightly be called a historian. *Because Acts was a new venture, a new task, "Luke" needed to use a new style.*[146] Due to the lack of an underlying framework, the

---

[139] Ibid., p. 10.   [140] Ibid.   [141] Ibid.

[142] Ibid., pp. 5f. Dibelius theorizes the third section is an underlying collection of itinerary notices of stations where Paul stopped, supplemented by additions from the author-editor or from other traditional sources.

[143] Ibid., pp. 7f. notes the fourth section is marked by numerous speeches not influencing movement or action but rather amplifying the epideictic quality of their content.

[144] Martin Dibelius, "The First Christian Historian" in Greevan, *Studies in the Acts of the Apostles.*

[145] See page 75 above.   [146] Dibelius, "First Christian Historian," pp. 124f.

Dibelius: Acts summaries and short, independent sentences at the end of narratives
1:13–14; 2:42, 43–47; 4:4, 32–35; 5:12-16, 42; 6:7; 9:31; 12:24
Dibelius: Acts bridge passages
7:58; 8:1, 3, 4, 25; 11:19.

Figure 2.8 Dibelius' list of summaries, independent sentences, and bridge passages in Acts

first half of Acts (1–12) presented a greater challenge to the formation of a continuous narrative than the second half. Narrative-summaries help serve that purpose, observes Dibelius, because they allow the author-editor to arrange traditions about *individuals* into a flowing narrative that creates a *general* sense of early Christian community development:

> Another means of establishing a continuity is offered by the so-called narrative-summaries which are to be found throughout the first part of Acts . . . *these are little cross-sections of a general nature which, for the very reason that they are of this type, must have originated with Luke* [emphasis added].[147]

In light of *Formgeschichte*, Dibelius reconfirms the authorial nature of summaries, which connect traditional forms or individualized stories and whose function in effect "turns stories into history."[148] The idea that summaries in Acts come from the hand of the author-editor, that their content signals intentional generalization, and that they link traditional material all contribute to their significance in the compositional process. Figure 2.8 shows the entire Dibelius list.

As Dibelius worked on the style of Acts, Henry J. Cadbury published "The Summaries in Acts" in *The Beginnings of Christianity*,[149] in which he defines the function of Acts summaries by investigating, first, their analogical relation to those in the synoptic gospels and, second, the various patterns of parallelism among them. By showing the author-editor of Luke freely used, repeated, and rearranged the summaries in Mark, Cadbury contends an analogous situation exists for the summaries of Acts, even though no sources are extant. That is to say, Cadbury

---

[147] Ibid., p. 127.   [148] Ibid., p. 129.
[149] Cadbury, "The Summaries in Acts," pp. 392–402.

is persuaded certain summaries in Acts are pre-"Lukan," having been simply repeated or rearranged:

> How far the summaries came to our author along with his materials cannot now be determined. Whether thus derived or whether added by the final author, they give us tantalizing suggestions for determination of sources . . . But at whatever stage they arose they are undoubtedly pieces of editorial workmanship, devised by the author or his predecessor for the creation of a continuous narrative out of the raw materials.[150]

Cadbury assumes "Lukan" authorship for Acts, so naturally he understands "Luke's" treatment of Markan summaries as a control on how "Luke" would have either redacted existing summaries in the inherited tradition or composed what he considered suitable summaries where none had before existed.

As a result, Cadbury identifies five defining characteristics of summaries in Acts, under the assumption they had a similar history to those in Luke. First, summaries are "later than the intervening panels."[151] Compositional activity on the part of the author-editor in joining narrative complexes or individual stories occurs subsequent to the composition of the complexes or stories themselves. In other words, literary sutures and summaries, which unite previously unconnected material, were composed at a *later* point in time than the material they connect in the formation of a continuous narrative. Second, summaries are "derived by generalization from some of the specific adjacent material."[152] In effect, summaries are composed in order to present a generality based on and developed from a specific event or events in adjacent material. To Cadbury, whether the specific adjacent material preceded or followed the summary is less important than the summary's *generalized content* and especially its adaptation in parallel or repeated contexts. Third, summaries are "peculiarly liable to free treatment by the final editor and especially to combination."[153] This aspect emphasizes the *independent nature of the editing or compositional process* performed by "Luke," who in Cadbury's view does not restrict himself to a sole literary formula for content, placement, or repetition. This serves as a prelude to the last two characteristics. Fourth, for any particular summary, whether independent composition or edited traditional material, it is not unusual to find there are *similarities between one summary's content and that in other summaries* "when similar to one another in subject matter they [summaries]

---

[150] Ibid., p. 401.   [151] Ibid., p. 396.   [152] Ibid.   [153] Ibid.

may be due to Luke's well-known tendency to express himself independently but similarly on the same theme, but also may be derived by repetition from an underlying written source."[154] Summaries containing similar or parallel content may derive from the creativity of the author-editor or from the repetition of content taken from an inherited written source. Either possibility is plausible. Fifth, assuming the author-editor repeated a summary inherited from a written source, a paraphrase of the inherited material would occur in the repeated summary. More importantly, it is likely *the original summary would be found farther from the beginning of the book than the repeated, paraphrased summary.* In other words, the repeated summary, although composed later than the original, would actually appear more forward in the text than the original, "in the latter case (if derived from a written source and repeated) the variation is due to the author's tendency to paraphrase. Of two similar summaries there is some probability . . . that the second occurrence represents the original position of the summary in the source."[155]

Cadbury gives examples of this "positional" phenomenon from the Hebrew Bible. The summary in 1 Kgs 10:23–29 is used as a written source for the two summaries in 2 Chr 1:14–17 and 2 Chr 9:22–28. The latter (2 Chr 9:22–28) is the original and the former (2 Chr 1:14–17) the repeated summary, which appears earlier in the text.[156] From these Jewish Bible examples and others in Matthew's use of Mark,[157] Cadbury extrapolates that a similar phenomenon occurs in Luke and Acts. Based on the five characteristics just outlined, Cadbury identifies several kinds of summary in Acts where a textual intersection – a literary "caesura" between panels or scenes in the continuous narrative – is revealed.

Summaries that demonstrate the clearest parallelism

What Dibelius classifies as "bridge" passages Cadbury describes as passages *parallel* in their literary content. While Dibelius focuses on the connection of distant material, Cadbury emphasizes the repetition – with variation – of parallel content. Thus, Acts 8:1b–c, 4, which depict the persecution of the Jerusalem church and the subsequent scattering of the disciples to other parts of Judea and Samaria after Stephen's martyrdom, closely parallel the content in 11:19–20. Although Cadbury admits the

---

[154] Ibid.   [155] Ibid.   [156] Ibid., pp. 394f.
[157] E.g., Mk 9:43–48 used in Mt 5:29–30 and 18:8–9, the latter its original place; also Mk 10:46–52 used in Mt 9:27–31 and 20:29–34, the latter its original place.

difficulty in deciding whether a summary begins or ends a scene,[158] he suggests the use of μὲν οὖν signals the start of a new section of material. Discussing 8:3 as a summary that anticipates Paul's conversion and baptism (9:1ff.), Cadbury observes how "general statements occur at some interval before or after the specific instance they deal with,"[159] a statement that coheres with Dibelius' concept of "bridge" passages.

Summaries that frame narrative panels

Cadbury builds on an article by C. H. Turner in the 1900 Hastings' *Dictionary of the Bible* in which six generalizing statements (Acts 6:7; 9:31; 12:24; 16:5; 19:20; 28:30–31) are considered "framing" passages for six narrative panels recounting the development of the early church. To limit the number to six, Cadbury concludes, or to require a schema based on such an ordered chronology or geography disregards the author-editor's use of sources and the range of information available to him.[160] First, to 6:7 he allows a general statement on both the growth in the number of disciples in the early Jerusalem community (6:7a) and new evidence of a large group of priests who joined the faith (6:7b).[161] Second, Cadbury understands 9:31, a description of peace in the church throughout Judea, Samaria, and Galilee, as a general preparatory passage: it anticipates a new section of Peter's specific healing and resuscitation miracles (9:32–35, 36–41), which result in a large increase of believers from Lydda, Sharon, and Joppa. Third, the short passage in 12:24 describes the spread and increase of the word of God (cf. 6:7; 19:20); it precedes the return of Barnabas and Saul after their relief mission (12:25, a summary discussed later by Cadbury).[162] Notwithstanding the story of Herod's death that intervenes (12:20–23), 12:24 may also conclude an antecedent passage on the relief collection for Judea to be delivered by Barnabas and

---

[158] Cadbury, "The Summaries in Acts," pp. 400f.   [159] Ibid., p. 401.

[160] Ibid., p. 392. With respect to the significance of Acts 28:30–31, see Daniel Marguerat, "The End of Acts (28:16–31) and the Rhetoric of Silence" in *Rhetoric and the New Testament: Essays from the 1992 Heidelberg Conference*, JSNT Sup 90 (Sheffield: Sheffield Academic Press, 1993).

[161] Cadbury, "The Summaries in Acts," p. 400. Although 6:7b contains a unique reference to priests and may possibly point to the trial of Stephen in front of the Sanhedrin (6:12), it seems more likely that 6:7 generalizes the particular scene, showing the need and selection of assistants (6:1–6). The selection of seven assistants frees the Twelve from performing table service so they may preach the word of God, and 6:7 summarizes the result of that disengagement, i.e., the word of God continued to spread and the number of disciples increased greatly.

[162] Ibid., p. 401.

Saul (11:27–30).[163] Fourth, 16:5, a generalized account of the day-by-day growth of the church in faith and number, Cadbury observes, is "an expression that ought to begin a new paragraph,"[164] but, he remarks, "It may be claimed that xvi.5 is neither at the beginning nor at the end of a section but in the middle."[165] Thus, 16:5 may summarize and anticipate: it summarizes antecedent material in 16:1–4, Paul's invitation to Timothy to join him on the journey, and anticipates the montage in 16:6–15, the holy Spirit's prevention of their preaching in Asia, and Paul's vision of a Macedonian mission, which begins a sea voyage into Europe and an encounter with Lydia, who along with her household was baptized. Fifth, 19:20, describing the spread of the word of the Lord in influence and power, caps the Jewish exorcists' story (19:13–19). Sixth, 28:30–31 describe Paul's two-year house arrest in Rome, where he received visitors and proclaimed the dominion of God with impunity. Cadbury cautiously suggests this summary may anticipate a third unknown or unwritten volume, but more importantly the verses generalize the specific events of Paul's days in Rome (28:17–28).

Besides Turner's six framing passages, Cadbury suggests four more summaries: 2:47b; 5:14; 11:21, 24.[166] The first two, 2:47b and 5:14, form part of Cadbury's reconstruction of the parallelism in the so-called three major summaries[167] and contain content parallel to Turner's six framing passages, that is, the growth of the early church. In the case of 11:21, Cadbury argues that 11:19–20 and 11:21 form a composite framing summary (11:19–21) with content parallel to 8:1b–c, 4. As for the last, 11:24 reveals a framing feature similar to others in its repetition of content on the growth of the early church.

Summaries that display complicated parallelism

Cadbury presents a three-column synoptic layout of the content in the so-called three major summaries: 2:41–47; 4:32–35; 5:11–14.[168] Using 2:41–47 as the basis of comparison, he proposes no fewer than eight distinct sets of parallelisms, while adding content from 1:14; 5:5b and omitting 4:33a; 5:13a: (1) 2:42; 1:14; 2:46; (2) 2:43a; 5:11; 5:5b; (3) 2:43b; 5:12a; (4) 2:44–45; 4:32, 34–35; (5) 2:46a; 5:12b; 1:14a;

---

[163] See Benoit, "La deuxième visite de saint Paul à Jérusalem," 778–792.

[164] Cadbury, "The Summaries in Acts," p. 401.

[165] Ibid. A valid question, however, is whether the author-editor's use of μὲν οὖν signals the start of a new scene.

[166] Ibid., p. 396.   [167] Ibid., pp. 397f.   [168] Ibid.

Cadbury: Acts summaries

1:14, 15; 2:41, 42, 43–47, and v. 47b; 4:4, 32–35; 5:5b, 11–14, 15–16 and v. 14; 6:1a, 7; 8:1b–c, 3, 4, 6–7; 9:31; 11:19 and vv. 19–20, 21, 24; 12:24, 25; 15:41b; 16:5; 18:23c; 19:11–12, 20; 28:30–31.

Figure 2.9 Cadbury's list of summaries in Acts

(6) 2:46b; 2:42 (essentially the same as 1); (7) 2:47a; 4:33b; 5:13b; (8) 2:47b; 5:14. Striking is the obvious repetition; in fact, Cadbury suggests 4:32–35 and 5:11–14, whose contents were repeated in the more composite 2:41–47, serve as summary "bookends" around the specifics of Barnabas' and Ananias' communal donations. In Acts 5:11–16, Cadbury actually differentiates two distinct summaries: one in 5:11–14 followed by another in 5:15–16, with the latter repeating content from 8:6–7; 19:11–12. The numerical nature of 2:41 is also repeated and paralleled with variation in 1:15; 4:4.

Summaries from causal participial constructions

Partial-sentence summaries attached to introductory or concluding passages include 6:1a; 15:41b; 18:23c. They depict the increase and strengthening of the disciples or the regional churches. A genitive absolute in 6:1a depicts an increasing number of disciples; the circumstantial participles in 15:41b; 18:23c show a strengthening by Paul of the churches (15:41b) and the disciples (18:23c).

In short, summaries as editorial activity from the hand of the author-editor exhibit no consistent structure, placement, or content. Structurally, they can be lengthy and perhaps composite, such as the three major summaries (2:41–47; 4:32–35; 5:11–14), or brief and partial sentences, such as 6:1a; 15:41b; 18:23c. Summaries are understood to occur either at the end of a scene to extrapolate from a specific preceding incident or before a scene to anticipate a specific incident (e.g., 12:25).[169] Shown in Figure 2.9, summaries most often contain general information but on occasion provide new and specific information: "Between those [summaries] which give definite new information and those which give mere generalities no line can be drawn. Sometimes we doubtless have both combined as at Acts vi.7 with its unique reference to the conversion of priests."[170]

---

[169] Ibid., p. 401 note 4.   [170] Ibid., p. 400.

When comparing the lists of Dibelius and Cadbury, the distinction between summaries and what we today call seams quickly blurs. Part of the vagueness may come from the view that functionally summaries recapitulate or anticipate. Although Dibelius specifies no seams or summaries at all in the second half of Acts, he and Cadbury identify these passages in common in the first half: 1:14 (Dibelius: 1:13–14); 2:42–47 (Dibelius: 2:42, 43–47; Cadbury: 2:41–47); 4:4; 4:32–35; 5:12–16 (Cadbury: 5:11–14, 15–16); 6:7; 8:1b–c; 8:3, 4; 9:31; 11:19 (Cadbury: 11:19–20); 12:24. As will be seen shortly, later scholars identify numerous other summaries (and seams) in the second half of Acts.[171]

Several decades after Dibelius and Cadbury, Pierre Benoit compiled a list of Acts summaries in an article on the literary composition of the three major summaries in Acts. He defines summaries as "a kind of broad outline which depict *in a general way* characteristics or attitudes of the community of which the adjacent narratives furnish *particular* illustrations [emphasis added].[172] Like Dibelius and Cadbury, Benoit emphasizes the generalized content in contrast to the specificity of adjacent material. Unlike them, however, Benoit suggests a two-tier distinction: summaries and notes. In the first tier, summaries, Benoit places only the three major Acts summaries: 2:42–47; 4:32–35; 5:12–16, distinguished especially by length. In the second tier, Benoit places: 1:15b; 2:41b; 4:4; 6:1a, 7; 9:31, 42; 11:21–24b; 12:24; 13:48f.; 14:1, 21; 16:5; 17:4, 12; 18:8; 19:10, 20, differentiated from summaries by length, not generality of content. Describing notes as verses "on the continuous growth of the community, which though scattered throughout the book are equally general but much briefer,"[173] Benoit defines them as "mere halts," textual pauses that mark the flow of the narrative, not to be equated with summaries. These brief statements on the growth of the community he likens to punctuation marks, which make the course of our speech intelligible,[174] in spite of the fact that Dibelius and Cadbury identify many of

---

[171] Because of the reasons already stated above, Johannis de Zwaan has not been included in the selected but representative group of experts. Responding to Turner as Cadbury did, de Zwaan specifies the following "incidents" as literary "stops": 2:42–43; 5:11–14; 19:17–20, as well as 1:14; 2:42, 47; 4:33; 5:14; 6:1, 7; 9:31, 42; 11:21, 24; 12:24; 13:48–49; 14:21; 15:41; 16:5; 17:4, 12; 18:8; 19:10–11, 20. The "feelings of amazement or of hostility" include these "stops": 2:12; 13:12 and quite possibly 2:37; 4:1–2, 23; 5:17–18; 7:54; 17:5, 13.

[172] Benoit, "Some Notes on the 'Summaries' in Acts 2, 4, and 5," p. 95.

[173] Ibid., p. 95 note 1. Benoit's list of eighteen notes appears in a footnote at the beginning of his article, unadorned by any further explanation. Benoit merely lists the references; he does not elaborate, since his article concentrates on the three major Acts summaries, not the notes.

[174] Ibid., p. 95.

Benoit: Acts summaries
2:42–47; 4:32–35; 5:12–16.

Benoit: Acts notes and suture
1:15b; 2:41b; 4:4; 6:1a, 7; 9:31, 42; 11:21–24b; 12:24, 25; 13:48f.; 14:1, 21; 16:5; 17:4, 12; 18:8; 19:10, 20.

Figure 2.10 Benoit's list of summaries, notes, and a suture in Acts

the "notes" as summaries. In addition, Benoit, in an article on the compositional structure of Paul's second visit to Jerusalem, identifies Acts 12:25 as a literary suture: "Que ce verset soit une suture. . ."[175] Figure 2.10 contains a list of all the Benoit-identified passages.

In the years following Benoit and the others, Hans Conzelmann compiled a *Hermeneia* commentary on Acts[176] and used "Luke's" treatment of Markan summaries as a control on how "Luke" would have either reworked summaries inherited from pre-Acts tradition or fashioned summaries where none had before existed. Like Cadbury, Conzelmann held the position that "Luke" made sense of the whole by extrapolating from specific episodes. He defines "summary" as "short summarizing statements easily recognizable as redactional constructions . . . as well as longer summaries . . . These passages introduce no new material but merely summarize."[177] The introduction to Conzelmann's commentary offers a few examples of "short summarizing statements" (1:14; 6:7; 9:31–32) and longer summaries (2:42–47; 4:32–35; 5:12–16).[178] Within the commentary itself, Conzelmann points out other verses. For example, he describes 8:1b–c; 16:5[179] as summaries and 8:12; 19:8; 28:23 as summaries "of the Christian message" based on the theme of βασιλεία τοῦ θεοῦ.[180] Mentioned exclusively by Conzelmann, the last three are characterized as "a typical Lukan summary of the Christian message," with the βασιλεία τοῦ θεου theme the theological common denominator. Further, although he avoided the term "seam," Conzelmann identifies 7:58b; 8:1a as redactional links and 8:25 as a literary connective, differentiating 8:1a and 8:1b–c as a literary link and a summary respectively.[181] Curiously, Conzelmann wrote no commentary at all on 11:24b; 12:24, both identified by Cadbury and Benoit. Figure 2.11 recapitulates the entire

---

[175] Benoit, "La deuxième visite de saint Paul à Jérusalem," 786.
[176] Conzelmann, *Acts of the Apostles.*   [177] Ibid., p. xliii.   [178] Ibid.
[179] Ibid., pp. 60f., 125.   [180] Ibid., pp. 60f., 227.   [181] Ibid., pp. 60f., 66.

Conzelmann: Acts summaries and summarizing statements
1:14; 2:42–47; 4:32–35; 5:12–16; 6:7; 8:1b–c, 12, 25; 9:31–32; 16:5; 19:8; 28:23.
Conzelmann: Acts redactional links and a connective
7:58b; 8:1a, 25.

Figure 2.11 Conzelmann's list of summaries, redactional links, and a connective in Acts

Conzelmann list; and after the work of the next scholar is consulted, a final tally of all the correspondences will be made.

In his recent Anchor Bible commentary on Acts (1998), Joseph Fitzmyer draws attention to the summaries in Acts. In fact, he declares the function and content of the summaries in Acts are such that they represent their own form-critical category:[182]

> one of the noteworthy differences in Acts is the number of verses or blocks of verses with summary statements linked to the narratives. *They are generalized reports on circumstances that create a chain of events punctuating the narratives and describing the growth and development of the early Christian community.* They serve as signals to the readers, reminding them of the progress that the Word of God is making despite the author's preoccupation with the narration of details. They constitute, then, a separate form-critical category in Acts [emphasis added].[183]

While the length of the three major summaries exceeds that of the others, Fitzmyer understands all summaries in Acts to perform a similar function, namely, to punctuate the narratives with descriptions of the growth and development of the early Christian community.[184] More to the point, Fitzmyer distinguishes three types of "summary" in Acts, as shown in Figure 2.12. First, he identifies the *major summaries*, recognized by virtually all scholars: 2:42–47; 4:32–35; 5:12–16; they are singled

---

[182] Fitzmyer, *Acts of the Apostles*, p. 97. [183] Ibid.

[184] The major Acts summaries have been shown to be consistent with summary descriptions of ethically intense religious or philosophical schools in fairly contemporaneous Greco-Roman and Hellenistic Jewish prose literature; see Sterling, "Athletes of Virtue." Also, since Fitzmyer assumes single authorship of Luke and Acts, a legitimate area of future investigation is whether the form-critical category of "summary" applies to summaries in Luke.

Fitzmyer: Acts major, minor, and numerical summaries
1:14; 2:41, 42–47; 4:4, 32–35; 5:12–16 and v. 14; 6:1, 7; 9:31; 11:21, 24; 12:24; 14:1; 16:5; 19:20; 28:30–31.
Fitzmyer: Acts sutures
12:25; 15:1–2, 35.

Figure 2.12 Fitzmyer's list of summaries and sutures in Acts

out on account of length and probable composite nature.[185] Second, *minor summaries* of shorter length describe the progress and growth in the early Christian community: 1:14; 6:7; 9:31; 12:24; 16:5; 19:20; 28:30–31; these witness to the early community's expansion in geography, number, and strength of faith. Although they may frame narrative panels, says Fitzmyer in acknowledgment of Turner's work,[186] he questions whether the author-editor of Acts intended such a partitioning; rather, summaries testify to the flourishing of early Christianity. Third, *numerical summaries* quantify the growth in the first communities: 2:41; 4:4; 5:14; 6:1, 7; 9:31; 11:21, 24; 12:24; 14:1; 19:20.[187] Some, already included in the list of major and minor summaries (e.g., 5:14; 6:7; 9:31; 12:24; 19:20), show evidence of growth (e.g., 2:41; 4:4) or allusions to plenteous counts (e.g., 5:14; 6:1, 7; 9:31; 11:21, 24; 12:24; 14:1; 19:20). Finally, Fitzmyer specifies several "sutures" or seams, passages that link but do not summarize: 12:25; 15:1–2, 35.[188]

Based on the work of Dibelius, Cadbury, Benoit, Conzelmann, and Fitzmyer, few of whom it must be said highlight seams in great detail, a final set of summaries (and likely seams) in Acts, agreed on by a majority, may be identified. As with Luke, the Acts preface (Acts 1:1–5) has been included in the list of seams and summaries;[189] it is an example of

---

[185] See, e.g., Cadbury, "The Summaries in Acts," pp. 397f.; Benoit, "Some Notes on the 'Summaries' in Acts 2, 4, and 5"; Co, "Major Summaries in Acts." See Sterling, "Athletes of Virtue."

[186] Fitzmyer, *Acts of the Apostles*, pp. 97f.   [187] Ibid.   [188] Ibid., pp. 86f.

[189] Debate exists as to the length of the Acts preface, e.g. Acts 1:1; 1:1–2; 1:1–5; 1:1–8; 1:1–11; 1:1–14; 1:1–26; 1:1–2:41; 1:1–2:47. I have chosen Acts 1:1–5, so Aune, *Literary*, p. 117. Even these verses lack "a clear closure formula to indicate the end of the preface," according to Walton, "Where Does the Beginning of Acts End?" p. 447.

independent authorial composition that, with the Lukan preface, forms a literary hinge. Therefore, the final list is a compilation of summaries (and seams) plus preface, *whose references are provided again in the footnotes and augmented by references to works of other noted scholars, as available*: Acts 1:1–5;[190] 1:14;[191] 2:41;[192] 2:42–47;[193] 4:4;[194] 4:32–35;[195]

[190] See footnote 188. See also Foakes Jackson and Lake, *Beginnings of Christianity*, vol. II, pp. 133–137, 489–510; Vernon K. Robbins, "The Claims of the Prologues and Greco-Roman Rhetoric: The Prefaces to Luke and Acts in Light of Greco-Roman Rhetorical Strategies," in Moessner, *Jesus and the Heritage of Israel*; and Schmidt, "Rhetorical Influences and Genre." For a full treatment of the Lukan preface and Acts 1:1, see Alexander, *Preface to Luke's Gospel*.

[191] Dibelius, "Style Criticism," p. 9 and Conzelmann, *Acts of the Apostles*, p. 9 see vv. 13–14 as the summary; Cadbury, "The Summaries in Acts," pp. 397f.; Fitzmyer, *Acts of the Apostles*, p. 212; Haenchen, *Acts of the Apostles*, pp. 154f. sees vv. 12–14 as the transitional summary; Ó Fearghail, *Introduction to Luke-Acts*, p. 70.

[192] Cadbury, "The Summaries in Acts," p. 397; Benoit, "Some Notes on the 'Summaries' in Acts 2, 4, and 5," p. 95 note 1, who limits the summary to v. 41b; Fitzmyer, *Acts of the Apostles*, pp. 98, 264, 267. See also Co, "Major Summaries in Acts," pp. 58ff.

[193] Cadbury, "The Summaries in Acts," pp. 397f.; Benoit, "Some Notes on the 'Summaries' in Acts 2, 4, and 5," pp. 94–103; Fitzmyer, *Acts of the Apostles*, pp. 268–269. For a description of various scholarly designations, see Haenchen, *Acts of the Apostles*, 193–196. See also Cerfaux, "La composition de la première partie du livre des Actes," pp. 673–680, and "La première communauté chrétienne à Jérusalem: Act. II, 41–V, 42," ETL 16 (1939), pp. 5ff.; Gerd Lüdemann, *Early Christianity According to the Traditions in Acts: A Commentary* (Minneapolis, Minn.: Fortress Press, 1987), p. 47; Co, "Major Summaries in Acts," pp. 58–61; Lindemann, "The Beginnings," pp. 203–209. For Acts 2:41–47 and its relation to first-century religious-philosophical tradition, see Sterling, "Athletes of Virtue," pp. 679–696. For an argument that the author-editor of Acts intended the summaries to describe the detachment of the early Christian community from the Temple and the "establishment," see S. K. Kisirinya, "Re-Interpreting the Major Summaries (Acts 2:42–46; 4:32–35; 5:12–16)," *African Christian Studies: The Journal of the Faculty of Theology of the Catholic Higher Institute of Eastern Africa, Nairobi* 18 (2002), 67–74.

[194] Dibelius, "Style Criticism," p. 10; Cadbury, "The Summaries in Acts," p. 397; Benoit, "Some Notes on the 'Summaries' in Acts 2, 4, and 5," p. 95 note 1; Fitzmyer, *Acts of the Apostles*, pp. 98, 298.

[195] Dibelius, "Style Criticism," p. 9; "First Christian Historian," p. 128; Cadbury, "The Summaries in Acts of the Apostles," p. 397f.; Benoit, "Some Notes on the 'Summaries' in Acts 2, 4, and 5," pp. 95ff.; Conzelmann, *Acts of the Apostles*, pp. xliii, 36; Fitzmyer, *Acts of the Apostles*, pp. 97, 312. See also Haenchen, *Acts of the Apostles*, pp. 193–196; Ó Fearghail, *Introduction to Luke-Acts*, p. 76, who sees 4:31 as a summary; Lüdemann, *Early Christianity*, pp. 47, 61f.; Co, "Major Summaries in Acts," pp. 61f.; Lindemann, "The Beginnings," pp. 209–212. For a discussion of this summary's relation to first-century religious-philosophical tradition, see Sterling, "Athletes of Virtue," pp. 679–696. For a discussion of the inner coherence of Acts 4:32–5:16, see S. J. Noorda, "Scene and Summary: A Proposal for Reading Acts 4,32–5,16" in J. Kremer (ed.), *Les Actes des Apôtres: traditions, rédaction, théologie*, BETL 48 (Leuven: Leuven University Press, 1977), pp. 475–483.

5:12–16;[196]   6:1a;[197]   6:7;[198]   7:58b;[199]   8:1b–c;[200]   8:25;[201]   9:31;[202]
11:21,[203] 24b;[204] 12:24;[205] 12:25;[206] 16:5;[207] 19:20.[208]

Toward an authorship analysis

An objective and robust authorship analysis depends on valid data. The
collected sets of seam and summary data in Luke and Acts, in which

[196] Dibelius, "Style Criticism," p. 9; Benoit, "Some Notes on the 'Summaries' in Acts 2, 4, and 5," pp. 95ff.; Conzelmann, *Acts of the Apostles*, pp. xliii, 39; Fitzmyer, *Acts of the Apostles*, pp. 97, 327. See also Haenchen, *Acts of the Apostles*, p. 242; Lüdemann, *Early Christianity*, pp. 66f.; Co, "Major Summaries in Acts," pp. 62f.; Lindemann, "The Beginnings," pp. 212f. For the suggestion that Acts 5:15–16 may depend on Mk 6:55–56, see Sterling, "Athletes of Virtue," p. 685.

[197] Cadbury, "The Summaries in Acts," p. 400; Benoit, "Some Notes on the 'Summaries' in Acts 2, 4, and 5," p. 95 note 1; Fitzmyer, *Acts of the Apostles*, p. 98. Lüdemann, *Early Christianity*, p. 74 designates it an "introductory phrase" and a "general indication of time."

[198] Dibelius, "Style Criticism," p. 10; "First Christian Historian," p. 127; Cadbury, "The Summaries in Acts," pp. 400–401; Benoit, "Some Notes on the 'Summaries' in Acts 2, 4, and 5," p. 95 note 1; Conzelmann, *Acts of the Apostles*, p. xliii; Fitzmyer, *Acts of the Apostles*, pp. 97, 344, 351. See also Haenchen, *Acts of the Apostles*, p. 264.

[199] Dibelius, "Style Criticism," p. 10; Conzelmann, *Acts of the Apostles*, p. 60; Fitzmyer, *Acts of the Apostles*, p. 390 ("[Saul's] name appears to be adventitious, added at the end of the sentence").

[200] Dibelius, "Style Criticism," p. 10; Cadbury, "The Summaries in Acts," pp. 394, 396; Conzelmann, *Acts of the Apostles*, pp. 60f.; Fitzmyer, *Acts of the Apostles*, pp. 390, 397. See also Haenchen, *Acts of the Apostles*, pp. 82–83; Lüdemann, *Early Christianity*, p. 91, who calls it a "Lukan generalization."

[201] Dibelius, "Style Criticism," p. 10; Conzelmann, *Acts of the Apostles*, p. 66; Fitzmyer, *Acts of the Apostles*, p. 407.

[202] Dibelius, "Style Criticism," p. 10; "First Christian Historian," p. 127; Cadbury, "The Summaries in Acts," pp. 396, 401; Benoit, "Some Notes on the 'Summaries' in Acts 2, 4, and 5," p. 95 note 1; Conzelmann, *Acts of the Apostles*, xliii, pp. 75f.; Fitzmyer, *Acts of the Apostles*, pp. 98, 438, 441. See also Ó Fearghail, *Introduction to Luke-Acts*, p. 79; Lüdemann, *Early Christianity*, pp. 119f., who designates it a "redactional summary."

[203] Cadbury, "The Summaries in Acts," p. 396; Benoit, "Some Notes on the 'Summaries' in Acts 2, 4, and 5," p. 95 note 1, who sees 11:21–24b as the summary; Fitzmyer, *Acts of the Apostles*, p. 98.

[204] Cadbury, "The Summaries in Acts," p. 396; Benoit, "Some Notes on the 'Summaries' in Acts 2, 4, and 5," p. 95 note 1; Fitzmyer, *Acts of the Apostles*, pp. 98, 477.

[205] Dibelius, "Style Criticism," p. 10; Cadbury, "The Summaries in Acts," pp. 396, 401; Benoit, "Some Notes on the 'Summaries' in Acts 2, 4, and 5," p. 95 note 1; Fitzmyer, *Acts of the Apostles*, pp. 86, 98, 492f., who sees 12:24 as a summary and 12:25 as a suture. See also Haenchen, *Acts of the Apostles*, p. 387; Ó Fearghail, *Introduction to Luke-Acts*, p. 75.

[206] Cadbury, "The Summaries in Acts," p. 401; Benoit, "La deuxième visite de saint Paul à Jérusalem," p. 786; Fitzmyer, *Acts of the Apostles*, pp. 83, 86.

[207] Cadbury, "The Summaries in Acts," pp. 396, 401; Benoit, "Some Notes on the 'Summaries' in Acts 2, 4, and 5," p. 95 note 1; Fitzmyer, *Acts of the Apostles*, pp. 97, 574. See also Haenchen, *Acts of the Apostles*, p. 479; Lüdemann, *Early Christianity*, p. 174.

[208] Cadbury, "The Summaries in Acts," p. 396; Benoit, "Some Notes on the 'Summaries' in Acts 2, 4, and 5," p. 95 note 1; Fitzmyer, *Acts of the Apostles*, p. 97.

the author-editor expresses his compositional and stylistic preferences and tendencies, has now been identified as a control. If the same author-editor is responsible for both, we can expect coherence in certain patterns of compositional and stylistic preferences and tendencies. Before the analysis may be performed, however, we must determine exactly what to look for. The next stage answers the question: What elements and conventions of ancient prose composition should be used to analyze the seams and summaries in Luke and Acts?

3

AUTHORIAL CRITERIA: GREEK PROSE COMPOSITIONAL CONVENTIONS

Indeed, it is above all necessary to stress today what Streeter once wrote years ago, that Luke "though not, as has been rashly alleged, 'a great historian' in the modern sense, is a consummate literary 'artist' (*The Four Gospels*, 548). For he composed his narrative (*diēgēsis*) not merely as an ancient historian of the Hellenistic mode, nor merely as a theologian of the early church writing in a biblical mold, *but also as a conscious littérateur of the Greco-Roman period* [emphasis added].[1]

That the style of Luke and Acts was influenced by the literary milieu of the first century is rarely disputed. Scholars point to the preface of Luke (Lk 1:1–4), the author-editor's remarkable stylistic range, or the rhetorical character of the Acts speeches. Hellenistic or κοινή Greek,[2] the

---

[1] Fitzmyer, *Luke: I–IX*, p. 92. The full reference to Streeter is: B. H. Streeter, *The Four Gospels: A Study of Origins, Treating of the Manuscript Tradition, Sources, Authorship, & Dates* (London: Macmillan, 1924), p. 548.

Nota bene: Unless otherwise noted, English translations of the Latin and Greek quotations have been taken or revised from books in the LCL series, as well as W. Rhys Roberts, *Demetrius: On Style: The Greek Text of Demetrius* De elocutione *Edited after the Paris Manuscript* (Cambridge: Cambridge University Press, 1902), and *Dionysius of Halicarnassas: On Literary Composition: Being the Greek Text of the* De compositione verborum (London: Macmillan and Co., 1910). Further, text variants in ancient language quotations are noted only if they significantly alter the sense of the text.

[2] For a perspective on the origin and development of Hellenistic or κοινή Greek in general, see J. de Zwaan, "The Use of the Greek Language in Acts" in Foakes Jackson and Lake, *Beginnings of Christianity, vol. II*, pp. 32f. For a treatment of general literary and rhetorical developments in antiquity, see Heinrich Lausberg, *Handbook of Literary Rhetoric: A Foundation for Literary Study*, trans. Matthew T. Bliss, Annemiek Jansen, and David E. Orton (Leiden: Brill, 1998); Stanley E. Porter, *Handbook of Classical Rhetoric in the Hellenistic Period: 330 B.C.–A.D. 400* (Boston, Mass.: Brill Academic Publishers, 2001); and Jeffrey T. Reed, "Greek Grammar since BDF: A Retrospective and Prospective Analysis," *FN* 4 (1991), 143–164; and Philip E. Satterthwaite, "Acts against the Background of Classical Rhetoric" in Bruce W. Winter and Andrew D. Clarke (eds.), *The Book of Acts in Its Ancient Literary Setting* (Grand Rapids, Mich.: William B. Eerdmans Publishing Company, 1993).

vernacular of that era, was used not only on the street or in marketplace transactions but also in literary works whose language and style at times reflect an awareness of a more elevated style of Greek.[3]

Adolf Deissmann defines the term "literature" as "that which is written for the public, or for a public, and which is cast in a definite artistic form."[4] Deissmann argues that early Christian literature, in which he includes Luke and Acts, was "on the whole, popular literature."[5] In language, style, and subject matter, he classifies the gospels and Acts as popular and literary, though not professionally literary.[6] Shortly after Deissmann, Henry Cadbury describes the language of Luke and Acts as follows:

> Luke's Greek is neither classical Greek nor modern Greek. It is Hellenistic Greek, sometimes called Koine, – the Greek that was employed in the first century when Luke wrote . . . From extremes of style Luke may certainly be excluded. He is not of the lowest cultural grade on the one hand, nor on the other does he belong with the Atticists of the time, who by rigid rules and conscious imitation attempted to write in a style comparable to that of the classical masters of Greek prose.[7]

---

[3] By no means an exhaustive list, the following references describe literary elements of the Greek language and style that scholars find in [a] Luke; [b] Acts; or [c] both. [a] LUKE: Bovon, *Luke 1*, pp. 2–5; Fitzmyer, *Luke I–IX*, pp. 109–113; W. C. van Unnik, "Éléments artistiques dans l'évangile de Luc" in Neirynck, *L'Évangile de Luc*, pp. 129–140; Norden, *Die antike Kunstprosa*, vol. II, pp. 480–492. [b] ACTS: Henry J. Cadbury, *The Book of Acts in History* (London: Adam and Charles Black, 1955), pp. 32–57; Conzelmann, *Acts of the Apostles*, pp. xxxv–xxxvi; David P. Moessner, "The Appeal and Power of Poetics (Luke 1:1–4)" in Moessner, *Jesus and the Heritage of Israel*, pp. 84–126; Eckhard Plümmacher, "Cicero und Lukas: Bemerkungen zu Stil und Zweck der historischen Monographie," in Verheyden, *Unity of Luke-Acts*, pp. 759–775; Earl Richard, *Acts 6:1–8:4: The Author's Method of Composition*, SBLDS 41 (Missoula, Mont.: Scholars Press, 1978); Satterthwaite, "Acts against the Background of Classical Rhetoric," pp. 337–379; de Zwaan, "The Use of the Greek Language in Acts," pp. 30–44. For discussion of the influences of first-century historiography on Acts, see W. C. van Unnik, "Luke's Second Book and the Rules of Hellenistic Historiography" in Kremer, *Les Actes des Apôtres*, pp. 37–60. [c] BOTH LUKE AND ACTS: Alexander, "Formal Elements and Genre," pp. 9–26; *Preface to Luke's Gospel*; Aune, *Literary*, pp. 116–157; Thomas Louis Brodie, "Greco-Roman Imitation of Texts as a Partial Guide to Luke's Use of Sources" in Charles H. Talbert (ed.), *Luke-Acts: New Perspectives from the Society of Biblical Literature* (New York: Crossroad: 1984), pp. 17–46; Cadbury, *Making of Luke-Acts*, pp. 113–126; *Style and Literary Method*, especially pp. 4–39; Robbins, "The Claims of the Prologues and Greco-Roman Rhetoric," pp. 63–83; Daryl D. Schmidt, "Rhetorical Influences and Genre: Luke's Preface and the Rhetoric of Hellenistic Historiography" in David P. Moessner (ed.), *Jesus and the Heritage of Israel: Luke's Narrative Claim upon Israel's History* (Harrisburg, Pa.: Trinity Press International, 1999), pp. 27–62; Talbert, *Literary Patterns*, pp. 67–88.

[4] Adolf Deissmann, *New Light on the New Testament: From Records of the Græco-Roman Period*, trans. Lionel R. M. Strachan (Edinburgh: T. & T. Clark, 1907), pp. 50f.

[5] Ibid., p. 62.   [6] Ibid., pp. 50, 62f.   [7] Cadbury, *Making of Luke-Acts*, p. 114.

A general view of style in Luke and Acts must not ignore the influences from Semitic sources such as the LXX, the Hebrew Bible, and perhaps the Aramaic language – scholars hold various opinions on the degree of Aramaic influence – but it is the Hellenistic Greek literary and educational milieu of the first century that provides guidance for this investigation of prose composition. George A. Kennedy writes a fitting summation:

> The books of the New Testament were written in Greek by and for speakers of Greek, many of whom were familiar with public address in Greek or had been educated in Greek schools. They thus employ some features of classical rhetoric combined with Jewish traditions and are modified by beliefs and values of Christianity.[8]

While a stylistic comparison of Luke and Acts has been carried out by many scholars in well-known monographs, articles, and commentaries,[9] the meaning of "style" actually varies, ranging in significance from a writer's choice of vocabulary, to details of grammar and syntax, to the use of literary figures, or to any combination thereof. In a vintage article,[10] W. Rhys Roberts taps the works of ancient critics in order to elucidate various Greek words for "style," for example, λέξις, ἑρμηνεία, φράσις, and ἀπαγγελία. Aristotle (*Rh.* 3.1.2) and his successor Theophrastus, whose treatise on style remains unrecovered aside from mentions in works by later rhetoricians, both refer to the best-known term, λέξις, while Dionysius of Halicarnassus, Longinus, and others also use φράσις, in all likelihood a less formal word than λέξις.[11] In addition, Dionysius (*Vet. Cens.* 2.4) and Plutarch (*Vit. Demosth.* c.2) use ἀπαγγελία in reference to historical narrative. More unsettled is the term ἑρμηνεία, whose meanings in Demetrius' *De elocutione* (περὶ Ἑρμηνείας, *On Style*) come to cover a wide range of "formal literary expression."[12]

That said, what have yet to be studied vis-à-vis Luke and Acts are the "stylistic" patterns of euphony, rhythm, and certain structural elements.

---

[8] George A. Kennedy, *Classical Rhetoric & Its Christian & Secular Tradition from Ancient to Modern Times* (Chapel Hill, N.C.: University of North Carolina Press, 1999), p. 143. See also Cecil W. Wooten, (ed.), *The Orator in Action & Theory in Greece & Rome: Essays in Honor of George A. Kennedy* (Leiden: Brill, 2001). For a comprehensive study of twentieth-century scholarship, see Frederick W. Danker, *A Century of Greco-Roman Philology* (Atlanta, Ga.: Scholars Press, 1988).

[9] See Chapter One: Background and Methodology, for a discussion of style in Luke and Acts.

[10] W. Rhys Roberts, "The Greek Words for 'Style' (with Special Reference to Demetrius περὶ Ἑρμηνείας)," *TCR* 15 (1901), 252–255.

[11] Ibid., 253.   [12] Ibid.

Because the seams and summaries identified in Chapter Two were written in Hellenistic Greek, it is naturally assumed the anonymous author-editor was educated in reading and writing, an area rich with scholarship;[13] however, the pedagogy, time, locale, or amount of education are unknown. Nevertheless, we do know in a general way how education took place in antiquity, and Dionysius of Halicarnassus himself describes one pedagogical approach in *De compositione verborum* (περὶ Συνθέσεως ὀνόματων, *On Literary Composition*):

> When we are taught to read, first we learn by heart the *names of the letters*, then *their shapes and their values*, then, in the same way, *the syllables and their effects*, and finally *words and their properties*, by which I mean the ways they are lengthened, shortened, and scanned, and the like. And when we have acquired knowledge of these things, we begin to write and read, syllable by syllable and slowly at first. And when a considerable lapse of time has implanted firmly in our minds the forms of words we execute them with the utmost ease, and we read through any book that is given to us unfalteringly and with incredible confidence and speed. *It must be assumed that something of this kind happens with accomplished littérateurs* [παρὰ τοῖς ἀθληταῖς τοῦ ἔργου] *when they come to deal with literary composition and the harmonious arrangement of clauses* [emphasis added].[14]   (Dion. Hal. *Comp.* 25)

---

[13] Comprehensive modern treatments of the educational process in antiquity include: Raffaella Cribiore, *Gymnastics of the Mind: Greek Education in Hellenistic and Roman Egypt* (Princeton, N.J. and Oxford: Princeton University Press, 2001); *Writing, Teachers, and Students in Graeco-Roman Egypt* (Atlanta, Ga.: Scholars Press, 1996); Yun Lee Too (ed.), *Education in Greek and Roman Antiquity* (Leiden: Brill, 2001); H. Gregory Snyder, *Teachers and Texts in the Ancient World: Philosophers, Jews and Christians* (London: Routledge, 2000); James L. Crenshaw, *Education in Ancient Israel: Across the Deadening Silence*, ABRL (New York: Doubleday, 1998). See also Ronald F. Hock and Edward N. O'Neil (eds.), *The Chreia and Ancient Rhetoric: Classroom Exercises* (Atlanta, Ga.: Society of Biblical Literature, 2002).

[14] τὰ γράμματα ὅταν παιδευώμεθα, πρῶτον μὲν τὰ ὀνόματα αὐτῶν ἐκμανθάνομεν, ἔπειτα τοὺς τύπους καὶ τὰς δυνάμεις, εἶθ᾽ οὕτω τὰς συλλαβὰς καὶ τὰ ἐν ταύταις πάθη, καὶ μετὰ τοῦτο ἤδη τὰς λέξεις καὶ τὰ συμβεβηκότα αὐταις, ἐκτάσεις τε λέγω καὶ συστολὰς καὶ προσῳδίας καὶ τὰ παραπλήσια τούτοις· ὅταν δὲ τὴν τούτων ἐπιστήμην λάβωμεν, τότε ἀρχόμεθα γράφειν τε καὶ ἀναγινώσκειν, κατὰ συλλαβὴν [μὲν: Sadée] καὶ βραδέως τὸ πρῶτον· ἐπειδὰν δὲ ὁ χρόνος ἀξιόλογος προσελθὼν τύπους ἰσχυροὺς αὐτῶν ἐν ταῖς ψυχαῖς ἡμῶν ἐμποιήσῃ, τότε ἀπὸ τοῦ ῥᾴστου δρῶμεν αὐτὰ καὶ πᾶν ὅ τι ἂν ἐπιδῷ τις βιβλίον ἀπταίστως [ἀπταίστω: Usener] διερχόμεθα ἕξει τε καὶ τάχει ἀπίστῳ [ἀπίστω: Usener omitted]. τοιοῦτο δὴ καὶ περὶ τὴν σύνθεσιν τῶν ὀνομάτων καὶ περὶ τὴν εὐέπειαν τῶν κώλων ὑποληπτέον γίνεσθαι παρὰ τοῖς ἀθληταῖς τοῦ ἔργου.

Thus, if attended to, the seams and summaries of Luke and Acts should reveal the author-editor's characteristic patterns of euphonic arrangement, rhythmic cadence, sentence structure, and word order, as classical philologist Thomas Dwight Goodell rightly opines in his examination of Greek word order: "The individuality of an author is as plainly legible *in his order* as in his diction [choice of words] [emphasis added]."[15]

Prose composition in antiquity

Classicist D. A. Russell reminds us that the Greek of the classical and post-classical eras is decidedly remote from modern linguistic sensibilities; it is more judicious therefore to accept early critical methods than to evaluate them.[16] Of literary critical output, Russell notes, "this material provides a special insight into the attitudes and presuppositions of the creative writers of antiquity. We seem to glimpse the inside of the workshop."[17] From the "workshops" of the early critics we may retrieve a brief historical sketch of the linguistic sensitivities learned, practiced, and appropriated by writers of Hellenistic Greek.[18] In the pre-fourth-century BCE era, literary criticism on composition was by and large focused on poetry,[19] on the efficacy of compositional devices that entertain or persuade an audience. By the time of Aristotle, however, prose composition apart from poetry qualified as an area to be evaluated stylistically.

---

[15] Thomas Dwight Goodell, "The Order of Words in Greek" in *TAPA 1890*, vol. XXI (New York: reprint, Johnson Reprint Corporation; Kraus Reprint Corporation, 1964), p. 47.

[16] Russell, *Criticism in Antiquity*, p. 131.

[17] Ibid., p. 5. For a full treatment of ancient literary criticism, see also G. M. A. Grube, *The Greek and Roman Critics* (Toronto: University of Toronto Press, 1965, 1968); D. A. Russell and Michael Winterbottom (eds.), *Ancient Literary Criticism* (Oxford: Clarendon Press, 1972); George A. Kennedy, *The Art of Rhetoric in the Roman World: 300 B.C.– A.D. 300* (Princeton, N.J.: Princeton University Press, 1972); *A New History of Classical Rhetoric* (Princeton, N.J.: Princeton University Press, 1994). See also D. A. Russell and Michael Winterbottom (eds.), *Classical Literary Criticism* (Oxford: Oxford University Press, 1989) and Kenneth Dover, *The Evolution of Greek Prose Style* (Oxford: Clarendon Press, 1997).

[18] In addition, I examined other ancient critics and sources (e.g., Aristoxenus, Dionysius Thrax, Hermagoras, Philodemus, *Rhetorica ad Herennium*) but did not include them because the contributions of the four critics chosen offer the most robust prose composition criticism and explicit examples. For a review of the historical formation of grammar as an object of study in antiquity, see Pierre Swiggers and Alfons Wouters, "Poetics and Grammar: From Technique to Τέκνη" in *Greek Literary Theory after Aristotle: A Collection of Papers in Honor of D. M. Schenkeveld* (Amsterdam: VU University Press, 1995), pp. 17–41.

[19] Modern scholars often point to an early example from the *Frogs* by Aristophanes (427 BCE). In the final scene, the Chorus sings: "It's bad form, then to sit chatting with Socrates; *to discard the rules of composition* [ἀποβαλόντα μουσικήν], and to neglect the chief canons of tragedy [emphasis added]" (Aristophanes, *Frogs* 1491). For other examples, see Grube, *The Greek and Roman Critics*, pp. 1–45.

Technically, prose composition came to be comprised of two aspects: diction (word choice) and word arrangement, but the distinction developed gradually. In *The Greek and Roman Critics*, classicist George M. A. Grube describes Aristotle's differentiation in his *Rhetorica* (περὶ τέχνης ῥητορικῆς, *The "Art" of Rhetoric*) as casual and implicit rather than specifically spelled out. For Aristotle, both diction and word arrangement were associated with the idea of λέξις (*Rh.* 3.8.1).[20] In the second and first centuries BCE, the distinction became more formal and sharp, as critics differentiated diction (ἐκλογή ὀνομάτων) and word arrangement (σύνθεσις)[21] as two separate aspects of composition. In his discussion of Demetrius' *De elocutione*, Grube points to the extant text in which this differentiation is first spelled out:

> the further subdivision of style itself into word-choice (λέξις, later ἐκλογή ὀνομάτων) and word-arrangement (σύνθεσις), which is here [in *De elocutione*] used explicitly for the first time, may well puzzle a modern reader. Word-choice in ancient critics not only refers to the use of current or unusual words, neologisms, compound words and the like, but also to the use of words expressing passion and character, so that writing in character is partly a matter of word-choice. It also includes the use of different forms, cases or tenses, the use of loaded words, metaphors and similes, and even the use of few words or many. *Synthesis* or word-arrangement, on the other hand, is mainly concerned with three things: the sound of music of words in juxtaposition, the structure of clauses and sentences, and above all the resulting rhythm.[22]

Further, W. Rhys Roberts informs us that, as an aspect of style, euphony (εὐφωνία) or harmony among the sounds, syllables, and words in a sentence was often expressed in Greek by terms such as εὐρυθμία, λειότης, ἁρμονία, and σύνθεσις.[23] Roberts shows that euphony, rhythm (ῥυθμός),[24]

---

[20] Ibid., p. 97 note 3. The abbreviations for ancient writers and their works have been taken from *The Oxford Classical Dictionary*, Simon Hornblower and Antony Spawforth (eds.), 3rd edition (Oxford: Oxford University Press, 1996), pp. xxix–liv.

[21] Literally "set together." [22] Grube, *Greek and Roman Critics*, p. 112.

[23] See Roberts, *Demetrius: On Style*, s.v. "εὐφωνία," pp. 283f., who suggests εὐφωνία is a late word. Roberts sees different shades of meaning in the work of Dionysius of Halicarnassus between εὐφωνία and εὔστομος (e.g., Dion. Hal. *Dem.* 13.42; *Comp.* 7.12, 11.5).

[24] See also, e.g., Friedrich Blass, "On Attic Prose Rhythm" in *Hermathena: A Series of Papers on Literature, Science, and Philosophy* 32 (1906), 18–34, whose methodology has now been updated; A. W. de Groot, *A Handbook of Antique Prose-Rhythm* (The Hague: J. B. Wolters – Groningen, 1919); Stanislas Skimina *État actuel des études sur le rythme*

and word order[25] pertain to both the written and spoken word, a principle that dates at least to Aristotle: "Ὅλως δὲ δεῖ εὐανάγνωστον εἶναι τὸ γεγραμμένον καὶ εὔφραστον· ἔστι δὲ τὸ αὐτό. [Generally speaking, that which is written should be easy to read or easy to utter, which is the same thing]" (*Rh.* 3.5.6). Today it is not uncommon to find σύνθεσις translated as either "composition" or "word arrangement" (Lat. *collocatio*; cf. Cicero, *De oratore* 3.171). Here, use of the term "prose composition" refers to the arrangement of syllables into words and words into clauses and sentences, with special attention to the aspects of euphony, rhythm, and word order.

Early critics of prose composition

As mentioned above, it is from the "workshops" of early critics that we retrieve an array of linguistic sensitivities and conventions available to writers of Hellenistic Greek. With regard to the style of Luke or Acts, it would be highly speculative and methodologically unsound to find the influence of any particular classical or Hellenistic school of criticism; nevertheless, literary criticism on prose compositional elements may serve as a *guide* when the seams and summaries of Luke and Acts are examined. To those who learned to compose Hellenistic Greek or emulated Greek littérateurs, the early critics provide evidence and examples. Four early critics of prose composition stand out for their contribution: Aristotle, Pseudo-Demetrius, Dionysius of Halicarnassus, and Pseudo-Longinus. The bulk of this chapter, an extensive summary of their critical views, follows the brief introduction of each.

Aristotle

Aristotle (fourth century BCE) is one of the early critics who describe the principles of prose composition. In *Rhetorica* 3,[26] his discussion of

---

de la prose grecque II, Eussup 11 (Lwów: Subventionnée par le Ministère de l'Instruction Publique Société Polon Paris, 1930), a study of ancient Greek prose rhythm and its relation to accentuation; Donald F. McCabe, *The Prose-Rhythm of Demosthenes* (New York: Arno Press, 1981), whose dissertation from Harvard University presents a full historical review of what ancient authors wrote on prose-rhythm and hiatus.

[25] See also, e.g., Herman Louis Eberling, "Some Statistics on the Order of Words in Greek" in *Studies in Honor of Basil L. Gildersleeve* (Baltimore, Md.: Johns Hopkins University Press, 1902), pp. 229–240; J. D. Denniston, *Greek Prose Style* (Oxford: Clarendon Press, 1952; reprint, 1960, 1965), pp. 41–59; Goodell, "The Order of Words in Greek," pp. 5–47.

[26] See Aristotle, *The "Art" of Rhetoric*, trans. John Henry Freese, Aristotle, vol. XXII, LCL 193 (Cambridge, Mass.: Harvard University Press, 1926; reprint 1939, 1947, 1959,

prose composition, Aristotle pays attention to prose rhythm and sentence structure but does not explicitly discuss aspects of euphony. The written style, he states, is the most refined, requiring knowledge of good Greek and precision (*Rh.* 3.12.2).[27] Although his discussion concentrates on sentences in the periodic style, Aristotle briefly treats the continuous style (λέξις εἰρομένη), which he regards as more ancient than the periodic (Arist. *Rh.* 3.9.1) and which he defines as sentences joined by connecting particles stopping only when the sense is complete (*Rh.* 3.9.1–2). From a modern perspective, G. A. Kennedy studies Aristotle's notion of a period in its historical context and recommends revising the elevated concept of a period developed in later antiquity.[28] Kennedy argues that, based on an overall lack of rhetorical attention to sentence arrangement in the sources of Aristotle's era, the two types of Aristotelian periods, one composed of clauses (κῶλα) and one called simple, may consist of short units such as a phrase or a line[29] or the pairing of words, phrases, or clauses.[30] Historically authentic, this sense of the period has come to seem out of step in light of later, more elaborate definitions of the periodic style. Aristotle's principles of prose composition, subsumed under the idea of λέξις (style), were later differentiated in more complex and categorical ways.[31]

Pseudo-Demetrius

Placed by most scholars a century or two after Aristotle, the so-named Pseudo-Demetrius (third or second century BCE) wrote *De elocutione*,[32] a literary critical work with an uncertain past. Until the latter part of the twentieth century, this work was dated to the first century CE; today agreement tends toward a second century BCE dating, which makes *De elocutione* one of the only extant critical pieces from the Hellenistic

---

1967, 1975, 1982, 1991, 1994, 2000). Relevant passages from Aristotle's *Poetics* are also used, e.g., Aristotle, *Poetics*, trans. Stephen Halliwell (ed.), Aristotle, vol. XXIII, LCL 199 (Cambridge, Mass.: Harvard University Press, 1995; reprint 1999), pp. 1–141. Classical scholars believe that Aristotle's *Rhetorica* was written in Athens about 330 BCE, or at the earliest 335. Most pertinent is Book 3, because it addresses style.

[27] Also, Arist. *Poet.* 20–21 lists the components of prose "style" (λέξις), which he catalogues without elaboration as the particulars of "element, syllable, connective, noun, verb, conjunction, inflection, statement"; i.e., στοιχεῖον, συλλαβή, σύνδεσμος, ὄνομα, ῥῆμα, ἄρθρον, πτῶσις, λόγος.

[28] George A. Kennedy, "Aristotle on the Period," *HSCP* 63 (1958), 284.

[29] Ibid., 286. [30] Ibid., 287f. [31] Grube, *Greek and Roman Critics*, p. 97 note 3.

[32] See Demetrius, *On Style*, trans. Doreen C. Innes (ed.), LCL 199 (Cambridge, Mass.: Harvard University Press, 1995; reprint 1999), pp. 309–525. See also Roberts, *Demetrius: On Style*.

period.[33] Its authorship is also disputed. The writer's name, often written as "Pseudo-Demetrius," alerts the reader to a disputed authorial attribution.[34] For the sake of simplicity, hereafter the name will be written as "Demetrius," although use of this shortened name does not imply ignorance of or indifference to the authorship debate. Demetrius addresses prose composition directly in *Eloc.* 38–44, 48–58, 68–74, 105, 117–118, 139, 179–185, 189, 204–208, 238, 241, 245–246, 255–258, 299–301, 303. He lays out the principles and conventions of prose composition in a structured, prescriptive schema based on four styles (χαρακτῆρες): the grand (μεγαλοπρεπής), the plain (ἰσχνός), the forceful (δεινός), and the elegant (γλαφυρός), each of which has a faulty or imperfect counterpart.[35] A distinguishing aspect of each style is its "suitable composition" (τὸ συγκεῖσθαι προσφόρως), meaning the use of rhythm, clause length, word order, cacophony, and hiatus.

Dionysius of Halicarnassus

A century later, Dionysius of Halicarnassus (first century BCE) in *De compositione verborum*[36] laments that those who have written on style misguidedly emphasize word choice or diction (ἐκλογή ὀνομάτων) over word arrangement, the latter of which, he insists, more than diction, gives discourse its pleasing, persuasive, or powerful effect (*Comp.* 2, 4).[37] In contrast to Demetrius' four-style schema, Dionysius describes

---

[33] See also Grube, *Greek and Roman Critics*, pp. 110, 120f., who argues convincingly for a third-century BCE dating (pp. 120f.).

[34] In her LCL introduction, Innes (Demetrius, *On Style*, trans. Doreen C. Innes (ed.), LCL 199 [Cambridge, Mass.: Harvard University Press, 1995; reprint 1999], pp. 312ff.) notes that in a tenth-century manuscript (P³), *De elocutione* (Δημητρίου περὶ ἑρμηνείας) was apparently attributed by mistake to the famous Demetrius of Phaleron (ca. 360–280 BCE), a student of Aristotle, who ruled Athens 317–307 BCE. In the same manuscript, there is a simpler and more original subscription that reads Δημητρίου περὶ ἑρμηνείας, which cannot solve the authorship issue either. Always possible is that either the author's name was not Demetrius or Demetrius was so common a name in antiquity as to obfuscate the attribution (pp. 312f.).

[35] For Demetrius on prose composition in the grand style, see *Eloc.* 38–44, 48–58, 68–74, 105); in the elegant style, *Eloc.* 139, 179–185; in the plain style, *Eloc.* 204–208; and in the forceful style, *Eloc.* 241, 245–246, 255–258, 299–301). The faulty counterpart to the grand style is the frigid style (ψυχρός); for the conventions of composition, see *Eloc.* 117–118. The counterpart to the elegant style is the affected (κακόζηλος); see *Eloc.* 189. The counterpart to the plain style is the arid (τὸ ξηρός); see *Eloc.* 238. And the counterpart to the forceful style is the repulsive (ἄχαρις); see *Eloc.* 303.

[36] Dionysius of Halicarnassus, "On Literary Composition."

[37] For a similar sentiment, cf. Cic. *Orat.* 150: (*Quamvis enim suaves gravesue sententiae tamen, si inconditis verbis effereuntur, offendent auris, quarum est iudicium superbissimum.*

three styles: the austere (αὐστηρά) (*Comp.* 22),[38] the polished (γλαφυρά) (*Comp.* 23),[39] and the well-blended (εὔκρατος) (*Comp.* 24), the third a combination of the first two.

Dionysius defines composition (σύνθεσις) as a certain arrangement of the parts of speech (μόρια τοῦ λόγου)[40] so that they establish an appropriate order, fit together properly in clauses, and suitably divide the discourse into periods (*Comp.* 2–3):[41]

> It may well be thought that composition [word arrangement] bears the same relation to selection [word choice] as words do to ideas: for just as fine thought is of no use unless one invests it with beautiful language, so here too *it is pointless to devise pure and elegant expression unless one adorns it with the proper arrangement* [emphasis added]. (*Comp.* 3)[42]

Dionysius argues this position by providing examples in which he rearranges the words in a sentence to show how their character and effectiveness can be greatly diminished (*Comp.* 4).[43] He gives an

Quod quidem Latina lingua sic observat, nemo ut tam rusticus sit quin vocalis nolit coniungere) [For however agreeable or important thoughts may be, still if they are expressed in words which are ill arranged, they will offend the ear, which is very fastidious in its judgment. The Latin language, indeed, is so careful on this point that no one is so illiterate as to be unwilling to run vowels together]; see Cicero, *Orator*, trans. H. M. Hubbell, LCL 342 (Cambridge, Mass.: Harvard University Press, 1971).

[38] Cf. Dion. Hal. *Dem.* 38–39. Demetrius' grand style, Usher suggests, corresponds to Dionysius' austere style; see Dionysius of Halicarnassus, "On Literary Composition," p. 169 note 2.

[39] Cf. Dion. Hal. *Dem.* 40.

[40] Dionysius reviewed the historical development of the parts of speech: Theodectes and Aristotle proposed three primary parts of speech: nouns (ὀνόματα), verbs (ῥήματα), and conjunctions (σύνδεσμα). Over the next few centuries, subsequent grammarians proposed at least nine primary parts of speech: nouns, verbs, conjunctions, articles (ἄρθρα), appellatives (προσηγορικά), pronouns (ἀντονομάσιαι), adverbs (ἐπιρρήματα), prepositions (προθέσεις), and participles (μετοχαί) (*Comp.* 2). Whether three or more, the combination (πλοκή) or juxtaposition (παράθεσις) of these primary parts of speech results in the formation of clauses (κῶλα) (*Comp.* 2), and the joining of clauses forms what are known as periods (περίοδοι), the final element of discourse. See also Dion. Hal. *Dem.* 48. For the suggestion that Dionysius was influenced by Stoic sources, see Dirk M. Schenkeveld, "Linguistic Theories in the Rhetorical Works of Dionysius of Halicarnassus," *Glotta* 61 (1983), 89.

[41] Cf. Dion. Hal. *Dem.* 37–41; *Thuc.* 22, 24, where he provides much of the same information.

[42] ὥσπερ γὰρ οὐδὲν ὄφελος διανοίας ἐστὶ χρηστῆς, εἰ μή τις αὐτῇ κόσμον ἀποδώσει καλῆς ὀνομασίας, οὕτω κἀνταῦθα οὐδέν ἐστι προὔργου λέξιν εὑρεῖν καθαρὰν καὶ καλλιρήμονα, εἰ μὴ καὶ κόσμον αὐτῇ τις ἁρμονίας τὸν προσήκοντα περιθήσει.

[43] For a similar methodology, see, e.g., Demetr. *Eloc.* 46; Longinus *Subl.* 39.4; Cic. *De or.* 1.16.70; Quint. *Inst.* 9.4.14–15.

example by Thucydides in the speech of the Plataeans (3.57.4): ὑμεῖς τε ὦ Λαδεδαιμόνιοι ἡ μόνη ἐλπίς, δέδιμεν μὴ οὐ βέβαιοι ἦτε ("And we fear, men of Sparta, lest you, our only hope, may fail in resolution") (*Comp.* 7). If rearranged, writes Dionysius, deficiencies in structure are revealed: ὑμεῖς τε, ὦ Λαδεδαιμόνιοι, δέδιμεν μὴ οὐ βέβαιοι ἦτε, ἡ μόνη ἐλπίς ("And we fear, men of Sparta, lest you may fail in resolution, that are our only hope"). He provides another example from Demosthenes (*De cor.* 119): τὸ λαβεῖν οὖν τὰ διδόμενα ὁμολογῶν ἔννομον εἶναι, τὸ χάριν τούτων ἀποδοῦναι παρανόμων γράφῃ ("The acceptance of the offerings, then, you admit as legal, but the rendering of thanks for them you indict as an illegal proposal") (*Comp.* 7). Inferior, notes Dionysius, would be a disorganized arrangement such as: ὁμολογῶν οὖν ἔννομον εἶναι τὸ λαβεῖν τὰ διδόμενα, παρανόμων γράφῃ τὸ τούτων χάριν ἀποδοῦναι ("Admitting therefore that the acceptance of the offerings is legal, you indict as illegal the rendering of thanks for them"). Just as Homer's Athene could make the same Odysseus appear in different forms, different arrangements cause the same words to appear sometimes "misshapen, beggarly and mean, and at other times sublime, rich and beautiful" (*Comp.* 4). Good composition, he states, produces two necessary effects: delightfulness (ἡδονή)[44] and beauty (τὸ καλόν) (*Comp.* 10),[45] which are themselves derived from melody (μέλος), rhythm (ῥυθμός), and variety (μεταβολή), accompanied by appropriateness (πρέπον) (*Comp.* 11).[46]

Complemented by his other critical essays,[47] *De compositione verborum* provides the most comprehensive treatment of prose composition

[44] See, e.g., Roberts, *Dionysius of Halicarnassas: On Literary Composition*, pp. 97, 119, where he translates ἡδονή as "charm"; whereas Usher, in Dionysius of Halicarnassas, "On Literary Composition," pp. 45, 69, translates it as "attractiveness." I find neither translation totally satisfying. Although "charm" is closer than "attractiveness" to the idea of delight, enjoyment, and pleasure, I have chosen to translate ἡδονή as "delightfulness" for two reasons. First, "delightfulness" better captures the sense of response on the part of the hearer or reader, and second, "delightfulness" distinguishes it more readily from the other aim of composition, beauty (τὸ καλόν).

[45] For a treatment of Dionysius' inconsistent theory of evaluation when distinguishing ἡδονή and τὸ καλόν, see Dirk M. Schenkeveld, "Theories of Evaluation in the Rhetorical Treatises of Dionysius of Halicarnassus," in R. Browning and G. Giangrande (eds.), *Museum Philologum Londiniense*, vol. I (Amsterdam: Adolf M. Hakkert, 1975).

[46] Russell, *Criticism in Antiquity*, p. 134 reminds us that pairing delightfulness and beauty is not as unusual as it might first appear: the two qualities are opposed to each other in the ethical sense of "pleasure" and "honor."

[47] See critical essays in *Dionysius of Halicarnassas: Critical Essays*, vol. I, trans. Stephen Usher, LCL 465 (Cambridge, Mass.: Harvard University Press, 1974; reprint, 2000) as well as those in vol. II, whose full reference may be found in note 168, Chapter One. For an in-depth examination of Dionysius' three styles of word arrangement, see Karin Pohl, "Die Lehre von den drei Wortfügungsarten: Untersuchungen zu Dionysios von Halikarnaß, *De compositione verborum*," unpublished PhD thesis, Eberhard Karls University, Tübingen

of any extant literary critical work in antiquity. A most valuable aspect of Dionysius' work is the abundance of specific examples of euphony, rhythm, and sentence structure – those to emulate and those to avoid. S. F. Bonner echoes others when he writes that Dionysius "produced more actual criticism of Greek literature than any other writer whose works have survived."[48] *De compositione verborum* serves not so much as a treatise on literary criticism as a tractate on literary theory.[49] Although critiquing the style of individual authors in other critical essays, Dionysius focuses primarily on word arrangement (σύνθεσις) in *De compositione verborum*. The merits of this treatise, notes Bonner, are based on the depth of detailed analysis, as well as the extent to which Dionysius shows how charm and beauty may be detrimentally affected.[50] In the crisp words of Dirk M. Schenkeveld, Dionysius' work may be characterized as "practical criticism,"[51] grounded in pedagogy and paradigm. Despite this, the value of Dionysius' critical contribution remains a matter of dispute. Bonner, for example, takes issue with Dionysius' simple binary approach to composition criticism; in other words, to argue that a compositional effect derives from *either* "choice of words" *or* "word arrangement" is to limit the possibilities. Bonner seems to view Dionysius as a "product of rhetorical training" with a mind that lacks "mental elasticity."[52] Indeed, André Hurst sums up the intermittent, cyclical nature of modern interest in Dionysius, "Au-delà des querelles sur la médiocrité ou le génie de Denys d'Halicarnasse, ses écrits attirent aujourd'hui, une fois de plus, des lecteurs."[53] Hurst notes, as do others, that Dionysius cites no Latin writer, although he relocates to Rome and learns the Latin language.[54] Nonetheless, it is George A. Kennedy who best captures the gist of Dionysius' contribution to education on the aesthetics of prose composition:

(1968). For the standard text-critical edition of Dionysius' literary critical essays, see H. Usener and L. Radermacher (eds.), *Dionysii Halicarnasei Opuscula*, 2 vols. (Stuttgart: B. G. Teubner, 1965). For discussion of the composition date of *De compositione verborum* and *De Demosthene*, see S. F. Bonner, *The Literary Treatises of Dionysius of Halicarnassus: A Study in the Development of Critical Method* (Cambridge: Cambridge University Press, 1939), pp. 31ff., 71. Dionysius is believed to have written *De compositione verborum* between 20 and 10 BCE.

[48] Bonner, *Literary Treatises of Dionysius of Halicarnassus*, p. 15.   [49] Ibid., p. 71.

[50] Ibid., p. 74ff.   [51] Schenkeveld "Theories of Evaluation," p. 93.

[52] Bonner, *Literary Treatises of Dionysius of Halicarnassus*, pp. 71ff.

[53] André Hurst, "Un critique grec dans la Rome d'Auguste" in Wolfgang Haase (ed.), *Principat*, vol. II, Part 1, *Aufstieg und Niedergang der römischen Welt* (Berlin: Walter de Gruyter, 1982), p. 839.

[54] Ibid., p. 841.

On Composition is the most detailed account we have of how educated Greeks reacted to the beauties of their native language. This subject, Dionysius thought, should fascinate the young and would be, more than argumentation, the most suitable object of their study. In none of his works does Dionysius show much interest in rhetoric as an art of persuasion; to him it is an aesthetic, literary subject.[55]

Pseudo-Longinus

In *De sublimitate* (περὶ Ὕψους, *On the Sublime*),[56] a work dated by most scholars to the first century CE, Pseudo-Longinus, for simplicity's sake hereafter referred to as "Longinus," provides not so much a treatise on style, types of style, or development of style as one on the "tone of writing, attainable only as a consequence of a developed intellectual and emotional response to life."[57] Although he disapproves of trying to teach criticism by means of rules or precepts,[58] Longinus identifies "dignified and elevated word-arrangement" (ἡ ἐν ἀξιώματι καὶ διάρσει σύνθεσις) as the "fifth source of sublimity" in great writing (*Subl.* 8).[59] Reflecting the non-prescriptive tendency of this treatise, Longinus' abbreviated treatment of composition focuses on rhythm (*Subl.* 39–42).[60]

These four critics, only briefly introduced above, describe and sometimes prescribe the elements of euphony, rhythm, and structure that a writer

---

[55] Kennedy, *Classical Rhetoric & Its Christian & Secular Tradition*, p. 132.

[56] See Longinus, *On the Sublime*, trans. W. Hamilton Fyfe (ed.), rev. Donald Russell, LCL 199 (Cambridge, Mass.: Harvard University Press, 1995; reprint 1999), pp. 143–307. *De sublimitate* is generally thought to have been written in the first century CE by an anonymous author. The tenth-century manuscript (Parisinus 2036) shows the title as Διονυσίου Λογγίνου, but the table of contents shows Διονυσίου ἢ Λογγίνου. Which is the more original title is disputed (pp. 145–148). Treatment of prose composition in *De sublimitate* may be found in *Subl.* 39–42. Although authorship uncertainty makes "Pseudo-Longinus" a more technically correct designation, I have opted hereafter to refer to the author simply as "Longinus."

[57] Russell, in Longinus, *On the Sublime*, p. 153.

[58] Russell, *Criticism in Antiquity*, p. 9.

[59] The first four sources of the sublime include: (1) the power of grand conceptions (*Subl.* 9); e.g., Hom. *Il.* 4.442; 21.338/20.61–5; 13.18/20.60/13.19, 27–9; *Gn* 1:3–9, and Hom. *Od.* 3.109–11; (2) the inspiration of vehement emotion (*Subl.* 10); e.g., Sappho fr. 31 in Campbell; Aristeas of Proconnesus fr. 1 Kinkel, fr. 7 Bolton, fr. 11 Bernabé; Hom. *Il.* 15.624–8; Aratus *Phaenomena* 299; (3) proper construction of figures of thought and speech (*Subl.* 16–29); and (4) nobility of language in the choice of words, use of metaphor, and elaborated diction (*Subl.* 31–32, 37–38).

[60] Apparently Longinus wrote two books on σύνθεσις (*Subl.* 39.1), both of which have been lost.

ought to consider when composing a Greek prose sentence. These elements are the rudiments of composition that traverse a variety of stylistic contexts. Hiatus, for example, an element of euphony, is discussed by Demetrius in the context of one stylistic schema and by Dionysius of Halicarnassus in the context of another schema. As the works of these four early critics are examined, there emerges a set of prose compositional conventions that may be used to analyze the seams and summaries of Luke and Acts. The author-editor composed the seams and summaries in accordance with the methods he learned, appropriated, and practiced. The amount of early criticism on euphony, rhythm, and structure suggests that each area be treated separately.

Euphonic elements in prose composition

Although a Latin literary style critic, Quintilian (first century CE) eloquently speaks to the "judgment of the ear" when describing the effects of artistic prose composition (*compositione*):

> For in the first place, *nothing can penetrate to the emotions that stumbles at the portals of the ear*, and secondly man is naturally attracted by harmonious sounds. Otherwise, it would not be the case that musical instruments, in spite of the fact that their sounds are inarticulate, still succeed in exciting a variety of different emotions in the hearer [emphasis added].
>
> (Quint. *Inst.* 9.4.10)

Moreover, when early critics described the effects of melody, sweet sounds, and harmony in prose composition, specific examples of euphonic and cacophonic conventions were frequently given.[61] Of the arrangement of syllables, words, and clauses, those composed most pleasingly attend to two key conventions: hiatus and dissonance, that is, dissonant sound combinations. Hiatus (σύγκρουσις or the verb συγκρούω) means a "clash, collision, or concurrence"[62] of two collocated vowel sounds, while dissonance, avoided in certain eloquent styles, is used to provide vividness in the plain style or vigor in the forceful style

---

[61] E.g., Aristotle (*Rh.* 3.8.4) refers to the "harmony" (ἀρμονία) of "ordinary conversation," known to favor lack of hiatus; Longinus *Subl.* 43 uses κακόστομον to describe the inharmonious sound of "ζεσάσης δὲ τῆς θαλάσσης" ("the sea seething").

[62] Also used was σύγκρουσις φωνηέντων (e.g., Demetr. *Eloc.* 68, 299); see Roberts, *Demetrius: On Style*, p. 302, s.v. "σύγκρουσις."

(Demetr. *Eloc.* 219, 255). Demetrius and Dionysius offer concrete and pragmatic advice on both.[63]

Hiatus

Demetrius defines two aspects of hiatus: frequency of occurrence and "type," the latter falling into three categories: that occurring between (a) two long vowels or diphthongs (δίφθογγοι), (b) a diphthong or long vowel and a short vowel, or (c) two short vowels. He also points out how well-known writers or orators use hiatus; Isocrates, for example, carefully avoids hiatus, but others admit it without any hesitation. Demetrius advocates a path between the two extremes (*Eloc.* 68),[64] where hiatus should not occur so frequently as to produce a jerky style, nor be avoided so frequently as to produce an excessively smooth composition. Ordinary speech, in fact, tends toward euphony (*Eloc.* 69).[65]

To satisfy the present authorship analysis, hiatus examples illustrative of prose style, not poetry, have been culled from *De elocutione*. In the grand style, hiatus between long vowels or diphthongs is favored. Exemplified by the two ω sounds in λᾶαν ἄνω ὤθεσκε ("he kept pushing up the stone," Homer *Od.* 11.596),[66] this type of hiatus lengthens the line and affords a sense of movement and heavy effort (*Eloc.* 72). Other examples of hiatus suitable to the grand style include that between the two η sounds in μὴ ἤπειρος εἶναι ("not to be mainland" Thuc. 6.1.2) and between the two οι diphthongs in ταύτην κατῴκησαν μὲν Κερκυραῖοι· οἰκιστὴς δὲ ἐγένετο . . . ("its colonists were Corcyrean, its founder was . . . " Thuc. 1.24.2) (*Eloc.* 72). Note well the latter spans a mark of punctuation (·). Variety is introduced when the prose writer collocates different long vowels or diphthongs, e.g., between η and ω in ἠώς or between οι and η in οἵην (*Eloc.* 73). Again note well both occur within a word.

---

[63] Cf. Quint. *Inst.* 9.4.13f. For a review of word order as it affects the "judgment of the ear," see Henri Weil, *The Order of Words in the Ancient Languages Compared with that of the Modern Languages*, Amsterdam Studies in the Theory and History of Linguistic Science, Series 1: Amsterdam Classics in Linguistics, 1800–1925 (Amsterdam: John Benjamins B. V., 1978) and Elaine Fantham, *Roman Literary Culture: From Cicero to Apuleius* (Baltimore, Md. and London: Johns Hopkins University Press, 1996).

[64] Perhaps the Aristotelian mean, as found in Arist. *Eth. Nic.* 2.5, 1106b 8; *Pol.* 3.13, 1284b 7–13; *Eth. Eud.* 2. 1220b 21; see also Usher's references in Dionysius of Halicarnassus, "On Literary Composition," p. 205 note 5.

[65] See Innes, in Demetrius, *On Style*, p. 395 note a, who explains that vowel-laden but euphonic Εὔιος is the god of the bacchant cry εὐοῖ (Dionysius).

[66] Cf. Dion. Hal. *Comp.* 20, who analyzed the entire passage in detail (Hom. *Od.* 11.593–596).

By contrast, the plain style avoids hiatus between long vowels and diphthongs, since lengthening causes the style to possess an uncharacteristic stately (ὀγκηρός) quality (*Eloc*. 207). If hiatus is used, it should occur between short vowels or between a long and a short, as in these two examples: (1) πάντα μὲν τὰ νέα καλά ἐστιν ("all that is young is beautiful," author unknown), where hiatus occurs between two short vowels in the word νέα and at the juncture of the words καλὰ and ἐστιν; and (2) ἠέλιος ("sun"), where hiatus occurs between the first two syllables, ἠ and έ, a long and short vowel, as well as between the third and fourth syllables, λι and ος, two short vowels (*Eloc*. 207).

In the forceful style, a dynamic effect results from erratic and varied hiatus, seen in this example from Demosthenes:[67] τοῦ γὰρ Φωκικοῦ συστάντος πολέμου, οὐ δι' ἐμέ, οὐ γὰρ ἔγωγε ἐπολιτευόμην πω τότε ("when the Phocian war broke out, through no fault in me, as I at that time was not yet active in public life," Dem. *De cor.* 18).[68] Here Demosthenes uses a variety of hiatus types: between two long vowels or diphthongs (πολέμου, οὐ), a short and a long (ἐμέ, οὐ), and two short vowels (ἔγωγε ἐπολιτευόμην), the last of which includes an internal collocation between a diphthong and a short vowel (ἐπολιτευόμην). Avoiding hiatus diminishes forcefulness (*Eloc*. 299), Demetrius counsels.

A century later, Dionysius of Halicarnassus offers guidelines for hiatus in a decidedly detailed but much less prescriptive schema. W. Rhys Roberts suggests that Dionysius provides many examples, but in no case does he propose rigid formulae:[69]

> His [Dionysius'] task is to investigate the emotional power of the sound-elements of language when alone and when in combination – their euphonic and their symphonic effects. Hence the constant recurrence, throughout the treatise, of words like εὐφωνία, εὐρυθμία, λειότης, ἁρμονία, σύνθεσις . . . Dionysius himself formulates no invariable rules upon the subject.[70]

Dionysius opines it is the "senses, untutored by reason" (ταῖς . . . ἀλόγοις αἰσθήσεσιν) that distinguish what is pleasant from what is not (*Dem.* 24). Although scholars do not agree on the overall value of Dionysius' essays,

---

[67] See Innes' comment on jerky hiatus in Demetrius, *On Style*, p. 521 note b.
[68] Ibid., p. 520.
[69] Roberts, *Dionysius of Halicarnassus: On Literary Composition*, pp. 27f.
[70] Ibid., p. 27. For Dionysius' contribution to our knowledge of ancient Greek pronunciation, see W. Sidney Allen, *Vox Graeca: A Guide to the Pronunciation of Classical Greek*, 3rd edition (Cambridge: Cambridge University Press, 1987).

W. B. Stanford favorably credits him with writing the most complete extant discussion of Greek euphony:[71]

> Whether any previous author had ventured to be quite so precise and so detailed in defining the euphonic properties of individual letters, we cannot now tell. Some critics in his time . . . said that people like Dionysios went too far in his speculations . . . But even if Dionysios is overenthusiastic in his theories, he is also a man of judicious taste and acute critical observation, and we can learn much from him.[72]

Use of hiatus or the avoidance thereof characterizes the austere and polished styles of Dionysius' schema. For examples in the austere style, Dionysius examines the first two periods (here separated by "|") in Thucydides' book on the Peloponnesian War (*Comp.* 22):

> Θουκυδίδης Ἀθηναῖος ξυνέγραψε τὸν πόλεμον τῶν Πελοποννησίων καὶ Ἀθηναίων, ὡς ἐπολέμησαν πρὸς ἀλλήλους, | ἀρξάμενος εὐθὺς καθισταμένου καὶ ἐλπίσας μέγαν τε ἔσεσθαι καὶ ἀξιολογώτατον τῶν προγεγενημένων [Thucydides, an Athenian, recorded the war between the Peloponnesians and the Athenians, writing how they waged it against each other and beginning his work as soon as the war broke out in expectation that it would be a major one and notable beyond all previous wars]. (Thuc. 1.1)[73]

There is a rough and rugged sense to this passage, lacking a smooth or euphonious effect. For example, in the first period, hiatus between καὶ and Ἀθηναίων effects a break in the continuity; in the second, hiatus interrupts the continuity three times in close succession, namely, between καὶ and ἐλπίσας, between τε and ἔσεσθαι, and between καὶ and ἀξιολογώτατον. In *Comp.* 22, Dionysius quotes the complete text of Thuc. 1.1, dividing it into twelve periods and thirty clauses, and, of the latter, he says an overwhelming majority manifests the same rough and rugged features. In the entire passage, Dionysius finds over thirty examples of hiatus,

---

[71] W. B. Stanford, *The Sound of Greek: Studies in the Greek Theory and Practice of Euphony* (Berkeley and Los Angeles, Calif.: University of California Press, 1967), pp. 51–60.

[72] Ibid., p. 51.

[73] Based on *Thucydides: The Peloponnesian War*, trans. Steven Lattimore (Indianapolis, Ind.: Hackett Publishing Co., 1998), p. 3. For a fascinating analysis of Thucydides's style in speeches, see Daniel P. Tomkins, "Stylistic Characterization in Thucydides," unpublished Phd thesis, Yale University (1968).

	Two long vowels or diphthongs	A long vowel or diphthong and a short vowel or *vice versa*	Two short vowels
Luke	*Between:* καὶ ἦν (1:80) *Within:* ἐκραταιοῦτο (1:80)	*Between:* L-S: καὶ ἐπιτιμῶν (4:41) S-L: εἴα αὐτὰ (4:41) *Within:* L-S: εἴα (4:41) S-L: θεοῦ (4:41)	*Between:* τὸ ὄρος (21:37) *Within:* διεπορεύετο (13:22)
Acts	*Between:* ἁγίου οὖς (1:2) *Within:* ἐποιησάμην (1:1)	*Between:* L-S: καὶ ὀχλουμένους (5:16) S-L: τινὶ αὐτῶν (5:15) *Within:* L-S: σημεῖα (5:12) S-L: λαῷ (5:12)	*Between:* τε ἀριθμὸς (11:21) *Within:* κύριον (11:21)

Figure 3.1 Hiatus examples in Luke and Acts

including: αι-α, αι-ε, ε-ε, ο-αυ, α-ε, α-η, αι-ου, η-ου, οι-υ, οι-ο, α-ο, ου-α, and οι-ε. Avoiding hiatus in the polished style ensures words will be able to "keep on the move, swept forward and riding along on top of one another, all sustained in their movement by mutual support, like the current of a stream that never rests" (*Comp.* 22). Appropriately, it seems, he gives no examples.

Hiatus in Luke and Acts

Based on the early critics' examples given above, the quantification of hiatus breaks down into three aspects: frequency, type, and location. Whereas "frequency" refers to the *number* of occurrences, "type" refers to particular *categories*, namely, hiatus between (1) two long vowels or diphthongs (long-long); (2) a long vowel or diphthong and a short vowel or *vice versa* (long-short or short-long); and (3) two short vowels (short-short). Location indicates whether hiatus occurs within a word (intra-word) or between words (inter-word). See Figure 3.1 for examples.

Further, the matter of diphthongs in hiatus must be clarified. All diphthongs, including the so-called improper diphthongs with an iota subscript (αι, ει, οι, ᾳ, ῃ, ῳ, αυ, ευ, ου, ηυ, υι), are considered naturally long,[74]

---

[74] Herbert Weir Smyth, *Greek Grammar*, rev. Gordon M. Messing (Cambridge, Mass.: Harvard University Press, 1920, 1956; renewed, 1984), §5.

Hiatus

- Frequency: number of occurrences
- Type: (1) long-long; (2) long-short or short-long; (3) short-short
- Location: (1) Inter-word or between words; (2) Intra-word or within a word

Figure 3.2 Hiatus conventions

even though in terms of accent, for example, the final -οι, -αι in the mas-
culine and feminine plural nominative make the syllable quantity short.[75]
The present analysis understands diphthongs in their natural, not accentual, state; hence, the inter-word hiatus in πολλοὶ ἐπεχείρησαν (Lk 1:1)
is given to the "long-short," not "short-short," category.[76] Finally, hiatus
in the final syllable of a clause or sentence needs clarification. Philologist
Eugene G. O'Neill, Jr., who investigates final syllables in Greek verse,
also examines them in the Greek prose works of Plato (*Apology, Crito,
Phaedo*) and Xenophon (*Anabasis*), both of whom "seem not to have cul-
tivated rhythmical effects to any great extent."[77] With respect to hiatus,
O'Neill justifiably ponders when a hiatus is really a hiatus and when it is
not.[78] Instances of hiatus between words written in the ancient text may
well have been elided when orally read. More to the point, however, for
comparison purposes, O'Neill disregards hiatus at the end of clauses or
sentences when the next clause or sentence begins with a vowel.[79] While
this disregard of final hiatus has been considered for the present authorial
analysis, it will not be used as a control for two reasons: (1) the early
critics *do* take it into account; and (2) disregarding it seems designed
to satisfy O'Neill's purposes of comparing Greek verse and Greek
prose. Therefore, in the present analysis, final hiatus is not disregarded.
Figure 3.2 shows the criteria to be studied in the full stylometric analysis
of hiatus presented in Chapter Four.

---

[75] Ibid., §169.

[76] For classicists who understand it this way, see Norden, *Die antike Kunstprosa*, vol. II,
p. 414, where ἄνδρες φίλοι is scanned as ‾ ‿ ‾ ‾. See also Usher, in Dionysius of Halicarnassus, "On Literary Composition," p. 140 note 1; p. 215 note 2, where ἄνδρες Ἀθηναῖοι is
scanned as ‾ ‿ ‿ ‾ ‾.

[77] Eugene G. O'Neill, Jr., "The Importance of Final Syllables in Greek Verse," *TPAPA*
70 (1939), 260.

[78] Ibid., 261.   [79] Ibid.

Dissonance

Demetrius says that "ugly sounds" (δυσφωνία) bring the grandeur of a subject to the foreground. In the example, Αἴας δ' ὁ μέγας αἰὲν ἐφ' Ἕκτορι χαλκοκορυστῇ ("mighty Ajax [aimed] always at bronze-helmeted Hector," Hom. *Il.* 16.358), the clash of sounds is harsh yet brings out the hero's greatness by its very excess (*Eloc.* 48, 105). The whole clause, Demetrius suggests, lacks a sense of euphony. Not only does the hiatus in Αἴας and αἰὲν provide dramatic vividness, but presumably also the cacophonic λκ combination in χαλκοκορυστῇ.[80] Rough-sounding combinations of consonants are often vivid, as in two more examples: (1) κόπτ', ἐκ δ' ἐγκέφαλος ("he struck them down and out spurted their brains," Hom. *Od.* 9.289–90) and (2) πολλὰ δ' ἄναντα, κάταντα ("over and over, up and down," Hom. *Il.* 23.116) (*Eloc.* 219). Although not specific as to which combinations they are, Demetrius appears to refer at a minimum to κδ and perhaps γκ in the first example and ντ in the second. Discordant sounds are rightly emphatic, he says, to render a sense of forcefulness (*Eloc.* 246).

Dionysius of Halicarnassus, in examining Thucydides' austere style, again analyzes the first two periods in Thuc. 1.1 with regard to dissonant sound combinations (*Comp.* 22). The Greek quotation is repeated here (with periods separated by "|"):

Θουκυδίδης Ἀθηναῖος ξυνέγραψε τὸν πόλεμον τῶν Πελο-
ποννησίων καὶ Ἀθηναίων, ὡς ἐπολέμησαν πρὸς ἀλλήλους, |
ἀρξάμενος εὐθὺς καθισταμένου καὶ ἐλπίσας μέγαν τε ἔσεσθαι
καὶ ἀξιολογώτατον τῶν προγεγενημένων, ...   (Thuc. 1.1)

In the first period, Ἀθηναῖος preceding ξυνέγραψε creates a discordant break because a final σ is not usually placed before ξ as if it were being pronounced in the same syllable. The sense is rough and dissonant. Further, there is a clash of sounds in four successive consonant combinations, namely, νπ, ντ, νπ, and νκ. According to Dionysius, these combinations annoy the ear and disrupt the rhythm of the sentence. Quoting Thuc. 1.1 in full in *Comp.* 22, Dionysius divides it into twelve periods and thirty clauses. He finds certain collocations (παραβολαί) of semi-vowels[81]

---

[80] See Innes' remarks on harshness in Demetrius, *On Style*, p. 381 note a.

[81] Today we usually refer to Dionysius' semi-vowels as consonants. According to Dionysius, there are eight semi-vowels (ἡμίφωνα): five are simple (ἁπλᾶ): λ, μ, ν, ρ, ς, and σ; and three are double (διπλᾶ): ζ, ξ, and ψ. Of the simple semi-vowels, the ς and σ are distinguished here because Dionysius distinguished them (*Comp.* 14). Of the double ones,

and voiceless consonants[82] that exhibit the qualities of dissonance (ἀντιτύπων), harshness (πικρῶν), and difficulty in pronunciation (δυσεκφόρων). Although from the text it is unclear, he most likely refers to a semi-vowel *followed* by a voiceless consonant, not a semi-vowel *preceded* by one. In all, Dionysius provides the following examples of dissonance: κδ, κλ, νδ, νθ, νκ, νλ, νξ, ντ, ντ, νχ, and σξ (*Comp.* 22).

For the polished and well-blended styles, he gives no specific examples, but the polished style aims at an arrangement in which all words are melodious, smooth, and soft: "In this respect the style resembles finely woven net, or pictures in which the lights and shadows melt into one another" (*Comp.* 22). The well-blended style, striking a mean between the austere and polished styles, reveals the use of hiatus and cacophony neither too little nor too much (*Comp.* 24).

Dissonance in Luke and Acts

Based on the examples given by early critics, an analysis of dissonant sound clusters in the seams and summaries entails determining their presence or absence, both between words and within words. While in the examples of Demetrius and Dionysius, discordant combinations are identified, the list shown in Figure 3.3 is of course not exhaustive; it merely consists of the *explicit* examples found in the works of these early critics.

Again, no inference or suggestion will be made that the presence or absence of dissonance patterns indicates an intention on the part of the author-editor to compose in a particular style. Chapter Four presents the analysis itself.

Rhythmic elements in prose composition

The best-documented aspect of early prose compositional theory, rhythm, is discussed by almost every literary critic because of its close connection

---

ζ is a composite of σ – δ, ξ of κ – σ, and ψ of π – σ. Like many others, Usher, in Dionysius of Halicarnassus, "On Literary Composition," p. 98 note 1 points out that ζ is composed of σδ, not δσ, and thus is the reverse of the English "dz" sound. Dionysius says the sweetest semi-vowel is λ. In contrast, ρ has a roughening effect. Offensive when used to excess, σ is neither graceful nor sweet. Of the double semi-vowels, ζ is most pleasing to the ear (*Comp.* 14).

[82] There are nine voiceless letters (ἄφωνα), declares Dionysius. Three are smooth (ψιλά): π, τ, κ; three rough (δασέα): φ, θ, χ; and three intermediate (μεταξύ): β, δ, γ (*Comp.* 14). The metaphor comes from the qualities of animal skin as hairy or smooth; see Usher's remarks in Dionysius of Halicarnassus, "On Literary Composition," p. 103 note 1.

Dissonance		
Explicit examples of dissonance from antiquity:		
γκ, κδ, κλ, λκ, νδ, νθ, νλ, νκ, νξ, νπ, ντ, νχ, σξ		
	Examples in Luke	**Examples in Acts**
γκ	Between: none Within: none	Between: none Within: none
κδ	Between: none Within: none	Between: none Within: none
κλ	Between: none Within: none	Between: none Within: κλάσει (2:42)
λκ	Between: none Within: none	Between: none Within: none
νδ	Between: αὐτῶν δοξαζόμενος (4:15) Within: none	Between: Ἦσαν δὲ (2:42) Within: ἐνδεής (4:34)
νθ	Between: none Within: ἀνθρώποις (2:52)	Between: τὸν θεὸν (2:47) Within: none
νλ	Between: τὸν λαόν (3:18) Within: none	Between: πρῶτον λόγον (1:1) Within: none
νκ	Between: ὧν κατηχήθης (1:4) Within: none	Between: γυναιξὶν καὶ (1:14) Within: none
νξ	Between: none Within: none	Between: none Within: none
νπ	Between: διήγησιν περὶ (1:1) Within: none	Between: μὲν πρῶτον (1:1) Within: none
ντ	Between: λόγων τὴν (1:4) Within: ἡγεμονεύοντος (3:1)	Between: ποιεῖν τε (1:1) Within: πάντων (1:1)
νχ	Between: τὸν χριστὸν (4:41) Within: none	Between: τῶν χειρῶν (5:12) Within: none
σξ	Between: none Within: none	Between: none Within: none

Figure 3.3 Dissonance conventions and examples in Luke and Acts

to poetry.[83] Thrasymachus (fifth to fourth century BCE) is generally recognized as the "inventor" of prose rhythm (Cic. *Orat.* 174–175; cf. Arist. *Rh.* 3.8.4; Cic. *Orat.* 39). Later, Aristotle, whose prose rhythm discussion centers on political oratory,[84] counsels that the form (σχῆμα) of prose style should be neither metrical nor lacking rhythm (*Rh.* 3.8.1). Prose must be rhythmical in moderation, but not metrical; otherwise it becomes poetry.[85] The general view of "rhythm in moderation" was held by subsequent prose critics through the first century CE and beyond. Moreover, by the fourth or fifth century CE, a transition from quantitative to accentual clausulae had gradually developed, which affected final rhythms. The early twentieth-century scholar, G. L. Hendrikson, analyzes the *Letter of Clement to the Corinthians* (1908) as a late first-century text: "the accent has lengthened practically all short syllables upon which it stands, but it has not yet produced a throrough-going shortening of adjacent long syllables."[86] Hendrikson understands long, unaccented syllables, as well as accented ones, long or short, to be the starting-point of rhythmical groupings.[87] While Hendrikson may have evidence of the transition from quantitative to accentual clausulae, for the purposes of the present analysis, the ancient Greek critics herein studied do not address clausulae this way, nor does accent play a prominent role in their explanations of prose rhythm.

In *Rh.* 3, Aristotle describes four prose rhythms and the qualities they suggest (*Rh.* 3.8.4–7).[88] First, the *dactyl* (‾ ˘ ˘),[89]

---

[83] For a condensed history of Greek prose rhythm to the time of Augustus, see Norden, *De antike Kunstprosa*, vol. I, pp. 41–50.

[84] Cf. Dion. Hal. *Comp.* 25, who summarizes Aristotle's views on rhythm for political oratory.

[85] Prose that is too metrical lacks persuasiveness because it appears artificial and distracting to the hearer, who ends up waiting for the recurrence of some metrical pattern (Arist. *Rh.* 3.8.1). Wilfried Neumaier, *Antike Rhythmustheorien: Historische Form und Aktuelle Substanz* (Amsterdam: B. R. Grüner, 1989), pp. 25–32 comprehensively summarizes Aristotle's theory on rhythm for poetry and prose, and supplements it with grammatical theory from Dionysius Thrax.

[86] G. L. Hendrickson, "Accentual Clausulae in Greek Prose of the First and Second Centuries of our Era," *AJP* 29 (1908), 284.

[87] Ibid.

[88] See Blass, "On Attic Prose Rhythm," 22, who mentions Cicero's reference to Theophrastus' lost book (Cic. *De or.* 3.185), specifically that Theophrastus added a fifth rhythm, the anapaest, to the four of Aristotle, i.e., the dactyl, iambus, trochee, and paean.

[89] The notation for syllable quantity is standard: a long syllable is designated " ‾ " and a short " ˘ ." See Freese's claim in Aristotle, *The "Art" of Rhetoric*, p. 384 note a, which adds the *spondee* (‾ ‾) and the *anapaest* (˘ ˘ ‾) to the heroic rhythms. Cf. Cic. *Orat.* 192: *Quod longe Aristoteli videtur secus, qui iudicat heroum numerum grandiorem quam desideret soluta oratio, iambum autem nimis e volgari esse sermone* [Aristotle held quite a different opinion: he thought the heroic measure [dactyl] too lofty for prose, and the iambic too close to ordinary conversation]

the so-called heroic rhythm, is dignified in stature, beyond the harmonious rhythm of common speech. Because the quantity of one long syllable ($-$) is equivalent to two short ones ($\smile$ $\smile$), Aristotle explains that the dactyl forms a one ($-$) to one ($\smile$ $\smile$) ratio (1:1) (*Rh.* 3.8.4). Second, the *iambus* ($\smile$ $-$), an example of "the language of the many" (ἡ λέξις ἡ τῶν πολλῶν), is the most commonly used rhythm in ordinary speech,[90] which ought to be directed toward stateliness. Third, the opposite of the *iambus* is the less than stately *trochee* ($-$ $\smile$), which Aristotle compares to a dance called the cordax, belonging to old Comedy (*Rh.* 3.8.4). Because the quantity of one long syllable ($-$) is said to be equivalent to two short ones ($\smile$ $\smile$), the iambus ($\smile$ $-$) and trochee ($-$ $\smile$) form a ratio of 1:2 and 2:1 respectively. Fourth, the *paean* in its *primus* ($-$ $\smile$ $\smile$ $\smile$) or *posterior* ($\smile$ $\smile$ $\smile$ $-$) form is Aristotle's preferred prose rhythm, because it is the only one not adapted to a poetic metrical system and thus the least likely to be detected. The *primus* paean ($-$ $\smile$ $\smile$ $\smile$) is suitable for the beginning of a period and the *posterior* paean ($\smile$ $\smile$ $\smile$ $-$) for the end, where a final long syllable is appropriate.[91] For Aristotle, the end of a period should be indicated by the rhythm itself rather than marked by a scribe (γραφεύς) or a punctuation mark (παραγραφή) (*Rh.* 3.8.4–7).[92] The posterior paean ($\smile$ $\smile$ $\smile$ $-$) forms a three ($\smile$ $\smile$ $\smile$) to two ($-$) ratio (3:2); conversely, the primus paean a two ($-$) to three ($\smile$ $\smile$ $\smile$) ratio (2:3). The paeanic ratios are equivalent to 1½:1 or 1:1½ respectively. Aesthetically and technically, then, 1½:1 or 1:1½ is the *mean* of the dactylic ratio (1:1) and either the trochaic (2:1) or the iambic (1:2) respectively. With a clear preference for the *mean*, Aristotle emphasizes that prose composition should be rhythmic but not metrical.

A century or so later, Demetrius elaborates on Aristotle's discussion of prose rhythms in particular as they relate to his own schema of styles. When paeans are used, Demetrius remarks, composition in the grand style is majestic (σεμνός) (cf. Aristotle *Rh.* 3.8.4). To create a dignified beginning and end of a clause, a long syllable should be used, because it is grand by nature (*Eloc.* 39). If a paean cannot be put at the beginning or end of a clause, the composition should be made "roughly paeanic" with

---

[90] Like Aristotle, Demetrius also observes that people speak in iambic rhythm without even knowing it (Demetr. *Eloc.* 43; cf. Quint. *Inst.* 9.4.88).

[91] There was disagreement among early critics whether the final syllable should be considered long in spite of its quantity. For the positions of some early critics, see Chapter Four.

[92] According to Freese in Aristotle, *The "Art" of Rhetoric*, p. 386 note a, the punctuation mark to indicate the end of a sentence was a dash below the first word of a line.

the addition of a long syllable at the beginning and ending of the clause. Demetrius gives an example, without unfortunately specifying the precise rhythms (he presumes reader familiarity in identifying syllable quantity): τῶν μὲν περὶ τὰ μηδενὸς ἄξια φιλοσοφούντων ("those who are philosophers about what is worthless," author unknown, used by Theophrastus) (*Eloc.* 41).[93] A possible scansion below supports Demetrius' opinion that "It [this clause] is not formed from paeans with any precision, yet it is roughly paeanic":

— —	˘ ˘ ˘	— ˘ ˘	— ˘ ˘	˘ ˘ ˘ —	—
τῶν μὲν	περὶ τὰ	μηδενὸς	ἄξια	φιλοσοφούν	των

The paeanic sense is based on the four syllables following the first, that is, ‾ ˘ ˘ ˘, and the four preceding the last, ˘ ˘ ˘ ‾. Still another paeanic impression occurs in the ninth to twelfth syllables, ‾ ˘ ˘ ˘.

In contrast, frigidity occurs when a clause is composed almost exclusively of long syllables (*Eloc.* 117). Demetrius gives the example: ἥκων ἡμῶν εἰς τὴν χώραν, πάσης ἡμῶν ὀρθῆς οὔσης ("arriving inside our land, since it now is all stirred up," author unknown). Because he does not record how he scans it, whether spondees or molossi prevail is unclear. The fact remains that of the sixteen syllables none is short:

— —	— —	— —	— —	— — —	— — —	— —
ἥκων	ἡμῶν	εἰς τὴν	χώραν	πάσης ἡ	μῶν ὀρθῆς	οὔσης

The elegant style, according to Demetrius, has rhythmic patterns not easily described (*Eloc.* 179). Plato's elegant style comes directly from rhythm (*Eloc.* 183), being neither completely metrical nor completely unmetrical. Demetrius gives three examples from Plato where there is an absence of long sequences of long syllables (*Eloc.* 183) or, for that matter, noticeable hiatus. For none of the examples does Demetrius record exact scansions, again presuming reader familiarity. The first example is: νῦν δὴ ἐλέγομεν ("We were saying just now" Pl. *Resp.* 411a):

— —	˘ ˘ ˘ —
νῦν δὴ	ἐλέγομεν

If scanned as shown above, this example of elegance begins with a spondee and ends with a posterior paean. The second example is: μινυρίζων τε καὶ γεγανωμένος ὑπὸ τῆς ᾠδῆς διατελεῖ τὸν βίον ὅλον

---

[93] See Innes' comments in Demetrius, *On Style*, p. 377 notes a, b for citation of Theophrastus F 703 Fortenbaugh.

("warbling and radiant under the influence of song he passes his whole life" Pl. *Resp.* 411a):

˘ ˘ —	˘ —	˘ ˘ —	˘ ˘ ˘	˘ — —	— ‖	˘ ˘ ˘ —	— ˘ ˘	˘
μινυρίζων	τε καὶ	γεγανω	μένος ὑ-	πὸ τῆς ᾧ	δῆς ‖	διατελεῖ	τὸν βίον ὅλ	ον

If scanned as shown, both clauses (separated by the double bar) begin with a posterior paean, and the first possesses a paeanic sense in the ninth to twelfth syllables. Noticeable is the absence of long sequences of long syllables. The third example is: τὸ μὲν πρῶτον, εἴ τι θυμοειδὲς εἶχεν, ὥσπερ σίδηρον ἐμάλαξεν ("first, if he had any symptom of passion he would like iron temper it" Pl. *Resp.* 411b). Although Demetrius does not detail how he scans it, a possibility is offered:

˘ —	— ˘ —	˘ ˘ ˘ —	— ˘ — ‖	— — ˘	— ˘ ˘ ˘	—˘
τὸ μὲν	πρῶτον, εἴ	τι θυμοει	δὲς εἶχεν, ‖	ὥσπερ σί	δη ρον ἐμά	λαξεν

The rhythm of this example is described simply as elegant and musical. If scanned as shown, there is an identical, "roughly paeanic" pattern in the two clauses (— — ˘ — ˘˘˘ —˘), from the second to tenth syllables in the first and the entire second. Furthermore, at the risk of reading too much into the patterns, there is actually a rhythmic palindrome formed by the two clauses, the fourth to the eleventh syllables in the first clause (˘—˘˘ —˘—) mirroring the second to ninth syllables in the second (—˘—˘˘˘—˘).

Flawed or meretricious elegance becomes the affected (κακόζηλος) style, noticeable when anapaestic patterns (˘ ˘ —) are present (*Eloc.* 189). Demetrius gives two examples from Sotades but does not provide details of his scansions.[94] The first example is: σκήλας καύματι κάλυψον ("having dried in the heat, cover up" Sotades 17 Powell). If scanned as shown, it becomes anapaestic and thus undignified (ἄσεμνος):

— —	— ˘	˘ ˘ —	˘
σκήλας	καύμα	τι κάλυ	ψον

In the second example, Demetrius criticizes Sotades' rhythm as feebly effeminate: σείων μελίην Πηλιάδα δεξιὸν κατ' ὦμον ("brandishing the ash spear Pelian to the right over his shoulder" Sotades 4a Powell). If

---

[94] Sotades (third century BCE), a Hellenistic poet, was judged by many to write affected verse. Roberts, *Demetrius: On Style*, p. 244 notes that use of "Sotadean" to refer to weak and affected rhythms developed after Sotades' own time. Cf. Dion. Hal. *Comp.* 4; Quint. *Inst.* 1.8.6.

scanned as shown, the indignity of the rhythmic structure is unclear, except for the anapaest:

— —	‿ ‿ —	— ‿ ‿	— — ‿	— ‿	— ‿
σείων	μελίην	Πηλιά	δα δεξι	ὸν κατ'	ῶμον

As if to spotlight the extremes, Demetrius compares Sotades' flawed rhythmic structure to the elegant dactylic shape of the almost parallel line from Homer: σείων Πηλιάδα μελίην κατὰ δεξιὸν ῶμον ("brandishing the Pelian ash spear over his right shoulder" Hom. *Il.* 22.133), which may be scanned as shown:

— —	— ‿ ‿	— ‿ ‿	— ‿ ‿	— ‿ ‿	— — [95]
σείων	Πηλιά	δα μελί	ην κατα	δεξιὸν	ῶμον

As these examples of elegance and affectation demonstrate, Demetrius holds the paean and the dactyl in highest regard and disdains the anapaest.

While giving scant attention to rhythm in the plain style, Demetrius favors a new-fashioned terribleness (ἡ νῦν κατέχουσα δεινότης) in the forceful style (*Eloc.* 245). He gives this example: ὡμολόγησα τούτοις, ὡς ἄν οἷός τε ὦ, συνερεῖν ("I have agreed to speak to the best of my ability in their support" Dem. *Lept.* 1), which may be scanned as shown below:

— ‿ ‿	— — —	— — ‿	— — ‿	— ‿ ‿	—
ὡμολό	γησα τού	τοις, ὡς ἄν	οἷός τε	ὦ, συνε	ρεῖν

Here the powerful, intense quality is produced by many long syllables, but not a lengthy sequence of long syllables.

In sharp contrast to Demetrius, Dionysius of Halicarnassus presumes little or no knowledge on the part of his audience and builds his opinions on prose rhythm from the ground up. Every noun, verb, or other part of speech greater than one syllable, he says, is spoken in some sort of rhythm (*Comp.* 17). All rhythmic feet (πόδες), two-syllable and three-syllable sequences, are described by Dionysius in terms of qualitative attributes. He presents the two-syllable sequences first and, as shown in Figure 3.4, there are four possibilities.

Describing their qualities, Dionysius suggests the spondee has great worthiness and grandeur, although the iambus does not lack stature, implying it may be sufficiently impressive. The trochee represents weakness and ignobility. The pyrrhic, being neither imposing nor solemn, also

---

[95] The last syllable is considered long here, and the elegance is furthered because of the beginning and ending spondee.

Notation	English	Greek
ˇ ˇ	*hegemon* or *pyrrhic*	ἡγεμών or πυρρίχιος
— —	*spondee*	σπονδεῖος
ˇ —	*iambus*	ἴαμβος
— ˇ	*trochee*[†]	τροχαῖος

[†] The name trochee was not used consistently. Quint. *Inst.* 9.4.80 refers to this foot as a choree: *huic contrarium et longa et brevi choreum, non ut alii trachaeum nominemus.*

Figure 3.4 Two-syllable rhythms

Notation	English	Greek
ˇ ˇ ˇ	*choree*[†]	χορεῖος
— — —	*molossus*	μολοττός
ˇ — ˇ	*amphibrach*	ἀμφίβραχυς
ˇ ˇ —	*anapaest*	ἀνάπαιστος
— ˇ ˇ	*dactyl*	δάκτυλος
— ˇ —	*cretic*[‡]	κρητικός
— — ˇ	*bacchius*	βακχεῖος
ˇ — —	*hypobacchius*	ὑποβάκχεῖος

[†] The name choree was used inconsistently. See note in Figure 3.4. Quint. *Inst.* 9.4.82 refers to this foot as a trochee: *Tres breves trochaeum, quem tribrachyn dici volunt, qui choreo trochaei nomen imponunt.*
[‡] The name cretic was also used inconsistently. Quint. *Inst.* 9.4.81 refers to this foot as a *amphimacus*, although he acknowledges it is often called a cretic: *Media inter longas brevis faciet amphimacrum, sed frequentius eius nomen est creticus.*

Figure 3.5 Three-syllable rhythms

suggests weakness (*Comp.* 17).[96] Next Dionysius defines and describes each of the eight possible three-syllable forms, as shown in Figure 3.5.

Evaluating their qualities, Dionysius suggests the molossus (— — —) is lofty, dignified, and strong. The anapaest (ˇ — —) is solemn, reflecting

[96] See Usher's comment on syllable qualities in Dionysius of Halicarnassus, "On Literary Composition," p. 125 note 2.

dignity or pathos – a marked contrast to Demetrius' unfavorable opinion of the anapaest. The dactyl (¯ ˘ ˘), basis for the heroic rhythm in poetry, is august and effective at creating beautiful language. The bacchius (¯¯˘) and hypobacchius (˘¯¯) are virile, solemn, dignified, and noble, and the cretic (¯˘¯) is not poor in stature, implying impressiveness. Contrariwise, the choree (˘ ˘ ˘) lacks both grandeur and stature.[97] The amphibrach (˘¯˘) is not at all graceful but languid, effete, and displeasing (*Comp.* 17). While Dionysius claims he does not offer anything new, he has laid out an organized, systematic foundation of prose rhythm.

Fortunately, Dionysius' critical essays record specific scansions to explain his examples, providing a bonanza for modern readers. For example, he scans text from two funeral orations. First, to Pericles' funeral oration in Thucydides, Dionysius gives high marks for dignified rhythms: Οἱ μὲν πολλοὶ τῶν ἐνθάδε ἤδη εἰρηκότων | ἐπαινοῦσι τὸν προσθέντα τῷ νόμῳ τὸν λόγον τόνδε, | ὡς καλὸν ἐπὶ τοῖς ἐκ τῶν πολέμων θαπτομένοις ἀγορεύεσθαι αὐτόν ("Most of those who have already spoken here praise the man who made this speech part of the custom, saying that for this address to be made at the burial of those lost in war is a fine thing," Thuc. 2.35.1). His scansion is shown below.

— —	— —	— —	˘ ˘ —	— —	— ˘ —
Οἱ μὲν	πολλοὶ	τῶν ἐν	θάδε ἤ	δη εἰ	ρηκότων

˘ — —	˘ — —	— — —	˘ ˘ —	˘
ἐπαινοῦ	σι τὸν προσ	θέντα τῷ	νόμῳ τὸν	λόγον τόν	δε

— ˘ —	˘ ˘ —	— —	˘ ˘ —	— ˘ ˘	˘ ˘ ˘	— —	— — ˘
ὡς καλὸν[98]	ἐπὶ τοῖς	ἐκ τῶν	πολέμων	θαπτομέ	νοις ἀγο	ρεύεσ	θαι αὐ	τόν.

To introduce the first clause, Dionysius scans three spondees, then an anapaest, another spondee, and a cretic. The second clause begins with two hypobacchii, then a cretic, then two more hypobacchii, and a final syllable. The third clause is introduced by a cretic followed by an anapaest, a spondee, another anapaest, two dactyls, two spondees, and the catalectic

---

[97] See ibid., p. 127 note 5, where Usher notes that sequences of short syllables are often used to show excitement; for example, in Eur. *Bacch.* 578–581.

[98] See ibid., p. 134 note 3. Usher notes the lengthening of this last syllable in καλὸν may be due to license taken in accord with that found in Homeric verse. Alternatively, the last syllable signaled a pause and therefore lengthened the syllable.

syllable (*Comp.* 18). Based on Dionysius' analysis, it appears he tries to respect word boundaries and strong rhythms. On the one hand, the two spondees that introduce the first clause may be evidence of his respect for word boundaries. On the other hand, the two hypobacchii beginning the second clause do not respect word boundaries, but they provide evidence of the weight he may give to strong three-syllable rhythms over weak two- or three-syllable ones, as all rhythms except the catalectic syllable are three-syllable feet. In the third clause, he favors strong three-syllable feet – and respects word boundaries, initially at least, unless a spondee is found. Reckoning Dionysius' scanning methodology is complicated at best, almost impossible to decipher at worst.

In the second example, a funeral oration written by Plato, Dionysius describes the rhythms as beautiful and again records the specifics of his scansion: ἔργῳ μὲν ἡμῖν οἵδε ἔξουσιν τὰ προσήκοντα σφίσιν αὐτοῖ | ὧν τυχόντες πορεύονται τὴν εἰμαρμένην πορείαν ("These men already have from us their due in deed; and having received it they are going their appointed way," Pl. *Menex.* 236 d):

— — ˘	— —	— ˘ ˘	— —	˘ —	— —	˘ ˘ —	—
ἔργῳ μὲν	ἡμῖν	οἵδε ἔ	ξουσιν	τὰ προσή	κοντα	σφίσιν αὐ	τοῖς

— ˘ —	— ˘ —	— —	— —	— ˘ —	˘ — —
ὧν τυχόν	τες πορεύ	ονται	τὴν εἰ	μαρμένην	πορείαν

He scans the first clause as a bacchius followed by a spondee, a dactyl with hiatus preserved, and another spondee. For τὰ προσή he reads a cretic, making τὰ a long syllable. After that, he reads a spondee (— —), which makes the τα in κοντα long, followed, he allows, by either a hypobacchius (˘ — —) or an anapaest (˘ ˘ —) and the catalectic syllable at the end. The second clause is introduced by two cretics, then two spondees, another cretic, and a hypobacchius. The result is a Platonic composition made up entirely of beautiful rhythms (*Comp.* 18),[99] which are the bacchius, spondee, dactyl, cretic, hypobacchius, and anapaest. As in the prior example, Dionysius' method appears to respect word boundaries initially and then read strong three-syllable feet unless a spondee is found.

Finally, Dionysius gives an example of a sentence of Demosthenes, whom he considers the most brilliant writer: πρῶτον μέν, ὦ ἄνδρες

---

[99] Ibid., p. 136 note 1.

Ἀθηναῖοι, τοῖς θεοῖς εὔχομαι πᾶσι καὶ πάσαις | ὅσην εὔνοιαν ἔχων ἐγὼ διατελῶ τῇ τε πόλει καὶ πᾶσιν ὑμῖν, | τοσαύτην ὑπάρξαι μοι παρ᾽ ὑμῶν εἰς τουτονὶ τὸν ἀγῶνα ("First of all, men of Athens, I pray to all the gods and all the goddesses | that as much good will as I have continuously shown toward the city and all of you | may be accorded to me in full measure by you in this present trial," Dem. *De cor.* 1.1):

‒ ◡	‒ ‒	◡ ◡	‒ ‒	‒ ◡ ‒	‒ ◡ ‒	‒ ◡ ‒	‒ ◡ ‒
Πρῶτον μέν,	ὦ ἄν	δρες Ἀθη	ναῖοι,	τοῖς θεοῖς	εὔχομαι	πᾶσι καὶ	πάσαις,

◡ ‒ ‒	‒ ◡ ◡	‒ ‒	◡ ◡ ◡	‒ ◡ ◡	‒ ◡ ‒	‒ ‒
ὅσην εὔ	νοιαν ἔ	χων ἐγὼ	διατελῶ	τῇ τε πόλει	καὶ πᾶσιν	ὑμῖν

◡ ‒ ‒	◡ ‒ ‒	‒ ◡ ‒	‒ ‒	‒ ◡ ‒	‒ ◡ ‒	◡
τοσαύτην	ὑπάρξαι	μοι παρ᾽ ὑ	μῶν εἰς	τουτονὶ	τὸν ἀγῶν	α

The first clause is introduced by a bacchius followed by a spondee, an anapaest, another spondee, three cretics, and a spondee. The second clause begins with a hypobacchius, then a bacchius or a dactyl, he allows, followed by a cretic, two paeans, a molossus or bacchius, he again allows, and a spondee. The third clause is introduced by two hypobacchii followed by a cretic, a spondee, another bacchius or, he allows, a cretic, followed by a cretic, and the catalectic syllable. All these rhythms reflect nobility, being among them no weak rhythm such as a pyrrhic, iambus, amphibrach, choree, or trochee (*Comp.* 18).[100] It is not that Thucydides, Plato, or Demosthenes never used weak rhythms, Dionysius observes, it is rather they concealed them so artfully that they were not detected.[101]

Dionysius severely criticizes writers whose reputation for composition is less than stellar. In doing so, he singles out Hegesias.[102] In

---

[100] See ibid., p. 140 note 1. Usher notes the "apparent irregularities" with the possible lengthening of the last syllable of εὔνοιαν, the second syllable of τουτονὶ, and τὸν. In addition, it appears that there may be further irregularities in the shortening of the last syllable of πόλει and the possible lengthening of the last syllable of πᾶσιν, the first syllable in ὑμῖν, and the third syllable of τουτονὶ.

[101] Cic. *Orat.* 65.220 suggests that if early historians such as Herodotus and Thucydides wrote anything rhythmical it was not on purpose but due to word arrangement.

[102] Cf. Cic. *Orat.* 69.230 also maligns Hegesias' work. For the reference to Hegesias' material, i.e., K. Müller, *Fragments of the Lost Historians of Alexander the Great*, p. 141 of Hegesias Magnes, see Roberts, *Dionysius of Halicarnassus: On Literary Composition*, p. 191. See also Norden, *Die antike Kunstprosa*, vol. II, pp. 134–138. Usher in Dionysius of Halicarnassus, "On Literary Composition," p. 141 note 2 suggests that Dionysius seems to find the greatest fault in jerky, monotonous rhythms and affected word order.

Comp. 4, Dionysius scans three passages he claims resemble Hegesias' "degenerate, effeminate way of arranging words," but he provides no specifics on how he scans them. The first example is: Ἐξ ἀγαθῆς ἑορτῆς ἀγαθὴν ἄγομεν ἄλλην ("After a goodly festival another goodly one we celebrate"). If scanned as shown, that is, favoring strong three-syllable rhythms as Dionysius is wont to do, the example paradoxically *appears* strong rather than weak with its dactyls, a cretic, and a hypobacchius:

— ˘ ˘	— ˘ —	— ˘ ˘	— ˘ ˘	˘ — —
Ἐξ ἀγα	θῆς ἑορ	τῆς ἀγα	θὴν ἄγο	μεν ἄλλην

Weakness may lie in other features, but Dionysius does not give us any clues. There are several possibilities: the alliteration of four words beginning with α (ἀγαθῆς . . . ἀγαθὴν ἄγομεν ἄλλην); all six words of the example terminate in the sound of either ς or ν; or the clause contains a series of four three-syllable words. Unfortunately, Dionysius provides no specifics. The second Hegesias example is: Ἀπὸ Μαγνεσίας εἰμὶ τῆς μεγάλης Σιπυλεύς ("From Magnesia am I, the mighty land, a Sipylean"). If scanned as shown, it is weak compositionally:

˘ ˘ —	˘ ˘ ˘	— ˘ —	˘ ˘ —	˘ ˘ —
Ἀπὸ Μα	γνεσίας	εἰμὶ τῆς	μεγάλης	Σιπυλεύς

The choree (˘ ˘ ˘) implies weakness, or, if the first word boundary were respected, the example would begin with a pyrrhic (˘ ˘), a weak rhythm. Further, weakness may be indicated by the fact that four of the six words end in the sound ς. The third example Dionysius presents includes two clauses: Οὐ γὰρ μικρὰν εἰς Θηβαίων ὕδωρ ἔπτυσεν ὁ Διόνυσος· ἡδὺ μὲν γάρ ἐστι, ποιεῖ δὲ μαίνεσθαι ("It was not a small drop that into Theban waters Dionysius spewed: sweet it is indeed, but it makes men mad"). If scanned as shown, a weak rhythmic effect is produced:

— —	— ˘ —	— — —	˘ — —	˘ ˘ ˘	˘ ˘ ˘	˘
Οὐ γὰρ	μικρὰν εἰς	Θηβαίων	ὕδωρ ἔ	πτυσεν ὁ	Διόνυ	σος.

— ˘ —	˘ — ˘	— — ˘	— — —
ἡδὺ μὲν	γάρ ἐστι,	ποιεῖ δὲ	μαίνεσθαι

The first clause contains two chorees and the second an amphibrach, both of which are weak and ineffectual rhythms. Indeed, if the first clause were scanned differently as a molossus (— — —), then hypobacchius (˘ — —) and two bachii (˘ ˘ — | — — ˘), the weakness indicated by two chorees (˘˘˘ | ˘˘˘) would still exist. Further, if the second clause began as three trochees (‾ ˘ | ‾ ˘ | ‾ ˘), weakness would also continue to occur.

Noteworthy in all Dionysius' examples is his lack of emphasis on the paean, the Aristotelian favorite.[103] Instead, he pays attention to strong three-syllable rhythms and the spondee. He advises that charming, rhythmic composition avoids a succession of short-syllabled words (*Comp.* 12), yet recommends avoiding an over-accumulation of polysyllabic words and the monotony of word combinations with the same accent or time length (ὁμοιόχρονα) (*Comp.* 12). It is true one finds inconsistencies in Dionysius' work; Bonner comments on the difficulties faced by modern scholars trying to understand the way Dionysius scanned prose rhythm.[104] Bonner and others who probe Dionysius' methods occasionally find what seems to be arbitrariness in assigning syllable quantities. Despite the occasional obscurity of Dionysius' scanning method, he has given us one of the most detailed rhythmic analyses of his time.

About a century after Dionysius, Longinus offers a brief but valuable discussion of prose rhythm in *De sublimitate*.[105] Longinus affirms the fifth source of literary sublimity is "the arrangement of the words themselves in a certain order" (τῶν λόγων αὕτη ποιὰ σύνθεσις) (*Subl.* 39). Melody (ἁρμονία) is a natural instrument of persuasion and pleasure (ἡδονή), but it is also an instrument of grandeur (μεγαληγορία) and emotion (πάθος). Like the melody of the flute and harp, word arrangement creates "a kind of melody in words" (ἁρμονίαν τινὰ οὖσαν λόγων) that can reach to a person's soul, carrying the speaker's actual emotion into the heart of the hearer. Phrase upon phrase soon builds a sublime whole (*Subl.* 39.3).

Longinus gives two examples, one from Demosthenes, the other from Euripides. In neither, however, does Longinus record the specifics of how he scans the rhythms. The first example is: τοῦτο τὸ ψήφισμα τὸν τότε τῇ πόλει περιστάντα κίνδυνον παρελθεῖν ἐποίησεν ὥσπερ νέφος ("This decree made the peril at that time encompassing the country pass away like a cloud," Dem. *De cor.* 188). Because the grandeur of this

---

[103] See Arist. *Rh.* 3.8, who favors the *paean* (˘ ˘ ˘ ‾) or (‾ ˘ ˘ ˘) for clausulae beginnings and endings. He does not favor recognizable regular rhythm in prose. See also Cic. *De or.* 3.47.182, who does not favor more than two or a few more *dactyls*, *anapaests*, and *spondees* (the heroic feet) in a row in prose. Usher in Dionysius of Halicarnassus, "On Literary Composition," p. 132 note 1 suggests Dionysius may have been offering original and revolutionary work.

[104] Bonner, *Literary Treatises of Dionysius of Halicarnassus*, pp. 72ff.

[105] *Subl.* 39.1 seems to indicate that Longinus had already written two books on composition.

passage's rhythm, Longinus suggests, rests on dactyls (*Subl.* 39.4), a possible scansion is shown:

$$- \cup - \;|\; - - \cup \;|\; - \cup \cup \;|\; - \cup \;|\; - \cup \;|\; - - \cup \;|\; - \cup \cup \;|\; \cup - -$$

τοῦτο τὸ | ψήφισμα | τὸν τότε | τῇ πό | λει πε | ριστάντα | κίνδυνον | παρελθεῖν

$$\cup - - \;|\; \cup - \;|\; - \cup \cup$$

ἐποίη | σεν ὦ | σπερ νέφος

If scanned like this, the text contains three dactyls. When the effects of grandeur are scattered, Longinus says, sublimity is carried away with them (*Sub.* 40.1). In tacit agreement with Dionysius on the significance of word order, Longinus advises those who want to achieve a reputation for literary grandeur that *it is possible by word arrangement alone.*

For the second example, γέμω κακων δὴ κοὐκέτ᾽ ἔσθ᾽ ὅποι τεθῇ ("I am loaded with woes and have no room for more," Eur. HF 1245), again no specific rhythms were recorded, but it may be scanned as shown. Note the three occurrences of the iambus ($\cup -$):

$$\cup - \;|\; \cup - - \;|\; - \cup - \;|\; - \cup \;|\; \cup -$$

γέμω | κακων δὴ | κοὐκέτ᾽ ἔσθ᾽ | ὅποι | τεθῇ

Pace Aristotle's view of the iambic rhythm of everyday speech, Longinus explains that this clause, without the context of the slaughter of Heracles' children, gives the impression of extremely ordinary language. When contextualized, it becomes sublime. Furthermore, elevated language is spoiled by effeminate (κεκλασμένος) and agitated (σεσοβημένος) rhythms such as pyrrhics ($\cup \cup$), trochees ($\cup \cup \cup$), and dichorees ($- \cup - \cup$) (*Subl.* 41). Because the hearer concentrates on the rhythm more than the words, an excessively rhythmical passage is also unrefined. Further, passages that are too concise lack sublimity, because they appear to be broken up into tiny pieces, that is, short syllables with a jerky rhythm (*Subl.* 41.3). Although brief, Longinus' discussion of prose rhythm adds a first-century CE dimension to literary criticism on prose rhythm.

A broad-brush view of the critics' opinions shows all agree the dactyl is dignified, grand, and august – not surprising, since it occupies a revered status in Greek poetry. Other rhythms do not command such a high degree of agreement, sometimes because they are not discussed. Based on the commentary and examples, early critics evaluate the dactyl, paean, spondee, molossus, cretic, bacchius, and hypobacchius as strong, respectable rhythms, but the trochee, pyrrhic, choree, and amphibrach as weak ones to be avoided or concealed. The qualities of the iambus are more ambiguous, since Aristotle considered it extraordinarily common, but Dionysius gave it stature. The dichoree is mentioned by Longinus only. The anapaest is the only rhythm about which disagreement is significant. From Demetrius' perspective it is a weak rhythm, but from Dionysius' it is strong.

Rhythm patterns in Luke and Acts

Using the actual examples given by the early critics, an analysis of prose rhythmic patterns in the seam and summary data may be performed to discover the extent to which, if any, rhythm played a role in their composition. Of significance to using the works of Demetrius, Dionysius, and Longinus, however, are three caveats.[106] First, the tenor of the critique is naturally determined by how the early critic scans the rhythms, unfortunately unrecorded by Demetrius and Longinus but generally well documented by Dionysius. Whether an example contains strong or weak rhythms, appears roughly paeanic, seems governed by dactyls, or artfully conceals weak rhythms, *the ancient critic has scanned a precise sequence of rhythms*. To scan a precise sequence of rhythms in the seams and summaries of Luke and Acts, then, brings to light a problem, namely, *who* decides what the precise sequence of rhythms is? That is to say, *whether* a syllable is long or short is not overly problematic, since quantity is fairly well known; rather, the problem is into what individual rhythms the syllables should be divided. Acts 5:14 illustrates the problem: like any other Greek clause or sentence, it allows various scansions, depending on the rhythmic principles assumed by the composer or reader. As shown in the "Scansion 1" section of Figure 3.6, an ancient critic might have scanned a bacchius, followed by a posterior paean, a hypobacchius, a spondee, a bacchius, two spondees, a cretic and a hypobacchius. Or, *per* "Scansion 2," the eleventh to nineteenth syllables (ον-τες τῷ κυ-ρί-ῳ, πλή-θη ἀν-) would be scanned as a molossus, a cretic, and a molossus.

Furthermore, *pace* Dionysius, all rhythms are strong in Figure 3.6; if weak ones were permitted, the sequence possibilities grow numerous. In antiquity, diversity in scanning rhythms is freely admitted; in the modern era, it is impossible to recover any method with exactitude. Thus, identifying the *precise sequence* of rhythms in the Luke and Acts seams and summaries becomes a speculative, if not arbitrary, exercise

---

[106] In *Rh.* 3, Aristotle did not give explicit examples of the use of prose rhythm.

Scansion 1

— — ˘	˘ ˘ ˘ —	˘ — —	— —	— — ˘	— —	— —
μᾶλ-λον δὲ	προσ-ε-τί-θεν-	το πι-στεύ-	ον-τες	τῷ κυ-ρί-	ῳ, πλή-	θη ἀν-
— ˘ —	˘ — —					
δρῶν τε καὶ	γυ-ναι-κῶν,					

Scansion 2

— — ˘	˘ ˘ ˘ —	˘ — —	— — —	— ˘ —	— — —
μᾶλ-λον δὲ	προσ-ε-τί-θεν-	το πι-στεύ-	ον-τες τῷ	κυ-ρί-ῳ,	πλή-θη ἀν-
— ˘ —	˘ — —				
δρῶν τε καὶ	γυ-ναι-κῶν,				

Figure 3.6 Two possible rhythm sequences for Acts 5:14

biased by the understanding of the scholar. Described in more detail in Chapter Four, this predicament effectively disqualifies the analysis of clause and sentence scansions as a prose compositional convention for Luke and Acts.

A second caveat regarding prose rhythm observations by the early critics, notably Aristotle and Demetrius, is the significance of the clausula, the end of a clause or sentence. That is to say, the final syllables of each clause or sentence may be examined for patterns. In the Lukan preface, for example, the final syllables of the four clauses may be scanned: (1) $- - ˘ -$; (2) $- - ˘ -$; (3) $˘ ˘ ˘ ˘$; and (4) ($- ˘ - ˘$). Although the first two terminate in parallel manner, the others do not. Comparison with the clausulae of other clauses and sentences in the Luke and Acts seam and summary data may or may not reveal patterns. If rhythms play an essential role in seam and summary prose composition, then patterns should be visible. If not, it is entirely possible the author-editor paid little or no attention to rhythm. Here, patterns are key, not individual rhythms.

A third caveat of prose rhythm mentioned by early critics is the unpleasant or monotonous sound of long-syllable sequences (e.g., Demetr. *Eloc.* 117). An excessive number of long syllables in a series evokes compositional frigidity, even though they represent strong rhythms. Thus, the presence or absence of long sequences of long syllables, described in greater detail in Chapter Four, may function quite suitably as a prose compositional convention. In Luke 9:51, for example, the first clause attests a sequence of eight long syllables, both naturally and by position (ἐν τῷ συμ-πλη-ροῦ-σθαι τὰς[107] ἡ- . . .); in Acts 4:32, the first

---

[107] Compensatory lengthening of α; see Smyth, *Greek Grammar*, §37.

Prose rhythm
1. Syllable quantity in clausulae, that is, at the end of a clause or sentence
2. Long sequences of long syllables

Figure 3.7 Prose rhythm conventions

clause shows a sequence of nine (πλή-θους τῶν πι-στευ-σάν-των ἦν καρ-...). The caveat arises only when attempting to label the sequences in terms of particular rhythms. A fascinating modern-day precedent for long-syllable sequence analysis is A. W. de Groot's *Handbook of Antique Prose-Rhythm*, originally prepared as a series of nine lectures in which he studies the frequency of short-syllable and long-syllable sequences in Thucydides, Xenophon, Plato, Demosthenes, Isocrates, and Plutarch, and in certain Latin writers such as Cicero, Sallust, and Livy. With the best-available computational tools at the time, de Groot presents a "systematic statistic investigation" based on 12 groups of 1,000 syllables taken from each of the above writers.[108] De Groot meticulously studies rhythmic patterns within the body of the texts, as well as at the end of individual clauses and sentences. He shows that, on average, Plutarch tends to use the least number of "greater than four" (>4) long-syllable sequences. That is, Plutarch averages 6.9 five-long-syllable sequences per 1,000 syllables, whereas Isocrates averages 13.7 and Xenophon 12.8.[109] This tendency carries through longer sequences of long syllables too, for example, in strings of six, seven, eight, nine, and ten long syllables. Thus, grappling with such sequences in Luke and Acts may actually complement de Groot's efforts.

It must again be stressed, when quantifying the patterns in the seams and summaries, no suggestion is made that their presence or absence indicates an intention of the author-editor to compose according to a particular style. Figure 3.7 shows two modest but unambiguous prose rhythm conventions to analyze in the Luke and Acts seams and summaries.

Structural elements in prose composition

It is well known that, in antiquity, phrases (κόμματα), clauses (κῶλα), and sentences were discussed by the critics largely in relation to periods

---

[108] A. W. de Groot, *A Handbook of Antique Prose-Rhythm*, p. 1.   [109] Ibid., p. 172.

(περίοδοι); it is also well known the periodic style is not often found in Luke and Acts or even the New Testament. A contrast to the periodic style is what Aristotle calls the "continuous" style (εἰρομένη λέξις) (Arist. *Rh.* 3.9.1) and Demetrius the "disjointed" style (διηρημένη ἑρμηνεία) (Demetr. *Eloc.* 12). Except for the Lukan preface (Lk 1:1–4), the seams and summaries may be described best in terms of the Aristotelian "continuous" (εἰρομένη) style. Joined by connecting particles, a sentence in this style has no end in itself, observes Aristotle, but only stops when the sense (τὸ πρᾶγμα λεγόμενον) is complete (Arist. *Rh.* 3.9.1–3). Ungraceful in its lengthiness, the continuous style does not allow the reader or hearer to perceive an approaching end. Conversely, the periodic style consists of sentences with a beginning and end, which feature "a magnitude that can be easily grasped" (*Rh.* 3.9.3).[110] As noted above, Kennedy argues there was an overall lack of rhetorical attention to sentential arrangement in the sources of Aristotle's era, and the more elaborate definitions of the periodic style developed later.[111]

Aristotle provides guidelines for sentence construction such as: (a) add connecting particles in their natural order and in proximity to each other, e.g., μέν . . . δέ and ἐγω μέν . . . ὁ δέ (*Rh.* 3.5.2);[112] (b) maintain agreement in number, e.g., a plural subject with a plural verb (*Rh.* 3.5.2); (c) give each word its own article, as in τῆς γυναικὸς τῆς ἡμετέρας, except when conciseness is desired, as in τῆς γυναικὸς ἡμετέρας; and (d) use connecting particles, as in πορευθεὶς καὶ διαλεχθείς ("having gone and having conversed"), or for conciseness omit them but keep the connection, as in πορευθεὶς διαλέχθην ("having gone, I conversed") (*Rh.* 3.6.6).

Clauses and periods should be neither too long nor too short.[113] If too short, the hearer is apt to become confused; if too long, the hearer is left behind. Applied to periods, clauses may be "divided into parts" (διηρμένη) or opposed (ἀντικειμένη); the former is a partition into properly constructed parts, and the latter refers to antithesis, which Aristotle notes is pleasing because contraries are easily understood (*Rh.* 3.9.8). Intentional similarity in final syllables of clauses is called *paromoiosis*

---

[110] μέγεθος εὐσύνοπτον.   [111] Kennedy, "Aristotle on the Period," 284.

[112] Aristotle uses this example: ἐγὼ μέν, ἐπεί μοι εἶπεν (ἦλθε γὰρ Κλέων δεόμενός τε καὶ ἀξιῶν), ἐπορευόμην παραλαβὼν αὐτούς ("As for me, I, when he told me – for Cleon came begging a favor and supplicating – set out, taking them along," author unknown). Connecting words have been imposed between ἐγὼ and ἐπορευόμην. If the interval between ἐγὼ and ἐπορευόμην becomes too great, the result is obscurity.

[113] A simple (ἀφελής) period consists of one clause.

(παρομοίωσις) (*Rh.* 3.9.9)[114] and is seen in the final syllables themselves or inflections of the same word or repetition of the same word. With relevant parts underlined, an example of each includes respectively: (a) similar final syllables in ἐν πλείσταις δὲ φροντίσι καὶ ἐν ἐλαχίσταις ἐλπίσιν ("in the greatest anxiety and the smallest hopes," author unknown); (b) inflections of the same word in ἄξιος δὲ σταθῆναι χαλκοῦς, οὐκ ἄξιος ὢν χαλκοῦ ("worthy of a bronze statue, not being worth a brass farthing," author unknown); and (c) repetition of the same word in σὺ δ᾽ αὐτὸν καὶ ζῶντα ἔλεγες κακῶς καὶ νῦν γράφεις κακῶς ("while he lived you spoke ill of him, now he is dead you write ill of him," author unknown). These and the previous pragmatic guidelines, applicable to not only periods but also sentences in the continuous style, help to shape the standards for Greek prose composition in the Hellenistic age. Both Demetrius and Dionysius draw upon Aristotelian structural concepts.

Demetrius discusses clauses and phrases individually first (*Eloc.* 1–9)[115] and then examines them within a sentential framework (*Eloc.* 10–35). Prose, he remarks, is organized and divided by clauses (*Eloc.* 1), some of which are a complete thought, others partial thoughts (*Eloc.* 2). In all cases, whether the thought is complete or partial, a clause will shape it (*Eloc.* 3). Heir to Aristotle's literary legacy, Demetrius defines a clause in two ways: (1) "A clause is one of the two parts of a period" (*Eloc.* 34; cf. Aristotle *Rh.* 3.9.5);[116] and (2) "A clause is either a simple period or part of a compound period" (quotation of an unknown "Archedemus") (*Eloc.* 34).[117] Somewhat sanguinely, Demetrius defines a phrase (κόμμα) as "what is less than a clause" (*Eloc.* 9)[118] and includes as examples: Διονύσιος ἐν Κορίνθῳ in the sentence Λακεδαιμόνιοι Φιλίππῳ· Διονύσιος ἐν Κορίνθῳ ("The Spartans to Philip: Dionysius in Corinth")[119] and the imperatives γνῶθι σεαυτόν ("Know yourself") and ἕπου θεῷ ("Follow God") (*Eloc.* 9).

Like Aristotle, Demetrius advocates avoidance of very long or very short clauses. Long clauses make the composition unmeasured (ἄμετρος)

---

[114] See R. Dean Anderson, Jr., *Glossary of Greek Rhetorical Terms Connected to Methods of Argumentation, Figures and Tropes from Anaximenes to Quintilian* (Leuven: Peeters, 2000), s.v. "παρομοίωσις."

[115] Kennedy, *Classical Rhetoric & Its Christian & Secular Tradition*, p. 130 notes there is speculation that the original opening of *De elocutione* may have been lost.

[116] κῶλόν ἐστι τὸ ἕτερον μέρος περιόδου. The other part is a phrase (κόμμα).

[117] κῶλόν ἐστιν ἤτοι ἁπλῆ περίοδος, ἢ συνθέτου περιόδου μέρος.

[118] κόμμα ἐστὶν τὸ κώλου ἔλαττον.

[119] Also found in Demetr. *Eloc.* 8, 102, 241. See Innes' historical remarks in Demetrius, *On Style*, p. 351 note e.

and endless (*Eloc.* 4); yet exceptions abound. In this example of a twenty-seven-syllable clause, opines Demetrius, the length is justified, due to the elevation of the language: τὸ γὰρ δὴ πᾶν τόδε τοτὲ μὲν αὐτὸς ὁ θεὸς πορευόμενον συμποδηγεῖ καὶ συγκυκλεῖ ("Sometimes God himself helps to escort and resolve this whole universe on its circling way," Pl. *Plt.* 269c).

Short clauses are unbefitting, because they make a composition choppy, yet the example of an eleven-syllable clause indicates the smallness of the river and its charm, observes Demetrius (*Eloc.* 6): οὗτος δὲ ἦν μέγας μὲν οὔ, καλὸς δέ ("This [river] was not large, it was beautiful however," Xen. *An.* 4.4.3).

Elaborating on Aristotle's definition of a period as "a portion of speech that has a beginning and an end" (*Eloc.* 11; cf. Arist. *Rh.* 3.9.3), Demetrius writes: "In general terms, a period is nothing more nor less than a particular arrangement of words. If its circular form should be destroyed and the arrangement changed, the subject matter remains the same, but there will be no period" (*Eloc.* 11). Similar to the Aristotelian guidelines for *paromoiosis* (cf. *Rh.* 3.9.9), Demetrius discusses clause endings such as *homoeoteleuton*, that is, when clauses end with the same word or same syllable (*Eloc.* 26), as in: σὺ δ᾽ αὐτὸν καὶ ζῶντα ἔλεγες <u>κακῶς</u>, καὶ νῦν ἀποθανόντα[120] γράφεις <u>κακῶς</u> ("When he was alive, you spoke to his discredit, and now that he is dead, you write to his discredit," author unknown).[121] Further, Demetrius agrees with Aristotle (Arist. *Rh.* 3.9.8) that antithetical clauses form good periods (*Eloc.* 22).[122]

In the grand style, long clauses are justified, as shown in two examples, the first twenty-seven syllables long and the second twenty long: (1) Θουκυδίδης Ἀθηναῖος ξυνέγραψε τὸν πόλεμον τῶν Πελοποννησίων καὶ Ἀθηναίων "Thucydides the Athenian wrote the history of the war between the Peloponnesians and the Athenians," Thuc. 1.1.1); and (2) Ἡροδότου Ἁλικαρνασσῆος ἱστορίης ἀπόδεξις ἥδε ("The history of Herodotus of Halicarnassus is here set out," Hdt. 1.1) (*Eloc.* 44). A short clause appearing suddenly would diminish the grandeur, in spite of diction or subject matter.

---

[120] Note Arist. *Rh.* 3.9.9 does not show this word.

[121] This example is also used by Aristotle (*Rh.* 3.9.9).

[122] The antithesis may be in content only, language only, or content and language. In the example τοῦ μὲν ἐπίπονον καὶ φιλοκίνδυνον τὸν βίον κατέστησεν, τῇ δὲ περίβλεπτον καὶ περιμάχητον τὴν φύσιν ἐποίησεν ("The man's life he created for labors and dangers, the woman's beauty he formed for admiration and strife," Isoc. *Helen* 17) (*Eloc.* 23), Demetrius' analysis showed that article is in antithesis to article, connective to connective; everything is in parallel. Note that the LCL 199 text (p. 362) and Roberts, *Demetrius: On Style*, p. 80 disagree with the text of the Perseus project at Tufts University: the two verbs, κατέστησεν and ἐποίησεν, have been interchanged.

More significantly, Demetrius understands the end of clauses and sentences as the *terminus* of greatest emphasis. Thus, with regard to word arrangement (τάσσειν τὰ ὀνόματα), less vivid (ἐναργῆ) words are placed first, those more vivid next or last (*Eloc.* 50). In doing so, what comes first seems vivid, and the rest even more so. In this Platonic example of a vividness crescendo (*Eloc.* 51): ἐπὰν μέν τις μουσικῇ παρέχῃ καταυλεῖν καὶ καταχεῖν διὰ τῶν ὤτων ("when a man lets music play over him and flood through his ears," Pl. *Resp.* 411a), Demetrius points out the first verb καταυλεῖν ("play over him") is vivid, but κατ-αχεῖν ("flood through his ears") even more so.[123] Following these, Plato writes: ὅταν δὲ καταχέων μὴ ἀνῇ, ἀλλὰ κηλῇ, τὸ δὴ μετὰ τοῦτο ἤδη τήκει καὶ λείβει ("but when the flood fails to stop and enchants him, at that point he melts and liquefies"). Not only is the last effect the most vivid, but also λείβει ("liquefies") follows the less vibrant τήκει ("melts") (*Eloc.* 51).

As for connectives in the grand style, Demetrius advises μέν... δέ... should not be matched too precisely, "since there is something trivial about exact precision" (*Eloc.* 53).[124] Expletive particles such as δὴ or νυ or πρότερον are added for reasons of style or rhythm (*Eloc.* 55).[125] Moreover, dignity is created by the use of multiple opening words (*Eloc.* 56), and connectives increase grandeur (*Eloc.* 63). Not only does he recommend using a variety of cases (*Eloc.* 65), as in: καὶ πρῶτος ἀποβαίνων ἐπὶ τὴν ἀποβάθραν ἐλειποψύχησέ τε, καὶ πεσόν-τος αὐτοῦ ἐς τὴν παρεξειρεσίαν... ("the first step on the gangway, he fainted, and in his falling on the oars . . . " Thuc. 4.12.1) (*Eloc.* 65), but he also recommends repetition to create dignity, as in: δράκον-τες δέ που ἦσαν ἐν τῷ Καυκάσῳ < . . . > μέγεθος, καὶ μέγεθος καὶ πλῆθος ("there were serpents in the Caucasus, <vast> in size, yes in size and number")[126] where the repetition of μέγεθος adds weight (*Eloc.* 66).

Distinctive patterns also shape the elegant, plain, and forceful styles. Where elegance is concerned, word order (τάξις) becomes a source of charm (χάρις) (*Eloc.* 139), especially when the charming idea is placed at the end of the sentence, as in: δίδωσι δὲ αὐτῷ καὶ δῶρα, ἵππον καὶ στολὴν καὶ στρεπτόν, καὶ τὴν χώραν μηκέτι ἁρπάζεσθαι ("He gives him gifts too – a horse, a robe, a torque, and the assurance that his country

---

[123] Plato's words were καταχεῖν τῆς ψυχῆς.   [124] μικροπρεπὲς γὰρ ἡ ἀκρίβεια.

[125] See Innes' remarks in Demetrius, *On Style*, p. 385 note d.

[126] Origin uncertain; perhaps from Hdt. 1.203.1, according to Innes in Demetrius, *On Style*, p. 393 note b.

would no longer be plundered," Xen. *An.* 3.1.31). Had the last gift τὴν χώραν μηκέτι ἁρπάζεσθαι been placed at the beginning of the sentence, observes Demetrius, the charm would have been lost (*Eloc.* 139). In the plain style, word order follows natural order, but such rules need not be rigidly enforced (*Eloc.* 199). While it is proper to begin a sentence with the nominative or the accusative case to lessen confusion for the hearer (*Eloc.* 201), long clauses are to be avoided, since length implies grandeur (*Eloc.* 204); to wit, clauses of "trimeter length," i.e., fifteen or sixteen syllables,[127] are recommended. In the forceful style, however, clauses are often replaced by phrases, because brevity is more forceful and decisive than length (*Eloc.* 241). Force also derives from putting the most striking idea at the end (*Eloc.* 249); although normally avoided, ending with a connective (e.g., δέ, τέ) is sometimes forceful (*Eloc.* 257).[128] In sum, although occasionally tending toward the prescriptive or proscriptive, Demetrius describes a schema of distinctive stylistic structures that provide valuable evidence for authorship analysis.

As was Demetrius, who wrote a century or two earlier, Dionysius of Halicarnassus is heir to the Aristotelian literary conventions of prose composition. Dionysius offers advice on sentence structure and word order but recommends compositional variety and lack of rigid adherence to formulaic rules:

> Now no one should think that I am proclaiming these as universal laws which will invariably produce pleasure when obeyed and annoyance when ignored. I am not so foolish as to make this claim . . . I think we must in every case keep good taste in view, for this is the best measure of what is pleasurable and what is not. (*Comp.* 12)

Frequently vary the cases of substantives, he counsels, so the ear is not irritated (*Comp.* 12), and break the monotony when many nouns, verbs, or other parts of speech are lined up in close succession. Do not repeat words to a degree that exceeds the limits of good taste, he urges (*Comp.* 12). As for word order, the natural word order is best, placing nouns (ὀνόματα) before verbs (ῥήματα) (*Comp.* 5). Dionysius reasons this order is natural, since nouns indicate substance (οὐσία) and verbs accident (συμβεβηκός), and "in the nature of things the substance is prior to its accidents."[129]

---

[127] According to Innes in Demetrius, *On Style*, p. 471, note b this length is roughly fifteen to sixteen syllables.

[128] The idea of ending with a connective brings to mind the close of the gospel of Mark (Mk 16:8), which ends with γάρ.

[129] Dion. Hal. *Comp.* 5.

Variation (μεταβολή) in composition is accomplished by flexibility in structure: a period here, a non-period there; a large number of clauses in one period, a small number in another; a short clause here, a long one there; a coarsely constructed clause here, a refined one there; and one rhythm here and another there (*Comp.* 19). In a classic article, H. P. Breitenbach concludes that, whereas Aristotle considers intellectual substance or content to overshadow the practical art of compositional style, Dionysius places greater emphasis on the fine art of producing an effect on the audience.[130] Whether attributable to their eras, sources, audiences, or a combination thereof, the work of Aristotle distinctly favors the forensic as much as Dionysius' the aesthetic. Breitenbach grants a nod to later scholarship on these two theories of discourse wherein as far as possible the basic elements of both, he notes, become harmonized.[131]

Clausal structure in Dionysius' three styles (austere, polished, and well blended) is distinctive, though only briefly addressed. In the austere style, clauses are not often parallel in word order or sound arrangement – such clauses are not "slaves to a rigid sequence, but noble, conspicuous, and free" (*Comp.* 22).[132] There is flexibility in the use of cases,[133] singular and plurals, and use of few connectives and articles.[134] By contrast, the polished style is comprised of balanced periods with clauses limited in length so that none is immoderately long or short (*Comp.* 23), whereas clauses in the well-blended style fit the mean between the two extremes.

Finally, around the end of the first century CE, Longinus approaches sentence composition from an almost ethereal point of view. Whereas Demetrius' critical bias tends toward the prescriptive and Dionysius' toward the flexible, Longinus' critical bias is essentially shaped by its opposite, no bias. Although he disapproves of teaching composition by means of rules or precepts,[135] Longinus considers elevated word arrangement to be a key aspect of compositional sublimity. In emphasizing

---

[130] H. P. Breitenbach, "The *De Compositione* of Dionysius of Hall-Carnassus Considered with Reference to the Rhetoric of Aristotle," *CP* 6 (1911), 177f.

[131] Ibid., 179.

[132] οὔτε ἀνάγκῃ δουλεύοντα, ἀκόλουθα δὲ καὶ εὐγενῆ καὶ λαμπρὰ καὶ ἐλεύθερα.

[133] Cf. Longinus, *De subl.* 23–24.

[134] Cf. Dion. Hal. *Dem.* 39. For an instructive comparison of grammar and the study of speech in Aristotle and Dionysius of Halicarnassus, see Swiggers and Wouters, "Poetics and Grammar," pp. 21–37. Swiggers and Wouters argue that both Aristotle and Dionysius distinguish between "thought-contents" and "formal expression" (pp. 22f., especially p. 22 note 14), but that the general distinction between the technical aspects of grammar and style had not yet happened. There seems to be an absence of a "disciplinary boundary" (p. 23), in that grammar is tied up with literary or stylistic issues.

[135] See Russell, *Criticism in Antiquity*, p. 9.

hyperbaton, that is, word arrangement out of the normal sequence, he gives an example from Herodotus that contains intense emotion (*Subl.* 22): ἐπὶ ξυροῦ γὰρ ἀκμῆς ἔχεται ἡμῖν τὰ πράγματα, ἄνδρες Ἴωνες, εἶναι ἐλευθέροις ἢ δούλοις, καὶ τούτοις ὡς δραπέτησιν. νῦν ὦν ὑμεῖς ἤν μὲν βούλησθε ταλαιπωρίας ἐνδέχεσθαι, παραχρῆμα μὲν πόνος ὑμῖν, οἷοί τε δὲ ἔσεσθε ὑπερβαλέσθαι τοὺς πολεμίους ("Our fortunes stand upon a razor's edge, men of Ionia, whether we be free men or slaves, aye, and runaway slaves. Now, therefore if you are willing to endure hardship, at the moment there is toil for you, but you will be able to overcome your enemies," Hdt. 6.11). The natural word order, Longinus observes, would have been: ἄνδρες Ἴωνες, νῦν καιρός ἐστιν ἡμῖν πόνους ἐπιδέχεσθαι· ἐπὶ ξυροῦ γὰρ ἀκμῆς ἔχεται ἡμῖν τὰ πράγματα . . . ("O men of Ionia, now is the time for you to endure toil, for our fortunes stand upon a razor's edge . . ."). Herodotus, however, has created a passage that appears unpremeditated and intense with emotion by moving the vocative ἄνδρες Ἴωνες away from the beginning and by not beginning with an exhortation to toil.

Variety and liveliness are produced by changes in case, tense, person, number, or gender.[136] To make words that are singular unexpectedly plural suggests emotion (*Subl.* 23, 24). Similarly, multiple things that have been combined into an attractively formed singular give an effect of surprise (*Subl.* 24). Vividness is expressed by narrating past events as though happening in the present (*Subl.* 25). Change of person gives an equally powerful effect (*Subl.* 26). Longinus suggests periphrasis contributes to sublimity (*Subl.* 28), since it often gives a richer tone than the single verb, yet he cautions periphrasis may be easily over-used so as to sound trivial and unpleasant (*Subl.* 29).

As shown above, the early critics, Demetrius, Dionysius, and Longinus, inherited Aristotelian structural principles, yet the work of each stands on its own. Demetrius, who explicitly refers to Aristotle, agrees that (a) particles should be used in their natural order but not matched so precisely as to trivialize the sentence and (b) clauses should not be too long or too short but gives examples of justifiable exceptions where lengthy clauses may convey elevated language and short clauses charm. Clauses of fifteen or sixteen syllables fit the plain style, he says, whereas forcefulness is increased by clausal brevity. Like Aristotle, Demetrius suggests appropriate ways to begin and end clauses with the same words or syllables but emphasizes the weightiness of the end. Thus, in showing how vividness, charm, or striking ideas may build to a climax,

---

[136] Cf. Dion. Hal. *Comp.* 22.

Demetrius places the greatest import squarely at the end of the clause or sentence.

Drawing less explicitly on Aristotelian principles, Dionysius and Longinus discuss variety and word order. Dionysius recommends variety in cases, parts of speech, and length of clauses or sentences. Similarly, Longinus calls for variety in gender, tense, case, person, and number. Dionysius suggests a natural word order set in a harsh, jarring arrangement for the austere style, but a balanced arrangement for the polished style. Longinus encourages the use of hyperbaton to increase emotion. For Dionysius, the key is to avoid surpassing the bounds of good taste. For Longinus, prosal sublimity lies in seemingly unpremeditated vividness or powerful emotion, not in rigid structural precepts.

Structural elements in Luke and Acts

In this brief sketch of ancient literary criticism on sentence structure and word order, four features that affect good prose composition come to light: (1) clause length; (2) use of particles and connective devices; (3) the natural order of subject and verb; and (4) the syntax that begins and ends a clause or sentence. Considering these features in the analysis of the seams and summaries shows that one is immediately problematic, namely, clause length.

To determine clause length in the seams and summaries means clausal division *per* the early techniques. Whereas the ancient critics give examples of clauses in sentences, along with suitable and unsuitable lengths, it is unclear precisely how they determine that length. Classicist D. Innes notes, in the periodic style, clauses of fifteen or sixteen syllables often appear to be standard,[137] but in what Aristotle calls the "continuous" style (εἰρομένη λέξις) (Arist. *Rh.* 3.9.1) and Demetrius the "disjointed" style (διηρημένη ἑρμηνεία) (Demetr. *Eloc.* 12), clause length is much less well established. For instance, both Aristotle (*Rh.* 3.9.6) and Demetrius urge the avoidance of very long or very short clauses. As already mentioned, long clauses usually make the composition unmeasured (ἄμετρος) and endless (Demetr. *Eloc.* 4), yet there are instances when length gives language an elevation. Likewise, short clauses usually make a composition choppy, but in some circumstances they add an element of charm (Demetr. *Eloc.* 6). Further, an actual example is Dionysius' division of the second period of Thuc. 1.1–2 into two clauses (delineated by "|"): ἀρξάμενος

---

[137] Clauses of "trimeter length" are fifteen to sixteen syllables long, according to Innes in Demetrius, *On Style*, p. 471 note b.

Sentence structure

- Parataxis and post-positive particles as connective devices
- Subject and verb order
- Syntactic element that begins and ends a clause or sentence

---

Figure 3.8 Sentence structure conventions

εὐθὺς καθισταμένου | καὶ ἐλπίσας μέγαν τε ἔσεσθαι καὶ ἀξιολογώτατον τῶν προγεγενημένων (Dion. Hal. *Comp.* 22). The first clause is eleven syllables long, which is fairly short; the second is twenty-five, which is rather long.

To determine clausal division, then, for the present authorship analysis, sentences are divided at a gross level, based on the natural boundaries of or punctuation markers for main clauses and subordinate or dependent clauses in the Nestle-Aland *Novum Testamentum Graece*, 27th edition. Also used by others such as G. L. Hendrickson,[138] this method provides consistency in dividing clauses in the seams and summaries, since the boundaries of main and dependent clauses are usually, but not always, punctuated by major or minor stops. Whether or not the anonymous author-editor of Luke or Acts intended finer clausal delineation is unknown. Because delineating clauses is undertaken at a gross level only, clause length is not a suitably robust feature for authorial analysis.[139]

Contrariwise, patterns of the three other features *are* quantifiable, as shown in Figure 3.8. First, not only may post-positive particles such as μὲν οὖν, μέν . . . δέ, δὲ, δὲ καί, τε, and γάρ be tabulated in the seams and summaries but also connective devices such as the paratactic καί. For examples of the former, see Lk 1:80; 3:18; 4:41; 19:48; Acts 1:1, 5; 2:41, 46; 4:34; 5:16. For examples of the latter, among many, see Lk 1:80; 2:52; Acts 1:4; 2:41. If it is the case, *pace* Turner, that "his ['Luke's'] more characteristically Greek δέ replaces Mark's connecting particle καί,"[140] the present analysis ought to confirm that. Second, an area studied by early notable scholars such as T. D. Goodell and H. L. Eberling, subject and verb order in clauses and sentences is quantifiable.[141] For subject-verb (SV) order, for example, see, among many, Lk 1:1; Acts 2:41a. For verb-subject order (VS), see Lk 4:14; Acts 2:41b. Third, of significance is the syntactic element (e.g., subject, verb, a direct object, or

---

[138] Hendrickson, "Accentual Clausulae," p. 284 note 1.
[139] See the Appendix for clausal division of the Luke and Acts seams and summaries.
[140] Turner, "The Style of Luke-Acts," p. 57.   [141] See notes 15 and 25.

prepositional phrase) that begins and ends a clause or sentence. Although an initial subject, verb, direct object, or prepositional phrase may lend weightiness to the clause or sentence, the greater emphasis appears to lie on the final syntactic element, be it subject (e.g., Lk 5:17b; Acts 4:4b), verb (e.g., Lk 6:18b; Acts 2:43b), direct object (e.g., Lk 1:4; Acts 9:31a), or prepositional phrase (e.g., Lk 1:80b; Acts 8:25a).

From the literary critical works of Aristotle, Demetrius, Dionysius of Halicarnassus, and Longinus, three key aspects of prose composition criticism have been considered in this chapter: euphony, rhythm, and sentence structure. Differences among the critics as to schemas, emphases, and depth of coverage are evident, but all agree on the fundamental effectiveness of good prose composition to further the aim and pleasure of discourse. What has been drawn out in this chapter are the elements whose presence or absence in the seams and summaries may be tabulated, tested, and compared; hence, what follows is the analysis itself.

4

AUTHORIAL UNITY: ANALYSIS RESULTS AND PROBABILITIES[1]

Using, then, as my main criterion simply that the speeches of Lysias are composed in a pleasing style, I have come to suspect many of the speeches which have been commonly regarded as genuine. I put them to the test and found them spurious, not because there was anything wrong with them in a general way, but because they did not strike me with that characteristic Lysianic charm or with the euphony of that style.

(Dion. Hal. *Lys.* 12)[2]

Dionysius was concerned incidentally with problems of ascription and chronology throughout his career as a literary critic. In the early *Lysias* he shows how, in the absence of internal chronological or other evidence, a developed literary taste could be called into service as the final judge of authorship.[3]

Although the once solid theological, thematic, generic, structural, and narrative unity of Luke and Acts has been challenged as to the extent of the two books' interwoven textuality, authorial unity has remained virtually closed to scholarly scrutiny.[4] The paucity of modern inquiry into the single authorship hypothesis is worrisome at best, ill-considered at worst.

Both ancient and modern literary critics are intrigued by authorship issues. On the one hand, modern critics are at a disadvantage. We cannot

---

[1] The writer gratefully acknowledges the generous assistance of Dr. Martin Buntinas of Loyola University Chicago's Department of Mathematics and Statistics in the preparation of this chapter.

[2] Translation based on Stephen Usher's – see *Dionysius of Halicarnassus*.

[3] See *Dionysius of Halicarnassus: Critical Essays*, vol. II, p. 246, where Usher makes this observation in his introduction to *Dinarchus*.

[4] See, e.g., Verheyden, "The Unity of Luke-Acts," pp. 6–7 note 13: "Today, the discussion on the common authorship of Lk and Acts, which is to be distinguished from that on the identity of the author, is *closed* [emphasis added]."

possess the same "developed literary taste"[5] as the ancient critics, because the Greek of the classical and post-classical eras is decidedly remote from modern linguistic sensibilities. As mentioned in Chapter Three, D. A. Russell reminds us it is more judicious to accept early critical methods than to evaluate them.[6] On the other hand, modern critics are at an advantage. We may use computer technology to analyze literary style, and, more specifically, those aspects of literary taste and style critically significant to the ancients. Thus, as described in Chapter One, a three-stage method of reconfirming authorial unity suggests itself: (1) find valid authorial data to analyze, that is to say, the *Luke and Acts seams and summaries* identified in Chapter Two; (2) cull out style conventions used by ancient author-editors when composing, namely, the early Greek *prose compositional conventions* identified in Chapter Three; and (3) perform *a stylometric analysis* to reconfirm (or challenge) single authorship by examining the compositional preferences in the two books' seam and summary evidence.[7] Put simply, the present analysis seeks to determine the statistical probability that Luke and Acts were written by the same author-editor. Because testing focuses solely on the primary question of whether the seams and summaries corroborate single authorship, as they should, broad-spectrum questions about authorial identity, theological perspective, or genre investigation lie beyond the scope of this inquiry.

Raw data derived from the seams and summaries in Luke and Acts

Culled from the seam and summary evidence identified in Chapter Two,[8] the raw data numbers shown in Figure 4.1 are classified for each book by the total number of: seams and summaries, including the preface; sentences;[9] clauses;[10] words; and syllables.

Should an objection be raised the data appear less than abundant for a robust authorship analysis, it must be remembered a majority of selected

---

[5] See footnote 3.   [6] Russell, *Criticism in Antiquity*, p. 131.

[7] As noted in Chapter One, stylometry is the scientific analysis of literary style.

[8] See the Appendix for the entire data set, laid out by clause, syllable, and quantity.

[9] Sentences are determined by the punctuated Greek text of the Nestle-Aland 27th edition of *Novum Testamentum Graece*, which seems the most objective approach.

[10] Clauses are determined by the boundaries of main clauses and subordinate or dependent clauses, many of which – but not all – are marked by major or minor stops in the Greek text of the Nestle-Aland 27th edition of *Novum Testamentum Graece*. What can be said with a high degree of certainty is that there would not be fewer than the number of clauses delineated.

Total number of:	Luke	Acts
Seams and summaries, including the preface	25	19
Sentences	28 + 4 partial sentences	26 + 2 partial sentences
Clauses	76	69
Words	642	590
Syllables	1,460	1,333

Figure 4.1 Breakdown of SSD

but representative scholars of Luke and Acts are solidly agreed that the identified seams and summaries are texts that have come from the hand of the author-editor of each book. *They represent material whose authorial origin or source is least open to question.*

Although proof is an undeniably rare commodity in the field of biblical criticism, the present analysis seeks to attain the highest possible level of stylometric investigatory rigor. To that end, statistical testing of the seam and summary evidence brings the weight of scientific analysis to bear on the research equation, wherein the key factor is *differences*. If the differences observed in the two books' patterns of preference lie *within* the bounds of normal authorial stylistic variation, as they should, then single authorship remains undisputed. If, however, the differences lie outside or beyond the range of normal stylistic variation, then the differences require an explanation. In statistics, abnormal variation constitutes an actual, intrinsic, and material difference, *inexplicable by mere chance or random variability*. The statistical tool appropriate to test authorship analysis is the chi-square contingency table test,[11] whose requirements and function are explained later in this chapter. Inasmuch as the chi-square contingency table test requires a minimum amount of data but no maximum, the identified seam and summary data amply fulfill the test's minimum requirement.

Pre-analysis assumptions

The methodology used herein to re-examine single authorship begins with three assumptions:

[11] See Martin Buntinas and Gerald M. Funk, *Statistics for the Sciences* (Belmont, Calif.: Brooks/Cole, 2005), pp. 457ff.

1. Seams and summaries offer a fully legitimate window into the prose compositional patterns of an author-editor. Literary "sutures" offer not only sufficient but also the most valid evidence of an authorial "handprint," as argued at length in Chapter Two.

2. In any two compositions, there will naturally be a degree of stylistic variation, even in writings from the same author-editor composing in the same genre, in the same style, and at the same or approximately the same time. Variability in writing samples is intrinsic, normal, and expected. Statistics tools ably handle these circumstances.

3. When the degree of variation lies outside or beyond the range of what is considered "normal" and "expected," according to statistical theory, *the differences must be explained.* In light of this requirement, if it happens that statistically significant differences between Luke and Acts exist, at least three major explanations for them appear possible.

Incorporating stylometric testing in the research equation allows us to reach a conclusion about authorial unity with a high degree of confidence. As noted, if significant differences in the compositional preferences of the Luke and Acts seam and summary data (SSD)[12] are discovered, statistics requires that we attribute the variability to something else besides random and expected variability – that is, to an actual, intrinsic, material difference in the compositions.

Explaining differences: three possibilities

Significant differences observed in Luke and Acts will occasion at least three possible explanations: (1) the *same* author-editor wrote Luke and Acts but wrote each book in a different genre or style, which is reflected in the prose style of the SSD; (2) the *same* author-editor wrote Luke and Acts but the dates of composition are so distant from one another that radical stylistic differences occur, which are reflected in the SSD; (3) *different* author-editors wrote Luke and Acts, hence, distinctive stylistic patterns appear in the SSD.

---

[12] "SSD" abbreviates the phrase "seam and summary data." This is the set of seams and summaries from Luke (Luke SSD), Acts (Acts SSD), or both (Luke and Acts SSD).

Explanation 1: Same author-editor but different
genres or styles

The question of generic unity is a knotty problem in the study of Luke
and Acts. Before exploring the ramifications of the two books' composition in different genres or styles, the one-genre hypothesis must be
addressed. The premise of generic unity usually treats the two texts as
an original logical unity affiliated with one genre, wherein their canonical separation does not affect the document's unified status. David E.
Aune, in his well-regarded book *The New Testament in Its Literary Environment*, promotes this view: "The Gospel of Luke and the Acts of the
Apostles originally constituted a two-volume work by a single author."[13]
Shortly thereafter, Aune states: "Luke-Acts *must* be treated as affiliated
with *one* genre [emphasis added]."[14] For Aune, that genre is "general
history," which narrates "the important historical experiences of a single
national group from their origin to the recent past. This usually involved
contacts with other nations (mostly through warfare)."[15] Thus, "Luke"
is seen as a Hellenistic Christian historian who narrates "the early history of Christianity from its origins in Judaism with Jesus of Nazareth
through its emergence as a relatively independent religious movement
open to all ethnic groups."[16] Further, in a noteworthy article on teaching
and learning history and historiography in the ancient classroom, Craig
A. Gibson brings together research and evidence from various first- to
fourth-century CE treatises on the pedagogy of *progymnasmata* (e.g.,
the use of fable, narrative, anecdote, maxim, refutation, confirmation,
commonplace, encomium, invective, comparison, speech in character,
ecphrasis, thesis, and law).[17] Indeed, Gibson rightly asks how any ancient
author-editor of history could "ever write a single word" without relying
on the years of training in the progymnasmatic exercises that taught prose
composition in formulations that we today would consider only periph-
erally historical.[18] This question deservedly informs the author-editor of
Luke and Acts. Indeed, one of the most recent biblical scholars to tackle
Luke, Acts, and the *progymnasmata*, Mikeal C. Parsons in *Luke: Storyteller, Interpreter, Evangelist*, concludes that studying these devices in
Luke and Acts adds a narrative richness predicated on ancient rhetorical
tradition.[19]

---

[13] Aune, *Literary*, p. 77.   [14] Ibid., p. 80.   [15] Ibid., pp. 88f.   [16] Ibid., pp. 138f.
[17] Craig A. Gibson, "Learning Greek History in the Ancient Classroom: The Evidence
of the Treatises on Progymnasmata" *CP* 99 (2004), 103f.
[18] Ibid., 126.
[19] Mikeal C. Parsons, *Luke: Storyteller, Interpreter, Evangelist* (Peabody, Mass.: Hendrickson Publishers, 2007).

Another proponent of the one-genre hypothesis, Charles H. Talbert in *Literary Patterns, Theological Themes, and the Genre of Luke-Acts*, concludes the genre of Luke and Acts is a type of ancient biography similar to that of Diogenes Laertius' *Lives of Eminent Philosophers*. This type of ancient biography, sometimes called a succession narrative, presents the life of the founder of a philosophical school, followed by a narrative about his followers, followed by a summary of teachings.[20] "Luke-Acts belongs to that type of ancient biography in which the life of a philosophical founder is followed by a list or narrative of his successors and selected other disciples."[21]

With respect to the present analysis, the one-genre position is explained as follows: If Luke and Acts are affiliated with one genre, then the style of their seams and summaries will not differ by more than the random variability expected when a unitary author-editor is composing prose. In other words, *one author-editor composing a two-volume, one-genre work effectively assures the seams and summaries will reveal a commonality of prose compositional style.*

Different genres

Of those who understand the two books as different types of literature, Martin Dibelius argues Acts contains certain stories or accounts that would never be found in any gospel, for example, the first community in Jerusalem (Acts 1–2), or Peter's Pentecost speech (Acts 2:14b–36).[22] Because of this fact, Dibelius writes "there is an essential difference between the literary type of the Gospel on the one hand and that of Acts on the other – it exists although the evangelist Luke is also the author of Acts."[23] Other different-genre proponents, Mikeal C. Parsons and Richard I. Pervo, in *Rethinking the Unity of Luke and Acts*, argue the

---

[20] Talbert, *Literary Patterns*, pp. 125–140, especially 127f., 131–134.

[21] Ibid., p. 134. Aune, *Literary*, pp. 78f., evaluates Talbert's analysis. The merit of Talbert's work, concludes Aune, is that it tries to "find an analogy in genre to Luke-Acts as a whole." Parsons and Pervo, however, scrutinize a variety of one-genre proposals, including monograph, general history, antiquities, apologetic history, biblical historiography, or philosophical succession, none of which reflects the genre entirely successfully; see Parsons and Pervo, *Rethinking the Unity of Luke and Acts*, pp. 25–37. See also Parsons, "The Unity of the Lukan Writings: Rethinking the *Opinio Communis*," in N. H. Keathley (ed.), *With Steadfast Purpose: Essays on Acts in Honor of Henry Jackson Flanders, Jr.* (Waco, Tex.: Baylor University Press, 1990); and "Who Wrote the Gospel of Luke?" *Bible Review* 17 (2001), 12–21, 54–55.

[22] Dibelius, "First Christian Historian," pp. 123f.   [23] Ibid., p. 124.

Acts speeches, crafted in the manner of contemporary rhetorical models, serve as the defining criterion for generic divergence:[24]

> The presence of these numerous addresses remains a formidable obstacle to the case for generic unity. They are one of the most prominent indicators that in Acts Lukas ["Luke"] has other literary goals and thus possibly operated with a different set of generic conventions. The speeches of Acts mark the second book as different.[25]

With respect to the present analysis, the different-genre position is explained as follows: If Luke and Acts do not share generic unity, that is, if they belong to distinct literary genres, these key questions must be answered. Do the seams and summaries therein exhibit a parallel or similar prose compositional style? If not, does genre distinction best explain the observed stylistic differences?

The answers to these questions take two approaches. First, Russell suggests that genre is unfortunately not a very precise term. It is used to "denote classes [of literature] formed on various principles."[26] Assigning an ancient text to its generic class is believed to be the key to understanding it. In antiquity, certain types of literature, such as early Greek lyric poetry, were expected to follow prescriptive principles, but Russell notes:

> Historically, "genre-theory" is very much more a Renaissance inheritance than an ancient one; when we come to look for it in the critics of antiquity, as of course we must, it appears a much more patchy and incomplete thing than is commonly supposed. Moreover, the gap between theory and practice . . . is uncomfortably wide.[27]

The diversity of scholarly opinion as to the genre or genres of Luke and Acts means it cannot be determined with ease or certainty whether the author-editor(s) of Luke and Acts intended to write in any of the genres assigned by modern critics. Second and more crucial, in antiquity it was recognized that one prose style may *traverse* a variety of types of literature. As described in Chapter Three, Dionysius of Halicarnassus in *De compositione verborum* proposes three compositional styles,

---

[24] Parsons and Pervo, *Rethinking the Unity of Luke and Acts*, pp. 37f.   [25] Ibid., p. 38.
[26] Russell, *Criticism in Antiquity*, pp. 148f.
[27] Ibid. For a review of Luke and Acts in their historical-literary context, see Detlev Dormeyer, *The New Testament Among the Writings of Antiquity*, Stanley E. Porter (ed.), trans. Rosemarie Kossov (Sheffield: Sheffield Academic Press 1998).

namely, the austere, polished, and well blended, illustrating their features by examples from writers of various genres: history (ἱστορία), civil oratory (λόγοι πολιτικοί), and poetry (ποίησις).[28] The evidence presented by Dionysius shows that Thucydides wrote history in the austere style, but Herodotus wrote history in the well-blended (style). In like manner, Antiphon wrote oratory in the austere style, Isocrates in the polished, and Demosthenes in the well-blended.[29] The point is: *literary genre and prose compositional style do not logically cohere, given that prose compositional style relates to an individual writer, not to a particular genre.* One the finest exemplars is Plutarch, the first-century philosopher whose extensive works reflect a mastery of multiple genres, specifically, ancient biography (e.g., *Lives*), practical ethics (e.g., *Moralia*), and philosophical discourse. That Plutarch exhibits over his lifetime a compositional artistry and expertise in various genres is supported by ancient and modern scholars; indeed, his style is not only individual but also identifiable.[30] According to Russell, Plutarch, the master of many genres, is characterized as "a conscious artist in an elaborate manner, meticulous in his periodic structures, his studied word-patterns, *his avoidance of hiatus*, his carefully chosen vocabulary, and so on [emphasis added]."[31] Furthermore, Russell quotes an observation of the early physician, Galen, about Galen's own writings. Astute, educated, and well-read, Galen suggests his own compositional style is easily detectible because not only does he know his letters, but he is also well grounded in the rudiments of style (λέξις).[32] Thus, for Galen, style is an authorship indicator in addition to medical and philosophical vocabulary. Nonetheless, style-oriented scholarship on other roughly contemporaneous writers of multiple genres such as Philo of Alexandria or Flavius Josephus largely furnishes "macro-views," that is, wide-ranging studies of the author's rhetorical arguments, thematic structures, or diction, but it rarely offers

---

[28] Dion. Hal. *Comp.* 22. In *Comp.* 24, he notes other types, such as tragedy and philosophy, and mentions the lyric poet (μελοποιός) and the orator (ῥήτωρ).

[29] See Dion. Hal. *Comp.* 22–24.

[30] The entire second chapter of D. A. Russell, *Plutarch* (New York: Charles Scribner's Sons, 1973), pp. 18–41, is devoted to Plutarch's language, style, and form. See also Shigetake Yaginuma, "Plutarch's Language and Style," in *Principat*, Part 2, vol. 33.6, Wolfgang Haase (ed.), *Aufstieg und Niedergang der römischen Welt* (Berlin: Walter de Gruyter, 1992).

[31] Russell, *Plutarch*, p. 21.

[32] Ibid., p. 19 cites Galen, *On His [My] Own Books*, xix, 8–9 Kühn: ὠνουμένου δέ τινος ὡς ἐμὸν ὑπὸ τοῦ ξένου τῆς ἐπιγραφῆς κινηθείς τις ἀνὴρ τῶν φιλολόγων ἐβουλήθη γνῶναι τὴν ἐπαγγελίαν αὐτοῦ· καὶ δύο τοὺς πρώτους στίχους ἀναγνοὺς εὐθέως ἀπέρριψε τὸ γράμμα, τοῦτο μόνον ἐπιφθεγξάμενος, ὡς οὐκ ἔστιν ἡ λέξις αὕτη Γαληνοῦ καὶ ψευδῶ ἐπιγέγραπται τουτο τὸ βιβλίον.

"micro-views" that pinpoint the author's characteristic use of hiatus, rhythm, or syntax.[33]

Even if Luke and Acts differ generically, it does not follow that the prose compositional style of the seams and summaries must differ. In fact, based on the observations above, even as genre research in Luke and Acts argues for generic distinction under the single authorship hypothesis, the two books' prose compositional style will arguably be the same or similar. While obvious distinctions between Luke and Acts, such as the presence of speeches,[34] convince many of genre differentiation, the less rhetorically robust seams and summaries operate at a level effectively genre-neutral. No matter what genre the document is, seams and summaries provide editorial transitions, either initial or culminating, which link one pericope or complex of pericopes to another. *Postulating different genres for Luke and Acts, then, does not provide a sufficient explanation for prose compositional differences, if found.*

Differences in style but not necessarily in genre

The question of genre aside, may prose compositional differences in the seams and summaries be explained by pointing to "Luke's" masterful touch, his artistic license to choose two different styles? Charles Talbert describes "Luke's" impressive artistry, his capability to write a lengthy two-volume work in such an extraordinary variety of styles. Although long, the following quotation by Talbert captures the commonly held opinion of "Luke's" artistic touch:

> [it] is reflected, for example, in the remarkable variation in Luke's style in the separate parts of his two volume work. In the Gospel we find a preface written in irreproachable literary Greek followed by the infancy narratives written in the style of the LXX. This very transition has been thought to prove the

---

[33] For Philo, see: V. Nikiprowetzky, "Caractère et structure du Commentaire Philonien" in *Le Commentaire de l'Écriture chez Philon d'Alexandrie: son caractère et sa portée: observations philologiques* (Leiden: Brill, 1977), pp. 170–235; Manuel Alexandre, Jr., *Rhetorical Argumentation in Philo of Alexandria* (Atlanta, Ga.: Scholars Press, 1999); J. Leopold and T. Conley, "Philo's Style and Diction" in D. Winston and J. Dillon (eds.), *Two Treatises of Philo of Alexandria: Commentary on* De gigantibus *and* Quod Deus sit immutabilis, Brown Judaic Studies 25 (Chico, Calif.: Scholars Press, 1983). For Josephus, see: Shaye J. D. Cohen, *Josephus in Galilee and Rome: His Vita and Development as a Historian* (Leiden: Brill, 1979).

[34] In Acts, speeches display rhetorical sophistication and length, whereas in Luke, they frequently present a short and pithy message that lacks rhetorical structure; in short, they are different in form, function, and content.

author to be a conscious artist. In the Acts also the author chooses the style which is suitable for the different periods, places, and persons he is describing. He imitates the LXX in the first part of Acts and in the missionary speeches to Jews due to his feel for the Palestinian context of the earliest church. His speeches also employ old titles for Jesus and ancient kerygmatic formulae in accord with the archaizing tendency of antiquity. At other times, less solemn, the author is capable of "painting a scene easily and expansively, dwelling lovingly on details, in almost conversational tones." *Luke simply varies his style in terms of the situation he is depicting and the tone that situation requires. Indeed, it is the opinion of H. J. Cadbury that Luke's sensitivity to style is even more far-reaching than that of the literary men of antiquity who understood the imitation of classical models of style* [emphasis added].[35]

"Luke's" artistry at stylistic variation is based on the idea the author-editor of Luke and Acts alters his style and tone as different scenes and situations require. "Luke's" stylistic variation, however, may be *too* singular. The last sentence of Talbert's quotation tellingly recognizes an authorial stylistic range at variance with contemporaneous models. To repeat, Talbert says:

> Indeed, it is the opinion of H. J. Cadbury that Luke's sensitivity to style is even more far-reaching than that of the literary men of antiquity who understood the imitation of classical models of style.

Indeed, James Hope Moulton and Wilbert Francis Howard also observe there are surprisingly few, if any, models in the literature of that era exhibiting such wide-ranging variation:

---

[35] Talbert, *Literary Patterns*, p. 1. To support his statements, Talbert cites (1) Streeter, *The Four Gospels*, p. 548; (2) Wayne G. Rollins, *The Gospels: Portraits of Christ* (Philadelphia, Pa.: Westminster, 1963), p. 97; (3) H. F. D. Sparks, "The Semitisms of Acts," *JTS* n.s., 1 (1950), 16–28; (4) Haenchen, *Acts of the Apostles*, p. 74, 80; (5) John Martin Creed, *The Gospel according to St. Luke: The Greek Text with Introduction, Notes, and Indices* (London: Macmillan & Co., 1930), p. lxxvi; (6) Lucien Cerfaux, "The Acts of the Apostles" in A. Robert and A. Feuillet (eds.), *Introduction to the New Testament* (New York: Desclée, 1965), p. 366; (7) Eckhard Plümacher, *Lukas als hellenistischer Schriftsteller* (Göttingen: Vandenhoeck & Ruprecht, 1972), pp. 51, 63–64, 67–69, 72–78; and (8) Cadbury, *Making of Luke-Acts*, p. 221.

It would be *hard to find ancient parallels for the variation of style* he ["Luke"] shows as his story changes its scene [emphasis added].[36]

Opinions supporting the anomalous extravagance in stylistic variation given to "Luke," in fact, may need to be reconsidered. While it is *possible* that "Luke" composed in an array of styles beyond the ken of all his contemporaries, it is simply not probable. The point is: Even if "Luke's" disproportionate and sweeping stylistic variation were not an anomaly, there is little, if any, reason to postulate stylistically different seams and summaries in Luke and Acts for the reason *they function in a consistent and similar way in the two books*; hence, stylistic coherence is more plausible than radical variation. Finally, as noted in Chapter Two, Martin Dibelius justifies the variation in style in Luke and Acts by suggesting that "Luke" wrote his early Christian history (Acts) without the aid of the same amount of traditional material as he had for the gospel (Luke). Because Acts was a new venture, a new task, the writer "Luke" needed to use a new style.[37] This argument would engage us more strongly if we knew about the sources of Acts; though a creative description of a less than certain set of circumstances, it explains the stylistic differences between Luke and Acts by the "fresh start" approach.

In sum, neither different genres nor different styles will provide a sufficient explanation for significant compositional differences in the seams and summaries, if found. A second noteworthy explanation, however, was offered long ago.

Explanation 2: Same author-editor but different dates of composition

As mentioned in Chapter One, John C. Hawkins in *Horae Synopticae* postulates a considerable "time lapse" between the compositions of Luke and Acts in order to explain the striking linguistic differences he observes. These differences are often overlooked and yet are extensive enough, he suggests, to conclude that the two books could not have been written at or near the same time:[38]

---

[36] James Hope Moulton and Wilbert Francis Howard (eds.), *A Grammar of New Testament Greek*, vol. II (Edinburgh: T. & T. Clark, 1920; reprint 1968), pp. 7f. This quotation is also cited in Cadbury, *Making of Luke-Acts*, pp. 221f.

[37] Dibelius, "First Christian Historian," pp. 124f.

[38] Hawkins, *Horae Synopticae*, pp. 177–180.

Would it be at all likely that an author (unless he wished to conceal his identity, which we know from Acts i, 1 that this author did not wish) would so alter his style in two nearly contemporaneous books as, e.g., to drop εἶπεν δέ, ἐν τῷ with infinitive, and καὶ αὐτός, to take to μὲν οὖν, τε, κελεύειν, and συνέρχομαι, and to substitute the infinitive for the finite verb after ἐγένετο, to the extent that has now appeared? *We have thus some internal evidence in favour of placing Luke at a considerably earlier date than Acts, whatever the date of the latter book may be* [emphasis added].

The linguistic differences observed by Hawkins have commonly been considered representative of the stylistic variation found in Luke and Acts. Although Hawkins concentrates on word choice and syntax, *Horae Synopticae* has become a landmark work that offers a balanced analysis of "Luke's" style, addressing both similarities and differences. The substantial weight of linguistic differences, however, never prompted Hawkins to call out the possibility of different authorship.[39]

Is it feasible a chronological gap between the dates of composition would account for significant differences in prose compositional patterns, if found? On the one hand, Hawkins unfortunately proposes no extenuating circumstances or authorial situation on which to base his time-lapse theory, but what could they be? Assuming the priority of Luke, is it reasonable that, in the years prior to composing Acts, the author-editor of Luke received more training in Greek prose composition or relocated to a community where a different type of Greek compositional style was used or taught? The Acts speeches, for example, exhibit an obvious rhetorical excellence not found in Luke, no matter how justified that observation may be framed vis-à-vis sources, redaction, genre, or transmission. Thus, whereas stylistic development or improvement over time is certainly possible, there is as yet no evidence to suggest it; the possibilities remain mere speculation. Further, in the twenty-first century, applying reasons for noticeable improvements in style over time in the

---

[39] More recently, Richard I. Pervo, analyzing at length the internal and external evidence or early Christian and cognate writings, proposes a convincing date of ca. 115 CE for Acts; see Richard I. Pervo, *Dating Acts: Between the Evangelists and the Apologists* (Santa Rosa, Calif.: Polebridge Press, 2006), p. 343. Based on complex religious and cultural constellations in early Christianity, Pervo argues, the author-editor of Acts both defends and attacks, as appropriate, the issues of Jews and Judaism, Greco-Roman polytheism and culture, and "heretical" Christian stances. Yet, like Hawkins, Pervo does not support the idea that compositional distance between Luke and Acts could signal different author-editors.

works of a first-century author-editor risks anachronism.[40] *More convincing is the argument that consistency in authorial style is retained over time.* The ancient critics understood that an author-editor's style remains fairly consistent and recognizable. Indeed, they rely on that understanding when ascribing authorship to manuscripts whose authorship is unknown.

Because the time-lapse theory may not be substantiated by anything other than evidence of stylistic differences, the explanation of distant dates of composition may be construed as a case of special pleading. *Hawkins, however, has made us realize the differences must be accounted for*, which compels us to consider the third explanation, namely, different author-editors.

Explanation 3: Different author-editors?

If style markers based on euphony, rhythm, and syntactic features show evidence of significant differences in Luke and Acts, then statistical theory requires another intrinsic explanation. If the first two explanations, different genres and chronologically distant dates of composition, prove insufficient to explain the extreme variation in the pattern of these style markers, then it becomes difficult to conceive of or ascribe an explanation to this phenomenon other than different authorship of Luke and Acts. Of course, if no statistically significant differences come to light, the question is moot and the single authorship hypothesis is entirely validated, at least as regards these particular data. To that end, the rest of this chapter presents a stylometric analysis of prose composition style markers in the Luke and Acts SSD – specifically, a statistically measured survey of the euphonic, rhythmic, and structural patterns identified in Chapter Three.

Euphony analysis

Euphony in prose composition receives ample attention in the work of ancient critics such as Demetrius[41] and Dionysius of Halicarnassus. Demetrius, organizing his work in a practical but unfortunately not

---

[40] Because a writer today, for example, improves composition by learning to use restrictive and non-restrictive relative pronouns correctly does not provide sufficient explanation that a first-century writer's style might so improve. This argument appears in Robert C. Tannehill, "Response to Patricia Walters, 'The Gilded Hypothesis Revisited: Authorial Unity of Luke and Acts,'" unpublished paper presented at the annual meeting of the Society of Biblical Literature, Washington, D.C., November 2006, p. 3.

[41] Please recall that in lieu of the longer and more correct "Pseudo-Demetrius" I simply use "Demetrius."

example-rich format, understands hiatus and "ugly sounds" (δυσφωνία) as they apply to the grand, elegant, plain, and forceful styles described in *Eloc.*, whereas Dionysius, who gives free rein to descriptive images of aesthetically pleasing experiences that stem from euphony in composition, supplies us with not only more details than other ancient critics but also many concrete examples. According to Dionysius, it is with the "senses, untutored by reason" (ἀλόγοις αἰσθήσεσιν) that one always distinguishes what is pleasant from what is not (*Dem.* 24). Both Demetrius and Dionysius advise attention to hiatus, harsh sound combinations, and the effect on the reader's or hearer's perception of pleasantness or unpleasantness. What follows is a stylometric analysis of the two euphonic elements identified in Chapter Three, hiatus and dissonance, which frame in large part the euphonic character of any prose composition.

The analytical process includes the following four parts: (a) a brief recapitulation of the compositional element from the perspective of ancient critics; (b) a table of raw data numbers from the Luke and Acts SSD; (c) a bar graph illustrating the degree of similarity and difference in the two books' patterns; and finally, (d) the computer-generated output of the chi-square contingency table test. After analysis of all the stylistic conventions derived from Chapter Three, a prose compositional "big picture" of Luke and Acts will be formulated, drawing together what may be deduced *in toto*.

Hiatus is then the first convention to be analyzed, and, unlike the conventions that follow, a detailed explanation is given for each phase in the analytical process. After that, such an exhaustive account will not be necessary.

Hiatus

Vowel clashes (συγκρούσεις) occur when two vowels or diphthongs stand immediately adjacent to one another, either between or within words, causing a pause in time as the mouth changes from one position to another, thus interrupting the smoothness.[42] Herbert Weir Smyth describes *hiatus* as technically occurring between words, but both Demetrius and Dionysius offer examples of vowel clashes between *and* within words;[43] so the distinction appears somewhat terminological. Smyth specifies natural vowel quantity as follows: ε and o are always short; η and ω are always

---

[42] Dion. Hal. *Comp.* 22.
[43] Smyth, *Greek Grammar*, §§46f.; and e.g., Demetr. *Eloc.* 68–73, 207, 299; Dion. Hal. *Comp.* 20.

	L-L	L-S and S-L	S-S
Luke	*Between:* καὶ ἦν (1:80) *Within:* ἐκραταιοῦτο (1:80)	*Between:* L-S: καὶ ἐπιτιμῶν (4:41) S-L: εἶα αὐτὰ (4:41) *Within:* L-S: εἶα (4:41) S-L: θεοῦ (4:41)	*Between:* τὸ ὄρος (21:37) *Within:* διεπορεύετο (13:22)
Acts	*Between:* ἁγίου οὖς (1:2) *Within:* ἐποιησάμην (1:1)	*Between:* L-S: καὶ ὀχλουμένους (5:16) S-L: τινὶ αὐτῶν (5:15) *Within:* L-S: σημεῖα (5:12) S-L: λαῷ (5:12)	*Between:* τε ἀριθμὸς (11:21) *Within:* κύριον (11:21)

Figure 4.2 Examples of hiatus in the Luke and Acts SSD

long; and α, ι, and υ may be either short or long.[44] Diphthongs (αι, ει, οι, long ᾳ, ῃ, ῳ, αυ, ευ, ου, ηυ, υι) are always naturally long, according to Smyth:[45] "Length by position does not affect the natural quantity of a vowel. Thus, both λέ-ξω *I shall say* and λή-ξω *I shall cease* have the first syllable long by position; but the first vowel is short in λέξω, long in λήξω."[46] For the present analysis, *pace* Smyth, it should be remembered *vowel* quantity is not the same as *syllable* quantity.

As noted in Chapter Three and shown again in Figure 4.2, three types of hiatus vis-à-vis particular styles are delineated by ancient critics sensitive to this convention. The first type of hiatus, long-long, hereafter abbreviated "L-L," occurs when a long vowel or diphthong is immediately adjacent to another long vowel or diphthong. The second type of hiatus occurs when a long vowel or diphthong is immediately adjacent to a short vowel, for which there are two sequences, long-short and short-long, hereafter abbreviated "L-S" and "S-L" respectively. The third type of hiatus, short-short, abbreviated "S-S," occurs when two short vowels stand immediately adjacent to each other.

Furthermore, hiatus analysis must be performed on a syllable-by-syllable basis. To preview the totals given in Figure 4.4 and to serve

---

[44] See Smyth, *Greek Grammar*, §4.

[45] Ibid., §5. While §5 appears to contradict §169, wherein final –αι and –οι are sometimes regarded as short in terms of accent, the *natural* quantity of final –αι and –οι remains long, based on §5.

[46] Ibid., §144b.

	L-L	L-S and S-L	S-S
Luke	...αὐτοῦ. Ἤγγιζεν ... (Hiatus follows 21:38)	L-S: (None) S-L: ...Ἱεροσόλυμα. Εἶπεν... (Hiatus follows 13:22)	...λεγόμενα. Ἐγένετο... (Hiatus precedes 18:35a)
Acts	...Ἰακώβου. οὗτοι... (Hiatus precedes 1:14)	L-S: ...αὐτοῦ. Ἐγένετο... (Hiatus preceding 8:1b–c) S-L: ...εἰρήκατε. Οἱ... (Hiatus precedes 8:25)	...πέντε. Ἐγένετο... (Hiatus follows 4:4)

Figure 4.3 Examples of hiatus following or preceding a seam or summary

as an example for comparison calculations, it will be seen that: L-L hiatus occurs 58 times in Luke, 24 times in Acts; L-S and S-L hiatus occur 142 times in Luke, 100 in Acts; and S-S hiatus occurs 63 times in Luke, 59 in Acts.

Now, as they stand, these numbers cannot be accurately compared. To make sense of them, we must calculate each as a percentage of the total. Before that, however, a special case must be considered, namely, hiatus occurring with the word immediately (a) preceding a seam or summary or (b) following it, as shown in the examples in Figure 4.3. As noted in the previous chapter, G. L. Hendrickson disregards final hiatus in his analysis of Greek poetry and prose, but at least two reasons exist to include it. First, scholars agree the author-editor of Luke and Acts composed seams and summaries to link preceding and following text, so it makes sense to take such occurrences into account. Second, and more significantly, the early critics did not disregard it. Dionysius (*Comp.* 7) opines that clauses must be joined to one another so as to present an appearance of affinity and attachment, and a total euphonious effect is thus created. He also applies this harmonious fit to periods (*Comp.* 9). Figure 4.3 gives examples of hiatus across major stop boundaries.

Therefore, to calculate correct percentages, the total number of possible hiatus locations is needed. To obtain that number, the following steps are taken: first, start with the total number of syllables in the Luke SSD (1,460) and the Acts SSD (1,333); then augment the total by adding 1 for each seam or summary *except the preface*.[47] Since 25 seams and

---

[47] For a simple example of why "1," not "2," is added for each seam and summary except the preface, the following is a hypothetical six-syllable seam. There are seven possible locations where hiatus (marked by ◆) may occur. The number of words is irrelevant, since the calculation of all possible hiatus locations (needed to calculate an accurate percentage)

Hiatus	L-L	L-S and S-L	S-S	None
Luke	58	142	63	1,221
% of 1,484 (1,460 + 24) syllables	3.91%	9.57%	4.25%	82.28%[†]
(Between words; within a word)	(46; 12)	(67; 75)	(14; 42)	
Acts	24	100	59	1,168
% of 1,351 (1,333 + 18) syllables	1.78%	7.40 %	4.37%	86.45%
(Between words; within a word)	(20; 4)	(42; 58)	(23; 36)	

[†] Due to rounding, the percentages add up to 100.01% instead of 100.00%.

Figure 4.4 Hiatus in the Luke and Acts SSD

summaries were identified in Luke and 19 in Acts (see Figure 4.1), add 24 to the total in Luke and 18 to the total in Acts. The result is 1,484 possible hiatus locations for Luke and 1,351 for Acts, the most accurate numbers by which to calculate the percentages shown in Figure 4.4. The rightmost column shows the number of locations in which *no* hiatus or vowel clashes occur, a number needed later for statistical testing.

What may be observed about hiatus patterns in the two books? Notice L-L hiatus occurs about twice as often in Luke as in Acts: 58 to 24, or 3.91 to 1.78 percent. Of the locations where hiatus exists (Lk: 263; Acts: 183), the L-L type accounts for over one-fifth of the occurrences in Luke (58/263) but only about one-eighth in Acts (24/183). Furthermore, in Acts the L-L hiatus occurs less than half as often as the S-S, 1.78 and 4.37 percent respectively, not true in Luke. To compare these percentages visually, they may be formatted in a vertical bar graph where all three varieties of hiatus in Luke and Acts are placed side by side; see Figure 4.5.

In bar graph format, the differences *prima facie* look as though they may be significant, but are they? Or do the differences simply represent a normal variation to be expected in the prose compositional style of a unitary author-editor? A stylometric tool, the chi-square contingency table test, will provide an answer.

The chi-square contingency table test explained

In statistics, the single authorship of Luke and Acts is called the "null hypothesis," often denoted H_0, because it is the position presumed to be

takes into account syllables only, not whole words themselves. ◆ Syl-1 ◆ Syl-2 ◆ Syl-3 ◆ Syl-4 ◆ Syl-5 ◆ Syl-6 ◆ So "1" must be added to the seam's six syllables to obtain the precise total of seven *possible hiatus locations*.

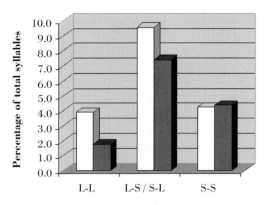

Figure 4.5 Hiatus patterns in vertical bar graph format [white = Luke; shaded = Acts]

true – the default position, if you will. Because the null hypothesis is presumed to describe the state of affairs accurately, it becomes the frame of reference against which the test results will be compared.[48] In the case of hiatus, the null hypothesis states:

> H_0: *There is no difference in the hiatus patterns of Luke and Acts beyond normal, random variability.*

This means variation in hiatus patterns between Luke and Acts is expected and will not militate against single authorship in any statistically significant way. When, however, statistically significant variation in the observed differences does occur, it has the potential to militate against single authorship *unless* the extreme variation can be explained in another way. Thus, in statistics, the "alternative hypothesis," often denoted H_a, describes the situation when the null hypothesis is false. In the case of hiatus, the alternative hypothesis states:

> H_a: *There is a difference in the hiatus patterns of Luke and Acts beyond normal, random variability.*

Hypothesis testing either rejects or retains the null hypothesis; the alternative hypothesis is never rejected, but rejecting the null hypothesis is equivalent to accepting the alternative hypothesis. What does this mean for hiatus? If the chi-square contingency table test results in statistically

---

[48] Marija J. Norušis, *SPSS 11.0: Guide to Data Analysis* (Upper Saddle River, N.J.: Prentice Hall, 2002), pp. 240ff.

significant differences in hiatus patterns between Luke and Acts, that is, beyond the range of normal and expected variability, *the null hypothesis is rejected and the alternative hypothesis is accepted*. Hence, as argued above, *different authorship may not be ruled out as an explanation for the extreme variation*.

The chi-square contingency table test calculates a decimal P-Value (probability value) from the observed data, that is, from the number of actual occurrences, not the percentages. The P-Value is used to decide whether or not the null hypothesis should be rejected.[49] When the P-Value is translated to a percentage and shown to lie *at or above 95 percent*, the evidence is said to be statistically "significant"; in this case, the null hypothesis is rejected and the alternative accepted at a 95 percent level of confidence. Lying beyond the range of normal, random variability, the observed differences require another intrinsic explanation. At an even higher level of assurance, when the translated P-Value is shown to lie *at or above 99 percent*, the evidence is said to be "highly significant"; in this case, the null hypothesis is rejected and the alternative accepted, because there is a 99 percent level of confidence the observed differences are *not* due to expected variation. Although the chi-square contingency table test generates the P-Value in decimal format (e.g., 0.001; see Figure 4.6), the value may be translated to a percentage (e.g., 1 percent), which, when subtracted from 100 percent, results in the level of confidence (e.g., greater than 99 percent). Any P-Value resulting in less than a 95 percent level of confidence indicates the observed differences are not statistically significant enough to reject the null hypothesis, and the evidence proves inconclusive. To understand how the chi-square contingency table test arrives at a P-Value and what the P-Value means entails a detailed statistical process; for those already familiar with the chi-square contingency table test or those who do not want to explore the statistical process in depth, please skip to page 160.

Details of the chi-square contingency table test

Using the MINITAB statistical software package[50] to run the chi-square contingency table test for hiatus generates the exact output shown in

---

[49] The chi-square statistic compares sample (categorical) observed data "with what would be expected if the data were generated from a sampling distribution" (Buntinas and Funk, *Statistics for the Sciences*, p. 450). Assuming the null hypothesis is true, Luke and Acts would constitute two random texts out of the entire set of writings of the single author-editor.

[50] MINITAB®: Statistical Software for Windows; Minitab, Inc., State College, Pa.

```
Expected counts are printed below observed counts.
Chi-square contributions are printed below expected counts.

          L-L       L/S      S-S      None   Total
   Lk      58       142       63      1221    1484
         42.92    126.68    63.86   1250.54
          5.296    1.854    0.012     0.698

   Ac      24       100       59      1168    1351
         39.08    115.32    58.14   1138.46
          5.817    2.036    0.013     0.766

Total      82       242      122      2389    2835

Chi-Sq = 16.491, DF = 3, P-Value = 0.001
```

Figure 4.6 Calculating the chi-square output for hiatus

Figure 4.6. The column headings are self-explanatory: L-L stands for long-long hiatus, and so forth. The column labeled "None" shows the number of locations between syllables where *no* hiatus exists. In a chi-square contingency table test, all possible locations where hiatus *could* occur must be evaluated, those where it exists and those where it does not.

The computed chi-square value ("Chi-Sq"), also referred to as "the chi-square statistic," examines the relationship between the row variable and the column variable. In the case of hiatus above, the row variable is Luke ("Lk") and Acts ("Ac"); the column variable is hiatus in its three varieties (L-L, L/S, S-S) and "None."

In the output of the chi-square test shown in Figure 4.6, the intersection of a row and column is called a cell, and each cell contains three numbers: (1) the "observed count"; (2) the "expected count"; and (3) the chi-square contribution. An explanation of the placement of these numbers relative to each other is always given under the title:

```
Expected counts are printed below observed counts.
Chi-Square contributions are printed below expected counts.
```

To make sense of the three numbers, we may look at the cell or intersection of the row "Lk" and the column "L-L," where the "observed count" is 58, the "expected count" 42.92, and the chi-square contribution 5.296. What follows is an explanation of how these numbers are calculated.

Observed count

As its name implies, the observed count refers to the *number of actual occurrences* of the L-L hiatus observed in the Luke SSD ("Lk"). In other words, an analysis of the seams and summaries in Luke shows there are 58 instances of the long-long type of hiatus; see Figure 4.4.

Expected count

The "expected count" refers to the number that *ought* to be in that cell if the null hypothesis were true, that is, if there were no difference between Luke and Acts beyond random variability. This is how it is arrived at. Referring to the bottom number of the rightmost "Total" column of Figure 4.6, we see that the number of all locations where hiatus could occur in Luke and Acts *combined* is 2,835, which is the sum of 1,484 in Luke ("Lk") and 1,351 in Acts ("Ac"). Now we can say, 1,484 ÷ 2,835 or 52.35 percent[51] of all possible hiatus locations are found in Luke and 1,351 ÷ 2,835 or 47.65 percent are found in Acts.

Referring to the bottom of the "L-L" column in Figure 4.6, we also see that the combined "Total" of the L-L hiatus in Luke and Acts is 82 (58 + 24) occurrences. If the null hypothesis were true, 52.35 percent of the 82 occurrences *ought* to occur in Luke and 47.65 percent in Acts. This is the "expected count." In this example, the expected count is 42.92, which is 52.35 percent of 82, rounded to two decimal points.[52] In equation-like language, the expected count is:

$$\frac{1,484}{2,835} \text{ of } 82 = 42.92$$

Each cell's expected count is calculated in the same way, by working out the proportionality. *Further, it is usually required that each cell contain an expected count equal to or greater than 5.0, since the chi-square test loses validity when the counts are too low.* A rule-of-thumb *exception* allows 20 percent or fewer of the cells to contain an expected count lower than 5.0.

---

[51] The result is actually calculated more precisely to more than two decimal places: 0.5234567.

[52] The more precise calculation of 0.5234567 is actually used. See footnote 51.

Chi-square contribution

The chi-square contribution for each cell is calculated by performing the following steps: (1) find the difference between the observed count, O, and the expected count, E, for a cell, j; (2) square the difference and (3) divide the squared difference by the expected count for the cell. Formally, this is shown by:

$$\chi^2 \text{ contribution} = \frac{(O_j - E_j)^2}{E_j}$$

Using the same example whose chi-square contribution is 5.296, we may show how the number is calculated: first, subtract the expected count from the observed count, $58 - 42.92^{53} = 15.08;^{54}$ second, using the more exact number, square the difference $(15.076551)^2 = 227.30239$; and third, divide the squared difference by the more exact expected count, $227.30239 \div 42.923449 = 5.2955294$, which when rounded to three decimal points is 5.296. The chi-square contribution for each cell is calculated in the same way.

The last line of the output contains three pieces of key information. First, the leftmost "Chi-Sq" value represents the sum of all the cells' chi-square contributions.[55] In the example shown in Figure 4.6, Chi-Sq = 16.491. Next to it, the "DF" ("Degrees of Freedom") value is given. This is merely the number calculated by multiplying the number of rows (r) minus 1 by the number of columns (k) minus 1, or in notation, DF = (r − 1)(k − 1). In this example, there are two rows and four columns, so DF = (2 − 1)(4 − 1) = (1) (3) = 3. Last, the rightmost number is the most important. It is the *P*-Value, which is obtained by using the Chi-Sq value and the DF value in conjunction with a chi-square statistical table available in statistics textbooks or on the Internet. The MINITAB software automatically looks up the *P*-Value and provides it. In this example, the *P*-Value is 0.001. This means that if the null hypothesis were true,

---

[53] The expected count is actually figured to a greater number of decimal places to obtain more precision; thus, 42.92 is actually 42.923449, which is the number used in the calculations.

[54] Thus, $58 - 42.923449 = 15.076551$.

[55] Formally, the sum of all the chi-square (χ^2) contributions is shown as:

$$\chi^2 = \sum_j \frac{(O_j - E_j)^2}{E_j}$$

	Null hypothesis = TRUE	Null hypothesis = FALSE[†]
Null hypothesis = Retained	CORRECT conclusion	Type 2 ERROR
Null hypothesis = Rejected	Type 1 ERROR	CORRECT conclusion

[†] This is actually the alternative hypothesis, H_a.

Figure 4.7 Null hypothesis testing chart

one would expect (with 3 degrees of freedom) to see a Chi-Sq value as large as 16.491 only 1 time in 1,000.[56]

Type 1 and Type 2 Errors. Rejection of the null hypothesis means a case *against* stylistic coherence, and hence single authorship, exists beyond a reasonable doubt. Figure 4.7 is a chart similar to one found in virtually every introductory statistics textbook; it shows the four possible outcomes of testing the null hypothesis. Two outcomes result in a *correct* conclusion, two in an *erroneous* conclusion.

A correct conclusion for hiatus testing is seen when: (1) the hiatus patterns in Luke and Acts show no differences beyond random variability, and so the null hypothesis is retained; and (2) there are differences in the hiatus patterns in Luke and Acts beyond normal, random variability, and so the null hypothesis is rejected.[57]

Two types of incorrect conclusion may also occur: (1) the null hypothesis is rejected when in fact it is true; or (2) the null hypothesis is retained when in fact it is false. The "Type 1 Error" means the null hypothesis has been rejected, when in fact it is true. In the case of hiatus, a Type 1 Error means there exist no differences in hiatus patterns in Luke and Acts beyond normal, random variability, but single authorship is rejected by mistake. At a 99 percent level of confidence, this situation might, *though not necessarily would*, happen on average 1 time in 100. An average of 1 time in 100 a perfectly good null hypothesis could, though not necessarily would, be rejected.

A "Type 2 Error" means the null hypothesis is really false, but it is retained. In the case of hiatus, a Type 2 Error means the differences between Luke and Acts in the hiatus patterns fall within the expected range of variability, but single authorship is in fact false. The null

[56] Norušis, *SPSS 11.0*, pp. 359ff.   [57] Ibid., p. 256.

```
Expected counts are printed below observed counts.
Chi-Square contributions are printed below expected counts.

            L-L      L/S      S-S      None    Total
   Lk        58      142       63      1221     1484
          42.92   126.68    63.86   1250.54
          5.296    1.854    0.012     0.698

   Ac        24      100       59      1168     1351
          39.08   115.32    58.14   1138.46
          5.817    2.036    0.013     0.766

Total        82      242      122      2389     2835

Chi-Sq = 16.491, DF = 3, P-Value = 0.001
```

Figure 4.8 Chi-square output for hiatus

hypothesis would not be rejected because there is insufficient evidence to do so.

Chi-square statistic for hiatus

In the case of hiatus in Figure 4.8, the *P*-Value is 0.001. When translated to a percentage format, the *P*-Value becomes 0.1 percent. In statistical terms, the confidence level therefore stands at or above 99 percent, making the evidence highly significant. The null hypothesis is thus rejected and the alternative hypothesis accepted with an especially high degree of confidence, meaning *the observed differences in hiatus cannot reasonably be explained by random variability. Another intrinsic explanation is needed.* Statistical theory requires the differences in hiatus patterns in Luke and Acts be explained by something other than mere happenstance; as argued, different authorship offers the most likely explanation.

Needless to say, highly significant differences in hiatus alone neither can nor should bear the entire weight of an authorship study. The remaining conventions and their preferences in the Luke and Acts SSD will now be analyzed to discover how they, together with hiatus, contribute to the larger prose compositional picture and, indeed, to the question of single or different authorship.

Dissonance

Produced by certain non-vowel sounds in close proximity, the harshness or "ugliness" of language gives prose composition a sense of not only heaviness with a rough texture but vividness as well. A degree of cacophony enhances the grandeur of language, suggests Demetrius (*Eloc.* 48, 105), yet he gives few explicit examples. Because he does not identify explicit combinations, the γκ, κδ, and λκ clusters have been deduced from his examples. In contrast, Dionysius gives numerous unambiguous examples of dissonant combinations, both jarring and difficult to pronounce: κδ, κλ, νδ, νθ, νκ, νλ, νξ, ντ, ντ, νχ, and σξ (*Comp.* 22). Although the examples from Demetrius and the lengthy list from Dionysius surely represent only a sub-set of sound combinations considered dissonant in antiquity, they do constitute actual examples. More to the point, they allow an investigation of dissonance in the Luke and Acts SSD, isochronal (or nearly so) with the early prose composition critics. Figure 4.9 contains examples of dissonant sound combinations both within words and between words, as well as totals for the combinations in the Luke or Acts SSD. Many combinations do not occur at all; others seldom. For the sake of completeness, the counts in Figure 4.9 have been separated into those occurring between words and within words.

For statistical testing, in the case of dissonant sound combinations, the null hypothesis of single authorship and the alternative hypothesis may be stated as follows:

H_0: *There is no difference in the dissonant sound combination patterns of Luke and Acts beyond normal, random variability.*

H_a: *There is a difference in the dissonant sound combination patterns of Luke and Acts beyond normal, random variability.*

Although individually categorized and totaled, the data as they stand in Figure 4.9 are unusable. For statistical purposes the chi-square contingency table test requires an "expected count" of 5.0 for each cell. When the "expected count" calculated for a particular sound combination in Luke or Acts does not equal at least 5.0, the chi-square contingency table test starts to lose validity. The "νχ" combination, for example, occurs only once in Luke and twice in Acts, so the "expected count" requirement cannot possibly be met for this combination. Therefore, further data distillation is required.

Statistical theory fortunately allows category combining. The categories in Figure 4.9 may be merged into six categories, shown in Figure 4.10, the totals for which satisfy the "expected count" requirement. As with hiatus, analysis is performed on a syllable-by-syllable basis. A

		Examples from the Luke and Acts SSD	No. between words	No. within words	Total
γκ	Luke:	None	0	0	0
	Acts:	None	0	0	0
κδ	Luke:	None	0	0	0
	Acts:	None	0	0	0
κλ	Luke:	None	0	0	0
	Acts:	Within: κλιναρίων (5:15)	0	5†	5
λκ	Luke:	None	0	0	0
	Acts:	None	0	0	0
νδ	Luke:	Between: ἦν διδάσκων (4:31)	6	0	6
	Acts:	Between: τῶν δὲ (5:13); within: ἀνδρῶν (4:4)	8	3	11
νθ	Luke:	Within: ἀνθρώποις (2:52)	0	1	1
	Acts:	Between: τὸν θεὸν (2:47)	1	0	1
νλ	Luke:	Between: τὸν λαόν (3:18)	1	0	1
	Acts:	Between: πρῶτον λόγον (1:1)	5	0	5
νκ	Luke:	Between: ὧν κατηχήθης (1:4)	33	0	33
	Acts:	Between: ἀποστόλων καὶ (2:42)	17	0	17
νξ	Luke:	None	0	0	0
	Acts:	None	0	0	0
νπ	Luke:	Between: πνευμάτων πονηρῶν (8:2)	9	0	9
	Acts:	Between: αὐτῶν παρὰ (7:58b)	13	0	13
ντ	Luke:	Between: ἐν ταῖς (1:80); within: ἅπαντες (4:40)	30	20	50
	Acts:	Between: πληθυνόντων τῶν (6:1a); within: ἐντειλάμενος (1:2)	28	37	65
νχ	Luke:	Between: τὸν χριστὸν (4:41)	1	0	1
	Acts:	Between: τῶν χειρῶν (5:12)	2	0	2
σξ	Luke:	None	0	0	0
	Acts:	None	0	0	0

† The five occurrences of "κλ" in Acts do *not* include three occurrences in various forms of the noun, ἐκκλησία (Acts 8:1b–3; 9:31; 16:5). Erring on the side of caution eliminates them due to the unknown treatment of the "κκλ" combination. Indeed, excluding them produces a more conservative numerical and statistical result than if they were included.

Figure 4.9 Examples and raw data totals of dissonance from the Luke and Acts SSD

Category	Luke		Acts	
	Number	**% of Total Syllables (1,484 = 1,460 + 24)**	**Number**	**% of Total Syllables (1,351 = 1,333 + 18)**
νπ : *Between* words	9	.61	13	.96
ντ: *Between* words	30	2.02	28	2.07
ντ: *Within* a word	20	1.35	37	2.74
νκ : *Between* words	33	2.22	17	1.26
νδ : *Between* words + *within* a word	6	.40	11	.81
Other: *Between* words + *within* a word	3	.20	13	.96

Figure 4.10 Six-category table of dissonant combinations

dissonant sound combination may appear within a syllable,[58] between syllables within a word, or between words. *No occurrence fits into more than one category.* As with hiatus, comparison is based on percentages. To calculate an accurate percentage, the total number of possible dissonance locations must be accurately calculated, including the special case of a dissonant combination occurring with the word immediately *preceding* a seam or summary or with the word immediately *following* it, except for the preface. As with hiatus, for each seam or summary except the preface, "1" is added to the total syllable count, which results in the correct number of syllables to calculate percentages. As above, the total number of syllables within which and between which dissonance may occur is adjusted to 1,484 for Luke (i.e., $1,460 + 24 = 1,484$) and 1,351 for Acts (i.e., $1,333 + 18 = 1,351$).

The table *prima facie* brings to light three noteworthy differences, notwithstanding six categories that show a frequency of less than 1 percent. First, the "ντ" pattern *within* a word occurs less than half as frequently in Luke as in Acts (Lk: 1.35 percent; Acts: 2.74 percent). Second, the "νδ" combination, both between words and within a word, occurs less than half as often in Luke as in Acts (Lk: .40 percent; Acts: .81 percent). Third, combinations in the "Other" category occur almost 5 times less frequently in Luke than in Acts (Luke: .20 percent; Acts: .96 percent). To compare the percentages visually, we may format them

---

[58] The κλ combination is the only one that occurs within a syllable; the rest occur between syllables.

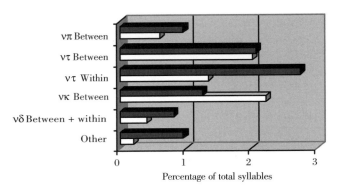

Figure 4.11 Horizontal bar graph of dissonant combinations [white = Luke; shaded = Acts]

in a horizontal bar graph where the six categories of dissonant sound combinations in Luke and Acts are placed side by side; see Figure 4.11.

Do the differences in dissonance, some of which appear substantial, simply reflect the expected variability of a unitary author-editor? Or do they require another explanation for the abnormal variation? Statistics will furnish the answer.

Chi-square statistic for dissonance

The chi-square contingency table test for the six categories in Figure 4.10 generates the output shown in Figure 4.12. Due to line limits in the computer-generated output, abbreviations have been used: (1) "n p" [with a space] designates the "νπ" combination occurring *between* words; (2) "n t" [with a space] the "ντ" combination *between* words; (3) "n-t" [with a hyphen] the "ντ" combination *within* words; (4) "n k" [with a space] the "νκ" combination *between* words; (5) "n d + n-d" [with a space and a hyphen] the "νδ" occurring both *between* and *within* words. "Other" obviously designates combinations not occurring in any of the above categories, and "None" holds the count of locations where no dissonant sound clusters occur at all.

As always, the *P*-Value delivers the punch, because it determines whether the null hypothesis is rejected or retained. In the case of dissonance, the *P*-Value is 0.004, a highly significant statistical finding. Translated into a percentage, it means with a (greater than) 99 percent level of confidence that not only is the null hypothesis rejected but also the abnormal variation in dissonance between Luke and Acts must be attributed to something other than coincidence in one writer's stylistic repertoire.

```
Expected counts are printed below observed counts.
Chi-square contributions are printed below expected counts.

         n p      n t      n-t      n k    n d+n-d    Other    Total
  Lk       9       20       33        6                  3      101
         10.10    26.63    26.17    22.95     7.80      7.35
         0.120    0.427    1.454    4.396    0.417      2.571

  Ac      13       28       37       17       11         13      119
         11.90    31.37    30.83    27.05     9.20      8.65
         0.102    0.363    1.234    3.731    0.354      2.182

Total     22       58       57       50       17         16      220

Chi-Sq = 17.350, DF = 5, P-Value = 0.004
```

Figure 4.12 Chi-square output for dissonant sound combinations

To recapitulate the chi-square contingency table test outcomes so far, the differences in euphony between Luke and Acts result in evidence of hiatus and dissonance patterns that lie *beyond* the range of normal, random, or expected variability. In both cases, the null hypothesis is rejected with a 99 percent level of confidence, a highly significant conclusion, statistically speaking. Indeed, it is proof beyond a reasonable doubt that happenstance does not account for the observed differences. In each case, accepting the alternative hypothesis *requires* an explanation for the actual, intrinsic, and material difference between Luke and Acts. As already argued, different authorship is the most likely.

Prose rhythm analysis

A better-defined aspect of ancient compositional theory than euphony, prose rhythm attends to the sequential patterns of long and short *syllables* of which sentences, clauses, phrases, or words are composed. Whereas euphony functions at the level of vowels and consonants within and between syllables, the "sub-syllable" level, if you will, prose rhythm operates at the whole-syllable level. Syllable quantity then is either long or short. Certain sequences of long and short syllables are called rhythmic feet, or simply "rhythms," and are used to create an effect on the reader or hearer. The modern scholar who tries to decipher how ancient prose critics scanned rhythms in clauses and sentences often finds the examples maddeningly ambiguous to interpret, unless the rhythmic sequences are laid out explicitly by the early critic.

More to the point, the ancient critics did not always agree among themselves. When analyzing Demosthenes' prose rhythm, for example,

Donald F. McCabe notes that ancient literary critics disagreed on such principles as whether a short syllable was lengthened before a major stop; or which mute+liquid combinations lengthened a preceding short syllable and which did not.[59] In the case of lengthening a short syllable before a major stop, Aristotle appears to regard both long and short syllables acceptable in the final position; Dionysius of Halicarnassus seems to believe there is lengthening at a pause; Cicero declares explicitly there is lengthening; and Quintilian suggests a final long syllable is better than a short one, although the latter is acceptable.[60] In the case of a mute+liquid making the preceding short syllable long (where the addition of further consonants would not guarantee lengthening), McCabe used computer-aided analysis to confirm that, in Demosthenes, π, κ, or τ before μ, ν, λ, or ρ do not appear to lengthen the preceding short syllable; the same holds true for φ, χ, and θ before μ, ν, λ, or ρ. The case of β, γ, or δ is different: before ρ the preceding short syllable remains short, but before μ and ν the preceding short syllable is lengthened; β, γ, or δ before λ is undetermined, although the analysis suggests lengthening.[61]

A modern scholar who attempts to scan as the ancients did must do so cautiously. Indeed, rhythm is not entirely separate from euphony, because it is affected by factors such as crasis, contraction, or elision; the first two cause lengthening, the last may or may not. Early prose critics such as those identified in Chapter Three write in varying degrees of detail about prose rhythm, but none suggests that rhythm should play an obtrusive role in prose composition; rather, it ought to be used with a sense of propriety, paying attention to the rhythmic sense but avoiding metrical or poetic composition. Determining syllable quantity, and hence rhythms, in the Luke and Acts SSD as precisely as possible must be informed by the propositions that early literary critics disagreed among themselves on certain rhythmic principles, and the author-editor(s) of Luke and Acts may not have actually paid attention to prose rhythm.

---

[59] McCabe, *Prose-Rhythm*, pp. 29ff., 119ff., 130ff.

[60] Ibid. See Arist. *Rh.* 3.8.6–7; Dion. Hal. *Comp.* 18; Cic. *Orator* 214; Quint. *Inst.* 9.4.93.

[61] McCabe, *Prose-Rhythm*, pp. 133ff. See also Allen, *Vox Graeca*, p. 108. Allen cites the dissertation by J. Schade, "De correptione Attica," unpublished PhD thesis, Greifswald (1908), in which Schade observes the tendency of Attic Greek *always* to lengthen short syllables before βλ, γλ, γν, γμ, δν, and δμ. See also W. Sidney Allen, *Accent and Rhythm: Prosodic Features of Latin and Greek: A Study in Theory and Reconstruction* (Cambridge: Cambridge University Press, 1973).

Clause	Quantity
1	‒ ◡ ◡ ◡ ‒ ‒ ‒ ‒ ◡ ◡ ‒ ‒ ‒ ◡ ‒ ◡ ‒ ◡ ‒ ◡ ‒ Καὶ ἐ-γέ-νε-το ἐν τῷ ἑ-ξῆς ἐ-πο-ρεύ-θη εἰς πό-λιν κα-λου-μέ-νην Να-ῒν
2	‒ ◡ ◡ ◡ ‒ ◡ ‒ ◡ ‒ ◡ ‒ ‒ ‒ ◡ ‒ ◡ ◡ καὶ συν-ε-πο-ρεύ-ον-το αὐ-τῷ οἱ μα-θη-ταὶ αὐ-τοῦ καὶ ὄ-χλος πο-λύς.

Figure 4.13 Syllable quantities in Lk 7:11

Prose rhythm problematics

With that in mind, as argued in Chapter Three, scanning the sequence of rhythms in a clause or sentence ultimately admits at least two measures of errancy unacceptable for the present authorship analysis. First, from a contemporary vantage point it is often unclear how ancient critics scanned prose rhythms, since scholarly hindsight is not twenty-twenty. Because the early critics disagree among themselves about syllable lengthening, it is unknown with whom the author-editor of Luke or Acts would have agreed. To illustrate how problematic this is, Figure 4.13 shows the two-clause summary in Lk 7:11 divided into syllables whose quantities appear above them.

To begin with, the last two words in the second clause, ὄχλος πολύς, highlight an ambiguity where ancient critics appear to disagree as noted previously. Is the final syllable of πο-λύς lengthened before a major stop? Is ὄ-, the first syllable in ὄ-χλος, lengthened before the mute+liquid, χλ? *For the purposes of this analysis, the following criteria hold: (a) a final short syllable immediately preceding a major stop is not lengthened automatically:* if it is naturally short and not followed by a consonant combination in the next word which causes lengthening by position, the final syllable is counted as short; and *(b) a mute+liquid combination does not automatically lengthen a preceding short syllable* except in the cases of β, γ, or δ before μ, ν, and λ; in addition, the mute+liquid must both occur in the same syllable, otherwise the preceding short syllable is lengthened.

Still, based on the works of Dionysius of Halicarnassus, who provides such well-documented examples of sequences, should not a clause-by-clause scanning technique for the authorial analysis be extractable? Each attempt to deduce a set of scanning principles brings up unanswerable questions. Does Dionysius look at the entire clause first and then divide it into individual feet? How does he divide the clause into individual feet? Does he look for the strong, respected rhythms first? At the beginning of a clause, when does he count the first two, three,

Clause	Scansion 1				
	— ‿ ‿ ‿	‿ — —	— — ‿	‿ — —	— ‿ —
1	Καὶ ἐ-γέ-νε-	το ἐν τῷ	ἐ-ξῆς ἐ-	πο-ρεύ-θη	εἰς πό-λιν
	‿ — ‿ —	‿ —			
	κα-λου- μέ-νην	Να-ῒν			

OR

Clause	Scansion 2				
	— ‿ ‿ ‿	‿ —	— — —	‿ ‿ —	— — ‿
1	Καὶ ἐ-γέ-νε-	το ἐν	τῷ ἐ-ξῆς	ἐ-πο-ρεύ-	θη εἰς πό-
	— ‿ —	‿ — ‿ —			
	λιν κα-λου- μέ-νην	Να-ῒν			

Figure 4.14 Possible rhythm sequences of Lk 7:11a

Clause	Scansion 1				
	— ‿ ‿ ‿	— — ‿	— — —	‿ — —	— — —
2	καὶ συν-ε-πο-	ρεύ-ον-το	αὐ-τῷ οἱ	μα-θη-ταὶ	αὐ-τοῦ καὶ
	‿ — ‿	‿			
	ὄ-χλος πο- λύς.				

OR

Clause	Scansion 2				
	— ‿ ‿ ‿	— —	‿ — —	‿ ‿ —	— — —
2	καὶ συν-ε-πο-	ρεύ-ον-	το αὐ-τῷ	οἱ μα-θη-	ταὶ αὐ-τοῦ
	— ‿ —	‿ ‿			
	καὶ ὄ-χλος πο-λύς.				

Figure 4.15 Possible rhythm sequences of Lk 7:11b

or four syllables as an individual foot? Does he make any attempt to have the individual rhythms follow word boundaries, or does he disregard them? Even if answers to these questions were available, how much do Dionysius' scanning methods cohere with those of other ancient critics? Moreover, with whom would the author-editor of Luke or Acts have agreed? Using the same Lk 7:11 example, attempts to scan the two clauses, Lk 7:11a and 7:11b, appear in Figure 4.14 and in Figure 4.15 respectively.

The initial paean seems obvious, but after that, how are individual rhythms determined? As shown in the upper part of Figure 4.14, is Clause 1 scanned as a paean followed by a hypobacchius, a bacchius, another hypobacchius, a cretic, and three instances of an iambus – or, in lieu of three instances of iambus, an amphibrach and a cretic (˘ — ˘ | — ˘ —)? Equally possible, as shown in the lower part, however, perhaps Clause 1 is scanned as a paean, followed by an iambus, then a molossus, an anapaest, a bacchius, a cretic, and two repetitions of an iambus – or, in lieu of the two repetitions of iambus (˘ — | ˘ —), an amphibrach and the catalectic syllable (˘ — ˘ | —). Because a number of other scansion possibilities also exist, it becomes impossible to know how Luke's author-editor would have scanned Clause 1. A parallel situation occurs in the second clause.

Shown in the upper part of Figure 4.15, is Clause 2 scanned as a paean, followed by a bacchius, then a molossus, a hypobacchius, another molossus, an amphibrach, and the catalectic syllable? Or, as the lower part shows, perhaps it is scanned as a paean, followed by a spondee, a hypobacchius, a cretic, a molossus, another cretic, and finally a pyrrhic. As these examples illustrate, identifying the sequence of individual rhythms in a clause or sentence does not offer enough control or reliability to be considered a tool for an authorship analysis.

A second measure of errancy unacceptable for the present analysis concerns clausulae. As noted in Chapter Three, a clausal ending is where prose rhythms are said to produce the greatest effect on the reader or hearer. Is there any evidence to suggest the author-editor of Luke or Acts intended to create a rhythmic effect at clausal or sentential endings? To find out, the final (four) syllables of a clause or sentence may be examined, for which there are the sixteen possible sequences or categories: (1) ˘˘˘˘, (2) ˘˘˘—, (3) ˘˘—˘ , (4) ˘˘——, (5) ˘—˘˘, (6) ˘—˘—, (7) ˘——˘, (8) ˘———, (9) —˘˘˘, (10) —˘˘—, (11) —˘—˘, (12) —˘——, (13) ——˘˘, (14) ——˘—, (15) ———˘, and (16) ———— . The number of occurrences, however, in each of the sixteen categories in the Luke and Acts SSD is insufficient to conduct a valid chi-square contingency table test. The recommended "expected count" of 5.0 for each category is not satisfied, because there are simply too few occurrences in most final sequences to fulfill the requirement. Therefore, as with dissonance, categories may be combined. In doing so, another circumstance comes to light. Because some ancient critics lengthen the last syllable before a major stop and others do not, it begs the question: would the author-editor of Luke or Acts have lengthened it? The answer is of course unknown. It follows, then, the final syllable of a clause or sentence may remain *undifferentiated*, allowing its quantity to be long or short. The number of sequences or categories thus decreases to eight, where "X" represents the undifferentiated long or short final syllable: (1) ˘˘˘ X, (2) ˘˘ ¯ X, (3) ˘ ¯˘ X, (4) ˘ ¯ ¯ X, (5) ¯˘˘ X, (6) ¯˘ ¯ X, (7) ¯ ¯˘ X, and (8) ¯ ¯ ¯ X. The number of occurrences of these patterns are respectively: (1) Lk: 6; Acts: 4; (2) Lk: 8; Acts: 10; (3) Lk: 12; Acts: 9; (4) Lk: 10; Acts: 6; (5) Lk: 5; Acts: 5; (6) Lk: 16; Acts: 18; (7) Lk: 10; Acts: 12; and (8) Lk: 9; Acts: 5. When the chi-square contingency table test is run, the results will be invalid, because there still exist too many "expected counts" less than 5.0.[62] The evidence is simply insufficient to support or militate against single authorship; perhaps the author-editor of Luke or Acts did not coordinate, repeat, or in any other way organize rhythm patterns at the end of clauses.[63]

Sequences of long syllables

Is it possible to discover whether rhythm played a role at all in the composition of Luke or Acts? Perhaps. A stylistic feature by which early literary critics judge the quality of prose is variety in strings of long syllables. Demetrius, for example, declares when a clause intended to express grandeur is composed almost exclusively of long syllables, it becomes frigid (*Eloc.* 117). Still, he suggests, a quality of forcefulness is produced by many long syllables, which show intensity when combined with succinct phrases. Demetrius believes Plato's compositional elegance comes directly from rhythm, being neither completely metrical nor unmetrical, and his three Platonic examples noticeably avoid long sequences of long syllables (*Eloc.* 183). Dionysius observes long words

---

[62] When the chi-square contingency table test is run, two cells have less than 5.0 for the "expected count" (i.e., in Acts, both ˘˘˘ X and ¯˘˘ X show an expected count of 4.76). Two is 25 percent of eight and thus, when the number of cells holding less than an "expected count" of 5.0 comprise more than 20 percent of the total number of cells, the test is invalid.

[63] Although clausal-ending rhythm patterns do not reveal statistically significant differences between Luke and Acts, it happens that, in certain seams and summaries in Luke, the author-editor appears to repeat clausal-ending rhythm patterns, though not necessarily in every clause. Curiously, the same phenomenon does not hold as noticeably for Acts. For example, both clauses of Lk 1:80 end with ˘ ¯˘ X, where "X" stands for the undifferentiated last syllable whose quantity, as suggested above, may be either long or short. Other Lukan examples include: (1) Lk 3:1–3a, of whose nine clauses four end with ˘ ¯ ¯ X and the last two with ˘ ¯˘ X; (2) Lk 4:14–15, whose three clauses end with ˘˘ ¯ X; (3) Lk 4:40–41, of whose seven clauses four end with ¯˘ ¯ X; and Lk 7:11, both of whose clauses end with ˘ ¯˘ X. In Acts, the most prominent example is 4:32–35, of whose ten clauses five end with ¯˘ ¯ X, and both clauses of Acts 4:4, with ˘ ¯ ¯ X.

with a high proportion of long syllables express an austerity of style (*Comp.* 22). Thus, discussed in the ancient critical theory highlighted in Chapter Three, the stylistic effect of multiple long syllables in sequence is a subject for investigation in the Luke and Acts SSD.

What constitutes a long sequence of long syllables? Although neither the early critics nor A. W. de Groot[64] give an explicit number, it seems reasonable that a sequence of one, two, or three long syllables does not imply "long" length, since in combination with short syllables they form individual rhythmic feet. For example, one long syllable plus two short ones is a dactyl (¯ ˘ ˘) or an anapaest (˘ ˘ ¯); one long syllable plus three short ones a paean (¯ ˘ ˘ ˘ or ˘ ˘ ˘ ¯); two long syllables plus a short one a bacchius (¯ ¯ ˘) or hypobacchius (˘ ¯ ¯); and three long syllables a molossus (¯ ¯ ¯). Moreover, a sequence of four long syllables may not automatically imply "long" length, since four long syllables in a row occur in the collocation of two feet, such as a hypobacchius followed by a bacchius (˘ ¯ ¯ | ¯ ¯ ˘) or a molossus followed by a primus paean (¯ ¯ ¯ | ¯ ˘ ˘ ˘). While it is certainly possible to construct a succession of five or more long syllables, for example a molossus followed by a bacchius (¯ ¯ ¯ | ¯ ¯ ˘) or two molossi (¯ ¯ ¯ | ¯ ¯ ¯), five or more long syllables begin to attract attention vis-à-vis the hearer or reader, who according to the early literary critics could sense the effect, be it pleasing, grand, forceful, or frigid.

It is necessary to analyze long-syllable sequences on a sentence-by-sentence basis, given that in antiquity a writer built up complete thoughts by joining clauses together, be they periodic or not. As a result, rhythms in one clause may affect those in adjacent clauses. Because sentences express complete thoughts, analysis on a sentence-by-sentence basis assures more valid results. As noted in Chapter Three, major and minor stops derive from the punctuation established in the Nestle-Aland *Novum Testamentum Graece*, 27th edition. To recapitulate, Figure 4.1 shows that the Luke SSD consists of 28 whole sentences and 4 partial ones, the Acts SSD of 26 whole sentences and 2 partial ones. Thus, tabulations of "non-long" sequences (i.e., strings of one, two, three, and four long syllables) and "long" sequences (i.e., strings of five, six, seven, eight, nine, and ten) result in the data in Figure 4.16. The *upper* part shows "non-long" sequences and their percentages, the *lower* part the "long" sequences.

---

[64] For a discussion of de Groot, *A Handbook of Antique Prose-Rhythm*, see Chapter Three.

"Non-long" sequences of:	Luke		Acts	
	Number of syllables [number of sequences]	Percentage of all long syllables (=810)	Number of syllables [number of sequences]	Percentage of all long syllables (=717)
One long syllable	158 [158]	19.51	162 [162]	22.59
Two long syllables	202 [101]	24.94	198 [99]	27.62
Three long syllables	141 [47]	17.41	156 [52]	21.76
Four long syllables	120 [30]	14.81	100 [25]	13.95
Total: Syllables [sequences]	621 [336]	76.67	616 [338]	85.91
"Long" sequences of:	Number of syllables [in number of sequences]	Percentage of all long syllables (=810) %	Number of syllables [in number of sequences]	Percentage of all long syllables (=717) %
Five long syllables	75 [15]	9.26	35 [7]	4.88
Six long syllables	60 [10]	7.41	42 [7]	5.86
Seven long syllables	28 [4]	3.46	7 [1]	.98
Eight long syllables	16 [2]	1.98	8 [1]	1.12
Nine long syllables	–	–	9 [1]	1.17
Ten long syllables	10 [1]	1.23	–	–
Total: Syllables [sequences]	189 [32]	23.33	101 [17]	14.09
Grand total: Syllables [Sequences]	810 [368]	100 [100]	717 [345]	100 [100]

Figure 4.16 Number of long syllables, in "long" and "non-long" sequences

"Non-long" sequences

In the Luke SSD, one, two, three, and four long-syllable sequences (the "non-long" sequences) appear 158, 101, 47, and 30 times, respectively. Multiplied out, they comprise 158, 202, 141, and 120 long syllables, or roughly 20, 25, 18, and 15 percent of all long syllables. When combined, they make up 76.67 percent of the long syllables in Luke (i.e., 621/810). In the Acts SSD, the "non-long" sequences appear 162, 99, 52, and 25 times, respectively. Multiplied out, they comprise 162, 198, 156, and 100 long syllables, or roughly 23, 28, 22, and 14 percent of the long syllables.

Added together, they make up 85.91 percent of all long syllables used in Acts (i.e., 616/717).[65]

"Long" sequences

In Luke, strings of five, six, seven, eight, nine, and ten long-syllable sequences (the "long" sequences) appear 15, 10, 4, 2, 0, and 1 times, respectively. When multiplied out, they represent 75, 60, 28, 16, and 10 long syllables for a total of 189, accounting for 23.33 percent of all long syllables (i.e., 189/810). In Acts, the "long" sequences occur 7, 7, 1, 1, and 0 times, respectively, accounting for a total of 101 long syllables, or 14.09 percent (i.e., 101/717). While the number of complete sentences is roughly equivalent in Luke and Acts, 28 and 26, respectively, Luke contains over twice as many five long-syllable sequences as Acts (Lk: 15; Acts: 7) and four times as many seven long-syllable sequences (Lk: 4; Acts: 1). Do these numbers and percentages represent expected differences, inherent in any author-editor's compositional repertoire? Or do they reveal significant distinctiveness? At first glance, not only do similar frequencies of the "non-long" sequences in Luke and Acts appear *not* to be distinctive, but also the differences in number and percentage of "long" sequences in Luke and Acts do *not* seem startling or significant. Yet the use of statistics sometimes reveals what appearances hide.

To visualize the differences, we may format the percentages from Figure 4.16 in a bar graph. Thus, Figure 4.17 compares the *percentage* of long syllables in "long" sequences to the *percentage* of long syllables in "non-long" sequences. In Luke, roughly 75 percent of all long syllables occur in "non-long" sequences, and in Acts, roughly 85 percent. In Luke, "long" sequences account for about 25 percent of all long syllables, and in Acts, about 15 percent. Similarities obtain, as differences *appear* moderate.

Chi-square statistic for sequences of long syllables

As in the case of hiatus or dissonance, to run a valid chi-square contingency table test, prose rhythm needs a null hypothesis (H_0) to test and an alternative hypothesis (H_a), in case the null hypothesis is rejected. For

---

[65] The ratio of long syllables to the total number of syllables – long or short – in the Luke and Acts SSD compares quite similarly; that is, in Luke, of the 1,460 total syllables, 810 or 55.48 percent are long; in Acts, of the 1,333 total syllables, 717 or 53.79 percent are long.

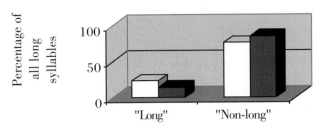

Figure 4.17 Long syllables as a percentage of "long" and "non-long" sequences [white = Luke; shaded = Acts]

long syllables in "long" and "non-long" sequences, the two hypotheses may be stated as follows:

> H_0: *There is no difference in the number of long syllables in "non-long" and "long" sequences in Luke and Acts beyond normal, random variability.*

> H_a: *There is a difference in the number of long syllables in "non-long" and "long" sequences in Luke and Acts beyond normal, random variability.*

Figure 4.18 shows the output of the chi-square test. The P-Value is 0.000, highly significant statistically. This result demands rejection of the null hypothesis with an extraordinarily high level of confidence; hence, the observed differences in the number of long syllables in "long" and "non-long" sequences may not be explained by coincidence. Another reason is required for the actual, intrinsic, and material difference.

The key difference lies in the number of long syllables in sequences of five to ten syllables in length. It appears that either, intentionally or unintentionally, the author-editor of Luke strings together more protracted long-syllable sequences than the author-editor of Acts, or the author-editor of Acts deliberately avoids extensive, lengthy sequences of long syllables. In the first case, the author-editor may have not paid attention to syllable quantity at all, or, if he did, perhaps he intended to infuse the prose with a particular quality or attribute. In the second case, the author-editor may have intentionally avoided extended sequences of long syllables for stylistic reasons or on the basis of an unknown rationale. In either case, statistics reveal highly significant differences that are not explainable by normal, expected variation in the stylistic repertoire of one author-editor.

```
Expected counts are printed below observed counts.
Chi-square contributions are printed below expected counts.

          Number      Number
            in          in
          "Long"     "Non-Long"    Total

  Lk        189         621         810
          153.83      656.17
          8.040       1.885

  Ac        101         616         717
          136.17      580.83
          9.083       2.129

Total       290        1237        1527

Chi-Sq = 21.138, DF = 1, P-Value = 0.000
```

Figure 4.18 Chi-square for no. of long syllables in "long" and "non-long" sequences

In sum, stylometric analysis of prose rhythm in Luke and Acts presents us with two difficulties and a success. First, it was shown that the rhythms in a clause or sentence rhythms may not be scanned with confidence because the early critics' methods are virtually unknown today. Second, analysis of rhythmic patterns at the end of clauses, especially in the final four syllables, returns inconclusive results, because statistically speaking the data are insufficient to provide valid evidence. Third, and most intriguing, analyzing the number of long syllables in various sequences in Luke and Acts nets significant evidence: namely, when compared with each other, it appears that either the author-editor of Luke intentionally concatenates long syllables into lengthy sequences or else pays little or no attention to them, or the author-editor of Acts purposely avoids composing with lengthy sequences of long syllables. In either case, statistical testing reveals highly significant differences, not explained by normal, expected variation in the stylistic range of one author-editor. It now remains to look at structural elements.

Sentence structure analysis

In prose composition criticism, the term "structural" recalls a variety of meanings about how words create a sentence. Taking a cue from the ancient critics, the term "structural" here means the syntactic elements comprising a sentence. Sensitivity to the arrangement of syntactic elements played a role in fulfilling the ancient hearer's or reader's expectations; for example, segues from one clause or sentence to the next either enhanced or compromised a hearer's or reader's understanding and pleasure.

Sentence structure problematics

Although less arbitrary than prose rhythm vis-à-vis stylometric analysis, problematic to sentence structure analysis are two conventions that do not fit statistical requirements: first, the ordered arrangement of "subject" and "verb" in a clause or sentence; and second, the genitive absolute.

In the case of the former, three categories of arrangement were examined: (1) Subject-Verb, where the subject is explicit; (2) Verb-Subject, also with an explicit subject; and (3) Verb-only, where the subject is implied in the verb. Indeed, various scholars have dealt with this stylistic convention. In his comprehensive study on syntax order, Hjalmar Frisk selects representative passages from Herodotus, Thucydides, Xenophon, Plato, Antiphon, Lysias, Demosthenes, Polybius, Plutarch, Philostratus, the gospel of Matthew, and "official" language (*Kanzleisprache*)[66] in order to analyze "subject-predicate" and "object-predicate" arrangements in main and dependent clauses. In the supplementary analysis of temporal and conditional clauses, Frisk searches the entirety of the other three New Testament gospels (Mark, Luke, John) and Acts of the Apostles. He finds a certain distinction between Luke and Acts in terms of object-predicate (OP) and predicate-object (PO) order (i.e., OP: Luke, 29 percent; Acts, 44 percent; PO: Luke 71 percent; Acts 56 percent).[67] It is unclear precisely how Frisk chooses the non-biblical samples, however. Different portions of Herodotus are used to analyze the subject-predicate arrangements (I.6–36; II.151–176; III.118–141; IV.118–142; V.82–102; VII.1–9, 121–137; VIII.113–144) and the object-predicate arrangements (I.6–41; II.151–180; III.118–149; IV.59–75, 118–142; V.69–102; VI.42–82; VII.1–9, 121–137; VIII.107–144; IX.1–30, 76–92),[68] yet the biblical material remains the same in both cases. Without analyzing precisely the same data, one runs the risk of skewing the results. This is not to imply a preferential outcome in Frisk's study, rather it is to suggest that rigorous data controls must always be the rule. In other scholarship on Greek word order in the New Testament synoptics and

---

[66] Hjalmar Frisk, *Studien zur griechischen Wortstellung*, Göteborgs Högskolas Årsskrift 39 (Gothenburg: Wettergren & Kerbers Förlag, 1933), pp. 16f.
[67] Ibid., pp. 28, 30f.   [68] Ibid., pp. 16f.

Acts, Eduard Schwyzer lays out the order of subject-verb in subordinate clauses wherein the verb tends to follow the pronoun or conjunction immediately rather than appearing elsewhere in the clause.[69] Providing a set of percentages for Matthew only, Schwyzer suggests the other synoptic gospels and Acts produce similar percentages, although he does not offer them. The implication is, therefore, no noticeable distinction exists between Luke and Acts. Although Greek word order has been studied by these and other scholars, overall agreement is less than evident.[70]

In the present analysis, the word order convention is problematic owing to clausal division and statistical requirements. Based on the clausal division shown in the Appendix, where partitions depend largely, though not exclusively, on major or minor stops, it is possible for more than one category to fit a clause, or conversely, one clause may fit into multiple categories, a statistical *non sequitur*. There are 7 clauses in Luke (Lk 1:4, 4:40b; 6:19b; 7:11a; 8:1a; 19:47b, 48a) and 4 clauses in Acts (Acts 1:2; 2:45b; 4:35b; 5:16c) containing both a main and a dependent part, due to the caution with which clausal divisions are determined. Dividing one of these full clauses into two to analyze structural elements becomes awkward for several reasons:

1. The dependent part occurs in the *middle* of the full clause, or in other words the main part serves as a "bookend" around the dependent part (Lk 1:4; 4:40b; Acts 1:2). Thus, ὧν κατηχήθης occurs in the middle of Lk 1:4 (ἵνα ἐπιγνῷς περὶ ὧν κατηχήθης λόγων τὴν ἀσφάλειαν), and οὓς ἐξελέξατο occurs in the middle of Acts 1:2 (ἄχρι ἧς ἡμέρας ἐντειλάμενος τοῖς ἀποστόλοις διὰ πνεύματος ἁγίου οὓς ἐξελέξατο ἀνελήμφθη). The middle or dependent part may not be simply lifted off without affecting the syntactic arrangement, as well as euphony and rhythm.

2. The main and dependent parts form an idiomatic expression not easily divided into two clauses (Lk 7:11a; 8:1a), that is, Καὶ ἐγένετο . . . ἐπορεύθη (Lk 7:11a) and Καὶ ἐγένετο . . . καὶ αὐτὸς διώδευεν (Lk 8:1a).

3. The dependent part seems too closely attached to the main part to be split off for the sake of making two clauses (Lk 19:48a;

---

[69] Eduard Schwyzer, *Griechische Grammatik: auf der Grundlage von Karl Brugmanns griechischer Grammatik*, vol. II (Munich: C. H. Beck'sche Verlagsbuchhandlung, 1950), pp. 695f.

[70] See also the vintage article, Eberling, "Some Statistics on the Order of Words in Greek."

Acts 2:45b; 4:35b). For instance, τὸ τί ποιήσωσιν in Lk 19:48a (καὶ οὐχ εὕρισκον τὸ τί ποιήσωσιν), or ἄν τις χρείαν εἶχεν in Acts 4:35b (διεδίδετο δὲ ἑκάστῳ καθότι ἄν τις χρείαν εἶχεν).

4.   Most problematic is that statistical testing results will be invalid when a clause fits into more than one category. In Lk 6:19b: ὅτι δύναμις παρ' αὐτοῦ ἐξήρχετο καὶ ἰᾶτο πάντας, both the Subject-Verb order (δύναμις . . . ἐξήρχετο) and the Verb-only order (ἰᾶτο) pertain. Allowing two categories of word order to apply to one clause nullifies the chi-square contingency table test. Further, a split subject may occur on both sides of the verb, as in Lk 19:47b: οἱ δὲ ἀρχιερεῖς καὶ οἱ γραμματεῖς ἐζήτουν αὐτὸν ἀπολέσαι καὶ οἱ πρῶτοι τοῦ λαοῦ, or in Acts 5:16c, οἵτινες ἐθεραπεύοντο ἅπαντες. In these examples, both the Subject-Verb category and Verb-Subject category apply to one clause, thereby invalidating the data statistically.

Without arbitrarily chopping up certain clauses into two or more subclauses, it is unclear how to classify them for a statistical analysis. Indeed, where should the "chopping" stop, and how is a "total" of possible occurrences confirmed and validated? The aim of statistics is of course to avoid a "fishing expedition."[71]

The second sentence structure convention that does not fit statistical requirements is the genitive absolute construction. In his study of Luke and Acts style outlined in Chapter One, Nigel Turner analyzes the use of genitives absolute in roughly equal passages taken from the infancy narrative, the Lukan version of "Q," the Markan sections of Luke, "Special L," the first part of Acts (1–15), the second part of Acts (16–28), and the "We"-Sections.[72] He compares the frequency of the genitive absolute

---

[71] Deserving of future study are two types of difference in the Luke and Acts SSD in clauses with finite verbs: first, occurrences of the Predicate-only category appear significantly more often in Luke than Acts (Lk: 50 percent; Acts: 33 percent); and, second, occurrences of the Predicate-Subject category appear considerably more frequently in Acts than Luke (Lk: 15 percent; Acts: 27 percent). Totals for finite verbs only, in contrast to including infinitival and participial constructions, allow a more valid, reliable, and controlled data set.

[72] Turner, "The Style of Luke-Acts," p. 59. The passages, each of approximately 260 lines of Nestle-Aland, include Lk 1:5–2:52 for the infancy narrative; 6:20–7:10; 7:18–35; 9:57–62; 10:2–15, 21–24; 11:2–4, 9–26, 29–36 for Luke's version of "Q"; 8:4–9:50 for the Markan section of Luke; 15:1–16:15; 16:19–31; 17:7–21; 18:1–14; 19:1–27 for "Special L"; Acts 3:1–5:42 for the first part of Acts; 17:1–19:40 for the second part of Acts; and 16:10–18; 20:5–15; 21:1–18; 27:1–28:16 for the "We"-Sections; see Turner, "The Style of Luke-Acts," p. 45.

	Luke and Acts SSD (75 verses)	Luke SSD (40 verses)	Acts SSD (35 verses)
Frequency	8	6	2
Ratio of genitive absolute to verses	1:9	1:7	1:18

Figure 4.19 Genitives absolute in Luke and Acts SSD

in these data samples with that in a variety of LXX and intertestamental books, and concludes that in the "We"-Sections the frequency of use exceeds that in the LXX, as well as the rest of the New Testament. In fact, as Turner observes, it actually meets classical standards. By examining samples from the Markan sections of Luke, "Special L," the first part of Acts (1–15), and the second part of Acts (16–28), Turner computes the ratio of genitives absolute to verses, and the result is one genitive absolute occurrence in 17 verses, or 1:17. In the present analysis of the Luke and Acts SSD, a different proportion results. The genitive absolute occurs six times in Luke (Lk 3:1–3 *quater*; 4:40; 8:4a) and twice in Acts (Acts 5:15; 6:1a). To compare roughly in terms of verses as Turner does, the ratios are shown in Figure 4.19. That four of the six genitives absolute in Luke come from Lk 3:1–3 mitigates the final ratio, but the Luke and Acts SSD ratio of 1:9 is roughly half of Turner's ratio of 1:17.

Most problematic is that the genitives absolute evidence does not meet the requirements for a chi-square contingency table test, because the "expected counts" are too small, less than 5.0; the data is simply insufficient.

Final syntactic element

Apart from subject and verb word order and genitives absolute, what *may* be analyzed is the syntactic element in the location of prominence, at the end of a sentence or clause. Although the beginning of a clause or sentence carries weight, Aristotle and Demetrius suggest the end bears greater significance.[73] Will the analysis of final syntactic elements in the Luke and Acts SSD reveal a significant difference between Luke and Acts?

---

[73] E.g., Ar. *Rh.* 3.9.1–4; Demetr. *Eloc.* 11, 18.

Final syntactic element	Luke SSD	Percentage of total clauses: 76	Acts SSD	Percentage of total clauses: 69
Prepositional phrase	38	50.00	23	33.33
Subject	12	15.79	8	11.59
Direct object	9	11.84	10	14.49
Finite/main verb	7	9.21	13	18.84
Indirect object	0	0.00	6	8.70
Other	10	13.16	9	13.04

Figure 4.20 Ending syntactic element

Figure 4.20 shows the raw data, organized by category, for the final syntactic elements in the clauses of the Luke and Acts SSD. In the order of most frequently occurring in Luke, the categories include: (1) prepositional phrase; (2) subject; (3) direct object; (4) finite/main verb; (5) indirect object; and (6) other, which includes all categories whose number of occurrences was too small to be considered separately, namely, vocative, dative of respect, dative of means, circumstantial participle I (i.e., agreement with the subject or object of the leading verb), infinitival clause, circumstantial participle II (i.e., genitive absolute), and adverb.

Of particular note in Figure 4.20 is the difference between Luke and Acts in the number of final prepositional phrases: 38 or 50 percent of the total in the Luke SSD, and 23 or 33.33 percent of the total in Acts. In other words, Luke ends with a prepositional phrase half the time, Acts a third. Note that a final prepositional phrase may be *simple*, as in Lk 1:80b (πρὸς τὸν Ἰσραήλ) or Acts 1:3a (ἐν πολλοῖς τεκμηρίοι), where the preposition is followed by its substantive and perhaps a modifier; or it may be quite complex because of embedding, such as in Lk 1:1a (περὶ τῶν πεπληροφορημένων ἐν ἡμῖν πραγμάτων), in which the ending prepositional phrase, περὶ . . . πραγμάτων, includes the embedding of the participial construction πεπληροφορημένων and its modifying prepositional phrase ἐν ἡμῖν. In addition to prepositional phrases, a subject, direct object, or indirect object may also contain embedding and thus exhibit more complex syntactic structure. Also noteworthy in Figure 4.20 are the differences in the final finite/main verb. Luke shows 7 instances or 9.21 percent, and Acts 13 or 18.84 percent. Acts is thus twice as likely as

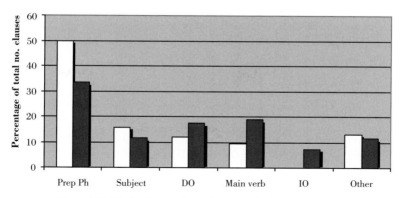

Figure 4.21 Vertical bar graph: ending syntactic element [white = Luke; shaded = Acts]

Luke to end a clause or sentence with a finite/main verb.[74] Still another difference shown in Figure 4.20 concerns a final indirect object: the Luke SSD shows 0 occurrences, and Acts 6, or 8.70 percent of the total. To help readers visualize all the differences, Figure 4.21 presents the percentages in bar graph format, where abbreviations include: "Prep Ph" for prepositional phrase, "DO" for direct object, and "IO" for indirect object.

Taken together, the differences *prima facie* appear to be considerable; the frequency of each category, especially ending prepositional phrases, finite/main verbs, and indirect objects, indicate clear differences. The chi-square contingency table test will determine whether the differences are statistically significant.

Chi-square statistic for ending syntactic element

As in the case of hiatus, dissonance, and prose rhythm, to run a valid chi-square contingency table test, a null hypothesis (H_0) and an alternative hypothesis (H_a) are needed. For ending syntactic elements, the two hypotheses may be stated as follows:

---

[74] Note that an ending participle in periphrasis fits in this category of finite/main verb, for example, in Lk 5:16 (αὐτὸς δὲ ἦν ὑποχωρῶν ἐν ταῖς ἐρήμοις καὶ προσευχόμενος) and 21:37a (Ἦν δὲ τὰς ἡμέρας ἐν τῷ ἱερῷ διδάσκων). In contrast, a participle as the final verb in a genitive absolute does not fit the category, because the participle is not part of a finite verb construction, for example in Lk 3:1e (καὶ Λυσανίου τῆς Ἀβιληνῆς τετρααρχοῦντος); so also the final participle in Lk 3:18a (Πολλὰ μὲν οὖν καὶ ἕτερα παρακαλῶν) and 19:48b (ὁ λαὸς γὰρ ἅπας ἐξεκρέματο αὐτοῦ ἀκούων), both circumstantial participles.

```
Expected counts are printed below observed counts.
Chi-square contributions are printed below expected counts.

        Prep Ph      S      DO      Vb      IO    Other   Total
   Lk        38     12       9       7       0       10      76
          31.97  10.48    9.96   10.48    3.14     9.96
          1.136  0.220   0.092   1.157   3.145    0.000

   Ac        23      8      10      13       6        9      69
          29.03   9.52    9.04    9.52    2.86     9.04
          1.252  0.242   0.102   1.274   3.464    0.000

Total        61     20      19      20       6       19     145

Chi-Sq = 12.084, DF = 5, P-Value = 0.034
2 cells with expected counts less than 5.†
```

†The two cells in the IO category do not meet the conservative requirement of an "expected count" of at least 5.0. However, according to statistical experts, when fewer than 20 percent of the cells fail to meet this requirement, the test should still be valid. Because the number of data cells in this chi-square test is 12, the test should still be valid when there are 2 cells with expected counts less than 5.0.

Figure 4.22 Chi-square output for ending syntactic elements

H_0: *There is no difference in the ending syntactic element of a clause or sentence in Luke and Acts beyond normal, random variability.*

H_a: *There is a difference in the ending syntactic element of a clause or sentence in Luke and Acts beyond normal, random variability.*

The output generated by the chi-square contingency table test is shown in Figure 4.22, where additional abbreviations include: "S" for subject and "Vb" for finite/main verb. As already noted, "Other" is a composite category, as not all types of syntactic elements occur in sufficient numbers to satisfy the "expected count" requirement of 5.0.

The *P*-Value is 0.034, a statistically significant number, because it means the differences between Luke and Acts in ending syntactic elements do not result from random variation; hence, the null hypothesis is rejected with a 95 percent level of confidence and the differences must be explained another way.[75] As argued, the statistically significant differences observed appear to be best explained by different authorship.

[75] One hypothesizes that apart from random variability there should be no difference between Luke and Acts in finding a prepositional phrase at the end of a clause or sentence, i.e., the null hypothesis. The chi-square contingency table test results show otherwise. Differences are, in fact, highly significant statistically:

Before, however, pulling together all the evidence for this authorship analysis, one more prose compositional element must be analyzed, namely, the manner in which clauses and sentences are interwoven. How is the transition from one to the next fashioned?

Clause and sentence segues

A well-studied difference between Luke and Acts is clause or sentence transition; that is, the use of connective devices such as post-positive particles (e.g., μέν, μέν οὖν, δέ, τε, τε καί), on the one hand, and the paratactic καί, on the other. Aristotle describes the continuous style (λέξις εἰρομένη), the most ancient (Arist. *Rh.* 3.9.1), as sentences joined by connecting particles and stopping only when the sense is complete (*Rh.* 3.9.1–2). He also advises adding connecting particles in their natural order and in proximity to each other, e.g., μέν . . . δέ and ἐγώ μέν . . . ὁ δέ (*Rh.* 3.5.2). By contrast, Demetrius seems more flexible on the strict match-up of connective pairs, "since there is something trivial about exact precision" (*Eloc.* 53).[76]

As noted in Chapter One, the differences between Luke and Acts in the use of τε and μέν (in two of its forms, μέν *solitarium* and μέν οὖν) form part of an earlier challenge to single authorship by Albert C. Clark. Indirectly supporting Clark is classicist J. D. Denniston, who, although he does not address the Greek New Testament, observes that τε as a single connective is "mainly confined to the historians . . . and Plato" rather than

```
Expected counts are printed below observed counts.
Chi-square contributions are printed below expected counts.

          Prep   No Prep   Total
   Lk       38        38      76
         31.97     44.03
         1.136     0.825

   Ac       23        46      69
         29.03     39.67
         1.252     0.909

Total       61        84     145

Chi-Sq = 4.122, DF = 1, P-Value = 0.042
```

The *P*-Value is 0.042, which indicates we can conclude with over a 95 percent level of confidence some other factor besides normal variability is at work.

[76] μικροπρεπὲς γὰρ ἡ ἀκρίβεια.

	Post-positive/ other particle	Paratactic καί	None
Luke	20	33	23
(Percentage of clauses with a connective device: 53)	(38%)	(62%)	
[Percentage of total clauses: 76]	[26%]	[43%]	[30%]†
Acts	37	16	16
(Percentage of clauses with a connective device: 53)	(70%)	(30%)	
[Percentage of total clauses: 69]	[54%]	[23%]	[23%]

† Due to decimal rounding differences, the "percentage of total clauses" percentages add up to 99 percentage rather than 100%.

Figure 4.23   Post-positive/other particle vs. paratactic καί

the orators.[77] Henry Cadbury observes that the writer "Luke" prefers δέ to καί (e.g., Lk 3:21; 4:43; 5:22, 33, 34),[78] and Joseph Fitzmyer notes that "Luke" frequently replaces καί with δέ or τε.[79] Numerical differences between the Luke and Acts SSD in the use of post-positive/other particles and the paratactic καί are shown in Figure 4.23. Not surprisingly, the numbers and percentages in Luke and Acts are nearly inversely proportional.

Luke shows 20 post-positive/other particles, constituting 38 percent of the clauses containing any kind of connective device and 26 percent of all clauses. Acts shows 37 post-positive/other particles, representing 70 percent of the clauses containing a connective device and 54 percent of all clauses. In clauses with a connective device, Acts is almost twice as likely as Luke to show a post-positive/other particle (Lk: 38 percent; Acts: 70 percent). Conversely, Luke is roughly twice as likely as Acts to show the paratactic καί in clauses containing a connective device (Lk: 62 percent;

[77] J. D. Denniston, *The Greek Particles* (Oxford: Clarendon Press, 1959), p. 497. A quick scan of τε in Acts shows that a majority of occurrences does not appear in the speech material.

[78] Cadbury, *Style and Literary Method*, p. 143. Other examples from Cadbury include: Lk 6:1, 2, 7, 8, 9; 8:10, 24, 25, 27, 28, 30, 33, 35, 54; 9:6, 7, 14, 16, 19, 25; 18:15, 31, 32; 20:5, 9; 22:54; 23:3, 34, 38, 45; 24:3.

[79] Fitzmyer, *Luke I–IX*, p. 108. Fitzmyer cites Eduard Schweizer, "Eine hebraisierende Sonderquelle des Lukas," *TZ* 6 (1950), 166 note 18. In the case of τε, Schweizer suggests one "Lukan" use in Luke (Lk 24:20) and twelve in Acts (Acts 15:39; 19:2, 3, 6, 10, 11; 28:23; in the "We"-Sections: 16:13; 27:1, 3, 5, 8).

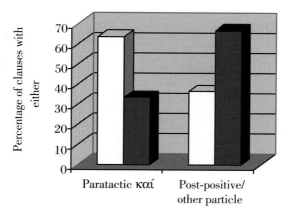

Figure 4.24 Vertical bar graph of post-positive/other particle use vs. paratactic καί [white-Luke; shaded-Acts]

Acts: 30 percent). The "None" column contains the number of clauses without a connective device; this number must be included in order to conduct a valid statistical test. To visualize the differences, Figure 4.24 shows in bar graph format the inverse proportionality of Luke and Acts. The chi-square contingency table test will specify to what degree the differences are significant.

Chi-square statistic for clause and sentence segues

Following the standard procedure for prior chi-square contingency table tests, both null and alternative hypotheses are required. They may be stated as follows:

> H_0: *There is no difference between Luke and Acts in the use of post-positive/other particles and the paratactic καί beyond normal, random variability.*

> H_a: *There is a difference between Luke and Acts in the use of post-positive/other particles and the paratactic καί beyond normal, random variability.*

The output of the chi-square contingency table test for clause and sentence segues is shown in Figure 4.25. The *P*-Value is 0.003, which means the null hypothesis is rejected with a 99 percent level of confidence in favor of the alternative hypothesis; thus, the differences between Luke and Acts *must* be explained by a reason other than random variability.

```
Expected counts are printed below observed counts.
Chi-square contributions are printed below expected counts.
        PP/Other  Paratactic   None   Total
          Part       Kai
  Lk        20        33        23      76
          29.88     25.68     20.44
          3.265     2.085     0.320

  Ac        37        16        16      69
          27.12     23.32     18.56
          3.596     2.296     0.353

Total       57        49        39     145

  Chi-Sq = 11.914, DF = 2, P-Value = 0.003
```

Figure 4.25 Chi-square output for post-positive/other particle and paratactic καί

Convention	*P*-Value	Statistical result
Hiatus	0.001	Highly significant
Dissonance	0.004	Highly significant
Long syllables in long sequences	0.000	Highly significant
Final syntax	0.034	Significant
Clause/sentence segues	0.003	Highly significant

Figure 4.26 Recapitulation of *P*-Values

One or two intrinsic differences between Luke and Acts do not argue forcefully for the explanation of different authorship; but when viewed all together, the tests appear to make a strong case. Pooling the results of each chi-square contingency table test allows for a broad prose compositional interpretation, one that not surprisingly generates more questions than answers.

Interpreting the differences: Is there a "big picture"?

The preceding tests reveal some unexpected differences with regard to five prose compositional conventions: hiatus, dissonance, long-syllable sequences, ending syntactic element, and clause and sentence segues. In the chi-square contingency table tests, the resulting *P*-Values recapitulated in Figure 4.26 show that *differences fall outside the range of normal variability expected in one author-editor's prose compositional style.*

P-Values in the tests of hiatus (0.001) and dissonance (0.004) indicate that the differences between Luke and Acts are "highly significant," and therefore the null hypothesis is rejected with a 99 percent level of confidence. The normal, expected variation inherent to single authorship simply does not hold, because *the differences fall outside the most probable statistical range allowed for normal variability.* In the case of the number of syllables in long-syllable sequences and sentence segues, the *P*-Values of 0.000 and 0.003, respectively are again "highly significant" statistically, more than sufficient to reject the null hypothesis. Finally, the *P*-Value in the test of final syntactic element (0.034) also indicates that the differences between Luke and Acts are statistically significant, and the null hypothesis is rejected with a 95 percent level of confidence.

While statistics cannot prove with absolute certainty, they can confirm beyond a reasonable doubt. When stylometric testing contradicts the foundations of a hypothesis that has been assumed true, then statistics matter, and they demand scholarly interpretation. Evidence of authorial unity in the seams and summaries of Luke and Acts, identified by a selected but representative group of scholars in Chapter Two, exhibit distinct patterns of the prose compositional conventions identified in Chapter Three, and the differences when measured statistically produce results that in every case are significant or highly significant. In light of the present analysis of the Luke and Acts SSD, what conclusions may we draw?

Euphony and prose rhythm

That hiatus, dissonance, and long-syllable sequences result in highly significant differences may indicate intentional sensitivity to euphonious composition on the part of the author-editor. Based on these conventions, three areas of investigation come to light. First, L-L hiatus, the most distinctive type, is used or allowed twice as frequently in Luke as Acts (see Figure 4.4). Yet puzzling is the fact that the eloquent Lukan preface (Lk 1:1–4) includes no L-L hiatus, but the less sophisticated Acts preface (Acts 1:1–5) includes five, four of which occur in the first two verses. Did the anonymous author-editor deliberately avoid L-L hiatus in the Lukan preface but make a point to use it elsewhere, in fact, twice as frequently as in Acts? Further, is it significant that, except for two inter-word L-L hiatus occurrences in Acts (Acts 11:21: καὶ ἦν; 12:24: θεοῦ ηὔξανεν), there are no instances in the second half of the Acts SSD (i.e., in Acts 9:31; 11:24b; 12:25; 16:5; 19:20)? Second, regarding dissonance, the fact is, except for two categories in Figure 4.10, dissonance is used or allowed in Acts from 30 percent to 50 percent or more frequently than in Luke (see Figure 4.10). Compared with Luke, then, does the fact that Acts attests the intra-word "ντ" cluster almost twice as often (Lk: 20 or 1.35 percent; Acts: 37 or 2.74 percent) imply perhaps a greater number of *participles* in Acts, wherein the "ντ" cluster would naturally appear? To answer, the "ντ" cluster in participles occurs 16 times in Acts and 10 times in Luke, but in percentage terms, the greater use of participles in Acts is *not* indicated, since 50 percent of the "ντ" clusters in Luke are participial constructions, but only 43 percent in Acts. (Most of the remaining "ντ" clusters occur in various forms of ἅπας and πᾶς.) Yet, we must wonder whether dissonance is used or allowed in Acts more than in Luke to further a stylistic purpose. Moreover, in regard to the "νκ" cluster, might the paratactic καί in Luke account for the κ? In certain cases (Lk 4:14–15; 5:17; 8:1–3), καί in parataxis exists but does not play an overwhelmingly key role. For example, in Lk 4:14–15 two of the three "νκ" clusters result from parataxis, in 5:17 two of four, and in 8:1–3 only one of six. Third, in the case of prose rhythm, Luke contains roughly twice as many "long" sequences as Acts (Lk: 32; Acts: 17), or roughly 25 and 15 percent respectively (see Figure 4.16). The elegant Lukan preface (Lk 1:1–4) shows two strings with five long syllables and one with six, but the Acts preface only one string of five. Other seams and summaries show elevated numbers of long-syllable sequences, for example, Lk 6:17–19; 8:1–3; 9:51; 19:47–48; Acts 4:32–35; 5:12–15(16). Are these more (or less!) carefully crafted than others with fewer?

Ending syntactic element, and clause and sentence segues

Other key differences beg questions. As seen in Figure 4.20, why does Luke's author-editor favor ending clauses or sentences with prepositional phrases 50 percent of the time while the Acts' author-editor favors it only somewhat (33 percent), preferring final finite verbs and indirect objects over 25 percent of the time to Luke's roughly 7 percent? Does this variety in Acts imply a distinctly more sophisticated style or not? The answer remains unclear. Lastly, although differentiating Luke and Acts, the inversely proportional use of the paratactic καί and post-positive particles in the Luke and Acts SSD respectively confirms scholars' long-standing and well-established agreement on transitions between clauses and sentences.

It is now evident that no facile compositional "big picture" emerges. Indeed, many more questions than answers arise. More particularly, *compared with Acts*, the compositional picture of Luke reveals an author-editor who uses or allows significantly more hiatus, long sequences of long syllables, final prepositional phrases, and the paratactic καί; or conversely, *compared with Luke*, the author-editor of Acts appears to avoid the deliberate use of these conventions. Furthermore, *compared with Luke*, the compositional picture of Acts reveals an author-editor who uses or allows significantly more dissonance, finite/main verbs in the final position of a clause or sentence, and post-positive particle or other connectives instead of the paratactic καί; conversely, *compared with Acts*, the author-editor of Luke appears to ignore or avoid assiduously the use of these conventions.

To sum up the entire analysis, stylometric testing has shown beyond a reasonable doubt the differences between Luke and Acts are not explainable by the normal variation expected in the prose compositional style of a unitary author. *These differences actually differentiate Luke and Acts.*

5

FINAL CONSIDERATIONS AND FUTURE DIRECTIONS

Among the writings of the New Testament one book occupies a special place, a fact which often receives too little attention. This is the Book of Acts, which tradition attributes to Luke, the author of the third Gospel; *there are some things to be said against this tradition*, but far more in favour of it, so that we may call the author by the name of Luke [emphasis added].[1]

Final considerations

The authorial unity of Luke and Acts is little argued in scholarly circles, since virtually everyone unanimously agrees the external and internal evidence confirm single authorship. That the external evidence is from the latter part of the second century and beyond or that the internal evidence tends to favor similarities over differences does not receive much attention.

The current project was undertaken to re-examine the evidence for the authorial unity of Luke and Acts by analyzing their seams and summaries in light of ancient prose composition criticism and modern stylometric methods. The statement to be tested may be expressed thus: *If the common authorship of Luke and Acts is true, their seams and summaries, genre-neutral text, will reveal the same or similar prose compositional features*. If differences of a statistically significant or highly significant nature are discovered, single authorship may, or better, must, be called into question. Given this, a three-stage analysis evolved as the most appropriate methodological approach.

1.   Considering the knotty source questions attached to Luke and Acts composition, *identify text that Luke and Acts scholars agree derives from the hand of the author-editor*. Seams and

---

[1] Dibelius, "First Christian Historian," p. 123.

summaries, the obvious choice, occupy a compositional stratum unaffected by traditional forms and are written later than the pericope or complexes of pericopes they connect.

2. In view of the prose compositional conventions familiar to many who learned to write Hellenistic Greek, *consult the works of key ancient literary critics to cull actual examples of compositional elements whose patterns may be analyzed in the seams and summaries.* The selected critical works comprise: (a) Aristotle *Rhetorica* 3; (b) Demetrius *De elocutione*; (c) Dionysius of Halicarnassus *De compositione verborum* and other critical essays; and (d) Longinus *De sublimitate.*

3. Using the results of the first two stages, *detect the presence or absence of prose compositional conventions in the Luke and Acts seams and summaries by tabulating and comparing patterns and then testing them with the chi-square contingency table test in the MINITAB statistical software.* Discovered were statistically significant differences in prose compositional patterns precisely where one would most expect a unitary author-editor to expose his own stylistic preferences, that is, in the seams and summaries. Because the patterns in one book's seams and summaries do not repeat the compositional preferences found in the other book – a set of circumstances one reasonably expects in the case of single authorship – it is confirmed with a high degree of confidence and beyond reasonable doubt that the compositional elements analyzed herein actually differentiate Luke and Acts.

The net result of this authorship analysis challenges the prevailing hypothesis of authorial unity held by a majority of biblical scholars who, it seems, accept it on the grounds of largely uncontested tradition. If different authorship were true, it would mean revamping certain entrenched historical and literary paradigms.

Implications of different authorship

The single authorship hypothesis has so dominated research that any doubt about the veracity of the hypothesis would require a transformation of the existing mindset. To be sure, a call to consider the *possibility* of different authorship may be resisted in many circles. So, what are the implications of different authorship? Three present themselves immediately.

The dating of Acts

Different authorship calls for reconsidering how the two books came to be linked together. Since neither a sole provenance nor a close chronological distance for the composition of the two books may be assumed, the circumstances surrounding their pre-connection status become even murkier. If Luke may no longer be used as a baseline, the dating of Acts is therefore affected. By and large, scholars date Luke and Acts to approximately the same time, giving priority to Luke; yet exceptions do exist. With regard to chronological proximity, Sir John Hawkins, discussed in Chapter One, argues for a significant time lapse between the composition of Luke and Acts. Regarding the question of priority, Henry G. Russell argues for Acts priority based on the abrupt ending, in which Paul is awaiting trial.[2] Further, scholars such as Joseph Tyson[3] and Richard Pervo[4] now argue convincingly for dating Acts to the second century CE. If Acts is that late, and if Luke was written first, as is generally believed, in the 80s, an obvious question must be answered: How *does* one account for the striking parallels in content, sequence, and theme between Luke and Acts? After all, the traditional single authorship hypothesis commands a far-reaching axis of scholarly assent and respect. Charles Talbert, for example, finds thirty-two content and sequence parallels between Luke and Acts; Joseph Fitzmyer details theological parallels in his commentaries on Luke and Acts; other scholars highlight coherences as well.[5] If different authorship is true, did the author-editor of Acts consult the gospel of Luke? The answer must be either no or yes. If no, Luke and Acts likely developed along completely separate trajectories until someone eventually noticed the two books' similarities and hinged them together, the position held by Albert C. Clark.[6] If yes, there exist two scenarios:

---

[2] Russell, "Which was Written First, Luke or Acts?" 171.

[3] Joseph B. Tyson, "The Date of Acts: A Reconsideration," *Forum* 5 (2002), 49, dates Acts to a second-century, post-Marcionite date. See also Tyson, "Why Dates Matter: The Case of the Acts of the Apostles," *The Fourth R* 18 (2005), 8–14.

[4] Richard I. Pervo, "Dating Acts," *Forum* 5 (2002), 53, dates Acts to ca. 110–120 CE. For an extensive and persuasive treatment, see Pervo, *Dating Acts*.

[5] Charles Talbert, *Literary Patterns*, pp. 15ff.; Joseph Fitzmyer, *Luke I–IX*, pp. 143–258. For details of other theological-thematic parallels between Luke and Acts, see Chapter One.

[6] Clark, *Acts of the Apostles*, p. 408. According to Clark, the linguistic evidence and the prologues to Theophilus point in different directions:

> If the linguistic proof is decisive, suspicion must fall on the prologue to Acts. *Can it be that in the early days of the Church someone who noticed the similarity in style, which undoubtedly exists, between Acts and Lk. as opposed to Mt., Mk., and Jn., added to Acts a prologue similar to that in Lk., in order to help out the identification? I see no other solution* [emphasis added].

Besides composing independently, either the author-editor of Acts used *only* Luke, or he used Luke *and* other extant traditions. With regard to these scenarios, the point is this: If different authorship is indeed true, and if Luke was written prior to Acts, it follows that Acts depends on Luke but not *vice versa*, barring a transmission process as yet undetected. That is, the author-editor of Acts may have imported thematic content, sequence, theology, or any combination thereof from the third gospel, but a reciprocal dependence does not exist.[7]

Arguments for and rebuttals of the above scenarios abound, many of them detailed in Chapter One. The later the date of Acts, the more likely the author-editor *knew* the gospel of Luke, simply because a later date provides more opportunities to encounter the circulating gospel. On the one hand, to propose totally separate compositional trajectories for Luke and Acts means the theological-thematic parallels come from common inherited tradition, implying the author-editor of Acts at some point noticed similarities and joined the two books together. In rebuttal, many quite reasonably argue the similarities in vocabulary, content, sequence, and theology are too remarkable to support separate development. On the other hand, proposing that the Acts author-editor used Luke *and* other extant tradition besides independent composition means the two books' parallels may come from deliberate, intentional correspondence-building to ensure they demonstrate a unified arrangement of material, or that, due to common tradition, the parallels may not have been so closely designed. The irrefutable fact remains: the determined search for similarities between Luke and Acts has eclipsed the study of differences. Challenging single authorship by no means contradicts a late date for Acts, which, if true, critically affects how we reconstruct the historical, social, and ideological contours of early Christianity.

"Luke-Acts," an afterthought?

Arguments for a unified theology or style, for example the theological continuity of salvation history from Luke through Acts, would have to accept the possibility that the union of the two books was an afterthought, not part of an original plan. Actually, any theology of the New Testament would have to acknowledge the two books' initially separated circumstances. Phraseology such as "Luke's" theology, or "Luke's" style,

---

[7] Parenthetically and notably, advocates of Proto-Luke discover many of Talbert's correspondences in content and sequence lie in the material corresponding to Mark.

or "Luke's" vocabulary to refer to both Luke and Acts should be revised. Under the different authorship hypothesis, unity at the level of genre (e.g., David E. Aune and Charles H. Talbert) or narrative (e.g., Robert C. Tannehill) derives from one of two compositional possibilities: (1) deliberate incorporation of Lukan tradition and themes *during* the composition of Acts or (2) *post*-unification redaction. According to the different authorship hypothesis, Luke was not originally composed as a prequel to Acts, nor Acts necessarily as a sequel to Luke.

Resolution of conundra

An unintended consequence of different authorship is the resolution of various conundra. Perhaps most puzzling are the conflicting ascension stories (Lk 24:50–53; Acts 1:6–12).[8] Special pleading, it seems, is required to reconcile the two accounts, whereas different authorship understands reconciliation is not needed, as different author-editors composed the two accounts. Moreover, linguistic differences would need no reconciliation; for example, of the three ἐγένετο constructions in Luke and Acts, two are used exclusively in Luke and one exclusively in Acts.[9] These differences and others related to sentence connectivity, particle use, and stylistic variation would need no compromise explanation.

If not pressed too far, there may exist a cautiously offered analogous situation between the single authorship of Luke and Acts and the Mosaic authorship of the Torah. Until the French Oratorian priest, Richard Simon, published *Histoire critique du Vieux Testament* (1678), Mosaic authorship of the Torah had been unquestioned.[10] Simon's suggestion that the final form of the Torah may have involved work by scribes at the time of Ezra was not well received, yet today after several centuries of critical scholarship Mosaic authorship is hardly the prevailing opinion. In a similar way, the possibility that Luke and Acts come from different author-editors, which is also not well received, may one day become a viable opinion.

---

[8] In Acts, the risen Jesus' forty-day earthly sojourn before his ascension appears to contradict the Lukan account, which implies the risen Jesus ascends on Easter Sunday night.

[9] Cf. Clark's challenge discussed in Chapter One: Background and Methodology, where it is noted there could be one questionable use of the third construction in Luke.

[10] See Joseph Blenkinsopp, *The Pentateuch: An Introduction to the First Five Books of the Bible*, ABRL (New York: Doubleday, 1992), p. 3.

Future directions

Projects too large in scope to be included in the current one are anticipated. In the case of Luke, a study of all Lukan redaction vis-à-vis euphony, rhythm, and sentence structure would further verify the compositional patterns found in the gospel's seams and summaries. These patterns ought to be mirrored in the redaction of all Markan material, assuming it could be confidently identified. Changes to the inherited text should result from and respect the author-editor's compositional prerogatives.

In the case of Acts, several large tasks are envisioned. First, long regarded as independent compositions by the author-editor, the speeches provide rich possibilities for an analysis of compositional patterns, because they ought to reflect the overall compositional picture in the Acts seams and summaries.[11] Second, the so-called "We"-Sections in Acts also comprise a textual stratum ripe for compositional analysis. If statistically *insignificant* differences in the "We"-Sections and the Acts seams and summaries are found, common authorship may not be ruled out. If, however, statistically significant differences exist, common authorship *may* be ruled out. Third, based on the different authorship hypothesis, a new investigation into the Christology of Acts is envisioned, one that is less attached to the third gospel. Fourth, the problem of the so-called "Western" text may need to be tackled.[12] Intriguing is the fact that the "Western" text of Acts is roughly 10 percent longer than the Alexandrian, a curiosity that scholars have tried to explain ever since the discovery of

---

[11] An analysis of compositional patterns in the Acts seams and summaries and in the Acts speeches should reveal statistically *insignificant* differences.

[12] See Metzger, *The Canon of the New Testament*, pp. 15*, 222. In brief, theories on the text traditions of Luke and Acts demonstrate that Luke manuscripts followed a development pattern similar to those of Mark and Matthew, but Acts manuscripts apparently diverged early into two distinct forms: (1) the Alexandrian text tradition; and (2) the so-called "Western" tradition. First, the Alexandrian text tradition is represented most significantly by $\mathfrak{P}^{45}$ (for Acts) $\mathfrak{P}^{50}$ (for Acts) $\mathfrak{P}^{74}$ ℵ A B C Ψ 33 81 104 326 and 1175. For a view on the transmission history of the New Testament text, the Alexandrian and other text type families, see Bruce M. Metzger, *A Textual Commentary on the Greek New Testament*, 2nd edition (Stuttgart: Deutsche Bibelgesellschaft, 1994), pp. 3*–10*. See also A. F. J. Klijn, *A Survey of the Researches into the Western Text of the Gospels and Acts: Part 2 1949–1969* (Leiden: Brill, 1969). Second, the "Western" text tradition is most importantly represented by D and $\mathfrak{P}^{29}$ (for Acts) $\mathfrak{P}^{38}$ (for Acts) $\mathfrak{P}^{48}$(for Acts) syr[h with]* (for Acts) h (for Acts) Cyp Aug. For discussion on "Western" as a misnomer due to the fact that early manuscripts have been found in the East, see the introduction in Clark, *Acts of the Apostles*, pp. xv–xix. See also Fitzmyer, *Acts of the Apostles*, pp. 69–70.

Codex Bezae (D) in the sixteenth century.[13] Since the "Western" text tradition in Acts, especially Codex Bezae, reveals some text variants in the seams and summaries, a project to analyze the compositional differences in the seams and summaries of the "Western" tradition should be undertaken, even though the *opinio communis* as yet considers it the later.

Concluding reflection

The present book is but a small beginning. If the hypothesis of different authorship is open to reconsideration, as I believe it must be, the search for truth will not be eclipsed by its implications. Faith in the inspired and revelatory nature of Scripture is neither negated nor nullified if Luke and Acts had different author-editors. Faith simply becomes more informed. In sincerity of purpose is truth sought.

---

[13] For an introduction to the text problems with Acts, see Metzger, *Textual Commentary*, pp. 222–236. For a discussion of the Alexandrian and "Western" traditions as two distinct revisions of one original composition, see M. Wilcox, "Luke and the Bezan Text of Acts," in Kremer, *Les Actes des Apôtres*, pp. 447–455. Until the 1980s the subject of priority had seemed fairly settled; see Delobel, "The Text of Luke-Acts," pp. 83–107. As a result of recent studies, text critics sometimes advocate an "eclectic" approach, which grants preference to neither the Alexandrian nor the "Western," but rather offers equal preference. For a discussion of the term "eclecticism" and its application, see Gordon D. Fee, "Rigorous or Reasoned Eclecticism – Which?" in Elliot, *Studies in New Testament Language and Text*, pp. 174–197. For an introduction to the text tradition problem of Acts as well as the eclectic approach, see also Metzger, *Textual Commentary*, pp. 222–236. To use the eclectic approach objectively is harder to achieve than it seems *prima facie*, because one text tradition, namely, the "Western," is relegated more often to the critical apparatus.

APPENDIX

For the purposes of the present authorship analysis, the Luke and Acts SSD identified in Chapter Two may be divided syllabically and by quantity as shown below. Sentence delineation follows the Greek text in the Nestle-Aland *Novum Testamentum Graece*, 27th edition. Clausal division is guided by the ancient prose composition critics, as well as the major and minor stop punctuation in the Nestle-Aland text. In general, in this schema an attributive participle does not enjoy separate clausal status, but a circumstantial participle does indicate a distinct dependent clause; see Smyth, *Greek Grammar*, §§2049–2053; 2054–2069. For syllable division criteria, see Smyth, *Greek Grammar*, §§138–141; for syllable quantity, see ibid., §§142–148, and for vowel length, see ibid., §§4–6, 144b; also Liddell and Scott, *Greek–English Lexicon*.[1] For clarification purposes, two numbers sometimes appear to the left of the Greek data: verse numbers are identified in the far left column labeled "v."; and clause numbers are adjacent to the Greek text.

Luke seams and summaries

Lk 1:1–4

v.

1 1 ἐ-πει-δή-περ πολ-λοὶ ἐπ-ε-χεί-ρη-σαν ἀ-να-τά-ξα-σθαι δι-ή-γη-σιν
    πε-ρὶ τῶν

    πε²-πλη-ρο-φο-ρη-μέ-νων ἐν ἡ-μῖν πραγ-μά-των

2 2 καθ-ὼς παρ-έ-δο-σαν ἡ-μῖν οἱ ἀπ-᾿ ἀρ-χῆς αὐτ-ό-πται καὶ ὑπ-η-ρέ-ται
    γε-νό-με-νοι τοῦ λό-γου,

---

[1] Smyth, *Greek Grammar*. H. G. Liddell and H. S. Jones and R. McKenzie and R. Scott, *A Greek–English Lexicon*, 9th edition, new supplement (Oxford: Clarendon Press, 1996).

[2] Short vowel before πλ does not make syllable long by position *per* criteria in Chapter Four.

⏑ — ⏑ — — ⏑ — ⏑ — — ⏑ ⏑ — — ⏑ — — ⏑ — — — — —
3 3 ἔ-δο-ξε κἀ-μοὶ³ πα-ρη-κο-λου-θη-κό-τι ἄν-ω-θεν πᾶ-σιν ἀ⁴-κρι-βῶς
καθ-ε-ξῆς σοι γρά-ψαι,

⏑ — — ⏑ ⏑ ⏑
κρά-τι-στε Θε-ό-φι-λε,

⏑ ⏑ ⏑ — ⏑ — — ⏑ — — — — ⏑ — — — ⏑ ⏑ ⏑
4 4 ἵ-να ἐ-πι⁵-γνῷς πε-ρὶ ὧν κατ-η-χή-θης λό-γων τὴν ἀ-σφά-λει-αν.

Lk 1:80

⏑ ⏑ — ⏑ ⏑ — ⏑ — ⏑ ⏑ — — — ⏑ ⏑
1   Τὸ δὲ παι-δί-ον ηὔ-ξα-νεν καὶ ἐ⁶-κρα-ται-οῦ-το⁷ πνεύ-μα-τι,

— — — — ⏑ — — ⏑ — — ⏑ ⏑ ⏑ — — — — — — ⏑ ⏑ —
2   καὶ ἦν ἐν ταῖς ἐ-ρή-μοις ἕ-ως ἡ-μέ-ρας ἀ-να-δεί-ξε-ως αὐ-τοῦ πρὸς τὸν Ἰσ-ρα-ήλ.

Lk 2:40

⏑ ⏑ — ⏑ ⏑ — ⏑ — ⏑ ⏑ — — — ⏑ ⏑ —
1   Τὸ δὲ παι-δί-ον ηὔ-ξα-νεν καὶ ἐ-κρα-ται-οῦ-το⁸ πλη-ρού-με-νον σο-φί-ᾳ,

— ⏑ — — — ⏑ ⏑ —
2   καὶ χά-ρις θε-οῦ ἦν ἐπ-' αὐ-τό.

Lk 2:52

— ⏑ — — — ⏑ — ⏑ ⏑ — — — ⏑ — ⏑ ⏑ — ⏑ ⏑ ⏑ — — — — —
1   Καὶ Ἰ-η-σοῦ προ-έ-κο-πτεν [ἐν τῇ]⁹ σο-φί-ᾳ καὶ ἡ-λι-κί-ᾳ καὶ χά-ρι-τι
πα-ρὰ θε-ῷ καὶ ἀν-θρώ-ποις.

Lk 3:1–3

v.
⏑ ⏑ — ⏑ — ⏑ — ⏑ — — — ⏑ — ⏑ ⏑ ⏑ — — ⏑ ⏑
1   1   Ἐν ἔ-τει δὲ πεν-τε-και-δε-κά-τῳ τῆς ἡ-γε-μο-νί-ας Τι-βε-ρί-ου Καί-σα-ρος,

— ⏑ — — — ⏑ ⏑ — — ⏑ ⏑ — ⏑ — — —
2   ἡ-γε-μο-νεύ-ον-τος Πον-τί-ου Πι-λά-του τῆς Ἰ-ου-δαί-ας,

---

³ Crasis classified as two words: καὶ μοί.

⁴ Short vowel before κρ does not make syllable long by position *per* criteria in Chapter Four.

⁵ Short vowel before γν makes the syllable long by position *per* criteria in Chapter Four.

⁶ Short vowel before κρ does not make syllable long by position *per* criteria in Chapter Four.

⁷ Short vowel before πν does not make syllable long by position *per* criteria in Chapter Four.

⁸ Short vowel before πλ does not make syllable long by position *per* criteria in Chapter Four.

⁹ Included in the Nestle-Aland *Novum Testamentum Graece*, 27th edition text.

‿ ⌣ ⌣ — — — — — ⌣ ⌣ — ⌣ — — —
3 καὶ τε[10]-τρα-αρ-χοῦν-τος τῆς Γα-λι-λαί-ας Ἡ-ρῴ-δου,

⌣ — — — — — — — ⌣ ⌣ — — — ⌣ — — — ⌣ ⌣ — —
4 Φι-λίπ-που δὲ τοῦ ἀ-δελ-φοῦ αὐ-τοῦ τε[11]-τρα-αρ-χοῦν-τος τῆς
   Ἰ-του-ραί-ας καὶ Τρα-χω-νί-τι-δος

— —
χώ-ρας,

— ⌣ ⌣ — — ⌣ ⌣ — — ⌣ ⌣ — — ⌣
5 καὶ Λυ-σα-νί-ου τῆς Ἀ-βι-λη-νῆς τε[12]-τρα-αρ-χοῦν-τος,

⌣ ⌣ — ⌣ ⌣ — — ⌣ ⌣ — ⌣
2 6 ἐ-πὶ ἀρχ-ι-ε-ρέ-ως Ἄν-να καὶ Κα-ϊ-ά-φα,

⌣ ⌣ ⌣ ⌣ — ⌣ ⌣ — — — — ⌣ — — ⌣ — — ⌣ ⌣ — —
7 ἐ-γέ-νε-το ῥῆ-μα θε-οῦ ἐ-πὶ Ἰ-ω-άν-νην τὸν Ζα-χα-ρί-ου υἱ-ὸν ἐν τῇ
   ἐ-ρή-μῳ.

— — ⌣ — — — — ⌣ ⌣ — — — ⌣ — ⌣ —
3 8 καὶ ἦλ-θεν εἰς πᾶ-σαν [τὴν][13] πε-ρί-χω-ρον τοῦ Ἰ-ορ-δά-νου

— — — — — ⌣ ⌣ ⌣ — ⌣ ⌣ ⌣ ⌣ — —
9 κη-ρύσ-σων βά-πτι-σμα με-τα-νοί-ας εἰς ἄ-φε-σιν ἁ-μαρ-τι-ῶν,[14]

Lk 3:18

— ⌣ — — ⌣ ⌣ ⌣ ⌣ ⌣ —
1 Πολ-λὰ μὲν οὖν καὶ ἕ-τε-ρα πα-ρα-κα-λῶν

— ⌣ ⌣ ⌣ ⌣ — ⌣ —
2 εὐ-ηγ-γε-λί-ζε-το τὸν λα-όν.

Lk 4:14–15

v.
— ⌣ — — ⌣ ⌣ — ⌣ — ⌣ ⌣ — — ⌣ — — — —
14 1 Καὶ ὑπ-έ-στρε-ψεν ὁ Ἰ-η-σοῦς ἐν τῇ δυ-νά-μει τοῦ πνεύ-μα-τος εἰς τὴν
       Γα-λι-λαί-αν.

— — — — — ⌣ ⌣ — ⌣ ⌣ — — ⌣ — — ⌣ —
2 καὶ φή-μη ἐξ-ῆλ-θεν καθ-᾽ ὅ-λης τῆς πε-ρι-χώ-ρου πε-ρὶ αὐ-τοῦ.

— — ⌣ — ⌣ — — ⌣ — — ⌣ — ⌣ ⌣ — —
15 3 καὶ αὐ-τὸς ἐ-δί-δα-σκεν ἐν ταῖς συν-α-γω-γαῖς αὐ-τῶν
       δο-ξα[15]-ζό-με-νος ὑ-πὸ πάν-των.

---

[10] Short vowel before τρ does not make syllable long by position *per* criteria in Chapter Four.

[11] Short vowel before τρ does not make syllable long by position *per* criteria in Chapter Four.

[12] Short vowel before τρ does not make syllable long by position *per* criteria in Chapter Four.

[13] Included in the Nestle-Aland *Novum Testamentum Graece*, 27th edition text.

[14] Although the Nestle-Aland *Novum Testamentum Graece* terminates Lk 3:3 with a minor stop, for the purposes of this analysis it is considered the end of the seamic text.

[15] Syllable quantity is short; see Smyth, *Greek Grammar*, §147c.

Lk 4:31–32

v.   — ◡ — ◡ — ◡ — ◡ — — ◡ — —
31   1   Καὶ κατ-ῆλ-θεν εἰς Κα-φαρ-να-οὺμ πό-λιν τῆς Γα-λι-λαί-ας.

         — — — ◡ — ◡ — — — ◡ —
     2   καὶ ἦν δι-δά-σκων αὐ-τοὺς ἐν τοῖς σάβ-βα-σιν·

         — — ◡ — — ◡ — ◡ — ◡ — — ◡ ◡ — —
32   3   καὶ ἐξ-ε¹⁶-πλήσ-σον-το ἐ-πὶ τῇ δι-δα-χῇ αὐ-τοῦ,

         ◡ ◡ — ◡ ◡ — — — ◡ — ◡ —
     4   ὅ-τι ἐν ἐξ-ου-σί-ᾳ ἦν ὁ λό-γος αὐ-τοῦ.

Lk 4:40–41

v.   ◡ — — ◡ — — ◡ —
40   1   Δύ-νον-τος δὲ τοῦ ἡ-λί-ου

         ◡ — ◡ — ◡ — ◡ — ◡ — — — ◡ — — — ◡ ◡ — ◡
     2   ἅ-παν-τες ὅ-σοι εἶ-χον ἀ-σθε-νοῦν-τας νό-σοις ποι-κί-λαις ἤ-γα-γον
         αὐ-τοὺς πρὸς αὐ-τόν·

         ◡ ◡ ◡ ◡ — ◡ — — — ◡ ◡ — ◡ — ◡ ◡ — ◡ — —
     3   ὁ δὲ ἑ-νὶ ἑ-κά-στω αὐ-τῶν τὰς¹⁷ χεῖ-ρας ἐ-πι-τι-θεὶς ἐ-θε-ρά-πευ-εν
         αὐ-τούς.

         — — ◡ ◡ — — ◡ ◡ ◡ ◡ — ◡ — — ◡ — ◡ ◡
41   4   ἐξ-ήρ-χε-το δὲ καὶ δαι-μό-νι-α ἀ-πὸ πολ-λῶν κρ[αυ-γ]¹⁸ἀ¹⁹-ζον-τα καὶ
         λέ-γον-τα

         ◡ ◡ ◡ — ◡ — — — ◡ —
     5   ὅ-τι σὺ εἶ ὁ υἱ-ὸς τοῦ θε-οῦ.

         — ◡ ◡ ◡ — — — ◡ ◡ — ◡ —
     6   καὶ ἐ-πι-τι-μῶν οὐκ εἴ-α αὐ-τὰ λα-λεῖν,

         ◡ ◡ — — ◡ — — ◡ — — ◡ —
     7   ὅ-τι ᾔ-δει-σαν τὸν χρι-στὸν αὐ-τὸν εἶ-ναι.

Lk 4:44

         — — — ◡ — — — — ◡ — — ◡ — —
1   Καὶ ἦν κη-ρύσ-σων εἰς τὰς²⁰ συν-α-γω-γὰς τῆς Ἰ-ου-δαί-ας.

Lk 5:15–16

v.   ◡ — — ◡ ◡ — ◡ ◡ — — ◡ — —
15   1   δι-ήρ-χε-το δὲ μᾶλ-λον ὁ λό-γος πε-ρὶ αὐ-τοῦ,

---

¹⁶ Short vowel before πλ does not make syllable long by position *per* criteria in Chapter Four.
¹⁷ Compensatory lengthening of α; see Smyth, *Greek Grammar*, §37.
¹⁸ Not included.
¹⁹ See Smyth, *Greek Grammar*, §147c.
²⁰ Compensatory lengthening of α; see Smyth, *Greek Grammar*, §37.

‿ ⏑ ‿ ‿ ⏑ ‿ ‿ ‿ ‿ ‿ ‿ ‿ ‿ ⏑ ‿ ‿ ‿ ‿ ‿ ‿ ‿ ‿
2 καὶ συν-ήρ-χον-το ὅ²¹-χλοι πολ-λοὶ ἀ-κού-ειν καὶ θε-ρα-πεύ-ε-σθαι
   ἀ-πὸ τῶν ἀ-σθε-νει-ῶν αὐ-τῶν·

‿ ‿ ‿ ⏑ ‿ ‿ ‿ ‿ ‿ ‿ ‿ ‿ ‿ ⏑ ‿ ‿ ‿
16 3 αὐ-τὸς δὲ ἦν ὑ-πο-χω-ρῶν ἐν ταῖς ἐ-ρή-μοις καὶ προσ-ευ-χό-με-νος.

Lk 5:17

‿ ⏑ ⏑ ⏑ ‿ ‿ ⏑ ‿ ‿ ‿ ‿ ‿ ⏑ ⏑ ‿ ‿
1 Καὶ ἐ-γέ-νε-το ἐν μι-ᾷ τῶν ἡ-με-ρῶν καὶ αὐ-τὸς ἦν δι-δά-σκων,

‿ ‿ ‿ ⏑ ‿ ‿ ⏑ ⏑ ‿ ‿ ‿ ⏑ ⏑ ‿ ‿
2 καὶ ἦ-σαν καθ-ή-με-νοι Φα-ρι-σαῖ-οι καὶ νο-μο-δι-δά-σκα-λοι

‿ ‿ ⏑ ‿ ‿ ⏑ ⏑ ‿ ‿ ‿ ‿ ‿ ‿ ‿ ‿ ⏑ ‿ ‿ ‿ ‿ ⏑ ⏑ ‿ ‿
3 οἵ ἦ-σαν ἐ-λη-λυ-θό-τες ἐκ πά²²-σης κώ-μης τῆς Γα-λι-λαί-ας καὶ
   'Ι-ου-δαί-ας καὶ 'Ι-ε-ρου-σα-λήμ·

‿ ⏑ ⏑ ‿ ‿ ⏑ ‿ ‿ ‿ ‿ ⏑ ‿ ‿ ‿ ‿
4 καὶ δύ-να-μις κυ-ρί-ου ἦν εἰς τὸ ἰ-ᾶ-σθαι αὐ-τόν.

Lk 6:17–19

v. ‿ ⏑ ⏑ ‿ ‿ ‿ ⏑ ⏑ ⏑ ‿ ‿ ‿
17 1 Καὶ κα-τα-βὰς μετ' αὐ-τῶν ἔ-στη ἐ-πὶ τό-που πε-δι-νοῦ,

‿ ⏑ ‿ ⏑ ⏑ ‿ ‿ ‿ ‿
2 καὶ ὅ²³-χλος πο-λὺς μα-θη-τῶν αὐ-τοῦ,

‿ ‿ ‿ ‿ ⏑ ⏑ ‿ ‿ ⏑ ‿ ‿ ‿ ‿ ‿ ‿ ⏑ ⏑ ‿ ‿ ‿ ‿
3 καὶ πλῆ-θος πο-λὺ τοῦ λα-οῦ ἀ-πὸ πά²⁴-σης τῆς 'Ι-ου-δαί-ας καὶ
   'Ι-ε-ρου-σα-λὴμ καὶ τῆς

⏑ ⏑ ⏑ ‿ ⏑ ‿ ‿ ⏑ ‿
πα-ρα-λί-ου Τύ-ρου καὶ Σι-δῶν-ος,

‿ ⏑ ⏑ ‿ ‿ ‿ ‿ ‿ ‿ ‿ ⏑ ⏑ ‿ ‿ ‿ ‿
18 4 οἵ ἦλ-θον ἀ-κοῦ-σαι αὐ-τοῦ καὶ ἰ-α-θῆ-ναι ἀ-πὸ τῶν νό-σων αὐ-τῶν·

‿ ‿ ‿ ⏑ ⏑ ‿ ‿ ⏑ ‿ ‿ ⏑ ⏑ ‿ ‿ ‿ ⏑ ⏑ ‿ ‿ ‿ ⏑
5 καὶ οἵ ἐν-ο²⁵-χλού-με-νοι ἀ-πὸ πνευ-μά-των ἀ-κα-θάρ-των
   ἐ-θε-ρα-πεύ-ον-το,

‿ ‿ ⏑ ‿ ⏑ ‿ ‿ ‿ ‿ ‿ ‿ ‿
19 6 καὶ πᾶς ὁ ὄ-χλος ἐ-ζή-τουν ἅ-πτε-σθαι αὐ-τοῦ,

⏑ ⏑ ⏑ ‿ ⏑ ‿ ‿ ⏑ ‿ ‿ ⏑ ⏑ ‿ ‿
7 ὅ-τι δύ-να-μις παρ' αὐ-τοῦ ἐξ-ήρ-χε-το καὶ ἰ-ᾶ-το πάν-τας.

---

²¹ Short vowel before χλ does not make syllable long by position *per* criteria in Chapter
Four.
²² Compensatory lengthening of α; see Smyth, *Greek Grammar*, §37.
²³ Short vowel before χλ does not make syllable long by position *per* criteria in Chapter
Four.
²⁴ Compensatory lengthening of α; see Smyth, *Greek Grammar*, §37.
²⁵ Short vowel before χλ does not make syllable long by position *per* criteria in Chapter
Four.

Lk 7:11

‿ ‿ ‿ ‿ — — — — ‿ ‿ — — — ‿ ‿ — ‿ — ‿ —
1 Καὶ ἐ-γέ-νε-το ἐν τῷ ἑ-ξῆς ἐ-πο-ρεύ-θη εἰς πό-λιν κα-λου-μέ-νην Να-ΐν

— ‿ ‿ ‿ ‿ ‿ — ‿ — — ‿ — ‿ ‿ ‿ — ‿ ‿ —
2 καὶ συν-ε-πο-ρεύ-ον-το αὐ-τῷ οἱ μα-θη-ταὶ αὐ-τοῦ καὶ ὅ²⁶-χλος πο-λύς.

Lk 8:1–3

v.
‿ ‿ ‿ ‿ ‿ — — ‿ — — ‿ — — ‿ ‿ — — — ‿ ‿ — — — —
1 1 Καὶ ἐ-γέ-νε-το ἐν τῷ καθ-ε-ξῆς καὶ αὐ-τὸς δι-ώ-δευ-εν κα-τὰ πό-λιν καὶ
      κώ-μην

— — — — — ‿ ‿ ‿ ‿ — ‿ ‿ — — — ‿ —
2 κη-ρύσ-σων καὶ εὐ-αγ-γε-λι-ζό-με-νος τὴν βα-σι-λεί-αν τοῦ θε-οῦ

— — — ‿ ‿ ‿ — ‿ — — — ‿ ‿
[2] 3 καὶ οἱ δώ-δε-κα σὺν αὐ-τῷ, [8·2] καὶ γυ-ναῖ-κές τι-νες

— — — ‿ ‿ — ‿ — ‿ — ‿ ‿ — — ‿ —
4 αἵ ἦ-σαν τε-θε-ρα-πευ-μέ-ναι ἀ-πὸ πνευ-μά-των πο-νη-ρῶν καὶ
   ἀ-σθε-νει-ῶν,

‿ ‿ ‿ — ‿ — ‿ — — —
5 Μα-ρί-α ἡ κα-λου-μέ-νη Μαγ-δα-λη-νή,

‿ — — — ‿ ‿ — ‿ — — —
6 ἀ-φ᾽ ἧς δαι-μό-νι-α ἑ-πτὰ ἐξ-ε-λη-λύ-θει,

— ‿ — ‿ ‿ — — — — — — ‿ — ‿ — — —
3 7 καὶ Ἰ-ω-άν-να γυ-νὴ Χου-ζᾶ ἐ-πι-τρό-που Ἡ-ρῴ-δου καὶ Σου-σάν-να
      καὶ ἕ-τε-ραι πολ-λαί,

— ‿ — ‿ — ‿ ‿ ‿ — ‿ — — ‿ —
8 αἵ-τι-νες δι-η-κό-νουν αὐ-τοῖς ἐκ τῶν ὑπ-αρ-χόν-των αὐ-ταῖς.

Lk 8:4a

‿ ‿ ‿ — ‿ ‿ — ‿ — ‿ — — ‿ — ‿
1 Συν-ι-όν-τος δὲ ὅ²⁷-χλου πολ-λοῦ καὶ τῶν κα-τὰ πό-λιν
   ἐ-πι-πο-ρευ-ο-μέ-νων πρὸς αὐ-τὸν . . .

Lk 9:51

‿ ‿ ‿ ‿ — ‿ — — — — ‿ — ‿ —
1 Ἐ-γέ-νε-το δὲ ἐν τῷ συμ-πλη-ροῦ-σθαι τὰς²⁸ ἡ-μέ-ρας τῆς
   ἀ-να-λήμ-ψε-ως αὐ-τοῦ

— ‿ — ‿ — ‿ ‿ ‿ — ‿ — ‿ — — — ‿ ‿ — ‿
2 καὶ αὐ-τὸς τὸ πρόσ-ω-πον ἐ-στή-ρι-σεν τοῦ πο-ρεύ-ε-σθαι εἰς
   Ἰ-ε-ρου-σα-λήμ.

---

²⁶ Short vowel before χλ does not make syllable long by position *per* criteria in Chapter Four.

²⁷ Short vowel before χλ does not make syllable long by position *per* criteria in Chapter Four.

²⁸ Compensatory lengthening of α; see Smyth, *Greek Grammar*, §37.

Lk 10:38a

1 ＿ ᵕ ＿ ᵕ ＿ ＿ ＿ ＿ ＿ ＿ ＿ ᵕ ＿ ᵕ ＿ ＿ ＿ ᵕ ᵕ
'Εν δὲ τῷ πο-ρεύ-ε-σθαι αὐ-τοὺς αὐ-τὸς εἰσ-ῆλ-θεν εἰς κώ-μην τι-νά . . .

Lk 13:22

1 ＿ ᵕ ᵕ ᵕ ＿ ᵕ ᵕ ᵕ ᵕ ＿ ＿ ＿ ＿ ᵕ ＿ ＿ ＿ ᵕ ＿ ＿ ＿ ＿ ᵕ ᵕ
Καὶ δι-ε-πο-ρεύ-ε-το κα-τὰ πό-λεις καὶ κώ-μας δι-δά-σκων καὶ πο-ρεί-αν
ποι-ού-με-νος

＿ ᵕ ᵕ ᵕ ᵕ ᵕ
εἰς 'Ι-ε-ρο-σό-λυ-μα.

Lk 14:25a

1 ᵕ ᵕ ᵕ ＿ ＿ ＿ ᵕ ᵕ ＿ ＿ ＿
Συν-ε-πο-ρεύ-ον-το δὲ αὐ-τῷ ὄ²⁹-χλοι πολ-λοί . . .

Lk 17:11

1 ＿ ᵕ ᵕ ᵕ ＿ ＿ ᵕ ＿ ＿ ＿ ＿ ᵕ ᵕ ＿ ᵕ ＿
Καὶ ἐ-γέ-νε-το ἐν τῷ πο-ρεύ-ε-σθαι εἰς 'Ι-ε-ρου-σα-λὴμ

2 ＿ ＿ ᵕ ᵕ ＿ ＿ ᵕ ᵕ ＿ ＿ ＿ ᵕ ＿ ＿ ＿ ᵕ
καὶ αὐ-τὸς δι-ήρ-χε-το δι-ὰ μέ-σον Σα-μα-ρεί-ας καὶ Γα-λι-λαί-ας.

Lk 18:35a

1 ᵕ ᵕ ᵕ ᵕ ＿ ＿ ᵕ ＿ ＿ ᵕ ＿ ᵕ ᵕ ＿
'Ε-γέ-νε-το δὲ ἐν τῷ ἐγ-γί-ζειν αὐ-τὸν εἰς 'Ι-ε-ρι-χὼ . . .

Lk 19:28

1 ＿ ＿ ＿ ＿ ＿ ᵕ ᵕ ＿ ᵕ ᵕ ＿ ＿ ᵕ ᵕ ＿ ＿ ᵕ ᵕ ᵕ ᵕ
Καὶ εἰ-πὼν ταῦ-τα ἐ-πο-ρεύ-ε-το ἔμ-προ-σθεν ἀ-να-βαί-νων εἰς
'Ι-ε-ρο-σό-λυ-μα.

Lk 19:47–48

v. ＿ ＿ ᵕ ＿ ＿ ᵕ ᵕ ＿ ᵕ ᵕ ＿ ＿ ᵕ ＿
47 1 Καὶ ἦν δι-δά-σκων τὸ καθ-' ἡ-μέ-ραν ἐν τῷ ἱ-ε-ρῷ.

＿ ＿ ᵕ ＿ ＿ ᵕ ᵕ ＿ ＿ ᵕ ᵕ ＿ ＿ ᵕ ＿ ＿ ＿ ＿ ＿ ᵕ ＿
2 οἱ δὲ ἀρχ-ι-ε-ρεῖς καὶ οἱ γραμ-μα-τεῖς ἐ³⁰-ζή-τουν αὐ-τὸν ἀπ-ο-λέ-σαι
καὶ οἱ πρῶ-τοι τοῦ λα-οῦ,

---

²⁹ Short vowel before χλ does not make syllable long by position *per* criteria in Chapter Four.

³⁰ Long by position; see Smyth, *Greek Grammar*, §144.

48 3 καὶ οὐχ εὕ-ρι-σκον τὸ τί ποι-ή-σω-σιν,

    4 ὁ λα-ὸς γὰρ ἅ-πας ἐξ-ε-κρέ-μα-το αὐ-τοῦ ἀ-κού-ων.

Lk 21:37–38

v.

37 1 ῏Ην δὲ τὰς[31] ἡ-μέ-ρας ἐν τῷ ἱ-ε-ρῷ δι-δά-σκων,

    2 τὰς δὲ νύ-κτας ἐξ-ερ-χό-με-νος ηὐ-λί-ζε-το εἰς τὸ ὄ-ρος τὸ
       κα-λού-με-νον ᾿Ε-λαι-ῶν·

38 3 καὶ πᾶς ὁ λα-ὸς ὤρ-θρι-ζεν πρὸς αὐ-τὸν ἐν τῷ ἱ-ε-ρῷ ἀ-κού-ειν αὐ-τοῦ.

Acts seams and summaries

Acts 1:1–5

v.

1 1 Τὸν μὲν πρῶ-τον λό-γον ἐ-ποι-η-σά-μην πε-ρὶ πάν-των, ὦ Θε-ό-φι-λε,

   2 ὧν ἤρ-ξα-το ὁ ᾿Ι-η-σοῦς ποι-εῖν τε καὶ δι-δά-σκειν,

2 3 ἄ[32]-χρι ἧς ἡ-μέ-ρας ἐν-τει-λά-με-νος τοῖς ἀ-πο-στό-λοις δι-ὰ
      πνεύ-μα-τος ἁ-γί-ου

      οὓς ἐξ-ε-λέ-ξα-το ἀν-ε-λήμ-φθη.

3 4 οἷς καὶ παρ-έ-στη-σεν ἑ-αυ-τὸν ζῶν-τα με-τὰ τὸ πα-θεῖν αὐ-τὸν ἐν
      πολ-λοῖς τεκ-μη-ρί-οις,

   5 δι᾽ -ἡ-με-ρῶν τεσ-σε-ρά-κον-τα ὀ-πτα-νό-με-νος αὐ-τοῖς καὶ λέ-γων τὰ
      πε-ρὶ τῆς βα-σι-λεί-ας

      τοῦ θε-οῦ·

4 6 καὶ συν-α-λι-ζό-με-νος παρ-ήγ-γει-λεν αὐ-τοῖς ἀ-πὸ ᾿Ι-ε-ρο-σο-λύ-μων
      μὴ χω-ρί-ζε-σθαι

   7 ἀλ-λὰ πε-ρι-μέ-νειν τὴν ἐπ-αγ-γε-λί-αν τοῦ πα[33]-τρὸς

---

[31] Compensatory lengthening of α; see Smyth, *Greek Grammar*, §37.

[32] Short vowel before χρ does not make syllable long by position *per* criteria in Chapter Four

[33] Short vowel before τρ does not make syllable long by position *per* criteria in Chapter Four.

8　ἦν ἠ-κού-σα-τέ μου,

5　9　ὅ-τι 'Ι-ω-άν-νης μὲν ἐ-βά-πτι-σεν ὕ-δα-τι,

10　ὑ-μεῖς δὲ ἐν πνεύ-μα-τι βα-πτι-σθή-σε-σθε ἁ-γί-ῳ οὐ με-τὰ πολ-λὰς
　　ταύ-τας ἡ-μέ-ρας.

Acts 1:14

1　οὗ-τοι πάν-τες ἦ-σαν προσ-καρ-τε-ροῦν-τες ὁ-μο-θυ-μα-δὸν τῇ
　　προσ-ευ-χῇ

2　σὺν γυ-ναι-ξὶν καὶ Μα-ρι-ὰμ τῇ μη-τρὶ τοῦ 'Ι-η-σοῦ καὶ τοῖς ἀ-δελ-φοῖς
　　αὐ-τοῦ.

Acts 2:41

1　οἱ μὲν οὖν ἀ-πο-δε-ξά-με-νοι τὸν λό-γον αὐ-τοῦ ἐ-βα-πτί-σθη-σαν

2　καὶ προσ-ε-τέ-θη-σαν ἐν τῇ ἡ-μέ-ρᾳ ἐ-κεί-νῃ ψυ-χαὶ ὡ-σεὶ τρι-σχί-λι-αι.

Acts 2:42–47

v.
42　1　῏Η-σαν δὲ προσ-καρ-τε-ροῦν-τες τῇ δι-δα-χῇ τῶν ἀ-πο-στό-λων καὶ
　　　τῇ κοι-νω-νί-ᾳ,

　　　τῇ κλά-σει τοῦ ἄρ-του καὶ ταῖς προσ-ευ-χαῖς.

43　2　ἐ-γί-νε-το δὲ πά[34]-σῃ ψυ-χῇ φό-βος,

　　3　πολ-λά τε τέ-ρα-τα καὶ ση-μεῖ-α δι-ὰ τῶν ἀ-πο-στό-λων ἐ-γί-νε-το.

44　4　πάν-τες δὲ οἱ πι-στεύ-ον-τες ἦ-σαν ἐ-πὶ τὸ αὐ-τὸ

　　5　καὶ εἶ-χον ἅ-παν-τα κοι-νὰ

45　6　καὶ τὰ κτή-μα-τα καὶ τὰς[35] ὑπ-άρ-ξεις ἐ-πί[36]-πρα-σκον

　　7　καὶ δι-ε-μέ-ρι-ζον αὐ-τὰ πᾶ-σιν καθ-ό-τι ἄν τις χρεί-αν εἶ-χεν·

---

[34] Compensatory lengthening of α; see Smyth, *Greek Grammar*, §37.
[35] Compensatory lengthening of α; see Smyth, *Greek Grammar*, §37.
[36] Short vowel before πρ does not make syllable long by position *per* criteria in Chapter Four.

46 8 ‿ — ‿ — — — ‿ — ‿ ‿ ‿ — ‿ ‿ — — ‿ ‿ —
        καθ-᾽ ἡ-μέ-ραν τε[37] προσ-καρ-τε-ροῦν-τες ὁ-μο-θυ-μα-δὸν ἐν τῷ
        ἱ-ε-ρῷ,

    9 — — ‿ ‿ — ‿ ‿ — —
        κλῶν-τές τε κατ-᾽ οἶ-κον ἄρ-τον,

    10 ‿ ‿ — ‿ — ‿ — ‿ — ‿ ‿ — ‿ ‿ — ‿ — ‿ ‿
        μετ-ε-λάμ-βα-νον τρο-φῆς ἐν ἀ-γαλ-λι-ά-σει καὶ ἀ-φε-λό-τη-τι
        καρ-δί-ας

47 11 — — — — — — — ‿ ‿ — ‿ ‿ ‿ — — ‿ ‿
        αἰ-νοῦν-τες τὸν θε-ὸν καὶ ἔ-χον-τες χά-ριν πρὸς ὅ-λον τὸν λα-όν.

    12 ‿ ‿ — ‿ ‿ — ‿ — — ‿ — ‿ — ‿ ‿ — ‿ — ‿ ‿ — —
        ὁ δὲ κύ-ρι-ος προσ-ε-τί-θει τοὺς σῳ-ζο-μέ-νους καθ-᾽ ἡ-μέ-ραν ἐ-πὶ
        τὸ αὐ-τό.

Acts 4:4

1 — — ‿ — — — — — ‿ ‿ — — —
   πολ-λοὶ δὲ τῶν ἀ-κου-σάν-των τὸν λό-γον ἐ-πί-στευ-σαν

   — ‿ ‿ — (˘) ‿ — — — — — (—) ‿ ‿ ‿ —
2 καὶ ἐ-γε-νή-θη [ὁ][38] ἀ-ριθ-μὸς τῶν ἀν-δρῶν [ὡς][39] χι-λι-ά-δες πέν-τε.

Acts 4:32–35

v. — ‿ — ‿ — — — — — — — — ‿ ‿ — — — ‿ ‿ ‿
32 1 Τοῦ δὲ[40] πλή-θους τῶν πι-στευ-σάν-των ἦν καρ-δί-α καὶ ψυ-χὴ μί-α,

   2 καὶ οὐ-δὲ εἷς τι τῶν ὑπ-αρ-χόν-των αὐ-τῷ ἔ-λε-γεν ἴ-δι-ον εἶ-ναι

   — — — — — — — ‿ ‿ ‿
   3 ἀλ-λ᾽ ἦν αὐ-τοῖς ἅ-παν-τα κοι-νά.

   — — — ‿ ‿ — ‿ — — — ‿ — ‿ ‿ — ‿ — — ‿ ‿ —
33 4 καὶ δυ-νά-μει με-γά-λη ἀπ-ε-δί-δουν τὸ μαρ-τύ-ρι-ον οἱ ἀ-πό-στο-λοι
       τῆς ἀν-α-στά-σε-ως

      — — — ‿ — — — —
      τοῦ κυ-ρί-ου ᾽Ι-η-σοῦ,

   ‿ — ‿ — ‿ ‿ — — — ‿ — — ‿ —
5 χά-ρις τε με-γά-λη ἦν ἐ-πὶ πάν-τας αὐ-τούς.

   — — — ‿ ‿ — ‿ — — ‿ ‿ —
34 6 οὐ-δὲ γὰρ ἐν-δε-ής τις ἦν ἐν αὐ-τοῖς

   — — — ‿ ‿ — — ‿ ‿ — — ‿ ‿ — ‿ — —
7 ὅ-σοι γὰρ κτή-το-ρες χω-ρί-ων ἢ οἰ-κι-ῶν ὑπ-ῆρ-χον,

---

[37] Short vowel before πρ does not make syllable long by position *per* criteria in Chapter Four.

[38] Not included; see Nestle-Aland *Novum Testamentum Graece* critical apparatus.

[39] Included in the Nestle-Aland *Novum Testamentum Graece*, 27th edition text.

[40] Short vowel before πλ does not make syllable long by position *per* criteria in Chapter Four.

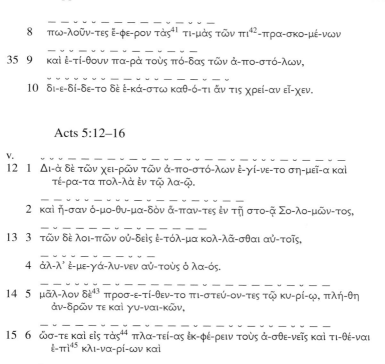

8 πω-λοῦν-τες ἔ-φε-ρον τὰς⁴¹ τι-μὰς τῶν πι⁴²-πρα-σκο-μέ-νων

35 9 καὶ ἐ-τί-θουν πα-ρὰ τοὺς πό-δας τῶν ἀ-πο-στό-λων,

10 δι-ε-δί-δε-το δὲ ἑ-κά-στω καθ-ό-τι ἄν τις χρεί-αν εἶ-χεν.

Acts 5:12–16

v.
12 1 Δι-ὰ δὲ τῶν χει-ρῶν τῶν ἀ-πο-στό-λων ἐ-γί-νε-το ση-μεῖ-α καὶ
τέ-ρα-τα πολ-λὰ ἐν τῷ λα-ῷ.

2 καὶ ἦ-σαν ὁ-μο-θυ-μα-δὸν ἅ-παν-τες ἐν τῇ στο-ᾷ Σο-λο-μῶν-τος,

13 3 τῶν δὲ λοι-πῶν οὐ-δεὶς ἐ-τόλ-μα κολ-λᾶ-σθαι αὐ-τοῖς,

4 ἀλ-λ’ ἐ-με-γά-λυ-νεν αὐ-τοὺς ὁ λα-ός.

14 5 μᾶλ-λον δὲ⁴³ προσ-ε-τί-θεν-το πι-στεύ-ον-τες τῷ κυ-ρί-ῳ, πλή-θη
ἀν-δρῶν τε καὶ γυ-ναι-κῶν,

15 6 ὥσ-τε καὶ εἰς τὰς⁴⁴ πλα-τεί-ας ἐκ-φέ-ρειν τοὺς ἀ-σθε-νεῖς καὶ τι-θέ-ναι
ἐ-πὶ⁴⁵ κλι-να-ρί-ων καὶ

κρα-βάτ-των,

7 ἵ-να ἐρ-χο-μέ-νου Πέ⁴⁶-τρου κἂν ἡ σκι-ὰ ἐ-πι-σκι-ά-σῃ τι-νὶ αὐ-τῶν.

16 8 συν-ήρ-χε-το δὲ καὶ τὸ⁴⁷ πλῆ-θος τῶν πέ-ριξ⁴⁸ πό-λε-ων
’Ι-ε-ρου-σα-λὴμ

---

⁴¹ Compensatory lengthening of α; see Smyth, *Greek Grammar*, §37.
⁴² Short vowel before πρ does not make syllable long by position *per* criteria in Chapter Four.
⁴³ Short vowel before πρ does not make syllable long by position *per* criteria in Chapter Four.
⁴⁴ Compensatory lengthening of α; see Smyth, *Greek Grammar*, §37.
⁴⁵ Short vowel before κλ does not make syllable long by position *per* criteria in Chapter Four.
⁴⁶ Short vowel before τρ does not make syllable long by position *per* criteria in Chapter Four.
⁴⁷ Short vowel before πλ does not make syllable long by position *per* criteria in Chapter Four.
⁴⁸ Syllable quantity is short; see Smyth, *Greek Grammar*, §147c.

˘ _ _ ˘ _ _ _ ˘ _ _ ˘ _ ˘ _ ˘ _ _ _

9   φέ-ρον-τες ἀ-σθε-νεῖς καὶ ὁ⁴⁹-χλου-μέ-νους ὑ-πὸ⁵⁰ πνευ-μά-των
     ἀ-καθ-άρ-των,

_ _ ˘ ˘ ˘ _ _ ˘ ˘ _ _ ˘

10   οἵ-τι-νες ἐ-θε-ρα-πεύ-ον-το ἅ-παν-τες.

Acts 6:1a

_ ˘ _ _ ˘ _ _ _ _ _ _ _ ˘ _ _

1   Ἐν δὲ ταῖς ἡ-μέ-ραις ταύ-ταις πλη-θυ-νόν-των τῶν μα-θη-τῶν . . .

Acts 6:7

_ ˘ ˘ _ _ ˘ _ _ ˘ _

1   Καὶ ὁ λό-γος τοῦ θε-οῦ ηὔ-ξα-νεν

_ _ ˘ _ ˘ ˘ ˘ _ _ _ ˘ ˘ _ ˘ _ _ _ ˘

2   καὶ ἐ⁵¹-πλη-θύ-νε-το ὁ ἀ-ριθ-μὸς τῶν μα-θη-τῶν ἐν Ἰ-ε-ρου-σα-λὴμ
     σφό-δρα,

˘ _ _ _ ˘ ˘ ˘ _ ˘ _ _ _ _ _ _

3   πο-λύς τε ὄ⁵²-χλος τῶν ἱ-ε-ρέ-ων ὑπ-ή-κου-ον τῇ πί-στει.

Acts 7:58b

_ _ ˘ ˘ _ _ _ ˘ ˘ _ ˘ ˘ _ ˘ _ _ ˘ ˘ _ ˘ _ ˘ _ _ ˘ _

1   καὶ οἱ μάρ-τυ-ρες ἀπ-έ-θεν-το τὰ ἱ-μά-τι-α αὐ-τῶν πα-ρὰ τοὺς πό-δας
     νε-α-νί-ου κα-λου-μέ-νου

_ _

Σαύ-λου, . . .

Acts 8:1b–c

˘ ˘ ˘ ˘ ˘ ˘ _ _ _ ˘ _ _ _ ˘ _ ˘ _ _ ˘ _ _

1   Ἐ-γέ-νε-το δὲ ἐν ἐ-κεί-νῃ τῇ ἡ-μέ-ρᾳ δι-ωγ-μὸς μέ-γας ἐ-πὶ τὴν
     ἐκ-κλη-σί-αν τὴν

˘ ˘ ˘ ˘ ˘ _

ἐν Ἰ-ε-ρο-σο-λύ-μοις,

_ _ ˘ _ _ ˘ _ ˘ _ _ _ _ ˘ _ ˘ ˘ _ _

2   πάν-τες δὲ δι-ε-σπά-ρη-σαν κα-τὰ τὰς⁵³ χώ-ρας τῆς Ἰ-ου-δαί-ας καὶ
     Σα-μα-ρεί-ας πλὴν

---

⁴⁹ Short vowel before χλ does not make syllable long by position *per* criteria in Chapter Four.
⁵⁰ Short vowel before πν does not make syllable long by position *per* criteria in Chapter Four.
⁵¹ Short vowel before πλ does not make syllable long by position *per* criteria in Chapter Four.
⁵² Short vowel before χλ does not make syllable long by position *per* criteria in Chapter Four.
⁵³ Compensatory lengthening of α; see Smyth, *Greek Grammar*, §37.

‾ ˘ ‾ ˘ ‾
τῶν ἀ-πο-στό-λων.

Acts 8:25

‾ ˘ ‾ ˘ ‾ ˘ ‾ ˘ ˘ ‾ ‾ ‾ ‾ ‾ ‾ ˘ ‾ ‾ ˘ ‾ ˘ ˘
1 Οἱ μὲν οὖν δι-α-μαρ-τυ-ρά-με-νοι καὶ λα-λή-σαν-τες τὸν λό-γον τοῦ
κυ-ρί-ου ὑπ-έ-στρε-φον

‾ ˘ ˘ ˘ ˘ ˘ ˘
εἰς Ἱ-ε-ρο-σό-λυ-μα,

‾ ‾ ˘ ‾ ‾ ‾ ˘ ˘ ‾ ‾ ‾ ˘ ˘ ‾ ˘
2 πολ-λάς τε κώ-μας τῶν Σα-μα-ρι-τῶν εὐ-ηγ-γε-λί-ζον-το.

Acts 9:31

‾ ˘ ‾ ‾ ‾ ˘ ˘ ˘ ‾ ˘ ˘ ‾ ‾ ‾ ˘ ˘ ‾ ‾ ‾ ˘ ˘ ‾ ˘ ‾ ˘
1 Ἡ μὲν οὖν ἐκ-κλη-σί-α καθ-᾽ ὅ-λης τῆς Ἰ-ου-δαί-ας καὶ Γα-λι-λαί-ας καὶ
Σα-μα-ρεί-ας εἶ-χεν

‾ ‾ ‾
εἰ-ρή-νην

‾ ˘ ‾ ˘ ˘ ‾ ˘ ˘ ‾ ‾ ˘ ‾ ‾ ‾ ˘ ‾ ‾ ˘ ˘ ‾ ‾ ‾ ˘ ˘ ‾
2 οἰ-κο-δο-μου-μέ-νη καὶ πο-ρευ-ο-μέ-νη τῷ φό-βῳ τοῦ κυ-ρί-ου καὶ τῇ
πα-ρα⁵⁴-κλή-σει τοῦ ἁ-γί-ου

‾ ˘ ˘ ˘ ‾ ‾ ˘ ˘
πνεύ-μα-τος ἐ⁵⁵-πλη-θύ-νε-το.

Acts 11:21

‾ ‾ ‾ ‾ ˘ ‾ ˘ ‾ ‾ ‾
1 καὶ ἦν χεὶρ κυ-ρί-ου μετ-᾽ αὐ-τῶν,

˘ ‾ ˘ ˘ ‾ ˘ ˘ ‾ ‾ ‾ ˘ ˘
2 πο-λύς τε ἀ-ριθ-μὸς ὁ πι-στεύ-σας ἐπ-έ-στρε-ψεν ἐ-πὶ τὸν κύ-ρι-ον.

Acts 11:24b

‾ ˘ ˘ ˘ ‾ ˘ ˘ ‾ ‾ ‾ ˘ ‾
1 καὶ προσ-ε-τέ-θη ὄ⁵⁶-χλος ἱ-κα-νὸς τῷ κυ-ρί-ῳ.

---

⁵⁴ Short vowel before κλ does not make syllable long by position *per* criteria in Chapter Four.
⁵⁵ Short vowel before πλ does not make syllable long by position *per* criteria in Chapter Four.
⁵⁶ Short vowel before χλ does not make syllable long by position *per* criteria in Chapter Four.

Acts 12:24

1   Ὁ δὲ λό-γος τοῦ θε-οῦ ηὔ-ξα-νεν καὶ ἐ[57]-πλη-θύ-νε-το.

Acts 12:25

1   Βαρ-να-βᾶς δὲ καὶ Σαῦ-λος ὑπ-έ-στρε-ψαν εἰς Ἰ-ε-ρου-σα-λὴμ

2   πλη-ρώ-σαν-τες τὴν δι-α-κο-νί-αν,

3   συμ-πα-ρα-λα-βόν-τες Ἰ-ω-άν-νην τὸν ἐ-πι-κλη-θέν-τα Μᾶρ-κον.

Acts 16:5

1   Αἱ μὲν οὖν ἐκ-κλη-σί-αι ἐ-στε-ρε-οῦν-το τῇ πί-στει

2   καὶ ἐ-πε-ρίσ-σευ-ον τῷ ἀ-ριθ-μῷ καθ-' ἡ-μέ-ραν.

Acts 19:20

1   οὕ-τως κα-τὰ[58] κρά-τος τοῦ κυ-ρί-ου ὁ λό-γος ηὔ-ξα-νεν καὶ ἴ-σχυ-εν.

---

[57] Short vowel before πλ does not make syllable long by position *per* criteria in Chapter Four.

[58] Short vowel before κρ does not make syllable long by position *per* criteria in Chapter Four.

BIBLIOGRAPHY

Alexander, Loveday, "Formal Elements and Genre: Which Greco-Roman Prologues Most Closely Parallel the Lukan Prologues?" in David P. Moessner (ed.), *Jesus and the Heritage of Israel: Luke's Narrative Claim upon Israel's History* (Harrisburg, Pa.: Trinity Press International, 1999).

The Preface to Luke's Gospel: Literary Convention and Social Context in Luke 1.1–4 and Acts 1.1, SNTSMS 78 (Cambridge: Cambridge University Press, 1993).

Alexandre, Jr., Manuel, *Rhetorical Argumentation in Philo of Alexandria* (Atlanta, Ga.: Scholars Press, 1999).

Allen, W. Sidney, *Accent and Rhythm: Prosodic Features of Latin and Greek: A Study in Theory and Reconstruction* (Cambridge: Cambridge University Press, 1973).

Vox Graeca: A Guide to the Pronunciation of Classical Greek, 3rd edition (Cambridge: Cambridge University Press, 1987).

Alter, Robert, *The Art of Biblical Narrative* (New York: Basic Books, 1981).

Anderson, R. Dean, Jr., *Glossary of Greek Rhetorical Terms Connected to Methods of Argumentation, Figures and Tropes from Anaximenes to Quintilian* (Leuven: Peeters, 2000).

Argyle, A. W., "The Greek of Luke and Acts," *NTS* 20 (1974), 441–445.

Aristotle, *The "Art" of Rhetoric*, trans. John Henry Freese, Aristotle, vol. XXII, LCL 193 (Cambridge, Mass.: Harvard University Press, 1926; reprint, 1939, 1947, 1959, 1967, 1975, 1982, 1991, 1994, 2000).

Poetics, trans. Stephen Halliwell (ed.), Aristotle, vol. XXIII, LCL 199 (Cambridge, Mass.: Harvard University Press, 1995; reprint, 1999).

Aune, David E., *The New Testament in Its Literary Environment* (Philadelphia, Pa.: Westminster Press, 1987).

Baur, Ferdinand Christian, *Paulus, der Apostel Jesu Christi*, 1845; ET: *Paul, the Apostle of Jesus Christ: His Life and Work, His Epistles and His Doctrine*, 2 vols., trans. Eduard Zeller (London: Williams and Norgate, 1873–1876).

Beck, B. E., "The Common Authorship of Luke and Acts," *NTS* 23 (1977), 346–352.

Benoit, Pierre, "La deuxième visite de saint Paul à Jérusalem," *Biblica* 40 (1959), 778–792.

"Some Notes on the 'Summaries' in Acts 2, 4, and 5" in *Jesus and the Gospel*, vol. II, trans. Benet Weatherhead (New York: Seabury Press, 1974); originally published as a paper contributed to the symposium *Aux sources de la tradition chrétienne, mélanges offerts à M. Maurice Goguel* (Neuchâtel-Paris, 1950).

Best, Ernest, *The Temptation and the Passion: The Markan Soteriology* (Cambridge: Cambridge University Press, 1965).

Bird, Michael F., "The Unity of Luke-Acts in Recent Discussion," *JSNT* 29 (2007), pp. 425–448.

Black, Matthew, *An Aramaic Approach to the Gospels and Acts*, 3rd edition (Oxford: Clarendon Press, 1967).

Blass, Friedrich, "On Attic Prose Rhythm" in *Hermathena: A Series of Papers on Literature, Science, and Philosophy* 32 (1906), 18–34.

Blenkinsopp, Joseph, *The Pentateuch: An Introduction to the First Five Books of the Bible*, ABRL (New York: Doubleday, 1992).

Boismard, M.-É., and A. Lamouille, *Texte occidental des Actes des Apôtres*, 2 vols. (Paris: Éditions Recherche sur les Civilisations, 1984).

Bonner, S. F., *The Literary Treatises of Dionysius of Halicarnassus: A Study in the Development of Critical Method* (Cambridge: Cambridge University Press, 1939).

Bovon, François, *Luke 1: A Commentary on the Gospel of Luke 1:1–9:50*, Helmut Koester (ed.), trans. Christine M. Thomas, Hermeneia (Minneapolis, Minn.: Fortress Press, 2002); originally published as *L'évangile selon saint Luc 1, 1–9, 50* (Geneva: Labor et Fides, 1991).

L'évangile selon saint Luc 9, 51–14, 35 (Geneva: Labor et Fides, 1996).

L'évangile selon saint Luc 15,1–19, 27 (Geneva: Labor et Fides, 2001).

Breitenbach, H. P., "The *De Compositione* of Dionysius of Hall-Carnassus Considered with Reference to the Rhetoric of Aristotle," *CP* 6 (1911), 163–179.

Brodie, Thomas Louis, "Greco-Roman Imitation of Texts as a Partial Guide to Luke's Use of Sources" in Charles H. Talbert (ed.), *Luke-Acts: New Perspectives from the Society of Biblical Literature* (New York: Crossroad, 1984).

Brown, Raymond E., Joseph A. Fitzmyer, and Roland E. Murphy (eds.), *The Jerome Biblical Commentary* (Englewood Cliffs, N.J.: Prentice Hall, 1968).

The New Jerome Biblical Commentary (Englewood Cliffs, N.J.: Prentice Hall, 1990).

Browning, R., and G. Giangrande (eds.), *Museum Philologum Londiniense*, vol. I (Amsterdam: Adolf M. Hakkert, 1975).

Bruce, F. F., *The Acts of the Apostles* (Grand Rapids, Mich.: Wm. B. Eerdmans, 1990).

Bruder, Carl Hermann, *Concordantiae omnium vocum Novi Testamenti graeci: primum ab Erasmo Schmidio editae, nunc secundum critices et hermeneutices nostrae aetatis rationes emendata auctae meliori ordine dispositae* (Lipsiae: Sumptibus Ernesti Bredtii, 1867).

Bultmann, Rudolf, *The History of the Synoptic Tradition*, trans. John Marsh from 3rd German edition (New York: Harper & Row, 1963); originally published as *Die Geschichte der synoptischen Tradition*, 3rd edition (Göttingen: Vandenhoeck & Ruprecht, 1957).

Buntinas, Martin, and Gerald M. Funk, *Statistics for the Sciences* (Belmont, Calif.: Brooks/Cole, 2005).

Cadbury, Henry J., *The Book of Acts in History* (London: Adam and Charles Black, 1955).

"Commentary on the Preface of Luke," in F. J. Foakes Jackson and Kirsopp Lake (eds.), *The Beginnings of Christianity, Part I: The Acts of the Apostles, vol. V: Additional Notes to the Commentary* (London: Macmillan and Co., 1933).

The Making of Luke-Acts, 2nd edition (Peabody, Mass.: Hendrickson Publishers, 1958; reprint, 1999).

The Style and Literary Method of Luke (Cambridge, Mass.: Harvard University Press, 1920 reprint, Eugene, Ore.: Wipf and Stock Publishers, 2001).

"The Summaries in Acts" in F. J. Foakes Jackson and Kirsopp Lake (eds.), *The Beginnings of Christianity, Part I: The Acts of the Apostles vol. V: Additional Notes to the Commentary* (London: Macmillan and Co., 1933).

"The Tradition," in F. J. Foakes Jackson and Kirsopp Lake (eds.), *The Beginnings of Christianity, Part 1: The Acts of the Apostles, vol. II: Prolegomena II: Criticism* (London: Macmillan and Co., 1922), pp. 210–211.

Cerfaux, Lucien, "The Acts of the Apostles" in A. Robert and A. Feuillet (eds.), *Introduction to the New Testament* (New York: Desclée, 1965).

"La première communauté chrétienne à Jérusalem: Act. II, 41–V, 42," *ETL* 16 (1939), 5–31.

"La composition de la première partie du Livre des Actes" (first published in *ETL* 13 (1936), pp. 667–691) in *Recueil Lucien Cerfaux: Études d'Exégèse et d'Histoire Religieuse de Monseigneur Cerfaux*, vol. II (Leuven: 1954).

Cicero, *Orator*, trans. H. M. Hubbell, LCL 342 (Cambridge, Mass.: Harvard University Press, 1971).

Clark, Albert C., *The Acts of the Apostles: A Critical Edition with Introduction and Notes on Selected Passages* (Oxford: Clarendon Press, 1933; reprint 1970).

Co, Maria Anicia, "The Major Summaries in Acts: Acts 2,42–27; 4,32–35; 5:12–16: Linguistic and Literary Relationship," *ETL* 68 (1992), 49–85.

Cohen, Shaye J. D., *Josephus in Galilee and Rome: His Vita and Development as a Historian* (Leiden: Brill, 1979).

Conzelmann, Hans, *Acts of the Apostles*, trans. James Limburg, A. Thomas Kraabel, and Donald H. Juel, Hermeneia (Philadelphia, Pa.: Fortress Press, 1987); originally published as *Die Apostelgeschichte* (Tübingen: J. C. B. Mohr, 1963, 1972).

The Theology of St. Luke, trans. Geoffrey Buswell (New York: Harper & Row, 1961); originally published as *Die Mitte der Zeit* (Tübingen: J. C. B. Mohr, 1953).

Creed, John Martin, *The Gospel According to St. Luke: The Greek Text with Introduction, Notes, and Indices* (London: Macmillan & Co., 1950).

Crenshaw, James L., *Education in Ancient Israel: Across the Deadening Silence*, ABRL (New York: Doubleday, 1998).

Cribiore, Raffaella, *Gymnastics of the Mind: Greek Education in Hellenistic and Roman Egypt* (Princeton and Oxford: Princeton University Press, 2001).

Writing, Teachers, and Students in Graeco-Roman Egypt (Atlanta, Ga.: Scholars Press, 1996).

Danker, Frederick W., *A Century of Greco-Roman Philology* (Atlanta, Ga.: Scholars Press, 1988).

Luke, Proclamation Commentaries (Philadelphia, Pa.: Fortress Press, 1987).

Dawsey, J., "The Literary Unity of Luke-Acts: Questions of Style – A Task for Literary Critics," *NTS* 35 (1989), 48–66.

Deissmann, Adolf, *New Light on the New Testament: From Records of the Græco-Roman Period*, trans. Lionel R. M. Strachan (Edinburgh: T. & T. Clark, 1907).

Delobel, Joël, "La rédaction de Lc. IV,14–16a et le 'Bericht vom Anfang'" in Frans Neirynck (ed.), *L'Évangile de Luc: problèmes littéraires et théologiques: mémorial Lucien Cerfaux*, BETL 32 (Gembloux: Duculot, 1978).

"The Text of Luke-Acts: A Confrontation of Recent Theories" in J. Verheyden (ed.), *The Unity of Luke-Acts*, BETL 142 (Leuven: Leuven University Press, 1999).

Demetrius, *On Style*, trans. Doreen C. Innes (ed.), LCL 199 (Cambridge, Mass.: Harvard University Press, 1995; reprint 1999).

Denniston, J. D., *The Greek Particles*, 2nd edition (Oxford: Clarendon Press, 1959).

Greek Prose Style (Oxford: Clarendon Press, 1952; reprint 1960, 1965).

Dibelius, Martin, "The First Christian Historian" in Heinrich Greevan (ed.), *Studies in the Acts of the Apostles*, trans. Mary Ling (London: SCM Press, 1956; reprint, Mifflintown, Pa.: Sigler Press, 1999).

From Tradition to Gospel, trans. Bertram Lee Woolf from the 2nd edition (New York: Charles Scribner's Sons, 1935); originally published as *Die Formgeschichte des Evangeliums* (Tübingen: Mohr/Siebeck, 1919).

"Style Criticism in the Book of Acts" in Heinrich Greevan (ed.), *Studies in the Acts of the Apostles*, trans. Mary Ling (London: SCM Press, 1956; reprint, Mifflintown, Pa.: Sigler Press, 1999); originally published as "Stilkritisches zur Apostelgeschichte" in H. Schmidt (ed.), *Eucharisterion: Studien zur Religion und Literatur des Alten und Neuen Testaments*, Festschrift Hermann Gunkel, vol. II (Göttingen: Vandenhoeck & Ruprecht, 1923).

Dionysius of Halicarnassas: Critical Essays, vol. I, trans. Stephen Usher, LCL 465 (Cambridge, Mass.: Harvard University Press, 1974; reprint, 2000).

Dionysius of Halicarnassus, "On Literary Composition" in *Dionysius of Halicarnassus: Critical Essays*, vol. II, trans. Stephen Usher, LCL 466 (Cambridge, Mass.: Harvard University Press, 1985).

Dormeyer, Detlev, *The New Testament Among the Writings of Antiquity*, Stanley E. Porter (ed.), trans. Rosemarie Kossov (Sheffield: Sheffield Academic Press, 1998).

Dover, Kenneth, *The Evolution of Greek Prose Style* (Oxford: Clarendon Press, 1997).

Dupont, Jacques, *The Sources of Acts*, trans. Kathleen Pond (New York: Herder and Herder, 1964).

Eberling, Herman Louis, "Some Statistics on the Order of Words in Greek" in *Studies in Honor of Basil L. Gildersleeve* (Baltimore, Md.: Johns Hopkins University Press, 1902).

Egger, Wilhelm, *Frohbotschaft und Lehre: Die Sammelberichte des Wirkens Jesu im Markusevangelium* (Frankfurt am Main: Josef Knecht, 1976).

Elliott, J. K. (ed.), *Studies in New Testament Language and Text: Essays in Honour of George D. Kilpatrick on the Occasion of his Sixty-Fifth Birthday* (Leiden: Brill, 1976).

Eusebius, *The Ecclesiastical History*, vol. I, trans. Kirsopp Lake, LCL 153 (Cambridge, Mass.: Harvard University Press, 1926; reprint 1949, 1953, 1959, 1965).

Fantham, Elaine, *Roman Literary Culture: From Cicero to Apuleius* (Baltimore, Md. and London: Johns Hopkins University Press, 1996).

Fee, Gordon D., "Rigorous or Reasoned Eclecticism – Which?" in J. K. Elliot (ed.), *Studies in New Testament Language and Text: Essays in Honour of George D. Kilpatrick on the Occasion of his Sixty-Fifth Birthday* (Leiden: Brill, 1976), pp. 174–197.

Fitzmyer, Joseph A., *The Acts of the Apostles: A New Translation with Introduction and Commentary*, AB 31 (New York: Doubleday, 1998).

"The Authorship of Luke-Acts Reconsidered" in *Luke the Theologian: Aspects of His Teaching* (New York: Paulist Press, 1989).

The Gospel According to Luke: I–IX, AB 28 (New York: Doubleday, 1970).

The Gospel According to Luke: X–XXIV, AB 28A (New York: Doubleday, 1985).

Luke the Theologian (New York: Paulist Press, 1989).

Foakes Jackson, F. J., and Kirsopp Lake (eds.), *The Beginnings of Christianity, Part 1: The Acts of the Apostles, vol. I: Prolegomena I: The Jewish, Gentile, and Christian Backgrounds* (London: Macmillan and Co., 1920).

The Beginnings of Christianity, Part 1: The Acts of the Apostles, vol. II: Prolegomena II: Criticism (London: Macmillan and Co., 1922).

The Beginnings of Christianity, Part 1: The Acts of the Apostles, vol. V: Additional Notes to the Commentary (London: Macmillan and Co., 1933).

"The Internal Evidence of Acts," *The Beginnings of Christianity: Part I: The Acts of the Apostles*, vol. II (London: Macmillan and Co., 1933), pp. 121–204.

Foster, Donald W., *Author Unknown: On the Trail of Anonymous* (New York: Henry Holt, 2000).

Elegy by W. S.: A Study in Attribution (Newark, Del.: University of Delaware Press, 1989).

Frisk, Hjalmar, *Studien zur griechischen Wortstellung*, Göteborgs Högskolas Årsskrift 39 (Gothenburg: Wettergren & Kerbers Förlag, 1933).

Fung, Glenn, *The Disputed Federalist Papers: SVM Feature Selection via Concave Minimization* (New York: ACM Press, 2003).

Gasque, W. Ward, *A History of the Criticism of the Acts of the Apostles* (Grand Rapids, Mich.: William B. Eerdmans, 1975).

Gibson, Craig A., "Learning Greek History in the Ancient Classroom: The Evidence of the Treatises on Progymnasmata," *CP* 99 (2004), 103–129.

Goodell, Thomas Dwight, "The Order of Words in Greek" in *TAPA 1890*, vol. XXI (New York: reprint, Johnson Reprint Corporation; Kraus Reprint Corporation, 1964).

Goodenough, Erwin R., "The Perspective of Acts," in Leander E. Keck and J. Louis Martyn (eds.), *Studies in Luke-Acts: Essays Presented in Honor of Paul Schubert, Buckingham Professor of New Testament Criticism and Interpretation at Yale University* (Nashville, Tenn.: Abingdon Press, 1966; London: SPCK, 1968, 1976, 1978; Philadelphia, Pa.: Fortress Press, 1980; reprint, Mifflintown, Pa.: Sigler Press, 1999), pp. 51–59.

Gregory, Andrew, "The Reception of Luke and Acts and the Unity of Luke-Acts" *JSNT* 29 (2007), pp. 459–472.

Groot, A. W. de, *A Handbook of Antique Prose-Rhythm* (The Hague: J. B. Wolters – Groningen, 1919).

Grube, G. M. A., *The Greek and Roman Critics* (Toronto: University of Toronto Press, 1965, 1968).

Haenchen, Ernst, *The Acts of the Apostles: A Commentary*, trans. Basil Blackwell (Philadelphia, Pa.: Westminster Press, 1971).

"Das 'Wir' in der Apostelgeschichte und das Itinerar," *ZTK* 58 (1961), 329–366.

Hahneman, Geoffrey Mark, *The Muratorian Fragment and the Development of the Canon* (Oxford: Clarendon Press, 1992).

Harnack, Adolf von, *The Acts of the Apostles*, 2nd edition, trans. J. R. Wilkinson (London: Williams & Norgate; New York: G. P. Putnam's Sons, 1909); originally published as *Die Apostelgeschichte*, BENT 3 (Leipzig: J. C. Hinrichs, 1908).

Luke the Physician: The Author of the Third Gospel and the Acts of the Apostles, trans. J. R. Wilkinson, 2nd edition (London: Williams & Norgate; New York: G. P. Putnam's Sons, 1909); originally published as *Lukas der Arzt, der Verfasser des dritten Evangeliums und der Apostelgeschichte* (Leipzig: 1906).

Sprüche und Reden Jesu: Die zweite Quelle des Matthäus und Lukas (Leipzig: 1907).

Hawkins, John C., *Horae Synopticae: Contributions to the Study of the Synoptic Problem*, 2nd edition (Oxford: Clarendon Press, 1909; reprint, 1968).

Hedrick, Charles W., "The Role of 'Summary Statements' in the Composition of the Gospel of Mark: A Dialog with Karl Schmidt and Norman Perrin," *NT* 4 (1984), 289–311.

Hemer, Colin J., *The Book of Acts in the Setting of Hellenistic History* (Winona Lake, Ind.: Eisenbrauns, 1990; reprint, 2001).

Hendrickson, G. L., "Accentual Clausulae in Greek Prose of the First and Second Centuries of our Era," *AJP* 29 (1908), 280–302.

Hills, Julian V., *et al.* (eds.), *Common Life in the Early Church: Essays Honoring Graydon F. Snyder* (Harrisburg, Pa.: Trinity Press International, 1998).

Hock, Ronald F., and Edward N. O'Neil (eds.), *The Chreia and Ancient Rhetoric: Classroom Exercises* (Atlanta, Ga.: Society of Biblical Literature, 2002).

Hurst, André, "Un critique grec dans la Rome d'Auguste" in Wolfgang Haase (ed.), *Principat*, vol. II, Part 1, *Aufstieg und Niedergang der römischen Welt* (Berlin: Walter de Gruyter, 1982).

Jeremias, J., *Die Sprache des Lukasevangeliums: Redaktion und Tradition im Nicht-Markus-Stoff des dritten Evangeliums* (Göttingen: Vandenhoeck & Ruprecht, 1980).

Johnson, Luke Timothy, "Literary Criticism of Luke-Acts: Is Reception-History Pertinent?" *JSNT* 29 (2007), pp. 159–162.

Kaestli, Jean-Daniel, "Luke-Acts and the Pastoral Epistles: The Thesis of a Common Authorship" in C. M. Tuckett (ed.), *Luke's Literary Achievement: Collected Essays*, JSNTSup 116 (Sheffield: Sheffield Academic Press, 1995).

Keck, Leander E., and J. Louis Martyn (eds.), *Studies in Luke-Acts: Essays Presented in Honor of Paul Schubert, Buckingham Professor of New Testament Criticism and Interpretation at Yale University* (Nashville, Tenn.: Abingdon Press, 1966; London: SPCK, 1968, 1976, 1978; Philadelphia, Pa.: Fortress Press, 1980; reprint, Mifflintown, Penn.: Sigler Press, 1999).

Kennedy, George A., "Aristotle on the Period," *HSCP* 63 (1958), 283–288.

   The Art of Rhetoric in the Roman World: 300 B.C.–A.D. 300 (Princeton, N.J.: Princeton University Press, 1972).

   Classical Rhetoric & Its Christian & Secular Tradition from Ancient to Modern Times (Chapel Hill, N.C.: University of North Carolina Press, 1999).

   A New History of Classical Rhetoric (Princeton, N.J.: Princeton University Press, 1994).

Kenny, Anthony, *A Stylometric Study of the New Testament* (Oxford: Clarendon Press, 1986).

Kisirinya, S. K., "Re-Interpreting the Major Summaries (Acts 2:42–46; 4:32–35; 5:12–16)," *African Christian Studies: The Journal of the Faculty of Theology of the Catholic Higher Institute of Eastern Africa, Nairobi* 18 (2002), 67–74.

Klarreich, Erica, "Bookish Math: Statistical Tests are Unraveling Knotty Literary Mysteries," *Science News* 164 (2003), 392–394.

Klijn, A. F. J., *A Survey of the Researches into the Western Text of the Gospels and Acts: Part 2 1949–1969* (Leiden: Brill, 1969).

Knox, Wilfred L., *The Acts of the Apostles* (Cambridge: Cambridge University Press, 1948).

   Some Hellenistic Elements in Primitive Christianity, The Schweich Lectures on Biblical Archaeology, 1942 (London: Oxford University Press, 1944; Munich: Kraus Reprint, 1980).

Kremer, J., *Les Actes des Apôtres: traditions, rédaction, théologie*, BETL 48 (Leuven: Leuven University Press, 1977).

Kümmel, Werner Georg, *The New Testament: The History of the Investigation of Its Problems*, trans. S. McLean Gilmour and Howard C. Kee (Nashville, Tenn.: Abingdon Press, 1972).

Lake, Kirsopp and Silva Lake, "The Acts of the Apostles," *JBL* 53 (1934), 34–45.

Larson, Kevin W., "The Structure of Mark's Gospel: Current Proposals," *CBR* 3 (2004), 140–160.

Lausberg, Heinrich, *Handbook of Literary Rhetoric: A Foundation for Literary Study*, trans. Matthew T. Bliss, Annemiek Jansen, and David E. Orton (Leiden: Brill, 1998).

Leopold, J., and T. Conley, "Philo's Style and Diction" in David Winston and J. Dillon (eds.), *Two Treatises of Philo of Alexandria* (1983).

Liddell, H. G. and H. S. Jones and R. McKenzie and R. Scott, *A Greek–English Lexicon*, 9th edition, new supplement (Oxford: Clarendon Press, 1996).

Lightfoot, Robert Henry, *Locality and Doctrine in the Gospels* (London: Hodder and Stoughton, 1938).

Lindemann, Andreas, "The Beginnings of Christian Life in Jerusalem According to the Summaries in the Acts of the Apostles (Acts 2:42–47; 4:32–37; 5:12–16)" in Julian V. Hills *et al.* (eds.), *Common Life in the Early Church: Essays Honoring Graydon F. Snyder* (Harrisburg, Pa.: Trinity Press International, 1998).

Lohmeyer, Ernst, *Galiläa und Jerusalem* (Göttingen: Vandenhoeck & Ruprecht, 1936).

Longinus, *On the Sublime*, trans. W. Hamilton Fyfe (ed.), rev. Donald Russell, LCL 199 (Cambridge, Mass.: Harvard University Press, 1995; reprint, 1999).

Lüdemann, Gerd, *Early Christianity According to the Traditions in Acts: A Commentary* (Minneapolis, Minn.: Fortress Press, 1987).

MacRory, J., "The Authorship of the Third Gospel and the Acts," *ITQ* 2 (1907), 190–202.

Marguerat, Daniel, "The End of Acts (28:16–31) and the Rhetoric of Silence" in *Rhetoric and the New Testament: Essays from the 1992 Heidelberg Conference*, JSNTSup 90 (Sheffield: Sheffield Academic Press, 1993).

Marxen, Willi, *Mark the Evangelist: Studies on the Redaction History of the Gospel*, trans. James Boyce, Donald Juel, William Poehlmann with Roy A. Harrisville (Nashville, Tenn.: Abingdon Press, 1969); originally published as *Der Evangelist Markus – Studien zur Redaktionsgeschichte des Evangeliums* (Göttingen: Vandenhoeck & Ruprecht, 1956, 1959).

McCabe, Donald F., *The Prose-Rhythm of Demosthenes* (New York: Arno Press, 1981).

Mealand, David L., "Luke-Acts and the Verbs of Dionysius of Halicarnassus," *JSNT* 63 (1996), 63–86.

Metzger, Bruce M., *The Canon of the New Testament: Its Origin, Development, and Significance* (Oxford: Clarendon Press, 1987).

A Textual Commentary on the Greek New Testament, 2nd edition (Stuttgart: Deutsche Bibelgesellschaft, 1994).

Moessner, David P., "The Appeal and Power of Poetics (Luke 1:1–4)" in David P. Moessner (ed.), *Jesus and the Heritage of Israel: Luke's Narrative Claim upon Israel's History* (Harrisburg, Pa.: Trinity Press International, 1999).

Moessner, David P. (ed.), *Jesus and the Heritage of Israel: Luke's Narrative Claim upon Israel's History* (Harrisburg, Pa.: Trinity Press International, 1999).

"The Lukan Prologues in the Light of Ancient Narrative Hermeneutics: Παρηκολουθηκότι and the Credentialed Author" in J. Verheyden (ed.), *The Unity of Luke-Acts*, BETL 142 (Leuven: Leuven University Press, 1999).

Morgenthaler, R., *Statistik des neutestamentlichen Wortschatzes* (Zurich: Gotthelf-Verlag, 1958).

Mosteller, Frederick and David L. Wallace, "Deciding Authorship," in J. M. Tanur *et al.* (eds.), *Statistics: A Guide to the Unknown* (San Francisco, Calif.: Holden-Day, 1972), pp. 207–219.

Moulton, James Hope (ed.), *A Grammar of New Testament Greek*, vol. IV (Edinburgh: T. & T. Clark, 1976).

and Wilbert Francis Howard (eds.), *A Grammar of New Testament Greek*, vol. II (Edinburgh: T. & T. Clark, 1920; reprint 1968).

Moulton, W. F., and A. S. Geden, *A Concordance to the Greek Testament*, 3rd edition (Edinburgh: T. & T. Clark, 1926).

Müller, K. (ed.), *The Fragments of the Lost Historians of Alexander the Great: Fragmenta Scriptorum de Rebus Alexandri Magni, Pseudo-Callisthenes, Itinerarium Alexandri* (Chicago, Ill.: Ares Publishers, 1979).

Neirynck, Frans (ed.), *L'Évangile de Luc: problèmes littéraires et théologiques: mémorial Lucien Cerfaux*, BETL 32 (Gembloux: Duculot, 1978).

"La matière Marcienne dans l'évangile de Luc," in Frans Neirynck (ed.), *L'Évangile de Luc: The Gospel of Luke*, BETL 32 (Leuven: Leuven University Press, 1989).

and F. van Segbroeck, "Caractéristiques stylistiques," *ETL* 61 (1984), 304–339.

Nestle, Eberhard and Erwin Nestle and Barbara Aland and Kurt Aland, *et al.* (eds.), *Novum Testamentum Graece*, 27th edition (Stuttgart: Deutsche Bibelgesellschaft, 1993, 1994).

Neumaier, Wilfried, *Antike Rhythmustheorien: Historische Form und Aktuelle Substanz* (Amsterdam: B. R. Grüner, 1989).

Nikiprowetzky, V., "Caractère et structure du Commentaire Philonien" in *Le Commentaire de l'Écriture chez Philon d'Alexandrie: son caractère et sa portée: observations philologiques* (Leiden: Brill, 1977).

Noorda, S. J., "Scene and Summary: A Proposal for Reading Acts 4,32–5,16" in J. Kremer (ed.), *Les Actes des Apôtres: traditions, rédaction, théologie*, BETL 48 (Leuven: Leuven University Press, 1977).

Norden, Eduard, *Agnostos Theos: Untersuchungen zur Formengeschichte religiöser Rede* (Leipzig: Teubner, 1913; reprint, Stuttgart: Teubner, 1923; reprint, Darmstadt: Wissenschaftliche Buchgesellschaft, 1956).

Die antike Kunstprosa von vi. Jahrhundert v. Chr. bis in die Zeit der Renaissance, 2 vols. (Stuttgart: B. G. Teubner Verlagsgesellschaft, 1958).

Norušis, Marija J., *SPSS 11.0: Guide to Data Analysis* (Upper Saddle River, N.J.: Prentice Hall, 2002).

Ó Fearghail, Fearghus, *The Introduction to Luke-Acts: A Study of the Role of Lk 1,1–4,44 in the Composition of Luke's Two-Volume Work*, Analecta Biblica: Investigationes Scientificae in Res Biblicas 126 (Rome: Editrice Pontificio Instituto Biblico, 1991).

O'Neill, Jr., Eugene G., "The Importance of Final Syllables in Greek Verse," *TPAPA* 70 (1939), 256–294.

Orton, David E. (ed.), *The Composition of Luke's Gospel: Selected Studies from "Novum Testamentum"* (Leiden: Brill, 1999).

The Oxford Classical Dictionary, Simon Hornblower and Antony Spawforth (eds.), 3rd edition (Oxford: Oxford University Press, 1996).

Oyen, Geert Van, *De summaria in Marcus en de compositie van Mc 1,14–8,26*, SNTA 12 (Leuven: Leuven University Press/Peeters, 1987).

Parsons, Mikeal C., *Luke: Storyteller, Interpreter, Evangelist* (Peabody, Mass.: Hendrickson Publishers, 2007).

"The Unity of the Lukan Writings: Rethinking the *Opinio Communis*" in N. H. Keathley (ed.), *With Steadfast Purpose: Essays on Acts in Honor of Henry Jackson Flanders, Jr.* (Waco, Tex.: Baylor University Press, 1990).

"Who Wrote the Gospel of Luke?" *Bible Review* 17 (2001), 12–21, 54–55.

and Richard I. Pervo, *Rethinking the Unity of Luke and Acts* (Minneapolis, Minn.: Fortress Press, 1993).

Pervo, Richard, *Dating Acts: Between the Evangelists and the Apologists* (Santa Rosa, Calif.: Polebridge Press, 2006).

"Dating Acts," *Forum* 5 (2002).

"Israel's Heritage and Claims upon the Genre(s) of Luke and Acts: The Problems of a History" in David P. Moessner (ed.), *Jesus and the Heritage of Israel: Luke's Narrative Claim upon Israel's Legacy* (Harrisburg, Pa.: Trinity Press International, 1999).

Profit with Delight: The Literary Genre of the Acts of the Apostles (Philadelphia, Pa.: Fortress Press, 1987).

Plümacher, Eckhard, "Cicero und Lukas: Bemerkungen zu Stil und Zweck der historischen Monographie" in J. Verheyden (ed.), *The Unity of Luke-Acts*, BETL 142 (Leuven: Leuven University Press, 1999).

Lukas als hellenistischer Schriftsteller: Studien zur Apostelgeschichte (Göttingen: Vandenhoeck & Ruprecht, 1972).

Plummer, Alfred, *A Critical and Exegetical Commentary on the Gospel According to S. Luke*, 5th edition (Edinburgh: T. & T. Clark, 1922; reprint, 1969).

Pohl, Karin "Die Lehre von den drei Wortfügungsarten: Untersuchungen zu Dionysios von Halikarnaß, *De compositione verborum*," unpublished PhD thesis, Eberhard Karls University, Tübingen (1968).

Porter, Stanley E., *Handbook of Classical Rhetoric in the Hellenistic Period: 330 B.C.–A.D. 400* (Boston, Mass.: Brill Academic Publishers, 2001).

and Jeffrey T. Reed, "Greek Grammar since BDF: A Retrospective and Prospective Analysis," *FN* 4 (1991), 143–164.

Quintilian, *Institutio Oratoria*, trans. H. E. Butler, 4 vols., LCL 124–127 (London: William Heinemann, 1920–1922).

Richard, Earl, *Acts 6:1–8:4: The Author's Method of Composition*, SBLDS 41 (Missoula, Mont.: Scholars Press, 1978).

Robbins, Vernon K., "The Claims of the Prologues and Greco-Roman Rhetoric: The Prefaces to Luke and Acts in Light of Greco-Roman Rhetorical Strategies" in David P. Moessner (ed.), *Jesus and the Heritage of Israel: Luke's Narrative Claim upon Israel's History* (Harrisburg, Pa.: Trinity Press International, 1999).

Robert, A., and A. Feuillet (eds.), *Introduction to the New Testament* (New York: Desclée, 1965).

Roberts, W. Rhys, *Demetrius: On Style: The Greek Text of Demetrius De elocutione Edited after the Paris Manuscript* (Cambridge: Cambridge University Press, 1902).

Dionysius of Halicarnassus: On Literary Composition: Being the Greek Text of the De compositione verborum (London: Macmillan and Co., 1910).

"The Greek Words for 'Style' (with Special Reference to Demetrius περὶ Ἑρμηνείας)," *TCR* 15 (1901), 252–255.

Rollins, Wayne G., *The Gospels: Portraits of Christ* (Philadelphia, Pa.: Westminster, 1963).

Russell, D. A., *Criticism in Antiquity* (Berkeley, Calif.: University of California Press, 1981).

and Michael Winterbottom (eds.), *Ancient Literary Criticism* (Oxford: Clarendon Press, 1972).

Classical Literary Criticism (Oxford: Oxford University Press, 1989).

Plutarch (New York: Charles Scribner's Sons, 1973).

Russell, Henry G., "Which Was Written First, Luke or Acts?" *HTR* 48 (1955), 167–174.

Satterthwaite, Philip E., "Acts against the Background of Classical Rhetoric" in Bruce W. Winter and Andrew D. Clarke (eds.), *The Book of Acts in Its Ancient Literary Setting* (Grand Rapids, Mich.: William B. Eerdmans Publishing Company, 1993).

Schade, J., "De correptione Attica," unpublished PhD thesis, Greifswald (1908).

Schenkeveld, Dirk M., "Linguistic Theories in the Rhetorical Works of Dionysius of Halicarnassus," *Glotta* 61 (1983), 67–94.

"Theories of Evaluation in the Rhetorical Treatises of Dionysius of Halicarnassus" in R. Browning and G. Giangrande (eds.), *Museum Philologum Londiniense*, vol. I (Amsterdam: Adolf M. Hakkert, 1975).

Schmidt, Daryl D., "Rhetorical Influences and Genre: Luke's Preface and the Rhetoric of Hellenistic Historiography" in David P. Moessner (ed.), *Jesus and the Heritage of Israel: Luke's Narrative Claim upon Israel's History* (Harrisburg, Pa.: Trinity Press International, 1999).

Schmidt, Karl Ludwig, *Der Rahmen der Geschichte Jesu: Literarkritische Untersuchungen zur ältesten Jesusüberlieferung* (Berlin: Nachdruck aus Ausgabe, 1919; reprint, Darmstadt: Wissenschaftliche Buchgesellschaft, 1965).

Schneckenburger, Matthias, *Über den Zweck der Apostelgeschichte* (Berne: Chr., Fischer, 1841).

Schneider, Gerhard, *Das Evangelium nach Lukas*, 2 vols. (Würzburg: Gütersloher Verlagshaus Gerd Mohn, Gütersloh und Echter Verlag, 1977).

Scholten, J. H., *Is de derde evangelist de schrijver van het boek der Handelingen? Critisch onderzoek* (Leiden: Academische Boekhandel van P. Engels, 1873).

Schweizer, Eduard, "Eine hebraisierende Sonderquelle des Lukas?" *TZ* 6 (1950), 161–185.

Schwyzer, Eduard, *Griechische Grammatik: auf der Grundlage von Karl Brugmanns griechischer Grammatik*, 3 vols. (Munich: C. H. Beck'sche Verlagsbuchhandlung, 1934 and 1939, 1950, 1953).

Skimina, Stanislas, *État actuel des études sur le rythme de la prose grecque II*, EUSSup 11 (Lwów: Subventionnée par le Ministère de l'Instruction Publique Société Polon Paris, 1930).

Smyth, Herbert Weir, *Greek Grammar*, rev. Gordon M. Messing (Cambridge, Mass.: Harvard University Press, 1920, 1956; renewed, 1984).

Snyder, H. Gregory, *Teachers and Texts in the Ancient World: Philosophers, Jews and Christians* (London: Routledge, 2000).

Sparks, H. F. D., "The Semitisms of Acts," *JTS* n.s., 1 (1950), 16–28.

Stanford, W. B., *The Sound of Greek: Studies in the Greek Theory and Practice of Euphony* (Berkeley and Los Angeles, Calif.: University of California Press, 1967).

Stein, Robert, *Gospels and Tradition: Studies on Redaction Criticism of the Synoptic Gospels* (Grand Rapids, Mich.: Baker Book House, 1991).

Sterling, Gregory E., "'Athletes of Virtue': An Analysis of the Summaries in Acts (2:41–47; 4:32–35; 5:12–16)," *JBL* 113 (1994), 679–696.

Streeter, B. H., *The Four Gospels: A Study of Origins, Treating of the Manuscript Tradition, Sources, Authorship, & Dates* (London: Macmillan, 1924).

Sundberg, A. C., Jr., "Canon Muratori: A Fourth-Century List," *HTR* 66 (1973), 1–41.

Swiggers, Pierre, and Alfons Wouters, "Poetics and Grammar: From Technique to Τέκνη" in *Greek Literary Theory after Aristotle: A Collection of Papers in Honor of D. M. Schenkeveld* (Amsterdam: VU University Press, 1995).

Talbert, Charles H., *Literary Patterns, Theological Themes, and the Genre of Luke-Acts* (Missoula, Mont.: Scholars Press, 1975).

(ed.), *Luke-Acts: New Perspectives from the Society of Biblical Literature Seminar* (New York: Crossroad, 1984).

Tannehill, Robert C., *Luke*, Abingdon New Testament Commentaries (Nashville, Tenn.: Abingdon Press, 1996).

The Narrative Unity of Luke-Acts: A Literary Interpretation, 2 vols. (Philadelphia, Pa.: Fortress Press, 1986).

"Response to Patricia Walters, 'The Gilded Hypothesis Revisited: Authorial Unity of Luke and Acts,'" unpublished paper presented at the annual meeting of the Society of Biblical Literature, Washington, D.C., November, 2006.

Tanur, J. M. *et al.* (eds.), *Statistics: A Guide to the Unknown* (San Francisco, Calif.: Holden-Day, 1972).

Thesaurus Linguae Graecae, CD ROM vol. E (University of California Irvine: 1990).

Thucydides, *The Peloponnesian War*, trans. Steven Lattimore (Indianapolis, Ind.: Hackett Publishing Co., 1998).

Tomkins, Daniel P., "Stylistic Characterization in Thucydides" unpublished PhD thesis, Yale University (1968).

Too, Yun Lee (ed.), *Education in Greek and Roman Antiquity* (Leiden: Brill, 2001).

Torrey, Charles Cutler, *The Composition and Date of Acts*, HTS 1 (Cambridge, Mass.: Harvard University Press, 1919; reprint, New York: Kraus reprint, 1969).

Tuckett, C. M., *Luke's Literary Achievement: Collected Essays*, JSNTSup 116 (Sheffield: Sheffield Academic Press, 1995).

Turner, Nigel, *Style*, vol. IV of James Hope Moulton (ed.), *A Grammar of New Testament Greek* (Edinburgh: T. & T. Clark, 1976).

"The Quality of the Greek of Luke-Acts" in J. K. Elliot (ed.), *Studies in New Testament Language and Text: Essays in Honour of George D. Kilpatrick on the Occasion of his Sixty-Fifth Birthday*, Supplements to *Novum Testamentum* 44 (Leiden: Brill, 1976).

"The Style of Luke-Acts" in James Hope Moulton (ed.), *Style*, vol. IV of *A Grammar of New Testament Greek* (Edinburgh: T. & T. Clark, 1976).

Tyson, Joseph B., "The Date of Acts: A Reconsideration," *Forum* 5 (2002), 33–51.

"Why Dates Matter: The Case of the Acts of the Apostles," *The Fourth R* 18 (2005), 8–14.

Unnik, W. C. van, "The 'Book of Acts' – The Confirmation of the Gospel" in David E. Orton (ed.), *The Composition of Luke's Gospel: Selected Studies from "Novum Testamentum"* (Leiden: Brill, 1999).

"Éléments artistiques dans l'évangile de Luc" in Frans Neirynck (ed.), *L'Évangile de Luc*, BETL 32 (Leuven: Leuven University Press, 1989).

"Luke's Second Book and the Rules of Hellenistic Historiography" in Jacob Kremer (ed.), *Les Actes des Apôtres: traditions, rédaction, théologie*, BETL 48 (Gembloux: J. Duculot; Leuven: Leuven University Press, 1979).

Usener, H., and L. Radermacher (eds.), *Dionysii Halicarnasei Opuscula*, 2 vols. (Stuttgart: B. G. Teubner, 1965).

Verheyden, J. (ed.), *The Unity of Luke-Acts*, BETL 142 (Leuven: Leuven University Press, 1999).

"The Unity of Luke-Acts" in J. Verheyden (ed.), *The Unity of Luke-Acts*, BETL 142 (Leuven: Leuven University Press, 1999).

Vogel, T., *Charakteristik des Lukas nach Sprache und Stil: eine philologische Laienstudie*, 2nd edition (Leipzig, 1899).

Walton, Steve, "Where Does the Beginning of Acts End?" in J. Verheyden (ed.), *The Unity of Luke-Acts*, BETL 142 (Leuven: Leuven University Press, 1999).

Weil, Henri, *The Order of Words in the Ancient Languages Compared with that of the Modern Languages*, Amsterdam Studies in the Theory and History of Linguistic Science, Series 1: Amsterdam Classics in Linguistics, 1800–1925 (Amsterdam: John Benjamins B. V., 1978).

Wellhausen, Julius, *Nachrichten von der königlichen Gesellschaft der Wissenschaften zu Göttingen, Philosophie-Historie Klasse* (1907), 1–21.

Wenham, J., "The Identification of Luke," *EvQ* 63 (1991), 3–44.

Wilcox, M., "Luke and the Bezan Text of Acts," in J. Kremer (ed.), *Les Actes des Apôtres: traditions, rédaction, théologie*, BETL 48 (Leuven: Leuven University Press, 1977), pp. 447–455.

Williams, C. B., *Style and Vocabulary: Numerical Studies* (London: Charles Griffin, 1970).

Windisch, H., "The Case Against the Tradition" in F. J. Foakes Jackson and Kirsopp Lake (eds.), *The Beginnings of Christianity: Part 1: The Acts of the Apostles, vol. II: Prolegomena II: Criticism* (London: Macmillan and Co., 1922).

Winston, D., and J. Dillon (eds.), *Two Treatises of Philo of Alexandria: Commentary on* De gigantibus *and* Quod Deus sit immutabilis, Brown Judaic Studies 25 (Chico, Calif.: Scholars Press, 1983).

Winter, Bruce W., and Andrew D. Clarke (eds.), *The Book of Acts in Its First-Century Setting*, vol. I of *The Book of Acts in Its Ancient Literary Setting* (Grand Rapids, Mich.: William B. Eerdmans, 1993).

Wooten, Cecil W. (ed.), *The Orator in Action & Theory in Greece & Rome: Essays in Honor of George A. Kennedy* (Leiden: Brill, 2001).

Yaginuma, Shigetake, "Plutarch's Language and Style" in *Principat* Part 2, vol. 33.6, Wolfgang Haase (ed.), *Aufstieg und Niedergang der römischen Welt* (Berlin: Walter de Gruyter, 1992).

Zimmermann, Heinrich, "Die Sammelberichte der Apostelgeschichte," *BZ* 5 (1961), 71–82.

Zwaan, J. de, "The Use of the Greek Language in Acts" in F. J. Foakes Jackson and Kirsopp Lake (eds.), *The Beginnings of Christianity: Part I: The Acts of the Apostles*, vol. II (London: Macmillan & Co., 1922).

"Was the Book of Acts a Posthumous Edition?" *HTR* 17 (1924), 95–153.

INDEX OF BIBLICAL AND OTHER ANCIENT SOURCES

INDEX OF MODERN AUTHORS AND SUBJECTS